CHINESE NATIONAL CINEMA

What does it mean to be 'Chinese'? This controversial question has sparked off a never-ending process of image-making in Chinese and Chinese-speaking communities throughout the twentieth century. This introduction to Chinese national cinema, written for scholars and students by a leading critic, covers three 'Chinas': mainland China, Hong Kong and Taiwan. It traces the formation, negotiation and problematization of the national on the Chinese screen over ninety years. Historical and comparative perspectives bring out the parallel developments in the three Chinas, while critical analysis explores thematic and stylistic changes over time.

As well as exploring artistic achievements and ideological debates, *Chinese National Cinema* also emphasizes industry research and market analysis. The author concludes that despite the rigid censorship systems and the pressures on filmmakers, Chinese national cinema has never succeeded in projecting a single unified picture, but rather portrays many Chinas.

Yingjin Zhang is Professor of Chinese, Comparative Literature, and Cultural Studies at the University of California-San Diego. His publications include *Screening China* (2002) and Routledge's *Encyclopedia of Chinese Film* (1998) which he co-authored and edited with Zhiwei Xiao.

CHINESE NATIONAL CINEMA

Yingjin Zhang

Routledge
Taylor & Francis Group

NEW YORK AND LONDON

First published 2004
by Routledge
270 Madison Avenue, New York, NY 10016

Simultaneously published in the UK
by Routledge
2 Park Square, Milton Park, Abingdon, Oxon, OX14 4RN

Reprinted 2005, 2006

Routledge is an imprint of the Taylor & Francis Group

© 2004 Yingjin Zhang

Typeset in Galliard by RefineCatch Limited, Bungay, Suffolk
Printed and bound in Great Britain by MPG Books Ltd, Bodmin

Library of Congress Cataloging in Publication Data
Zhang, Yingjin.
Chinese national cinema / Yingjin Zhang. – 1st ed.
p.   cm. – (National cinemas)
Includes bibliographical references and index.
(paperback: alk. paper)
1. Motion pictures – China – History.   2. Motion pictures – Taiwan –
History.   I. Title.   II. Series: National cinemas series.
PN1993.5.C4Z49   2004
791.43′0951 – dc22   2003023574

British Library Cataloguing in Publication Data
A catalogue record for this book is available from the British Library

ISBN 0–415–17289–6 (hbk)
ISBN 0–415–17290–X (pbk)

TO SU, MIMI AND ALEX

FOR LOVE, HOPE AND FUN WE
HAVE SHARED TOGETHER

CONTENTS

CONTENTS

ILLUSTRATIONS

TABLES

ACKNOWLEDGMENTS

The planning of this book began in 1996 when I was working on *Encyclopedia of Chinese Film* (Routledge, 1998) and *Cinema and Urban Culture in Shanghai, 1922–1943* (Stanford, 1999). Since then I have moved from the Midwest to the Pacific Coast of the US. I would like to acknowledge major institutional support I received during these years: to the University of California (UC) at San Diego for a faculty fellowship from the Center for the Humanities, course reduction from the Department of Literature, and research and travel grants from the Division of Arts and Humanities, the Academic Senate, as well as the UC Pacific Rim Research Program in 2001–3; to the Pacific Cultural Foundation, Taiwan, for a research grant in 1999–2000; to the National Endowment for the Humanities for a summer faculty stipend in 1999; to Indiana University at Bloomington for an Outstanding Junior Faculty Award in 1996–7, a sabbatical leave in the autumn of 1999, and a summer faculty fellowship in 2000. The archival research was undertaken on both sides of the Pacific. I specifically thank the Chinese Taipei Film Archive (Taiwan) and the Hong Kong Film Archive for granting generous access in 1999–2003. Thanks are also due to the centers for Chinese or East Asian studies at the University of Chicago, the University of Michigan at Ann Arbor, as well as the Harvard-Yenching Library for library travel grants in 1996–9.

For encouragement and support I am grateful to my colleagues and friends Dudley Andrew, Ru-Shou Robert Chen, Cheng Jihua, David Desser, Michael Curtin, Eugene Chen Eoyang, Joseph Esherick, Yi-Tsi Mei Feuweuerker, Wendy Larson, Perry Link, Lisa Lowe, Sheldon Hsiao-peng Lu, Paul Pickowicz, Stanley Rosen, Julian Stringer, David Der-Wei Wang, Jing Wang, Zhiwei Xiao and Zhang Longxi. I presented parts of the book in earlier drafts at the University of Southern California, Indiana University, the University of Notre Dame, the University of Wisconsin at Madison, the University of Maryland, Yale University, as well as the Ecole Normale Supérieure in Lyon, France, the City University of Hong Kong, and the Hong Kong Baptist University in 2000–3, and I remain appreciative to my hosts at these institutions. My thanks also to Zhu Tianwei of the China Film Archive (Beijing) for supplying photographs; to Paul Pickowicz for sharing his rare collection of early Chinese films; to Qin Liyan for timely research assistance in 2003; to Rebecca Barden and Susan Hayward for their confidence and patience; to four initial Routledge reviewers for endorsing the project years ago and four final reviewers for their comments, questions and suggestions, especially to Peter Rist for being so meticulous; and to Routledge's London staff – Lesley Riddle in particular – for seeing this book through reviewing, shortening (by 27,700 words), copy-editing, marketing, production and distribution.

This book is dedicated to my loving family: to Su for the twentieth anniversary of our marriage, to Mimi for her marvelous achievements in college education and to Alex for his growing appreciation of the power of images and words.

ABBREVIATIONS

b/w	black and white
CCP	Chinese Communist Party
CMPC	Central Motion Picture Company (Taiwan)
dir.	director
GIO	Government Information Office (Taiwan)
HKFA	Hong Kong Film Archive
HKIFF	Hong Kong International Film Festival
KMT	Kuomingtang (the Nationalist Party in China and Taiwan)
MP&GI	Motion Picture & General Investment (Hong Kong)
NFCC	National Film Censorship Committee (KMT, China)
PLA	People's Liberation Army (China)
PRC	People's Republic of China (mainland China)
RMB	Reminbi (PRC currency in yuan)
ROC	Republic of China (Taiwan)
ZDC	Zhongguo dianying chubanshe (China Film Press, Beijing)
ZDX	Zhongguo dianyingjia xiehui (China Film Association, Beijing)
ZDYYZ	Zhongguo dianying yishu yanjiu zhongxin (China Film Art Research Center, Beijing)
ZDZ	Zhongguo dianying ziliao guan (China Film Archive, Beijing)

1

INTRODUCTION
National cinema and China

'NATIONAL' CINEMA

At the start of the new millennium, the publication of another volume on national cinema may seem ironic for several reasons. First, in the age of globalization, operations of multinational corporations have increasingly criss-crossed and sometimes entirely obscured or bypassed national borders, while local, regional and transnational forces continue to undermine the legitimacy of any nation-state (Miyoshi 1993). Second, in response to the sweeping power of the 'global popular' (During 1997), media and cultural studies have looked to post-coloniality, postmodernity and transnationality for new conceptual frameworks, and any focus on a single national cinema appears rather narrow or even dated. Third, in the wake of new technological development, cinema itself is said to have entered its 'late' stage, and the current academic interest in early cinema and late cinema thus place in an unfavorable light a project that considers the entire history of a national cinema.

Admittedly, in regard to China, the national cinema paradigm seems utterly inadequate. China today consists of three territories: (1) The People's Republic of China (PRC) ruled by the Chinese Communist Party (CCP) in the mainland; (2) Hong Kong, formerly a British colony but since July 1997 a special administrative region of the PRC; (3) The Republic of China (ROC) controlled for decades by the Nationalists (KMT) but since 2000 ruled by the independence-minded Democratic Progressive Party (DPP) in Taiwan. The history of these territories further complicates the 'national' situation. The identification of mainland China as 'Communist' can only date back to 1949, the end of the KMT rule there. Similarly, the KMT control of Taiwan started only in 1945, at the end of half a century of Japanese occupation of the island (also known as 'Formosa', a term originated by Portuguese seafarers). For some, the history of the separation of film industries in China, Hong Kong and Taiwan 'has formed quite distinctive national cinemas within each territory' (Yeh 1998: 74). Such *territorial* concerns have occasioned a similar designation of national cinema status for Hong Kong and Taiwan. As Stephen Crofts notes, 'In Hong Kong, the national cinema outsells Hollywood by a factor of four to one' (1993: 55–6); Douglas Kellner

1

believes that 'the New Taiwan Cinema has produced an impressive succession of films comprising a distinctive national cinema' (1998: 101).

A closer scrutiny of Crofts' typology of national cinemas can help us locate its inadequacy vis-à-vis China. In 1993, he distinguished the following seven varieties (51–7). The first is European-model art cinema, characterized by art-house exhibition, state subsidy, a cultural mode of production, psychological characterization, narrational ambiguity and objective verisimilitude. The second is Third Cinema, distinct from the author's cinema and marked by its political oppositionality. The third is Third World and European commercial cinema, populist in nature and reliant on such genres as the thriller, comedy and soft-core pornography. The fourth are cinemas that ignore Hollywood, such as those in Hong Kong and India, with large domestic markets and stable export markets. The fifth are cinemas that imitate Hollywood, as in several Anglophone countries, but with limited success. The sixth are totalitarian cinemas, as in fascist Germany and Italy, Communist China and the former Soviet bloc. The seventh are regional or ethnic cinemas, produced by ethnic or linguistic minorities, as in Quebec, Canada. In 1998, Crofts revised his typology and offered eight varieties along with a chart to illustrate them by way of a vertical axis defined by such terms as 'industrial', 'cultural', 'political' and a horizontal axis reflecting the mode of production as regulated or controlled by the state. The newly added variety is United States cinema (including its medium-budget 'independent' films), and the list goes in a new sequence according to each cinema's relative place in relation to different modes of production: (1) United States cinema; (2) Asian commercial successes; (3) other entertainment cinemas in Europe and the Third World; (4) totalitarian cinemas; (5) art cinemas; (6) international co-productions; (7) Third Cinemas; and (8) sub-state cinemas (Crofts 1998: 389–90). Crofts' inclusion of the United States notwithstanding, his proposal – based on his conviction that nations and states have been drifting apart in recent decades – 'to write of states and nation-state cinemas rather than nations and national cinemas' (1998: 386) deserves careful evaluation in the case of Chinese cinema.

Although he does not mention Taiwan, it is worthwhile contemplating where Crofts may place Taiwan in his chart of national cinemas. The first possibility is to treat Taiwan as an example of 'Asian commercial successes'. This was indeed the case when Taiwan cinema did well domestically and in Southeast Asia in the 1960s (Lent 1990: 65; F. Lu 1998: 125–78). But this 'commercial mode' of production that ignores Hollywood is no longer in practice in Taiwan, for the sheer absence of a stable domestic market invalidates any attempt to construct a national cinema 'industry' in Taiwan nowadays. The second possibility is to treat Taiwan as an example of 'art cinema', which makes sense to a certain extent as Taiwan films have continued to win prestigious awards at international film festivals since the late 1980s. But a troubling question is that many such award-winning films are international co-productions and thus transnational in nature, and once again the national here becomes problematic. The third possibility is to

2

treat Taiwan cinema as a kind of 'totalitarian cinema', which is true for the majority of propaganda or 'policy films' (*zhengce pian*) from the state-run studios in the 1960s and 1970s (R. Huang 1994b). Yet, after the disintegration of the studio system, this 'political mode' of production is now a distant memory. The fourth possibility is to treat Taiwan films as an example of 'Third Cinema', distinguished by a radical oppositionality to the state on the one hand and to cultural and economic imperialism on the other. *Buddha Bless America* (Taiping tianguo, dir. Wu Nien-chen [Wu Nianzhen], 1996) is just one of very few such examples, which problematizes identity and identification in the era of postcoloniality (T. Lu 2002: 191–205).

Like Taiwan, Hong Kong and mainland China also challenge Crofts' paradigm. Although he explicitly qualifies Hong Kong as a 'nation-state cinema', how could Crofts ever explain that up to July 1997 Hong Kong remained a British colony and specifically lacked nation-state status? Further, how would he reconcile the fact that even after Hong Kong officially became a special administrative region of China in July 1997, the Taiwan government still classified Hong Kong films as 'guopian' (literally, 'national films')?[1] Similarly, Crofts solicits more questions when he twice mentions China's fifth generation in his 1993 typology. First, it is a kind of 'exile' filmmaking (included under Third Cinema) boosted by international funding but often 'banned' at home; second, it is 'political art cinema' peripheral to the core production of totalitarian cinema (1993: 54–7). Indeed, fifth generation films prove difficult to be pigeonholed in Crofts' typology because of a fundamental mutation. This group started as the state-subsidized production of an ideologically subversive 'art cinema' in the mid-1980s and has mutated to the internationally (or intra-nationally) funded co-production of 'ethnographic cinema' of 'authentic' Chinese culture and history since the early 1990s (Y. Zhang 2002: 220–51). Furthermore, where should we place the 'underground' filmmaking of China's sixth generation in the national cinema paradigm? Many of these films are not so much 'banned' in China as considered 'illegal' by the authorities because they did not wait for official approval for exhibition at international film festivals (Cui 2001). Ironically, the rumored 'banned' status often adds to the political capital of these films, which often win sympathy, prizes and future financial backing in the West and are acclaimed as 'truthful' depictions of contemporary Chinese life (Y. Zhang 2004).

Obviously, Chinese cinema does not sit easily in Crofts', or any national cinema paradigm, although I should clarify that the Chinese case as elaborated here is not meant to deny the validity of national cinema in many other countries. Here, I am tempted to follow Tom O'Regan and declare that Chinese cinema, like Australian cinema, 'is a messy affair', not the least because Chinese cinema is 'fundamentally dispersed' (1996: 2) – historically, politically, territorially, culturally, ethnically and linguistically. The messy state of Chinese cinema means that the question of the 'national' will not go away if we substitute 'national cinema' with 'nation-state cinema'. Indeed, the association with the nation-state is precisely what makes the term 'Chinese cinema' problematic.

'Chinese' cinema

Recently, the very term 'Chinese' has been put under intense interrogation, if not always 'under erasure' (Chow 1998: 24). Is 'Chinese' in 'Chinese cinema' meant as an ethnic, cultural, linguistic, political or territorial marker? If so, 'Chinese cinema' itself turns out to be a problematic designation. In ethnic terms, mainland China consists of the majority Han people and fifty-six officially classified national minorities, while Taiwan claims a long history of aboriginal peoples (*shandi ren*, literally 'mountain folks'), and Hong Kong has a multiracial, multi-ethnic population. In cultural terms, although most Chinese may choose to identify themselves with a civilization thousands of years old, in reality they are aware of regional differences such as those existing between northerners and southerners in the mainland, or mainlanders (*waisheng ren*) and islanders in Taiwan. Perhaps the most striking difference is the widespread, diverse, often mutually unintelligible dialects all over China. Thus, in linguistic terms, Mandarin cinema (*guoyu pian*) stands in opposition to Cantonese cinema in Hong Kong and to Taiwanese-dialect film (*Taiyu pian*) in Taiwan. In political terms, furthermore, ideological and institutional differences in the governments of mainland China, Hong Kong and Taiwan after 1949 have left indelible marks on film productions from what are often referred to as three Chinas.

The problematic nature of 'Chinese' as a signifier should suffice to demythify 'Chineseness' as a pre-given, monolithic and immutable essence. The question to be pursued further is whether we are content with speaking of Chineseness in the plural, as so many kinds of Chinese cinemas and their corresponding Chinesenesses. For Rey Chow, 'the problem of Chineseness is . . . not likely to be resolved simply by way of the act of pluralizing', and 'the poststructuralist theoretical move of splitting and multiplying a monolithic identity (such as *China* and *Chinese)* from within . . . is by itself inadequate as a method of reading' (1998: 24). Chow's warning of the theoretical inadequacy of pluralization notwithstanding, what we have seen since the mid-1990s is the apparent consensus that films from all three Chinas may be covered under the umbrella term 'Chinese cinema(s)', with or without the plural form.

The point at issue here is not that 'Chinese' will ever be an adequate marker. After all, critics like Yueh-yu Yeh (1998) can suggest no better term to replace 'Chinese cinema' than 'Chinese-language cinema' (*huayu dianying* or *Zhongwen dianying*). Anxiety about the equation of 'Chinese cinema' to 'Zhongguo dianying' (literally, 'cinema of the Chinese nation-state') finds a better articulation in Xiaobing Tang's explication of the term 'Chinese literature' (2000: 347):

> The history and vitality of Taiwan and Hong Kong literatures in the twentieth century . . . make an ever more compelling case that by 'modern Chinese literature' we understand not a narrow nation-state institution . . . nor just one geopolitically bounded literary production, but rather a vast literature written in modern Chinese and interacting with long and

uneven literary and cultural traditions – regional as much as national . . . 'Chinese literature' should be usefully broadened to mean 'Zhongwen wenxue' (literature in Chinese) and replace a narrowing 'Zhongguo wenxue' (literature of China, or even, of the Chinese nation-state).

Ideally, like 'literature in Chinese', 'Chinese-language cinema' should be a broader term than 'Chinese cinema' as the former may include Chinese-language films directed by the Chinese diaspora in Southeast Asia, West Europe and North America. However, 'Chinese-language cinema' may also be a *narrower* term because it is misleading to assume that what binds Chinese cinema together are its common linguistic features. A casual look at Chinese subtitles in many Hong Kong films since the 1980s would convince one that their intentionally *hybridized* linguistic practice – one that mixes standard written Chinese with invented characters to match spoken Cantonese – is meant precisely to highlight their regional difference and to subvert the myth of a unified, universal and unchanging Chinese script (Kam 1993). A new trend in the late 1990s also challenges an exclusively linguistic definition of Chinese cinema because several ethnic Chinese directors have made English-language films, sometimes with a separate soundtrack in Chinese.

It should be clear by now that a principal source of the anxiety about *Zhongguo dianying* is the association of *guo* in Chinese with the 'nation-state' or simply 'state'. But this problem is not as serious in Chinese as in English because, contrary to Crofts' proposal to envision a 'state cinema', we can strategically approach the 'Chinese' in 'Chinese cinema' in predominantly *cultural* and *historical* terms. For this book I prefer to use 'Chinese national cinema' to cover all films produced in mainland China (including those prior to 1949), Hong Kong and Taiwan, and instruct the reader to keep in mind all problematics or messiness – theoretical as well as geopolitical – surrounding 'China' and 'Chineseness'. This general and potentially *comparative* framework of Chinese national cinema enables us to trace the interactions between Beijing, Shanghai and Hong Kong (all marked by distinctive dialect uses) in early cinema and transnational cinema throughout the twentieth century. It also directs our attention to the remarkable similarities between nationalist state policies (such as film censorship and state subsidy) of the Chinese Communist Party (CCP) regime in the mainland and the Kuomingtang (KMT) regime in Taiwan after 1949. Rather than being constantly apprehensive about the unsettling, multifaceted Chineseness in Chinese national cinema, I believe it is the 'national' as historically constructed, circulated and contested in Chinese cinema that demands our in-depth investigation.

THE 'NATIONAL' AS CINEMATIC PROJECTS

Here, we must confront another kind of messiness unique to Chinese cinema: the Chinese language does not possess an exact equivalent to the English word 'nation'. A nation can be translated as both *minzu* (nation-people) or *guojia* (nation-state) in Chinese (Y. Zhang 2002: 152–7), and a national cinema thus means more than a nation-state cinema, for it also implies a cinema of, by or for the nation-people. The construction of the national has consequently become an ongoing project of contestation whereby the state and the people compete for the right to speak in the name of the nation.

Historically, this tension between people and state has resulted in a cyclical or spiral pattern of development in Chinese cinema: from cinemas of the nation-people during the 1920s through to the 1940s (e.g., early cinema and leftist cinema) to cinemas of the nation-state during the 1950s to the 1970s (e.g., socialist realism in mainland China and healthy realism in Taiwan) and back to cinemas of the nation-people during the 1980s and 1990s (e.g., New Chinese Cinema marked by its cultural reflection and New Taiwan Cinema marked by its rewriting of Taiwan history). The increasing interdependence of people and state in both mainland China and Taiwan at the turn of the new millennium thus lends legitimacy to *guo/zu* (nation/people), a shorthand new coinage originated from Taiwan. But even this new integrative term is built on an inherent split of the two fundamentally incompatible parts, thereby further foregrounding the messiness of the national in Chinese cinema.

I suggest that we take the messiness of Chinese cinema *positively*, as a sign that producers, filmmakers, exhibitors, state regulators, critics and audiences in different Chinese geopolitical regions and over different periods of time have aspired to different constructions of the national. Given the fundamentally messy and dispersed attributes of Chinese cinema, its enunciation of the national must be examined at multiple levels, historically, typologically and theoretically, all at once.

Theoretically, Chris Berry proposes that we study 'national agency' as a missing term in current scholarship on cinema and the national. For him, 'the nation is not merely an imagined textual object but a historically and socially contingent construction of a form of collective agency' (1998: 132). His source of inspiration is Judith Butler's theory of citation and iterability, 'a flexible conceptual framework that suggests any identity is infinitely plural because it exists only in its infinitely different citations' (Berry 1998: 146). From there he recommends 'recasting national cinema as a multiplicity of projects, authored by different individuals, groups, and institutions with various purposes, but bound together by the politics of national agency and collective subjectivity as constructed entities' (1998: 132).

Yet Berry's 'national agency' is itself an ambiguous term. How do we measure national agency – against regional or local agency, international or transnational forces? On what kind of the 'national' does national agency rely – the nation-state or the nation-people? And what is the relationship between individual subjectivity and national agency? Questions like these notwithstanding, I find Berry's reformulation of national cinema as multiple and heterogeneous projects particularly useful to a study of the national in Chinese cinema. Following Berry, we can entertain a vision of several distinct but equally valid Chinese national cinemas as 'socially, politically, and historically specific projects contesting each other in the construction of Chinese national agency, which is itself defined in various ways' (Berry 1998: 132). This vision allows for the possibility that a particular cinematic project of constructing national, regional or other collective agency or identity may exceed the unitary nation-state model, but it does not disqualify the project as belonging to a national cinema at the same time. Films like *Yellow Earth* (Huang tudi, dir. Chen Kaige, 1984), *City of Sadness* (Beiqing chengshi, dir. Hou Hsiao-hsien [Hou Xiaoxian], 1989) and *Centre Stage* (Ruan Lingyu, dir. Stanley Kwan [Guan Jinpeng], 1992) are just a few examples here. Moreover, the flexibility of this vision enables us not only to reformulate China (or Chineseness) as 'a discursively produced and socially and historically contingent collective entity' (Berry 1998: 131), but it also clears the way for strategic allegiance or permutation by means of boundary-crossing, *intra-national* and *intercultural* citations of images, themes, motifs, styles, genres and other cinematic or cultural conventions – strategies that historically characterize film production in all three Chinas.

FILM HISTORIOGRAPHY

A historical perspective is paramount to sorting out instances of allegiance and permutation as well as contestation and deconstruction in Chinese cinema. At the same time, we must remember that film history as a mode of inquiry has its own limits. 'The history of the cinema,' Gerald Mast asserts, 'will never be written; we shall simply have to be satisfied with histories of the cinema' (1976: 298). Histories of Chinese cinema were published as early as the 1920s and 1930s (ZDZ 1996a: 1320–5, 1355–80, 1385–1432), and the 1990s saw a proliferation of such writings in both Chinese and English. Rather than a full-fledged typology of Chinese film historiography (Y. Zhang 2000), I want to briefly differentiate several *types* of conventional historiography of national cinema here.

First, the *auteurist historiography* is dedicated to the study of a canon of masterpieces, and the historian's task is to locate outstanding careers, representative works and distinguished styles. As an early proponent of this approach, Mast thus justifies his practice: 'Just as the history of the novel is, to some extent, a catalogue of important novels, . . . the history of film as an art revolves around important films (1976: 298). For Mast, film is undoubtedly the most reliable textual source from which the historian can proceed to study the 'great film minds' in the history of cinema. In accordance with this model, Kwok-kan Tam and Wimal Dissanayake's *New Chinese Cinema* (1998) stages a hit parade of six great recent Chinese film minds – Chen Kaige, Zhang Yimou, Tian Zhuangzhuang, Hou Hsiao-hsien, Edward Yang (Yang Dechang) and Stanley Kwan. One problem with the auteurist approach is that it inevitably situates cinema in 'the province of the high art rather than popular culture' (Hayward 1993: 7), and the outcome is generally more biographical than historical.

7

Figure 1.1 Zhang Yimou: an auteur from China's fifth generation

Second, the *movement approach* aims at a similarly 'monumental' history, foregrounding moments of exception at the expense of a more comprehensive picture. Typically, the complexity and heterogeneity of a national cinema is systematically reduced, and the priority is given to narrating 'a select series of relatively self-contained quality film movements [that] carry forward the banner of national cinema' (Higson 1995: 22). Not surprisingly, the leftist film movement and the fifth generation have become virtually synonymous with pre-1949 and contemporary Chinese cinema in the mainland (J. Cheng *et al.* 1981; X. Zhang 1997), while New Taiwan Cinema stands for Taiwan film in general. What usually happens is that 'such cinema "movements" occupy a key position in conventional histories of world cinema, whose historiography is not only nationalist but also elitist in its search for the "best" films' (Crofts 1993: 62). One needs only to browse through the entries on China, Hong Kong and Taiwan in two recent film surveys to see the *reductive* nature of such a movement approach to film historiography (Hill and Gibson 1998: 543–81; Nowell-Smith 1996: 409–12, 693–713).

Third, the *theme-and-issues approach* concentrates on specific themes and genres in a national cinema (Elsaesser 1989: 1). The best recent example is perhaps Rey Chow's study of 'primitive passions' and auto-ethnography in contemporary Chinese cinema, albeit she intended it not so much as film history as a 'cultural history' of modern China (1995: x). A prominent advantage of this approach is its ability to diagnose 'symptoms' of an entire period by way of analyzing selected directors and films. An equally prominent disadvantage, however, is its narrow focus on textual evidence at the expense of film production, distribution, exhibition and reception.

In addition to the *text-based* and the *criticism-based* approaches (both exemplified by Chow), Andrew Higson mentions two other types of film historiography – the *industry* or *production-based analysis* and the *exhibition-led* or *consumption-based approach* (1989: 36–7). Higson advances 'an argument that the parameters of a national cinema should be drawn at the site of consumption as much as at the site of production of films; an argument, in other words, that focuses on the activity of national audiences and the conditions under which they make sense of and use the films they watch' (1989: 36). Chow's *Primitive Passions*, for instance, tells us little about how Chinese audiences make sense of the 'auto-ethnographic' films which they watch. For his study of the construction of a national cinema in Britain, Higson adopts a *case-study method* (1995: 272), using five films as a combined textual and contextual basis from which to unravel a fascinating history of film industry, filmmakers, film genres, film iconography, film audience and film criticism.

In Chinese film studies, production (industry) and consumption (audience) are two underdeveloped areas. Jay Leyda's chronology of film events and publications remains an isolated early attempt in English (1972), but there has been an increasing Chinese output in this area since the early 1990s, especially on Taiwan cinema (Chiao 1993; F. Lu 1998). A daunting problem facing the film historian has always been the lack of access to early films and film statistics. In the past decade, the publication of early film scripts and film reviews, together with the release of early films on VCDs (video compact disks) and extensive filmographies on mainland China and Hong Kong, have considerably eased the access problem. Such improvements of the research situation, admittedly still insufficient, should encourage Chinese film scholars to consider Higson's following argument more seriously (1989: 45–6):

> To explore national cinema . . . means laying much greater stress on the point of consumption, and on the *use* of film (sounds, images, narratives, fantasies), than on the point of production. It involves a shift in emphasis away from the analysis of film texts as vehicles for the articulation of national sentiment and the interpellation of the implied national spectator, to an analysis of how actual audiences construct their identity in relation to the various products of the national and international film and television industries, and the condition under which this is achieved.

Following Higson, I propose that we pay *sufficient* attention to archival material and historical evidence before or while committing ourselves to interpretations and speculations fashioned by theoretical or ideological positions. To say the least, a willing consideration of various issues at both production and consumption ends may compel us to re-examine lacunae, discrepancies and contradictions in film scholarship itself.

HISTORICAL PERIODIZATION

It is no surprise that different theoretical models hold sway at different times in film historiography in different geopolitical locales (Y. Zhang 1999a: 8–9). The ways in which ideological issues may alter our view of Chinese film history are illustrated by two examples from mainland China. First, based on the principles of 'Marxist' historiography, Li Shaobai divides Chinese film history into nine periods (1991: 43–63): (1) initial experiment, 1905–23, (2) early artistic exploration, 1923–6, (3) crisis and turning, 1927–32, (4) revolutionary change, 1932–7, (5) war time, 1937–45, (6) artistic enrichment, 1945–9, (7) socialist cinema, 1949–65, (8) prohibition, 1966–76, and (9) further exploration, 1976–89. Li's case is symptomatic of recent Chinese film historiography in general. In spite of his declared intention to write a history of Chinese *film art*, a project that would differ significantly from the heavily politicized history he collaborated with Cheng Jihua and Xing Zuwen in the early 1960s (J. Cheng *et al.* 1981), he cannot but subscribe to the officially sanctioned historical position. The labeling of his periods thus reflects a fundamental dilemma, which he manages to address by giving priority alternatively to artistic concerns and sociopolitical events, thereby striking at least a semblance of balance.

Paying little attention to balance, Ma Debo advances a revisionist scheme of periodization (1995: 1–32): (1) primitive commercial film, 1905–31, (2) leftist film, 1932–7, (3) realist film, 1947–9, (4) propagandist film, 1949–76, (5) social film, 1980–1, (6) film of life (*rensheng dianying*), 1982–6, (7) cultural film, 1984–7, and (8) modern commercial film, 1987 to present. Clearly,

10

Ma's scheme is not complete because it omits the war years (1938–46) and the immediate post-Mao years (1977–9). The imbalance of his scheme is evident in his preference for the 1980s, which includes four periods with overlapping years. Ma's scheme is designed to advance his argument in favor of a *cyclical model* of development in Chinese cinema, which recognizes an extraordinary coincidence of commercial film as the dominating mode at the beginning as well as the end of the twentieth century. In an uncanny way, Chinese cinema seems to have returned to its commercial basis (i.e., film as entertainment or *yule*) after sixty years of ideological battle and political control (i.e., film as vehicle of morality or *zaidao*).

Both Li's attempt to redress film art and Ma's attempt to reclaim commercial film signal new developments in Chinese film scholarship. Each periodization scheme necessarily fulfills a different objective in film historiography. For my part, since the focus of this book is the national in Chinese cinema, I have devised a larger scheme of periodization in order to accommodate parallel, divergent and diverse developments in mainland China, Hong Kong and Taiwan. The labels of my broad periodization are therefore more *thematic* in nature. I start with early cinema and national traditions (1896–1929) in Chapter 2, and move from cinema and the nation-people (1930–49) in Chapter 3 to the cinematic reinvention of the national in Taiwan (1896–1978) in Chapter 4 and the cinematic revival of the regional in Hong Kong (1945–78) in Chapter 5. I return to examine socialist cinema and the nation-state in the PRC (1949–78) in Chapter 6 and investigate cinema and national/regional cultures in all three Chinas (1979–89) in Chapter 7. I conclude with a discussion of cinema and the transnational imaginary and update developments in the new millennium (1990–2002) in Chapter 8. In all, my scheme aims to provide a flexible framework for a *comparative study* of cinema and the national in mainland China, Hong Kong and Taiwan in the twentieth century.

CHRONOLOGICAL HISTORY

Considering the fact that an up-to-date, comprehensive history of Chinese cinema in English is not yet available at the time of writing, I am convinced that a *chronological history* is the place to start in our endeavor to capture the richness of the national as cinematic projects in twentieth-century China. Such a history naturally follows the chronological order, and its approach is necessarily *synthetic* and interpretative, relying in turns on industry analysis, biographic sketch, stylistic consideration, textual criticism and audience study, among others. Given the fundamental diversity of Chinese cinema, I have devised a multi-layered, multi-focused scheme of presentation. In each chapter, I divide a period into phases, organizing information and offering analysis in regard to studios, producers, markets (distribution, exhibition, audience), genres, trends, artists (directors, screenwriters, stars), films, arts (aesthetics, style, technology), and sometimes also film publications and criticism.

My emphasis on a chronological history may depart from a new move in contemporary historiography: namely, the move from global history to sectorial or fragmentary history, from monumental history to diagrammatic history, from historicist history to structural history, and from documental history to conjectural history (Talens and Zunzunegui 1997). But my choice of a more conventional method in this book is conditioned by the current state of Chinese film scholarship in English. We must first of all explore a wide range of articulations of the national in Chinese cinema in order to appreciate, modify, challenge or subvert the conceptual frameworks of these articulations and the scholarship based on them. Simply put, we must be patient and willing to conduct primary research and complete the *constructive* phase of film historiography before we can proceed with deconstruction and reconstruction in any confident, meaningful way.

Ostensibly, this book does not attempt to embrace the totality of Chinese cinema, nor does it entertain the possibility of exploring all archival resources or exhausting all interpretive frameworks related to the national in Chinese cinematic projects. Similarly, this book does not dwell solely on the 'great film minds' or a body of canonized texts for an excavation of the essential Chineseness, nor does it privilege the marginal or the visionary merely for the sake of endorsing oppositional or alternative politics. Other caveats must follow. Given a limited space, this book concentrates primarily on feature films; documentary, animation and other types of film production – as valid articulations of the national themselves – regrettably have to await further investigation. The limited space also renders it unfeasible for me to cite all previous studies, although I appreciate their invaluable contributions, each in its own way, to our understanding of Chinese cinema in general. The access problem has prevented a more in-depth study of such topics as prewar Hong Kong cinema, the Japanese-sponsored Manchurian Motion Pictures, and wartime production in Japanese-occupied Shanghai. These imbalances, however, do not impact the overall picture of Chinese cinema narrated in the following chapters. As new archival material surfaces, a more comprehensive history will surely arrive to further our knowledge of Chinese cinema in all its diversity and complexity.

2

CINEMA AND NATIONAL
TRADITIONS, 1896–1929

INTRODUCTION: EARLY CINEMA

This chapter covers the period of early cinema in China. The period started in 1896, a year in which film was first exhibited in China, and ended in 1929, a year in which the crisis-ridden film industry struggled to restructure itself and the premiere of American talkies in a major Shanghai venue signaled the impending technological change.

This period witnessed several events that would fundamentally change the history of modern China. The Republican Revolution of 1911 overthrew the Qing court and terminated the imperial system of government in China. The newly created Republic of China, however, did not achieve central control as provincial and regional warlords fought against each other and ruled most of the nation. On the cultural and political fronts, the famous May Fourth movement, which introduced new ideas such as enlightenment and modernity by denouncing age-old Chinese traditions like Confucianism, began in Beijing in 1919 and spread to major cities around the country, and the CCP was founded in Shanghai in 1921. But these two events did not immediately impact the film industry, which reveled in traditional narratives and conservative ideologies. The Northern Expedition launched by the first KMT–CCP united front conquered much of Southern China and brought optimism to the war-torn nation. Yet the bloody crackdown on the CCP engineered by Chiang Kai-shek (Jiang Jieshi) in 1927 and the ensuing years of autocratic rule made the issue of political allegiance precarious for those engaged in film production and criticism. Nonetheless, 1928 marked the beginning of institutional changes favorable to centralized governance and economic development after the KMT government relocated the nation's capital to Nanjing (literally, 'southern capital') from Beijing (literally, 'northern capital', hence renamed Beiping until Beijing was reinstated as the capital of the PRC in 1949).

In terms of film history, this period can be divided into three phases. First, in the phase of *cinema as attractions* (1896–1921), Chinese filmmakers treated film as a new technology possessing an enormous appeal to the audience and hence with potential financial as well as educational benefits. Early short films were intimately wedded to traditional theater (*jiuju* or *xiqu*) and modern drama (*xinxi* or *xinju*), the latter widely known as the 'civilized play' (*wenmingxi*) from the late 1900s to the early 1920s. Second, in the phase of *cinema as narration* (1922–6), filmmakers began to treat film simultaneously as a business by organizing production companies with explicit objectives and investing in distribution and exhibition chains and as a profession by launching film magazines, establishing film schools and publishing film books. The success of feature-length films like *Orphan Rescues Grandfather* (Guer jiuzhu ji, dir. Zhang Shichuan, 1923; 10 reels), some of them influenced by a kind of popular urban fiction known as 'mandarin ducks and butterflies' (*yuanyang hudie*; 'butterfly' hereafter), strengthened the status of film as a legitimate art form. Third, in the phase of *cinema and speculations* (1927–9), cheap primitive genre films and the ferocious competition among studios overwhelmed the market and resulted in financial ruin for innumerable companies in Shanghai. The immense popularity of martial arts films like *The Burning of Red Lotus Temple, I–XVIII* (Huoshao honglian si, dir. Zhang Shichuan, 1928–31, 27 hours total) set a record for serial production and pushed this new genre to its market limits.

In general, early Chinese cinema did not establish itself as a full-fledged 'industry' because the security of a vertically integrated system was not in place and there was no concentrated ownership simultaneously coordinating the operations of investment, production, distribution and exhibition as a whole. Independent and under-funded in most cases, production companies rose and fell regardless of their ideological intentions, artistic visions or financial wellbeing, thus creating a chaotic film market not unlike that of France at the same time. In terms of film technology, especially camerawork and post-production, Chinese filmmakers relied heavily on foreign expertise at first but managed to learn the basics along the way. Similarly, exhibition venues changed from the teahouse through the opera theater to the modern cinema, as film itself evolved from a leisure attraction to a narrative art over these two decades.

Understandably, the period of early cinema in China is linked to its 'prehistory' as well. Generally, 28 December 1895 is regarded as the birthday of cinema, this being the day that the Lumière brothers showed their documentary shorts at the Grand Café in Paris. Shortly afterwards, on 11 August 1896, a French showman introduced 'Western shadowplays' (*xiyang yingxi*) amidst variety shows at the Xu Gardens (Xuyuan), an entertainment complex in Shanghai, thus marking cinema's first entrance in China. In July 1897 the American film made its debut in China when James Ricalton of New Jersey exhibited a program of Thomas Edison movies at the Tianhua Teahouse in Shanghai, charging tickets at four levels ranging from 0.1 to 0.5 yuan (Du 1988: 7) (see Tables 2.1 and 2.2).[1] In 1903 Spaniard Antonio Ramos took over the business started in 1899 by his countryman Galen Bocca and screened films at public venues in Shanghai such as a skating rink, teahouses and restaurants. Ramos' consistent effort

Table 2.1 Approximate value of Chinese currencies, 1920s–90s

General	Item	Equivalent
1927–9	1 yuan (silver coin)	US$0.38–0.45
Jan–Dec 1930	1 yuan (silver coin)	US$0.23–0.38
Jan 1931–Feb 1933	1 yuan (silver coin)	US$0.20–0.25
March 1933–May 1935	1 yuan (silver coin)	US$0.20–0.42
Nov 1935–July 1937	1 yuan (*fabi* or legal tender)	US$0.30
1960s–90s	HK$7.8	US$1
1980s–90s	RMB8.3	US$1

Specific	Item	Equivalent
1930	3 yuan	US$1
1934	2.4 yuan	US$1
1948	HK$4.5	US$1
1951–8	NT$32.28 (exchange to US$)	US$1
1951–8	NT$26.35 (exchange from US$)	US$1
1999	NT$32.27	US$1
2001	NT$33	US$1
1955–8	NT$7–8	HK$1

Sources: Y. Ding 1998: 105–24; GIO 2001: 154; J. Gong 1967: 479; R. Huang 2001: 40; Kubo 1986: 54; L. Lee 1999: 83; F. Lu 1998: 57; Z. Wang 1998: 64; Z. Zhang 1990: 303–4.

Note: After 1937, the unstable wartime situation and skyrocketing postwar inflation made it impossible to calculate exact equivalents between Chinese yuan and US dollars.

eventually made his programs at the Green Lotus Pavilion profitable (Leyda 1972: 2–3). Also in 1903 Lin Zhusan, who had studied in Germany, brought home a projector and reels of film and showed them at the Tianle Teahouse in Beijing (S. Cheng *et al.* 1927: chap. 2).

Just as foreign businessmen had to rely on traditional entertainment venues to attract Chinese audiences to the newly imported Western shadowplays, the Chinese on their part insisted on claiming certain credit for the invention of cinema by tracing comparable shadowplays in their *national traditions*. The inverted picture shown in a black box was said to exist in China as early as 475–221 BC and around 140 BC the Chinese invented the 'lighted shadow-play', in which papercut human figures were projected onto a screen for enjoyment. The lighted shadowplay reportedly had traveled to the Middle East and Southeast Asia by the thirteenth century, and between 1767 and 1776 it reached France (as *ombres chinoises*) and England (J. Cheng *et al.* 1981: 1: 4–5). The term 'shadowplay' (*yingxi*) – as well as its derivative, 'Western shadowplay' (i.e., film or *dianying*, literally 'electric shadows') – thus foregrounds a conscientious effort of the Chinese to treat film as historically related to and conceptually indebted to some kind of Chinese tradition. As shall be clearer below, institutionally as well as theoretically, early Chinese filmmakers depended on their experience with

15

Table 2.2 Sample ticket prices in China, 1890s–1940s

Year	Theater	Type of film	Prices (yuan)
1897	Tianhua Teahouse	Edison movies	0.1–0.5
1910s–20s	YMCA	domestic comic shorts	0.1
1910s–20s	Great World	midnight show	0.1–0.2
early 1920s	Embassy	foreign and domestic	1–5
1920s	Pavilion, Beijing	foreign	up to 2
1920s	Zhenguang, Beijing	weekend foreign matinee at student discount	0.1
1932	first-run venues, e.g., Capitol, Lanxin, Majestic	foreign sound	1–2
1932	first-run venues, e.g., Cathay, Carlton, Grand, Strand	foreign and domestic	0.6
1932	second-run venues, e.g., Paris, Iris, Odeon, Peking, Palace, Embassy, Apollo, Wiley	foreign and domestic	0.4
1932	second-run venues, e.g., Star, Guanghua, New Palace	foreign and domestic	0.3
1932	third-run venues, e.g., Empire, Carter, China, Hongkew	foreign and domestic	0.2
1932	others, e.g., Zhabei	unknown	0.1
1936	cheapest to highest	foreign and domestic	0.2–2
1940	first-run venues	foreign and domestic	3.2
1941	average venues, Manchuria	Japanese and domestic	0.2–1.5
1941	teahouse-type venues, Beijing	domestic silent	0.1–0.2
1942	first-run venues	Japanese and domestic	8
1945	first-run venues	domestic	60
1948	cheapest to highest	foreign and domestic	0.2–1.2 million

Sources: Y. Ding 1998: 105–24; Du 1988: 7; Fu 1997: 72–7; Fu 1998: 91–9; Hou 1996: 199–218; Leyda 1972: 2–3; S. Li and Hu 1996: 104; Manzhou zazhi she, March–April 1941; ZDZ 1996a: 191–8, 1496, 1509, 1569.

Note: All theaters are in Shanghai unless otherwise indicated.

theater-drama and deliberately validated 'play' or 'theater' (*xi*) as foundational to Chinese film practice.

CINEMA AS ATTRACTIONS, 1896–1921

For foreign exhibitors and Chinese filmmakers alike, the primary concern in the initial phase was to *attract* the Chinese audience to Western shadowplays as an acceptable form of modern entertainment. Zhang Shichuan thus remembered his first reaction to filmmaking in 1913: 'since it is making shadow "plays", I naturally associated it with traditional "plays" in China' (ZDZ

1996a: 401). Immersed in national traditions, Chinese theater thus provided a focus both as an institutional base and as an artistic model for early cinema in China.

Early exhibition: teahouse, tent and theater

To attract audiences, early exhibitors relied solely on old-fashioned venues like teahouses and theaters. Parallels between watching a traditional stage performance and early cinema can be drawn here. Characteristically of a teahouse, viewers sat at tables, while tea, snacks and occasionally hot towels were served (ZDZ 1996a: 1381). Since patrons came to such occasions as much to meet friends as to enjoy movies as exotic spectacles, they tended to drink, chat, laugh, shout, applaud, cough and spit at any time (ZDZ 1996a: 182–3, 608). This means that during a show the theater was a noisy or even chaotic place, a situation which did *not* bother the early audience too much. As reminisced by the eminent butterfly writer Bao Tianxiao, a small theater inside the Shanghai Great World Amusement Park regularly featured stage plays from eight o'clock in the evening to midnight at 0.3–0.4 yuan per ticket and showed movies from midnight to one-thirty in the morning at 0.1–0.2 yuan (see Table 2.2, p. 16). The midnight shows did brisk business because this was the time when courtesans arrived to enjoy themselves (ZDZ 1996a: 1509). Indeed, such a combination of film exhibition and theater performance had existed in China for decades. After its renovation in 1906, Beijing's Grand Shadowplay Theater (Daguanlou, 400 seats) featured both plays and movies. These examples confirm that the traditional theater seemed to provide the most reliable place to attract the Chinese and familiarize them with early cinema.

In addition to featuring movies amidst variety shows, some theaters developed what were known as 'chained-sequence plays' (*lianhuanxi* or *liansuoju*), a program of alternate live theatrical performances and film screenings (normally with five to six transitions). Modeled after its Japanese counterpart, the chained-sequence play sought to doubly satisfy the audience's needs by making the film and the theater complement each other. Just as the film might extend the theater through location shootings, the theater would heighten the artistic impact by introducing singing and chanting at the right moment, something cinema could not deliver in the silent era. But the requirement that the same actors appear both on stage and on the screen proved logistically too difficult to manage and financially too expensive to produce. Consequently, chained-sequence plays went out of fashion (M. He 1956: 49–50).

Fairy Maiden (Lingbo xianzi; 9 reels) and *Red Rose* (Hong meigui) were two chained-sequence plays jointly produced in 1925 by the Shanghai New Stage (Xin wutai) and Xu Zhuodai's Kaixin Film Company. Although Xu admitted these productions were financial disasters (ZDZ 1996a: 377), film historian Gu Jianchen believed that they foreshadowed the full-scale 'costume drama' (*guzhuang pian*). Gu also noted that in 1925 the Shared Stage (Gong wutai), another Shanghai theater, competed with the New Stage and produced a chained-sequence play, *Princess Lotus Flower* (Lianhua gongzhu; 9 reels) (ZDZ 1996a: 1365–6). Later that year, with some members from this production, Gu Wuwei established Great China (Da Zhongguo), which produced two sequels to *Princess Lotus Flower* (1926; 9 reels each). There is no indication whether these sequels were chained-sequence plays or entirely films. But what matters is that, in spite of its ephemeral existence, the chained-sequence play had served its function as a transitional, *hybrid* form of visual-performing arts that moved early Chinese audiences closer to a full screen experience.

As an alternative to the theater, an early exhibitor might rent an empty lot and set up a tent for screening, as an Italian expatriate A. E. Louros did in 1907. The audience paid a few coins to sit on rows of narrow benches placed on uneven, dirty and sometimes muddy ground. Ventilation was poor, and no heating or cooling system was installed inside the tent. As in a traditional theater, men and women were required to sit in separate seats, and the police was routinely invited inside to keep order (Hou 1996). In terms of creature comfort, these tents were worse than noisy theaters, and it was not long before enterprising businessmen started to invest in movie theaters in China.

In 1907 the first Chinese movie theater, the Pavilion Cinema (Ping'an), was built in Beijing.[2] As with most other cinemas to come, the venue was foreign-owned and served mostly foreign patrons (ZDZ 1996a: 177). A year later, but-tressed by a steady income from teahouse screenings, Ramos completed the Hongkou Cinema in Shanghai, a simple sheet-iron structure of 250 hard seats, yet the first among dozens of modern theaters to be erected in the treaty port in the following decades (S. Li and Hu 1996: 19–20).

Early audience: class, gender and motivation

Corresponding to the changes taking place in theaters, Chinese audiences of early cinema had also transformed themselves. In the early years, traditional theater fans might venture side trips into the exotic spectacles offered by Western shadowplays. Typically, these early shorts featured smiling female dancers, a woman bathing in a tub, passengers on a giant steamship, a bicycle race involving a head-on collision, and the police and passers-by chasing a troublemaker on the street (Leyda 1972: 2; Y. Zheng 1982: 1–2). As time went by, students, clerks and other educated urbanites were no longer content with action-filled slap-stick. Instead, they would join the gentry and other urban leisure classes in appreciating the screen equivalents of butterfly stories in the 1920s. The adaptation of traditional narratives of legendary heroes and historical figures further accustomed an audience of the literate and the illiterate alike to watching films as a satisfactory experience. More satisfied perhaps were those upper-class ladies who brought their tailors to a show and ordered them to custom-make any screen fashions that happened to catch their fancy (Cambon 1995: 34). In sum, from the turn of the century to the 1920s, the shadowplay evolved from an occasional visual treat to a staple in entertainment.

In 1927 Chen Dabei divided Beijing audiences into four groups: (1) the majority liked exciting stories with convoluted plots; (2) women liked sentimental tales and tear-jerkers; (3) more senior, experienced audiences liked characterization in depth; (4) a minority of intellectuals liked to study meaning in a film (ZDZ 1996a: 606). But even the last group might watch films simply for entertainment. A 1930 poll of eighty-five college sophomores demonstrated that seventy of them watched films for fun, compared to fifteen for learning English or for a taste of history (ZDZ 1996b: iv). The pressure of entertainment had engendered widespread opportunism in the film industry of the time, and even serious filmmakers had to concede to the market demand. Yang Xiaozhong admitted in 1926 that the most crucial thing was to cater to the taste of audiences of the middle and lower social strata. Zheng Zhengqiu was cognizant in 1925 of the necessity to adjust his goal of social education by adopting a pragmatic policy of 'commercialism with a dose of conscience' (ZDZ 1996b: v).

Early production: Yaxiya, Huanxian and Zhang Shichuan

As with early exhibition, it was a foreigner who established the first production company in China. Benjamin Brodsky (aka Brasky), a Jewish-American of Russian descent, founded Yaxiya (China Cinema Company, aka Asia Film) in Shanghai in 1909 and produced shorts in Shanghai and Hong Kong (Law 2000: 45–6). Nothing substantial came out until 1912, when Brodsky transferred his business to two compatriots, T. H. Suffert and a Mr Yashell. As manager of a life insurance company in Shanghai, Yashell knew little of the film business in China, so he entrusted production to his associate Jing Yingsan's nephew, Zhang Shichuan. At age 21 and speaking Pidgin English, Zhang recruited his playwright friend Zheng Zhengqiu to form Xinmin (literally, 'new people'), a film company based on Minming, a theater troupe organized by Zhang and Zheng and devoted to civilized plays. Since the stage performance took place in the evening and their employees had little to do during the day, Zhang and Zheng were particularly receptive to the film project, as their contract with Yaxiya had shifted the burden of their salaries to Yashell.

With Yaxiya responsible for funding (US$30,000) and technology, and Xinmin for screenplay, directing and acting, an example of *film co-production* was set in Chinese film history. Yashell first wanted to adapt *Wronged Ghosts in Opium Den* (Heiji yuanhun), a popular civilized play from the New Stage, but gave up the idea when he found out about its anti-drug theme and the theater owners' asking price (5,000 yuan). Instead, *The Difficult Couple* (Nanfu nanqi, dir. Zhang and Zheng; 4 reels), a comedy poking fun at traditional wedding rituals in Zheng's hometown in Guangdong province, became Yaxiya's first feature, which premiered at the New New Stage (Xinxin wutai) in September 1913.

Despite this successful cooperation, Zheng left Yaxiya to devote his energy to the civilized play and became known as a leading playwright and drama critic who would revive the genre in the mid-1910s (ZDZ 1996a: 398; Tan 1992: 1–216). Meanwhile, Zhang knew little about his work as film 'director' or *daoyan*, a Chinese term Lu Jie would invent in 1922. With Yashell standing behind a fixed camera, Zhang enjoyed directing his actors against a simple painted backdrop. In lieu of a full-scripted screenplay, early directors like Zhang used *mubiao*, something Zheng had adopted from the practice in the Beijing opera and the civilized play. A *mubiao* is divided in four parts: (1) number of acts; (2) indoor and outdoor settings in each act; (3) appearance of characters; and (4) main plots. Further details might be added to the plot section, such as gestures, facial expressions and main dialogue, but most actors *improvised* in the middle of shooting (ZDZ 1996a: 1574). Intertitles (*zimu*), sometimes *bilingual* in semi-literary Chinese and English, were added after the film was completed. Indeed, as Yaxiya's other American boss, Suffert was responsible for writing English intertitles and synopses (*benshi*).

Normally, Zhang shot a comic short in four to five days. Modeled after American slapsticks in style but drawn from funny acts preceding the feature civilized plays, these shorts were never welcomed by major theaters and had to be scheduled after the shows of civilized plays or at the YMCA at 0.1 yuan a ticket (ZDZ 1996a: 1569). A more reliable source of income came from the sales to Southeast Asia, where comedies were popular among the less educated Chinese diaspora. Yaxiya's fortune ran out as the outbreak of World War I in 1914 interrupted the supply of German film stock (ZDZ 1996a: 1388–91).

Zhang returned to manage Minming in addition to his uncle's amusement park, but he resumed film activities when American film stock arrived in 1916. With a few friends, he raised 6,000 yuan and established Huanxian. Since *Wronged Ghosts in Opium Den* continued to play to a capacity audience in Shanghai, Zhang rented equipment from Louros and directed a 5-reeler of the same title. This time, Zhang varied the position of the camera between takes, employing long, medium, close and extreme close-up shots. Although the picture had a decent theater run, Huanxian went out of business and became the first of innumerable 'one-picture companies' in China.

Commercial Press: popular education and national culture

A more prominent player in early cinema was the all-powerful Commercial Press based in Shanghai. In 1917 the company had acquired a Pathé camera, a printing machine and other equipment from an American for less than 3,000 yuan and installed them in its photography studio. In 1918 Commercial Press formally instituted the Motion Picture Department. Having obtained the recently invented lamps in 1919 after aiding the location shooting of a Universal picture in China, the board of trustees approved the funding for new equipment, set production policy and formalized exhibition and rental procedures. The Motion Picture Department produced over forty shorts in five distinct categories: scenery, newsreels, education, ancient plays (opera movies) and modern plays (short features). In particular, their education titles sought to complement a long list of popular primers, textbooks and magazines issued by Commercial Press since its establishment in 1903.

In 1919 Commercial Press justified its motivation in setting up the Motion Picture Department. While most foreign films shown in China were considered by the authorities to be harmful to Chinese custom and morality, those films shot in China and shipped abroad were often exposés of Chinese life at the lower social strata for the sake of ridiculing China. The envisioned products of Commercial Press, on the contrary, endeavored to battle on two fronts. Domestically, their films would be shipped to provincial capitals and commercial centers and shown at select sites as aids in *popular education* in resistance to morally detrimental foreign films. Internationally, their films would promote Chinese culture, abate foreigners' contempt for China and stir up *patriotism* among the overseas Chinese (J. Cheng *et al.* 1981: 1: 39).[3]

In spite of its solid financial support, new facilities (e.g., a glass-wall studio) and lofty rhetoric of *enlightenment*, feature productions from the Motion Picture Department were always substandard. Drawing mainly on traditional narratives, their early titles did not generate critical interest and failed to live up to the board's expectations of promoting modern education. On the other hand, by leasing equipment to small companies and shooting films on others' behalf, the Department claimed the credit for two spectacular successes: *Yan Ruisheng* (dir. Yang Xiaozhong; 10 reels) and *The Vampires* (Hongfen kulou, dir. Guan Haifeng; 14 reels). Together with *Sea Oath* (Haishi, dir. Dan Duyu; 6 reels), these three earliest Chinese feature-length films were all produced in 1921.

'Modern plays' as genre attempts: the three earliest long features

As one of the two categories Commercial Press set up for feature productions, 'modern plays' (i.e., films set in contemporary life) cover a range of possible genres, as illustrated by the three long features cited above. *Yan Ruisheng*, an adaptation of Zheng Zhengqiu's popular civilized play, was based on a sensational real-life case in which a renowned courtesan was murdered for money in 1920. Incidentally, Yan the real-life perpetrator admitted in court that foreign *crime films* had influenced his behavior (J. Cheng *et al.* 1981: 1: 13). Roughly similar to the fiction of social exposé or court cases fashionable among Chinese readers, the film sought to enhance its 'reel' impact by recruiting a former prostitute to play the victim and a former friend of the perpetrator to play Yan. The film premiered at the Embassy, a first-run Shanghai cinema that otherwise featured high-quality Western films, on 1 July 1921. In spite of paying 200 yuan in advertising fees and additional theater rental fees of 200 yuan per day, the film ran for a week and grossed over 4,000 yuan, with 1,300 yuan on the opening day alone (S. Li and Hu 1996: 70).

Bringing *romance* (*aiqing pian*) to the foreground, *Sea Oath* tells of a girl (Yin Mingzhu) who abandons her fiancé (a poor painter) and accepts the luxury provided by her rich cousin. But the film inserts a plot reversal by making the girl a runaway bride who regrets her 'sins' during her wedding at a church and chases the painter to a beach. When he refuses to accept her apology, she attempts suicide by jumping in the sea but is rescued by the painter. The film premiered at the Embassy on 23 January 1922 amidst media publicity, charging as high as 5 yuan a ticket. A 1922 review from the leading newspaper *Shenbao* praised Dan Duyu for capturing certain flavors of Western movies and the first-time actress Yin Mingzhu (aka Pearl Ing) for delivering a performance comparable to that of Mary Pickford. But the review also blamed the film for its Europeanized decors and unrealistic details (ZDZ 1996a: 1079). Nonetheless, Dan was praised for his dedication to quality because he had spent six months shooting *Sea Oath* and had discarded 15,000 feet of rushes to settle for a six-reeler of 6,000 feet (S. Li and Hu 1996: 73, 104).

The Vampires was an attempt at the *detective* and *thriller* genres. Based on a French detective story and originally titled *Ten Sisters*, the film devises a complicated plot of the kidnaps of a doctor and a lawyer by the Vampire Gang, whose members include ten gorgeous women. The locations of a hospital, a city park and an insurance company highlight the film's modern look, while the gang's secret cave and witchcraft intensify the ambience of mystery. The use of special effects and martial arts fights, along with a happy ending in which the lovers are united and married, further guaranteed the film's box-office success. For promotion, the producers sent a truck to tour the city, blasting its loud speakers and trumpets and distributing film plot sheets along the way. The scene of the gorgeous gangsters' meeting was staged live on the truck. When the film premiered at the Embassy on 10 May 1922, tickets were sold at three-tiered prices from 1 to 3 yuan (see Table 2.2, p. 16). Even foreigners joined the Chinese crowd in the theater, and the film was screened in Beijing, Tianjin and other large cities, as well as in such countries as Japan and Vietnam (ZDZ 1996a: 1496).

CINEMA AS NARRATION, 1922–6

The upshot of the success of the first three long features was the twin realization by Chinese filmmakers that film could be a profitable business in addition to a popular attraction and that feature-length modern plays had a better chance of attracting audiences than comic shorts. As a result, from the early to mid-1920s many studios were established, most of which specialized in producing films of contemporary life.

Mingxing: between entertainment and education

The most influential studio to emerge in the early 1920s was Mingxing (Star Motion Picture Company), founded in Shanghai in 1922 by Zhang Shichuan, Zheng Zhengqiu, Zhou Jianyun and two others with 10,000 yuan originally earmarked for stock speculations. The conflict between Zhang's profiteering mindset and Zheng's moralizing propensity surfaced immediately. While Zhang insisted on catering to the audience, Zheng proposed 'serious feature plays'; whereas Zhang declared that his films had no 'isms' (*zhuyi*) to speak of, Zheng insisted that films must have 'isms' (Luo *et al.* 1992: 1: 67). Their initial agreement was to bring out Zhang's preferred comic shorts, most of which proved unsuccessful. *Zhang Xinsheng* (dir. Zhang Shichuan, 1922; 8 reels), a more serious film about a real-life patricidal case, sold well at first but was chastised for its 'ruthless' depictions of murder and autopsy and was reportedly banned afterward (ZDZ 1996a: 403, 1520). Financial difficulty compelled Zhang to adopt Zheng's proposal in 1923, which materialized in *Orphan Rescues Grandfather*, a phenomenal success that took eight months to prepare but brought Mingxing an unexpected financial windfall (its assets now valued at 100,000 yuan) and secured its position as an industry leader (Du 1988: 70).

Between 1924 and 1928, Mingxing produced nearly sixty long features. A great number of these films portrayed suffering women of different ages and varied backgrounds. As with civilized plays, Zheng believed in education and wanted to promote *reform* through Mingxing's 'social films'. Nevertheless, Zheng was fully aware of the market and advocated a tripartite approach to 'social psychology': catering to (*yinghe*), adapting to (*shiying*) and improving (*gailiang*). Although a particular film might adopt all three, Zheng warned in 1925 that Chinese films must aim at the *majority* of audiences and must not be 'too profound' or 'too elevated' in thinking (ZDZ 1996a: 290).

From time to time the press would criticize Zheng's compromised solutions to social problems, but Zhang was happy to support Zheng for financial considerations. To cultivate a loyal following in the female audience, Zhang intended to churn out films that would elicit sympathetic tears and compensate his viewers with happy endings. Over the years, the maturation of Mingxing's family dramas was such that even old ladies were able to follow their convoluted plots, thus guaranteeing Mingxing's popularity across a wide spectrum of audiences (ZDZ 1996a: 1522).

Feature films: from attractions to narration

Perhaps fortuitously, Mingxing had engineered a quantum leap in early Chinese cinema from pure spectacular attractions to sophisticated narration, best illustrated in *Laborer's Love* (Laogong zhi aiqing, dir. Zhang Shichuan, 1922), now reputedly the earliest extant Chinese-made feature, and *Orphan Rescues*

Grandfather. A close reading of these two films will reveal the intricacies of this crucial transformation in Chinese film history.

Billed as a comic short, *Laborer's Love* tells the story of a carpenter-turned-street-vendor's romantic quest for the daughter of an ageing doctor whose business across the street goes downhill. The negotiation between the fruit-seller Zheng and debt-ridden Dr Zhu (Zheng Zhengqiu) leads to an agreement: once Zheng brings prosperity to the clinic, he can marry Zhu's daughter. Typical of the *cinema of attractions*, a form of early cinema Tom Gunning (1998) theorizes as characterized by a series of curious or novel views, *Laborer's Love* offers a quick succession of humorous scenes as spectacular visual treats. Zheng readies fruits for sale with the same precision as he handles carpentry. He swings a box of pears – his tokens of love – across the street to the daughter, who returns the box with her handkerchief and, by accident, her father's glasses. Zheng sees through the glasses and, in an optical point-of-view shot, everything goes out of focus. Some hooligans harass the daughter in a nearby teahouse, so Zheng comes to the rescue. He pushes a fat guy into a huge wok of boiling water and with a ladle pours water over the hooligans' heads. At night, Zheng's sleep is disrupted by a brawl in an upstairs nightclub, where two gamblers fight over a young woman. The climatic scene comes when Zheng devises an ingenious trick the next day by replacing the ladders and turning the stair into a controllable slide. He hides under the stairway and pulls the device when the nightclub patrons are about to descend, thus sending them tumbling down the stairway. As patients arrive at the clinic, Zheng volunteers to help Zhu. The two 'heal' the patients by pounding, pulling, pushing, turning and bending their heads, arms and legs (in fast motion). Upon hearing Zhu's marriage approval, Zheng kneels down and exclaims, 'My father-in-law!' The film ends with Zhu directly facing the camera in a fit of laughter, and his daughter covering her mouth with a handkerchief (ZDZ 1996a: 13–40).

These concluding images recall an earlier, frontal medium shot of Zheng shaking his head in a broad grin, while a superimposed image of him confessing love to the daughter is seen in the upper left-hand corner of the frame. A few shots later, Zheng's face turns miserable, as another superimposed image of Zhu refusing Zheng's proposal appears in the upper left corner. Clearly, by this film, Zhang Shichuan had mastered a number of specifically cinematic tricks. In addition to Zheng's fantasy sequences, a few extreme close-ups (e.g., of a clock or silver coins on Zhu's tray) highlight key narrative details. In spite of innovative camera work, though, the film ensures a fundamental familiarity to the audience by having characters enter and leave on both sides of the frame, thus simulating a viewing experience comparable to that of a stage play.

A closer scrutiny unravels several hidden layers of meaning in this otherwise simple comedy scripted by Zheng Zhengqiu. In its Chinese title, *Laborer's Love* pays lip service to the 'sanctity of working classes' (*laogong shensheng*), a typical May Fourth slogan. With its positive portrayal of the fruit-seller as a working-class member, the film also endorses the notion of 'love of one's free will' (*lian'ai*

Figure 2.1 Laborer's Love (1922): the earliest extant feature in China

ziyou), another standard May Fourth theme. Yet, the fact that Zheng must kneel to Zhu in gratitude at the end of the film implies an endorsement of *filiality*, thereby tactfully anchoring the film in a conservative ideology. The film's alternate Chinese title, *Zhiguo yuan* (literally, 'love occasioned by the throwing of fruits') contains a classical Chinese allusion thus further strengthening the film's claim to national traditions. On the other hand, the fact that the extant print of the film carries English intertitles indicates that the Mingxing producers were fully aware of the Western audience from the outset.

A mixture of disparate, sometimes contradictory elements, *Laborer's Love* embodies the confusion facing early Chinese filmmakers (Z. Zhang 1999). Since this was a transitional moment in Chinese films, the producers threw in pieces grabbed from various sources (e.g., lofty ideas, comic gestures and exaggerated acts). To Mingxing's relief, *Laborer's Love* opened at the Embassy to an enthusiastic crowd and anticipated the studio's fortune a year later (Tan 1992: 247–9).

A feature-length 'ethical drama', *Orphan Rescues Grandfather* starts with the tragic death of millionaire Yang Shouchang's only son, who is survived by his wife Yu Weiru (Wang Hanlun). Persuaded by his clansman, Yang adopts his nephew Daopei, a schemer who eyes Yang's riches. Since Yu is pregnant and a son may threaten Daopei's chance of acquiring a fortune, Daopei conspires with a friend and accuses Yu of infidelity. Yang believes them and kicks out Yu, who gives birth to a son named Pu and works hard to bring him up properly. In the meantime, Daopei squanders away money and gets himself in debt. Yang moves to a new house near a school built with his donations. One day, he is surprised to learn that Pu (Zheng Xiaoqiu, Zhengqiu's son) used what he learned from classical stories and rescued a child who had fallen into a large water pot. Yang pays for the broken pot and invites Pu to his house without knowing Pu's true identity. Debt-ridden Daopei demands money from Yang by force, but Pu who happens to pass by rescues Yang. Yu rushes to Yang's house to see the injured Pu and is shocked to meet Yang, her father-in-law. Before his death, Daopei admits his conspiracy against Yu, and Yang regrets his irresponsibility. The three generations reunite in tears. The ageing Yang entrusts all his fortune to Yu, who donates half of it for building new schools and extending free education to poor children like Pu (ZDZ 1996b: 1: 47–60).

Orphan Rescues Grandfather premiered at Shanghai's Shenjiang Theater on 21 December 1923 and set a box-office record for domestic films. Just as an orphan rescues his grandfather on screen, this film rescued Mingxing from its mounting debts and financed the studio's expansion. The significance of this film was both immediately felt and far-reaching. In 1923 Gu Kenfu judged the film to be extraordinary, the first domestic production to emotionally move the audience in a positive way, although he faulted the film for its excessive uses of intertitles and iris shots (ZDZ 1996a: 1080–1). In 1934 Gu Jianchen declared that the film had ushered in 'an unprecedented national film move-ment' (ZDZ 1996a: 1364). In 1992 Tan Chunfa regarded the film as the first Chinese 'art film', a work of 'idealized realism' laudable for its accessibility as popular education, its appropriate level of audience appreciation, its abundant humanism and its engaging narrative (1992: 270–84). Arguably, with *Orphan Rescues Grandfather*, early Chinese cinema had completed a number of sig-nificant transformations: artistically, from a cinema of attractions to a *narrative cinema*; conceptually, from film as leisure entertainment to social enlighten-ment; institutionally, from filmmaking as opportunist investment to a legitimate business.

Family drama: a 'Chinese' genre

Like Zheng's subsequent family dramas, *Orphan Rescues Grandfather* tackles social problems by exposing vices and eulogizing virtues. In film narratives of the 1920s, these vices included gambling, opium-smoking, prostitution, theft, robbery, grabbing others' inheritance, kidnap, infidelity, vanity and corruption, whereas virtues ranged from chastity, filiality, perseverance, diligence, patriotism, altruism, charity, risking one's life or giving up one's love for others (ZDZ 1996b). Given such clear-cut binaries, the family drama would foreground human *sufferings* (in particular those by miserable women and children) and resolve seemingly irresolvable problems by way of coincidences and compromises.

More than any other incipient genres of the 1920s, the family drama marks the maturing of Chinese film as a narrative cinema. First, in terms of narration, this genre typically structures a linear plot of conflict, climax and resolution, a plot punctuated by moments of obstacle, crisis, catastrophe and suspense. In terms of characterization, the family drama follows a few protagonists whose tribulations in life furnish both narrative momentum and emotional fluctuations through which the narrative attains a degree of psychological depth. In terms of ideology, this genre espouses traditional ethical values and upholds the sanctity and stability of family, thereby underscoring a conservative position vis-à-vis contemporaneous May Fourth radicalism.

Historically, the conservative position of the family drama might have resulted from a perception of social psychology shared by most Chinese filmmakers and their audiences: namely, each in their own ways had manifested a psychological need for a stable society amidst a rapidly changing environment. The *conservatism* in question does not mean that they did not wish for any change for the better, but that such changes would occur within the existing social and ethical structures. The tension generated by their yearning for a better future and their inability to imagine an alternative new society engendered constant conflicts between vices and virtues on the one hand and compromised solutions to social problems on the other. At the level of social psychology, family dramas like *Orphan Rescues Grandfather* sought to address the equilibrium of venting frustrations and observing conventions – an equilibrium believed to be characteristic of the 'Chinese mentality' (K. Hu 1996: 53).

The butterfly connection: conservatism and commercialism

Not surprisingly, the narrative compromise typical of the family drama paralleled Mingxing's ideological compromise between butterfly fiction and the May Fourth spirit. The studio's increased output demanded a new source of creative energy, and this led to Zhang and Zheng actively recruiting new talent. In 1924 Zheng enlisted Bao Tianxiao, whose successful stint inaugurated the subsequent participation of butterfly writers. Hong Shen joined in 1925, bringing his prestige as a Harvard-trained specialist in modern drama. A question thus arises as to why butterfly fiction had exerted more influence than May Fourth literature in early cinema.

The first factor to consider in formulating an answer to the question was the market timing. Early cinema arrived in a period when butterfly fiction, with its focus on various emotions or sentiments (*qing*), dominated the publishing world in spite of the heavy-handed intervention by May Fourth critics, who criticized butterfly writers as morally corrupt 'literary prostitutes' or 'literary beggars' (Y. Zhang 1997). The second yet more direct factor was the ideological affinity between the civilized play and butterfly fiction, both operating under conservatism and preferring compromised solutions to social problems instead of fundamental social changes propagated by May Fourth radicalism. In fact, in the late 1910s the civilized play borrowed extensively from butterfly fiction (B. Tian and Jiao 1993: 67). Since Zheng Zhengqiu and many other early filmmakers came from a background of the civilized play, their cooperation with butterfly writers in producing family dramas since the mid-1920s was a natural one. After all, these three modes of cultural production held on to traditional morality and ethical codes, at best endorsed reform instead of revolution and made no attempt to hide their *commercial* interests. The third factor might be the elitism of May Fourth writers. When writers from the Literary Association, a May Fourth stronghold, attacked butterfly writers, they manifested little interest in similarly 'vulgar' and 'escapist' genres in commercial films of the 1920s. The situation only changed in the early 1930s when the leftists sought to bring enlightenment to filmmaking.

Understandably, Zheng's family drama had a lot in common with butterfly fiction, and their mixture had healthy financial returns. *Lonely Orchid, I–II* (Konggu lan, dir. Zhang Shichuan, 1926; 20 reels), an adaptation of Bao Tianxiao's novel based on Japanese fiction, ran for two weeks at the Palace Theater and earned 132,300 yuan. This was a record for all silent films from Mingxing combined, including those in the 1930s (J. Li 1995: 39; Tan 1992: 324). In spite of its conservative ideology, butterfly fiction had played a *transitional role* in cultivating a new urban audience differing from that of slapstick comedies. Recruited to compose stories, synopses and intertitles, butterfly writers used their skills in semi-literary Chinese, which was cherished by many urban readers of the time, and helped bring them to modern cinema (Lee 1999: 82–119). Such *linguistic proximity*, coupled with visual and *narrative proximity* devised by early Chinese filmmakers in accordance with traditional Chinese narratives and arts, had successfully established film as a staple in urban entertainment by the end of the 1920s.

The May Fourth connection: Hong Shen and Hou Yao

Two filmmakers embodied the May Fourth connection in early Chinese cinema: Hong Shen and Hou Yao. Hong Shen had been interested in literature and theater before he attended Qinghua University in Beijing, which dispatched him to study at Harvard University in 1916. The May Fourth Movement at home convinced him to switch his studies from pottery to drama in 1919. He started writing plays at Harvard and in 1921 enriched his experience by taking classes in voice, acting and dance in Boston. He also worked as an intern at a theater, observing the entire procedure from rehearsals to programming and advertising. Hong returned to Shanghai in 1922 and wrote a call for screenplays for China Film (Zhongguo, a small company founded in 1919). 'Film is an effective vehicle for civilization', declared Hong, capable of 'spreading education and elevating the nation-people (*guomin*)'. To safeguard film's educational function, he specifically opposed certain subject matter. Frowned upon topics included pornography and robbery, those exposing human vices and the nation's short-comings, as well as those which admired foreign stories, and Chinese tales of

28

Figure 2.2 Lonely Orchid (1926): an adaptation of Bao Tianxiao's novel, an example of butterfly fiction

immortals and demons (ZDZ 1996a: 24). Significantly, the rhetoric Hong relied on here echoes the enlightenment discourse of Liang Qichao, a renowned late Qing reformer who in 1902 had advocated new fiction as an effective means of strengthening the Chinese nation.

Hong's stage plays of this time were groundbreaking in that they brought actors and actresses to the same stage. He was also praised for his *psychological* depiction of characters, something which was new to Chinese drama. His contribution to Chinese cinema was similarly substantial. In 1924 he published a script, *The Story of Lady Shen-Tu* (Shen Tu shi). Albeit never made into a film, this is the first complete Chinese screenplay, which structures the plot by units of 'scenes' (*jing*) rather than 'acts' (*mu*) and which emphasizes visual impact and emotional dynamics. This screenplay gradually encouraged many directors to discard the old-fashioned *mubiao* (ZDZ 1996b: viii–ix).

Hong's decision to join Mingxing in 1925 signaled the cooperation of the new and the old school of theater people. Although the film industry was regarded as a corrupting place and a friend had criticized his decision as an outrageous act of 'prostitution of art', Hong still saw his new challenge worth the risk. While teaching at Fudan University, Hong received a monthly salary of 40 yuan for his active role in Mingxing productions (Tan 1992: 339) (see Table 2.3). In subsequent years, he wrote and directed several films focusing on urban

Table 2.3 Salary comparison in China, 1910s–30s

Year	Monthly pay (in yuan)	Name	Job	Studio/city
1913	30–40	—	actor	Shanghai
1913	75	—	lead actor	Shanghai
early 1920s	20	Wang Hanlun	actress	Mingxing
early 1920s	150	Ye Xiangrong	cinematographer	Commercial Press
1925	40	Hong Shen	screenwriter	Mingxing
late 1920s	40	Yao Sufeng	title writer	Mingxing
late 1920s	100	Bao Tianxiao	screenwriter	Mingxing
late 1920s	1,000	Hu Die	lead actress	Mingxing
early 1930s	300	Bu Wancang	director	Lianhua
1935	4,500/title	Jin Yan	lead actor	Lianhua, loaned to Xinhua

Sources: Gongsun 1977: 1: 67, 2: 119; S. Li and Hu 1996: 30; Tan 1992: 272; ZDZ 1996a: 1438, 1456, 1510, 1523.

bourgeois life, in particular on female characters. Films like *Young Master Feng* (Feng da shaoye, 1925) were critically acclaimed as 'psychological films', distinctive in their characterization but far from successful at the box office, the latter attributed by Bao Tianxiao to the lowly taste of Shanghai audiences in general (ZDZ 1996a: 1516). One obvious challenge Hong posed to his audience was his drastically reduced use of intertitles. Compared with an average of 300 intertitles in films by Zhang and Zheng, Hong used merely 113 in *Young Master Feng* in an endeavor to foster a 'poetic' style different from that of the hyperbole in Zhang and Zheng's cinema (ZDZ 1996a: xii–iii).

Like Hong, Hou Yao was interested in new literature and joined the Literary Association in 1922. This connection resulted in two distinctive marks on Hou's career. First, he carried the Association's slogan 'art for life's sake' to his own filmmaking. Maintaining – à la Shakespeare – that 'life itself is a long play without an end', Hou promoted the functions of film in representing, interpreting, criticizing, purifying and beautifying life (Luo *et al.* 1992: 1: 48–9). Second, when he was put in charge of screenwriting at Great Wall (Changcheng) in 1924, Hou advocated 'problem films' as an equivalent to 'problem fiction' practiced by many May Fourth writers.

Hou admired Ibsen and tackled 'women's problems' in a way far more radical than that of his contemporaries. *Abandoned Woman* (Qifu, 1924; 11 reels), a film about a divorcee who fights for women's rights, concludes in an uncompromising manner, presenting the dead body of a career woman in protest against repressive patriarchy. After a few films, Hou moved from Great Wall to Minxin (China Sun Motion Picture Company) around 1926, and his mobility among studios, which was fairly common at the time, brings us to other prominent studios in the mid-1920s.

A crop of new studios

Unlike most other studios of the time, three brothers, Li Minwei (Lai Man-wai), Li Haishan (Lai Hoi-san) and Li Beihai (Lai Pak-hoi), established Minxin in Hong Kong in 1923. Born in Japan and educated in Hong Kong, Li Minwei was active in the civilized play, organizing two theater troupes in 1911 and 1913. When Brodsky passed through Hong Kong on his way to the United States in 1913, Li negotiated a deal with him and directed *Zhuangzi Tests His Wife* (Zhuangzi shiqi; 2 reels) as a release of Huamei (literally, 'Sino-American'). Based on Cantonese opera, the film features Li's brother Beihai as Zhuangzi, Li himself as the wife, and Li's wife Yan Shanshan (Yim Shan-shan) as the wife's maid (thus making her the first Chinese screen actress). The special effects of moving ghosts created by Brodsky's associate R.F. Van Velzer impressed the Li brothers and strengthened their determination to pursue a film career. The film was never shown in Hong Kong, but it was taken to the States by Brodsky and was reportedly screened in Los Angeles in 1917 (Law 2000: 46).

With their own company Minxin, the Li brothers produced documentaries, comprising of mostly sports and ethnographic spectacles. Notable among them were several celebrated episodes of Beijing opera performed by the star Mei Lanfang, shot in Beijing in 1924. Also noteworthy was the historical footage of Sun Yat-sen (Sun Zhongshan), the leader of the Republican Revolution. Minxin had purchased film equipment from overseas and appointed Moon Kwan (Guan Wenqing) as an adviser, but it had no luck with feature production in Hong Kong. Probably due to Li Minwei's ties to the Nationalists, the colonial government delayed processing Minxin's proposal for building a studio in the territory, forcing the Li brothers to set up shop across the border in Guangzhou and spend HK$9,000 shooting *Rouge* (Yanzhi, dir. Li Beihai, 1925). Adapted from *Liaozhai Record of Wonders* (Liaozhai zhiyi), a collection of classic fantasy and ghost stories, the film starred Li Minwei's other wife Lin Chuchu (Lam Cho-cho) as the female lead and had a decent ten-day run in Hong Kong, earning HK$10,000. Unfortunately, a prolonged labor strike from June 1925 to October 1926 paralyzed the entire region of Hong Kong and Guangdong (Fonoroff 1997: xiii–xiv).

Li Minwei was forced to bring part of their equipment to Shanghai and formed a new Minxin studio. Shanghai Minxin announced its *enlightenment* aims in a manifesto written by Ouyang Yuqian, a noted dramatist, in 1926: to produce high-quality films and to introduce to Europe and America the 'excellent ideas, pure morality and honest custom' of the Chinese people (ZDZ 1996a: 49). To these aims Minxin employed Ouyang Yuqian, Bu Wancang and Sun Yu, all rising stars in film directing and screenwriting. Minxin's seventeen features released in

Shanghai included some of the best films in the late 1920s, including *Romance of the West Chamber* (Xixiang ji, dir. Hou Yao, 1927; 10 reels).

A less influential industry player, Great Wall was established in Shanghai in 1924 by a group of overseas Chinese. As early as May 1921, several Chinese Americans were determined to learn film basics out of their irritation at humiliating portrayals of the Chinese in American films. They organized a film company named 'Great Wall' based in Brooklyn, New York, and produced two documentaries introducing Chinese costumes and martial arts. After shipping their equipment to Shanghai in 1924, these patriots were disappointed by the dismal reality at home and wanted to intervene in *social reform* by means of filmmaking (ZDZ 1996a: 85–6). Their rationale for producing 'problem films' was that, since China was fraught with various social problems in urgent need of solution, only by addressing these problems in films could they achieve the objectives of 'changing morale and criticizing society' (J. Zhang and Cheng 1995: 75). Each film was to focus on one social problem, and the problems taken up include love, marriage and women's careers, all reflected in the films Hou Yao directed for them.

In addition to Hou, Great Wall had on its payroll Cheng Bugao and Sun Shiyi, as well as Wan Laiming and Wan Guchan, the latter two producing the earliest Chinese cartoon shorts for the company. Great Wall titles were critically acclaimed for their forward-looking vision, and their combined artistic taste and moral integrity earned the appellation a 'Great Wall school' (ZDZ 1996a: 1065–6). However, their reputation as a distinct 'school' (*pai*) was short-lived as the company became involved in martial arts film production in 1927 against its original commitment to contemporary problems. Great Wall reportedly owned a distribution office in the US (ZDZ 1996a: 1362), but the company was financially insecure and had to close in 1930.

Like Great Wall, Shenzhou (Cathay Film Corporation) was established on a budget of 50,000 yuan in Shanghai in 1924 by Wang Xuchang (who studied at the Ecole du Cinéma in France) and his friends, with a specific policy: 'to subtly influence and change the audience' (*qianyi mohua*) (S. Li and Hu 1996: 91). Shenzhou filmmakers emphasized *humanism* and opposed sensationalism. As a result, their films paid special attention to the screenplay, acting, photography, art design, intertitles, as well as characters' psychology and a film's overall ambience. Although the company was shut down in 1927, the high standards of its melancholy, tragic films had earned the appellation a 'Shenzhou school' (ZDZ 1996a: 87, 1062). Like Great Wall, Shenzhou's operation was too short to have an impact on the industry. These two early 'schools' of filmmaking, therefore, existed more as collective aspirations than as viable industry forces.

Great China-Lily Pictures Company (Da Zhonghua baihe) was the result of a merger of two film companies in 1925: Great China Pictures and Lily. Feng Zhen'ou founded the former, and Wu Xingzai the latter, both in Shanghai in 1924. Financial difficulties compelled the two companies to merge after producing, respectively, two and four films. In their combined operations, Great

China-Lily produced around fifty titles in five years and claimed such talents as Lu Jie, Shi Dongshan and Wang Yuanlong. Initially, Great China-Lily exhibited a tendency towards a European style, best exemplified in Shi Dongshan's films of high *aestheticism*. Shi believed that film was the most comprehensive and most enchanting art form capable of expressing the beauty of sounds, colors, shapes and movements – in brief, natural and man-made beauty of all kinds (ZDZ 1996a: 371). In spite of their ideological affinity with bourgeois lifestyle, Shi's films were praised for their elegant looks and artistic details, which brought hope that Chinese film could finally become 'art' (ZDZ 1996a: 1145, 1268–72).

Dan Duyu, Yin Mingzhu and Shanghai Photoplay

An older studio that exhibited a similar tendency of Europeanization and aestheticism was Shanghai Photoplay Company, founded by Dan Duyu with a budget of 1,000 yuan in 1920. Dan was a well-known Shanghai painter who specialized in female figures, especially nudes, and ran a brisk business producing decorated commercial calendars that displayed fashionable beauties (S. Li and Hu 1996: 33, 270). A graduate of the Shanghai Academy of Fine Arts, Dan was skilled in oil painting and watercolors as well, and his hobby of photography led him to purchase a film camera from a foreigner. With no acquaintances around with any knowledge of cinematography, Du decided to disassemble the camera himself and reassemble the pieces. After a dozen times, he was able to handle the machine with ease.

Shanghai Photoplay was a typical family company not only because many employees lived with Dan's family in the studio complex but also because the studio employed several of his family members and relatives. The best known among them was Yin Mingzhu, a socialite studying at the East–West Women's School. Yin's fluent English, her Pearl White-type of clothing and her versatile skills in modern activities (e.g., dancing, swimming, horse-riding, bicycling and car-driving) had earned her the nickname 'Foreign Fashion', or 'Miss FF' for short. With her performance in Dan's debut *Sea Oath*, Yin became the first Chinese female movie star (Du 1988: 56).

Unfortunately, Yin's traditionally minded mother immediately forbade her from acting, sending her instead to serve as a clerk in a Japanese clinic. The loss of Yin prompted Dan Duyu to recruit Yin's equally fashionable schoolmate, Fu Wenhao, better known as 'Miss AA' (short for her English name, Anna) and the first woman to drive a private car in Shanghai, as the female lead in *The Revival of an Old Well* (Gujing chongbo ji, 1923; 6 reels). The film premiered at the Embassy to popular acclaim and was rush-ordered by Southeast Asian distributors. Miss AA became an instant star but her mother, like Yin's, forbade her to act. Fortunately for Dan, Yin had convinced her mother of the value of a film career by this time. After her leading roles in Dan's subsequent two films, Yin and Dan were married in Hangzhou in 1926, the first among many screen couples to come.

In addition to directing and screenwriting, Dan was also skillful with cinematography, lighting, editing and laboratory work. Once, while watching a foreign film in a theater, he detected from a flash on an actress's eyes that a reflector had been used to augment interior lighting. Back in the studio, he experimented with a silver sheet reflection board and successfully directed sunlight to where it was otherwise dark. In addition to experimenting with film techniques, Dan trained numerous up-and-coming film artists. Shi Dongshan, for instance, began his career as an art designer with Dan, played in a few films and then launched his directorial debut with Shanghai Photoplay.

The press consistently praised Dan's films for their distinctive aestheticism in set design, lighting and frame composition (ZDZ 1996a: 1069). In 1926 Zheng Zhengqiu acknowledged that the blooming Chinese film industry had owed much to Dan, a pioneering, multi-skilled artist who regarded film as 'an art of motion' and who 'had no equals' in China (ZDZ 1996a: vi, 1217–18).

Genre considerations: opera movies and comedies

Apart from the family drama, early Chinese cinema experimented with a number of incipient genres. Among them, opera movie and comedy came first, romance and family drama were popular in the early through to the mid-1920s, and costume drama/historical films and martial arts films took over the market in the late 1920s.

Opera movies (*xiqu pian*), based on existing stage plays, were among the earliest Chinese attempts at filmmaking (Farquhar and Berry 2001). This seemingly accidental choice was motivated by a kind of *cultural unconscious*. In terms of narrative, opera movies tell stories already familiar to the audience, thus posing little new challenge. In terms of visual style, the 'electric shadows' added a more exotic dimension to the familiar operatic acts and therefore appeared all the more attractive to the audience. In terms of price, the cheaper movie tickets translated into higher attendance rates since viewers otherwise prevented from seeing leading actors perform on stage were now able to watch them on screen.[4] In short, opera movies created a win–win situation for producers, exhibitors and audience alike.

This explains why opera movies came to be the first choice for several studios. The Fengtai Photography Shop in Beijing filmed the leading actor Tan Xinpei in *Conquering the Jun Mountain* (Ding Junshan, 1905; 3 reels), the first Chinese short feature, which premiered at the Grand Shadowplay Theater to public acclaim in 1905 and was shipped to southern provinces like Jiangsu and Fujian. Delighted at his unexpected success, the shop owner Ren Jingfeng arranged to have other popular operatic shorts filmed in the subsequent years. Similarly, among the early releases of the Motion Picture Department of Commercial Press were two opera movies directed and performed by Mei Lanfang in 1920. In most cases, early opera movies depended more on celebrity attraction than on cinematic means, although limited special effects were occasionally used, such as adding shots of clouds to accompany Mei's role as a fairy maiden flying in the sky.

The *comedy* was a genre that accounts for numerous shorts in the early years. *The China Cinema Year Book 1927* lists twenty-eight domestic comedies (*xiaoju*) – most in 2 to 3 reels – in a chapter separate from feature films (*zhuangju*, literally 'serious plays'). Early comedies were largely *slapsticks* (*da'nao xiju*), marked by a good deal of aggressive or violent action as the source of humor (ZDZ 1996a: 1390). Popular Western comedies featuring Max Linder, Charlie Chaplin and Buster Keaton were a direct source of inspiration, but humorous acts before or between Chinese stage plays also provided ready materials. In the silent era, humor was *situational* rather than verbal, and to engage the audience the filmmakers depended on exaggerated gestures and facial expressions.

Few studios took pride in the comedy, but in 1925 Xu Zhuodai and Wang Youyou named their company 'Kaixin' (literally, 'delighted') and specialized in comedies so as to achieve 'the sole goal of delighting the audience'. Their comedies (*huaji ju* or humorous plays) generated little interest in the press, which attributed the insufficiency of Chinese comedies to the lack of worthy screenplays and comic talents (ZDZ 1996a: 672–7).

Hong Shen defined the comedy (*xiju*) as a genre that pokes fun at a variety of contradictions in everyday situations. For him, there is a distinction between *huaji ju*, which provokes laughter through the absurd and the eccentric, and *xiju*, which aims at mild criticism and must avoid both the hyperbolic and the wearisome. He intended his *Roses in April* (Siyue lidi qiangwei chuchu kai, dir. Zhang Shichuan, 1926; 10 reels) to be a light comedy that ridicules enamored men and cunning women. To realize his vision of the comic, Hong employed long takes – with 5 to 6 shots each over 150-feet long – to get the best out of his cast (ZDZ 1996a: 309). A departure from the previous action-filled slapsticks, *Roses in April* expanded the comedy's critical functions and signaled the genre's maturity as a narrative form.

Beyond genres: allegory, feminization and Europeanization

A closer look at a typical urban romance here may help us better comprehend the multiple meanings that exceed a purely genre analysis as well as critical issues debated in the press of the 1920s. In lieu of setting the battle of vices and virtues in an ethical framework as in family drama, *Back Home from the City* (Chongfan guxiang, dir. Dan Duyu, 1925; 9 reels) allegorizes the perils of unbridled urban adventures. Time (Guangyin) sends her five daughters on a one-month tour of the city, and they stay with Aunt Indulgence (Ni'ai) and Uncle Coward (Queruo). Delighted at the arrival of pretty country maidens, Indulgence's prodigal son Money (Jinqian) frequents nightclubs and restaurants with Simplicity (Sunü, played by Yin Mingzhu), the eldest and most beautiful sister, while his playboy friends Flattery (Xianmei) and Seduction (Yinyou) date with Youth (Qingnian) and Vanity (Xurong). Only Chastity (Zhenjie) resists urban extravagances and finds it more interesting to visit the studio of Sincerity (Chengken, played by Shi Dongshan), Coward's nephew who is a Western-style painter (a narcissistic reference to Dan himself).

Shortly afterward, Beauty (Meili), one of the sisters, dies from excessive drinking, and Money has Chastity imprisoned in a secret room because he does not want her to interfere with his plots. As is characteristic of such urban tales, Money soon abandons Simplicity for Coquetry (Yaoye). After Coward's business goes bankrupt, Simplicity and Vanity stay with Scheme (Yinxian), who eventually steals all their belongings. In the meantime, Vanity has eloped with Seduction, and Youth has returned home. Coquetry now flirts with Flattery, who gets into a fight with Money that kills them both. Alone, Simplicity wanders to the mountains and realizes her mistakes in front of a Buddha statue. Finally, Chastity escapes and joins Simplicity on a trip 'back home from the city' (ZDZ 1996b: 1: 143–56).

Arguably, *Back Home from the City* functions only marginally as an old-fashioned cautionary tale. Conceptually as well as artistically, the film aligns itself with what Miriam Hansen terms *vernacular modernism* in international cinema, manifested at multiple levels ranging from its thematic concerns and narrative strategies to mise-en-scene, visual style, modes of performance, spectatorial identification and address to the film's potential horizon of reception (Hansen 2000: 13). Indeed, *Back Home from the City* is as much a star vehicle as a screen primer for everything *modern* (or Western) in cosmopolitan lifestyles: fashion, make-up, architecture, interior design, furnishing, mode of transportation and the like. Fundamental to the film's attractions is its spectacular display of modern images for mass consumption. As Money indulges in decadence and Coquetry flaunts her sexuality on screen, the film works as much to furnish new objects of desire as to generate new desires for the modern, not necessarily at the ideological level but more at the material level of everyday life. However, the 1920s horizon of reception was such that the film finds it obligatory to invoke conservatism by adding an anti-climatic closure where Simplicity and Chastity – two paragon female virtues – must return to the safe haven of their rural home.

Back Home from the City opened at the Embassy and received positive reviews. Bi Yihong praised the film for its 'philosophical' depth and its almost perfect execution of lighting and set design. Although he faulted the film for its all too obvious use of allegorical names and its obsessive close-ups of Yin Mingzhu, Bi believed that the film deserved a mention in the history of Chinese cinema (ZDZ 1996a: 1104).

Eulogies of aestheticism aside, several critics had enumerated problems in films of the contemporary life by the mid-1920s. In a 1926 article, Hu Zhifan divides current films into three types: the romantic, the social and the anecdotal (*tanci pai*). First, the 'romantic film' is the formulaic story of a scholar meeting a beauty drawn from traditional Chinese narratives, but filmmakers have modernized the formula by making the poor scholar a talented writer or artist, and the demure beauty a coquettish socialite. Second, the 'social film' is the exposé of social evils, dwelling excessively on playboys and prostitutes' 'modern' activities equally tempting to Shanghai residents. Third, the 'anecdotal film' is the adaptation of *tanci* narratives, and since *tanci* (or *pingtan*), a style of storytelling performed in lyrics and songs, was immensely popular in the Yangtze Delta region, *tanci* films are especially 'welcome by ladies and misses'. While mentioning moral tales (e.g., family dramas) and comedies as other types in passing, Hu opines that fragile beauties and bookish gentlemen will lend no assistance to a weak nation (Da Zhonghua Baihe 1926).

Implicit in Hu's article is a criticism of two tendencies – feminization and Europeanization – that dominated Chinese filmmaking in the mid-1920s. Hu's article was published as an endorsement of *The Migration Act* (Zhibian waishi, dir. Wang Yuanlong, 1926; 8 reels), a film that depicts the heroic act of southern farm workers migrating to the northern frontier. As Wang Yuanlong asserted in 1926, *The Migration Act* sought 'Easternization' by way of promoting 'indigenous Chinese culture' and thus represented a departure from his previous espousal of wholesale 'Westernization' (ZDZ 1996a: 303). In a film review, Zhou Shoujuan praised *The Migration Act* as a 'ground-breaking' film that delighted the audience with rural, natural beauty and exemplified a distinctive 'national characteristic' (ZDZ 1996a: 1160–1).

CINEMA AND SPECULATIONS, 1927–9

In a sense, what happened in the late 1920s was the return of 'Chineseness' with a vengeance – a kind of legendary, magical 'Chineseness' that spun out of control. As Bao Tianxiao predicted in 1926, 'the development of Chinese cinema would not materialize through the film romance where the so-called stars faked their feelings; it could only materialize through the historical film' (ZDZ 1996a: 629). He asserted that screen images of Chinese sages and heroes could benefit mass education on the one hand and correct the Western misconception of and contempt for the Chinese on the other. Albeit affiliated with Mingxing, Bao actually shared a conviction with the founders of a rising studio, Tianyi.

Tianyi and costume drama

The Shaw (Shao) brothers – Zuiweng (Renjie), Runde (Cunren), Runme (Renmei) and Run Run (Yifu) – founded Tianyi (Unique Film Production Company) in Shanghai in 1925 and intended their pictures to 'promote Chinese civilization and eschew Europeanization by emphasizing ancient morality and ethics' (Tan 1995: 18–19). A lawyer and businessman, Shao Zuiweng had collaborated with Zhang Shichuan and Zheng Zhengqiu in 1922 in managing the Laughter Stage (Xiao wutai) which specialized in the civilized play (ZDZ 1996a: 53). But contrary to Mingxing's focus on contemporary issues, Tianyi was interested primarily in adapting Chinese folk tales, myths and legends already popular among audiences, an interest in line with its *conservative* ideology (ZDZ 1996a: vii).

Under its pretext to advance national traditions, Tianyi released two noteworthy costume dramas in 1926, both directed by Shao Zuiweng. *The Lovers* (Liang Zhu tongshi; 12 reels), adopted from the *tanci* version of a popular folk tale about Liang Shanbo and Zhu Yingtai, fated lovers who were reunited only in death as two butterflies, took the nation by storm. A longer feature, *White Snake, I–II* (Yiyao baishe zhuan; 18 reels), broke all records of Chinese films in Southeast Asian markets, where tickets were sold as high as 6 yuan a piece (ZDZ 1996a: 89).

Admittedly an umbrella term, the *costume drama* might be extended to subsume genres such as the opera movie, the *historical film* and romances set in ancient times – all these also designated as 'ancient plays' by Commercial Press. But in a strict sense, the costume drama refers to a kind of historical film adapted from the *tanci* repertoires and a wealth of unofficial histories, traditional novels, vernacular stories and folk tales. Initially a reaction to Europeanization in domestic productions, costume dramas might have been triggered by imported epics like *The Ten Commandments* (dir. Cecile B. DeMille, 1923) (S. Hong 1995: 6). Most costume dramas dwelled on the narrative formula of either 'scholar meets beauty' (*caizi jiaren*), as in *The Lovers*, or 'hero loves beauty' (*yingxiong meiren*), as in *Sex Trap, I–II* (Meiren ji, dir. Lu Jie *et al.*, 1927; 24 reels). Since location shooting could be minimized and stage props, sets and costumes were readily available, the majority of costume dramas tended to be imitative in nature and, worse still, cheaply made. Historical accuracy was rarely an issue, and some producers rushed films to the market in a matter of a week or so. The Tianyi costume drama trend crested in 1927, bringing into its whirlpool other major studios.

There were, however, a few outstanding titles in this genre. *Sex Trap, I–II*, an adaptation of an episode from the classical novel *Romance of Three Kingdoms* (Sanguo yanyi), was a big-budget production. At a time when the average investment per film was 5,000 yuan, Great Wall-Lily poured 150,000 yuan into this two-part film that involved its four leading directors for an entire year in addition to thousands of extras (S. Hong 1995: 7). This attempt at producing 'well-made films' was aimed at driving low-priced imitations out of the market (ZDZ 1996a: 1418), but it could also backfire, as illustrated later.

Romance of the West Chamber: negotiating *wen* and *wu*

Before proceeding with the next commercial trend, we should pause now to consider another 'well-made' costume drama that anticipated the rise of martial arts films. Indebted to a long genealogy of literati writing and traditional theater (Harris 1999), *Romance of the West Chamber* is a Minxin release rich in literary quality, dramatic effect and cinematic artistry.

Scholar Zhang passes a scenic area. A sequence of shots shows a mountain, a pagoda, a temple, a pond and a bridge, and Zhang is surprised to run into Cui Yingying (Lin Chuchu) and her maid Hongniang inside Pujiu Temple. At a circle gate, Yingying looks over her shoulder, indicating her interest in the new visitor. Zhang rents a room in the temple and introduces himself to Hongniang. Spellbound by Yingying's beauty, he tries to satisfy his voyeurism by peeping at the latter praying for her parents. Zhang's recitation of a love poem is complemented by Yingying's poem recited across a wall. When Zhang climbs up the wall, two iris shots reveal Zhang's head and the retreat of Yingying and Hongniang behind the bushes.

The film cuts to the bandit chief Sun Feihu practicing martial arts in operatic routines. A long sequence of repeated shots follows Sun and his soldiers marching through mountains and heading toward the temple. This sequence cross-cuts with another showing the monks closing the temple doors and Yingying and her mother greatly alarmed. Sun demands that Yingying be his bride, but Yingying's widowed mother promises her hand to anyone who can rescue all. Zhang comes up with a plan, dispatching a letter to his friend General Du while convincing the bandits to wait for three days. Another set of crosscut sequences of Du's troops passing mountains and Sun's soldiers shouting outside the temple leads to a combat sequence of over five minutes. In succession, Du and Sun fight on horseback and on foot, using a spear and a knife respectively, in a stylized operatic fashion. A high-angle shot of opposing troops is repeated several times, and Du eventually kills Sun.

In a dream sequence unprecedented in Chinese film, Zhang falls asleep at his desk, and an iris shot opens to reveal Yingying. As the two lovers hold each other's hands, Sun arrives and grabs Yingying by force, her startled face shown in an extreme close-up. Zhang chases them with his brush pen, which is magically blown up to a size larger than a spear and carries him through the clouds. Just as Sun is about to force himself on Yingying by the roadside, Zhang arrives with his giant pen. Yingying covers her face as the two men battle, but she is overjoyed to see Sun dropping dead on the ground. The two lovers embrace, but all of a sudden Zhang is seen shaking his servant boy while dreaming.

For Hou, the dream sequence was meant to articulate the scholar's wish for *wen* (literary excellence) to conquer *wu* (military power), but he admitted that the film, which was designed to capture 'a sense of complete beauty', was but 'an ideal world for the literati' (ZDZ 1996a: 327). According to the original script published in a 1927 Minxin 'promotional magazine' (*tekan*), Yingying's mother recants her promise after the rescue and Zhang is deeply dejected. Hongniang serves as an intermediary between the heartbroken lovers, who express their longing for each other by music and poetry. A month after their secret consummation of love through Hongniang's audacious arrangement, Yingying's mother reluctantly approves the marriage on the condition that Zhang must succeed in imperial examinations and advance to officialdom (ZDZ 1996b: 1217–26).

39

Understandably, the extant 5-reel version (58 minutes), which was discovered at a Dutch film archive in 1981, differs considerably from the published script. The scenes of the lovers' outpouring of sentimental music and poetry and their sexual union are entirely absent. Instead, the film proceeds directly from Zhang's dream to the victory banquet hosted by Yingying's mother, and the lovers' ecstatic faces are cross-cut in two frontal shots. A farewell scene by a roadside bridge follows, and the long shot of the bridge dissolves into one of Zhang's return. The film ends with Hongniang watching the silhouette of the couple on the windowpanes. According to the script, however, the film ends with Yingying suffering the sorrows of separation, an ending in tune with standard literary and dramatic versions of the story.

Hou's skillful handling of shot composition and editing demonstrates the technical advancement early Chinese filmmakers had made in the 1920s. His use of iris shots integrates Western cinematic art and Chinese landscape painting. Effective cross-cutting helps generate tension on both narrative and emotional registers. The inclusion of a number of point-of-view shots and shot/reverse shot patterning further facilitates spectatorial identification and intensifies audience involvement. Remarkably, Hou incorporated elements of operatic performance of martial arts familiar to Chinese audiences, thereby engaging them in a gratifying experience that both excites and comforts.

Probably due to its thematic focus on romance and sexuality, its visual representation of Chinese landscape and theater and its relatively sophisticated use of cinematic techniques, *Romance of the West Chamber* was among a few early films chosen for export. The film was reportedly brought to Europe by a jewelry merchant and was shown in London on 26 September 1929 (M. Li 1993: 85). Earlier, a 5-reel version ran as *La Rose de Pu-Chui* from 20 April to 3 June 1928 in Paris, concurrently with *Ben-Hur* and *Joyless Streets*, generating certain media publicity in Europe (Harris 1999). If the extant film was a print of this export version, its focus on martial arts at the expense of romance foreshadowed the subsequent replacement of historical romance by martial arts film in China.

From martial arts to immortals and demons

Indeed, it was a small step from costume drama to *martial arts films* and *films of immortals and demons* (*shenguai pian*). Again, Western adventure films, especially those featuring Douglas Fairbanks, might have provided a genre model, while the reprints and the serialization of martial arts fiction in the popular press prepared the audience for the screen renditions of their favorite characters. Shortly after Mingxing launched *The Burning of Red Lotus Temple* in 1928, serial titles and cheap imitations began to flood the market. As famous knights-errant, immortals and historical figures roamed the screen to the audience's amazement, Tianyi formed six production units to churn out martial arts flicks.

Contrary to the ethos of *sentimentality* in costume drama, martial arts films concentrate on the *prowess* of their heroes and heroines who, in different narrative variations, kill off evil lords, avenge the deaths of their parents, deliver marvelous acts in competitions or retrieve stolen treasures (S. Hong 1995: 8–9). In addition to their superb *gongfu* skills, they are endowed with traditional virtues such as integrity, altruism, honesty, dependability, as well as abstinence from sex, money and officialdom (M. Chen 1996: 15–106). The public yearning for the 'new heroism' embodied in this genre reflected a collective dream of wish-fulfillment at a time when wars and massacres frequently immersed the nation in utter horror, and corrupt officials and evil landlords exploited the weak and the poor. In 1927, critic Lu Menshu went so far as to liken the calls for screen 'new heroism' to the nationalist revolution's slogan 'Down with imperialism' (ZDZ 1996a: 668, 1414).

If the martial arts film still fed on an illusion of effective *social intervention*, the film of immortals and demons presented fantasy and phantasmagoria as alternative routes of *escape* from existential crises. This hybrid subgenre mixed elements of martial arts with ingredients of immortals and demons drawn from vernacular stories as well as from myths, legends and folk tales. A typical film would feature swords dashing from the fingertip, lights emitting from the mouth, women flaunting half-naked bodies and men showing demonic faces. The screen would be criss-crossed by characters jumping into the air, traveling in the clouds or vanishing like smoke, as in the extant *Red Knight-Errant* (Hongxia, dir. Wen Yimin, 1929) (ZDZ 1996a: 666, 1037). Magical tricks and potent spells extended the limits of the supernatural, and special effects such as stop-motion camera, frame-by-frame shots, multiple exposures and cartoon animation, some of which are found in another extant – albeit incomplete – feature, *Swordswoman of Huangjiang, VI* (Huangjiang nüxia, dir. Chen Kengran *et al.*, 1930), further enhanced the ambience of sorcery and mystery (S. Hong 1995: 11).[5]

The craze for the hybrid genre lasted from 1928 to 1931 (Z. Zhang 2001).[6] Shortcomings like religious fanaticism and superstition were all too obvious in films of martial arts and immortals and demons. Numerous young viewers had reportedly left home to seek immortality in the mountains. A couple was spotted burning incense and praying in the middle of a theater show of *The Date of Nezha's Birth* (Nezha chushi, dir. Li Zeyuan, 1928; 10 reels) (ZDZ 1996a: 771), a Great Wall picture scripted by Sun Shiyi. As far back as 1926, Sun Shiyi had diagnosed this 'craze for ancient plays' as a troubling symptom and predicted that Chinese cinema was facing a crisis (ZDZ 1996a: 643–5). Indeed, even Zhang Shichuan was so afraid of haunting spirits in his films that he set up a shrine in the studio and regularly led his staff to worship the master immortals (ZDZ 1996a: 1529).

Market competition: 'a suicidal acceleration'

The unprecedented market competition wreaked havoc in the late 1920s as companies tried all conceivable means to undermine each other. An established studio, Mingxing was successful in boosting its resources. In October 1926 the studio claimed an asset of 500,000 yuan, 100,000 yuan of which might have come from a public offering of its stocks at 10 yuan per share in 1925. Mingxing received an additional 200,000 yuan from another stock offering at the same price per share in 1928 (ZDZ 1996a: 30–3). With such strong financial backing, Mingxing was able to lure top performers from other studios, such as Cheng Bugao and Hu Die (aka Butterfly Wu).

A relative newcomer, Tianyi tried to reduce costs to a minimum and thus put pressure on those studios like Minxin that still emphasized production value. For instance, in 1927 Minxin invested 30,000 yuan, sent a twenty-member crew to Northern China and enlisted four hundred army soldiers in shooting *Mulan Joins the Army* (Mulan congjun, dir. Hou Yao, 1928; 10 reels). Their six-month hard work proved a box-office disaster because Tianyi had released its *Hua Mulan Joins the Army* (Hua Mulan congjun, dir. Li Pingqian, 1927; 10 reels) four months ahead of Minxin. Tianyi had completed its production in less than a month and had used about a dozen people and some easily assembled sets inside its Shanghai studio (Du 1988: 127; M. Li 1993: 85).

Shanghai Photoplay was another studio emphasizing quality films, and its two releases in 1927 unveiled the mercurial nature of filmmaking at the time. *The Spider Cave* (Pansi dong, dir. Dan Duyu, 1927; 10 reels), an erotic episode from the classical novel *Journey to the West* (Xiyou ji), opened on Chinese New Year's Day to full houses in several Shanghai theaters and was immediately picked up by Southeast Asian distributors. Its popularity owed as much to the film's artistic appeal as to the studio's aggressive advertising. Apart from running large advertisements in major newspapers, the studio issued a promotional magazine edited by Yao Sufeng, which featured fantastic film stills. A surviving photograph displays a highly stylized sword fight between two females, both bare-foot and dressed in tank tops and shorts (ZDYYZ 1995: 56). The film raked in a record profit of 50,000 yuan, which enabled Dan to expand his studio, order new equipment and buy a second car (ZDZ 1996a: 85).

The success of *The Spider Cave* convinced Dan of the value of costume drama and led him to invest heavily in *Yang the Imperial Consort* (Yang guifei, dir. Dan Duyu, 1927; 20 reels), an ambitious project consisting of numerous exquisite palace scenes. For the intertitles, Dan invited the services of Zheng Yimei, who half a century later could recall in vivid detail Dan's elaborate methods of shooting key scenes: dancing in the moon palace, bathing in the Huaqing Pool and the chess game where court ladies serve as moving chess pieces (1982: 33–40). Unexpectedly, *Yang the Imperial Consort* was a flop despite Dan's advertising efforts, and it was not until after Yin had pawned her jewelry that the studio would turn to profit again a year later.

Some commentators have suggested that Dan's failure was due to the public interest in watching films of contemporary life as fashion shows, especially for those inland women who diligently followed Shanghai fashions (Y. Zheng 1982: 40). This market factor thus explains why Tianyi was flexible with its costume dramas and would dress historical characters either in ancient costumes or in modern fashions, and sometimes a mixture of both. Imitations soon followed, as in an adaptation of the classical novel *Dream of the Red Chamber* (Honglou meng, dir. Ren Pengnian, Yu Boyan, 1927; 20 reels) released by Fudan, a company founded in 1927. Otherwise a sickly beauty, the character Lin Daiyu now wears a long evening dance dress and high-heel shoes and lives in a room furnished with chandeliers and sofas (J. Cheng *et al.* 1981: 1: 89).

The market competition had affected all aspects of filmmaking. By 1930 small companies would choose *zhengpian* (the film stock for positive printing, at 0.05–0.06 yuan per foot) instead of *fupian* (the raw negative, at 0.2 yuan per foot). Only a few years before, the prices of these types of film were reported at 0.03 and 0.08 yuan per foot respectively, and the sudden increase of film prices was attributed to the Great Depression (ZDZ 1996a: 1369, 1423). The sharp rise in inflation compelled small companies to dump their products at huge discounts. While foreign-owned theaters typically refused to exhibit these films, many Chinese theaters that agreed to show domestic films had switched by 1926 their proportion of box-office revenue from 30 to 70 per cent (ZDZ 1996a: 104). The potential incomes from Southeast Asia were also down as profiteering distributors kept reducing prices per print, sometimes to as low as 400 yuan. In comparison, around 1928, an average film was budgeted at around 2,000 yuan, and a print could sell for between 500 and 600 yuan. In 1926 the price per print was 1,000 yuan, whereas a few years before it was as much as 4,000 yuan (ZDZ 1996a: 104, 1527). These figures show that, regardless of inflation, by 1930 the lowest prices per print were less than half of those in 1926 and about one tenth of those in the early 1920s. In other words, even with drastically reduced costs, filmmaking was no longer an easily profitable business in the late 1920s. As recently as 1925, with an average cost of 6,000 yuan per film, Mingxing was still able to count on a profit of 20,000 yuan from each of its releases (ZDZ 1996a: xiii) (see Tables 2.4 and 2.5).[7]

It is not surprising, then, that in 1928 a critic described the film industry as locked in 'a suicidal acceleration' (ZDZ 1996a: 117). Caught in a vicious circle, cheap features tended to lower the already low taste of the audience, and large studios were under pressure to churn out equally cheap features in competition. These factors combined to drive small companies into bankruptcy and forced medium-sized companies to merge or close shop (S. Hong 1995: 11–12; ZDZ 1996a: 1369–71). For instance, in 1926, due to the board members' determination to avoid external criticism of their substandard products, the Motion Picture Department was detached from Commercial Press to form a separate company, Guoguang. In spite of its decent funding (150,000 yuan), Guoguang closed in 1928 after releasing only five titles (ZDZ 1996a: 20, 1459–66).

Figure 2.3 A poster for *Dream of the Red Chamber* (1927): calligraphy by Bao Tianxiao

On the positive side, some industry leaders made a concerted effort to arrest the 'suicidal acceleration'. In 1926, at the outset of the market competition, Mingxing convinced Minxin, Great China-Lily, Shanghai Photoplay, Youlian and Huaju (the last two companies founded in Shanghai in 1925) to form a

Table 2.4 Production costs per film in China, 1920s–40s

Year	Studio or city	Cost (yuan)	Film
Average			
1925	Shanghai	4,000–6,000	—
early 1930s	Lianhua	40,000	—
mid-1930s	Mingxing	40,000–50,000	—
1936	Mingxing	30,000	—
1939	Shanghai	30,000	—
1940	Shanghai	100,000	—
1942	Shanghai	300,000	—
Jan 1945	Shanghai	10 million	—
post-1945	Shanghai	30 million	—
Specific			
1927	Great China-Lily	150,000	*Sex Trap, I–II*
1928	Minxin	30,000	*Mulan Joins the Army*
1931	Mingxing	120,000	*Sing-song Girl Red Peony* (sound)
1931	Huaguang	50,000	*Reconciliation* (sound)
1931	Tianyi	200,000	*A Singer's Story* (sound)
1932	Mingxing	1.2 million	*Fate in Tears and Laughter, I–VI* (partial sound)
1937	Central Film	50,000	*Secret Codes* (sound)

Sources: Du 1988: 127; Gongsun 1977: 2: 207; Fu 1997: 72–7; Fu 1998: 91–9; S. Li and Hu 1996: 375; ZDZ 1996a: xiii, 1378, 1418.

distribution company called United Six (Liuhe, aka United Film Exchange). Under Zhou Jianyun's management, United Six launched offensives on three fronts (ZDZ 1996a: 103). First, in terms of publicity, it established a magazine and defended the quality of national cinema by calling on audiences to resist cheap flicks, a resistance clearly directed against Tianyi, whose costume dramas owned a large share of domestic and overseas markets for Chinese films (Zhu 1998: 61–2). Second, in terms of distribution, United Six pressured domestic and overseas theaters to sign exclusive contracts with its members and to reject Tianyi's products. This strategy only partially succeeded in Shanghai but eventually backfired overseas. Third, in terms of production, United Six attempted to drive out its competitors by rushing to produce what they had planned to shoot, a strategy resulting in a direct confrontation with Tianyi (Gongsun 1977: 1: 177–83).

In two years, United Six's intervention in raising the stake of film production and distribution seemed to have some impact. More than twenty small companies were shut down in 1928. As recently as 1927, a source listed a total of 179 Chinese-owned film companies, 142 of them in Shanghai, eight in Guangzhou, six in Hong Kong and four in the US (S. Cheng *et al.* 1927:

Table 2.5 Film sales and rental prices, 1920s–60s

Year	Price	Film	Location
Per print			
pre-1925	up to 4,000 yuan	domestic title	Shanghai
1926	1,000 yuan	domestic title	Shanghai
1928	500–600 yuan	domestic title	Shanghai
1928	200 yuan	mediocre foreign title (rental)	Shanghai
1928	1,200 yuan	excellent foreign title (rental)	Shanghai
1930	400 yuan	domestic title	Shanghai
Per exhibition rights			
1923	9,000 yuan	*Orphan Rescues Grandfather*	Southeast Asia
late 1920s	2,400 yuan	quality domestic film	Singapore/Malaysia
late 1920s	1,800 yuan	quality domestic film	Thailand
late 1920s	2,700 yuan	quality domestic film	Indonesia
late 1920s	800 yuan	quality domestic film	Vietnam
1931	16,000 yuan	*Sing-song Girl Red Peony*	Indonesia
1931	18,000 yuan	*Sing-song Girl Red Peony*	Philippines
1930s	80,000 yuan	one Chaplin film	China
1937	HK$11,350	*The Critical Moment*	Southeast Asia
1937	HK$6,000	*The Critical Moment*	Hong Kong/Macao
1937	HK$3,500	*The Critical Moment*	North and South America
1948	US$10,000	*Orioles among Willow Leaves*	Philippines
1952	HK$80,000	Hong Kong film	overseas combined
1954	HK$50,000	Amoy-dialect film	overseas combined
1954	HK$20,000	Hong Kong Mandarin film	Taiwan
1955	HK$30,000	Cantonese title	overseas combined
1958	HK$19,000–21,000	Amoy-dialect film	Singapore
1958	HK$8,000–9,000	Amoy-dialect film	Philippines
1958	HK$11,000–13,000	Amoy-dialect film	Taiwan
1960s	NT$600,000	Hong Kong Mandarin film	Taiwan
1971	NT$300,000	Hong Kong Mandarin film	Taiwan
1960s	HK$30,000	Taiwan Mandarin film	Thailand/Vietnam
1960s	HK$30,000	Taiwan Mandarin film	Indonesia
1960s	HK$25,000	Taiwan Mandarin film	Philippines
1960s	HK$40,000	Taiwan Mandarin film	Hong Kong

Sources: Du 1988: 129–30, 618; M. Yu 1997: 142; M. Yu 2000: 71, 192; M. Yu 2001: 31, 166; ZDZ 1996a: 104, 185–6, 1363, 1527; Z. Zhang 1990: 1116.

chap. 3). In 1928 the number nose-dived to twenty, and fewer than a dozen were still in business by 1930. The rate of their disappearance was surely alarming, but the competition was such that even United Six fell apart in July

1929 due to internal disputes over Mingxing's apparent abuse of power (ZDZ 1996a: 1421).

The importance of Southeast Asia (*Nanyang*)

Tianyi prospered despite United Sixth's intervention and the press criticism of its *commercialism* (ZDZ 1996a: 88–9). One decisive factor that distinguished Tianyi from its competitors was its far-sighted venture in Southeast Asian markets. Often referred to as 'Nanyang' (literally, 'south ocean'), these markets included colonies along the Pacific Ocean such as Singapore, Kuala Lumpur (Malaysia) and Rangoon or Yangon (Burma) under Britain, Java (Indonesia) and Bangkok (Thailand) under Holland, Annam (Vietnam) under France, the Philippines and Honolulu under the US. Around 1926 many theaters in Southeast Asia had signed contracts with Mingxing and the United Six, but Tianyi sent Runme (age 25) and Run Run Shaw (age 19) to the region in order to develop their own network. They traveled to big cities as well as rural communities and soon convinced a number of distributors and exhibitors to join their cause (Du 1978: 157–9). Together they managed to exhibit Tianyi titles to overseas Chinese audiences, over 70 per cent of them merchants, coolies and plantation or farm workers (ZDZ 1996a: 1408). The popularity of their accessible films generated a huge demand for Tianyi products. By 1931, Tianyi managed 139 theaters in Southeast Asia (J. Zhang and Cheng 1995: 948) and thus commanded a leading edge that would facilitate its expansion to Hong Kong in the 1930s and restructuring as the all-powerful Shaw Brothers decades later.

Initially, Southeast Asia was intended as an alternative market because of a limited domestic ownership of theaters, which translated into a lower share of box-office returns in Shanghai (which averaged above 2,000 yuan per title for domestic features) and other Chinese regions and forced Chinese studios to seek additional incomes through the sales of film prints overseas.[8] As the Chinese diaspora welcomed domestic films out of nostalgia for the homeland and nationalistic pride, Southeast Asian distributors became regulars in the Shanghai industry. Yet, no single company dominated the overseas markets at first. As early as 1924, Mingxing signed a contract with a Singapore theater in an attempt to discourage the exhibition of films by other Shanghai studios. Starting in 1926, Tianyi increasingly shipped its films to Taiwan and other Southeast Asian communities (ZDZ 1996a: 117). According to one estimate, overseas sales of a quality film could generate 2,400 yuan from Singapore and Malaysia, 1,800 yuan from Thailand, 2,700 yuan from Indonesia, 800 yuan from Vietnam – a total of 7,700 yuan exclusive of the Philippines and other countries (Du 1988: 129–30). Although there is a lack of further statistics, it is probable that Southeast Asia might have become the mainstay or even the 'exclusive' market for many Shanghai companies in the second half of the 1920s.

However, by 1927, higher taxes and stricter censorship in Southeast Asia, as well as the lower production quality of commercial pictures, combined to reduce the Chinese diaspora's interest in domestic films. This was a fatal blow to the industry because, even with their intentionally apolitical titles which posed no ideological challenge to the colonial rule in the region, Shanghai companies could no longer automatically count on the overseas Chinese's patriotism for profits (ZDZ 1996a: 111, 170; Zhu 1998: 65).

The rise of the theater chains: Shanghai, Beijing and beyond

To restructure the domestic industry, Chen Dabei recommended building theaters in inland cities so that the Shanghai studios could rely less on Southeast Asian markets (ZDZ 1996a: 735). However, the problem was that the spread of cinemas across the nation was a slow process and foreigners who had little interest in domestic pictures controlled most of the theaters in China. According to one estimate, by the end of 1926 approximately 156 cinemas existed in China, and foreigners owned a majority of them (S. Cheng *et al.* 1927: chap. 33). The number reached 250 in 1930, of which only fifty or sixty showed domestic films (Zhu 1998: 61).

The city with the largest concentration of cinemas was Shanghai, with thirty-nine (i.e., 25 per cent of the national total) in 1927. Among Shanghai's most celebrated venues were the Carlton (Kaerdeng), Odeon (Aodi'an), Palace (Zhongyang), Pantheon (Baixing), Peking (Beijing) and Venus (Jinxing) theaters, as well as those owned by the Ramos Amusement Company and managed by W.N. Ginsburg, which included the Carter (Kate), Embassy (Xialingpeike), Empire (Enpaiya) and Victoria (Weiduoliya) theaters. Architecturally, most of these theaters featured European-style (e.g., art deco) exteriors and interiors. The contemporary photographs of the Odeon and Peking Theaters displayed interiors similar to that of a grand opera house, with central chandeliers, spacious balcony and comfortable seats throughout. As proprietor of the Peking Theater, the Shanghai Amusement Company ran an advertisement in *The China Cinema Year Book 1927*, boasting the theater's pillar-free structure, dim pathway lighting, effective ventilation and courteous staff.

Significantly, despite the dominant foreign ownership of distribution and exhibition, Chinese personnel managed many of the Shanghai cinemas. In the spring of 1926, Zhang Changfu and Zhang Juchuan established the first Chinese theater chain, Central Movie Company (Zhongyang) in Shanghai. They leased five theaters in Shanghai and one in Hankou – at the rate of 60,000 yuan a year – from the millionaire Ramos, who subsequently returned to Spain and concluded his two decades of pioneering show business in China. Together with Zhang's Palace, these theaters specialized in domestic films and were affiliated with Mingxing, whose distribution offices in Northern, Central and Southern China were under Zhou Jianyun's management. As Zhou reported in 1928, with an investment of 100,000 yuan, Central Movie Company made a profit of over 40,000 yuan in 1927, while the Peking Theater alone made a profit of

Figure 2.4 Hollywood in Shanghai: billboards outside the Peking Theater

over 60,000 yuan, which means that other theaters had deficits. In January 1928 the Carlton had an income of over 70,000 yuan (S. Li and Hu 1996: 105; ZDZ 1996a: 724).

In comparison with Shanghai, the capital city Beijing claimed merely fourteen cinemas in 1926, including the Popular Cinema (Tongsu) and the Star Cinema (Mingxing). As a rare example of what the Chinese could achieve in early film exhibition, Luo Mingyou deserves special attention. Born in Hong Kong in 1902, Luo attended the Law School of Peking University in 1918 and in 1919 started to manage Zhenguang (literally, 'truth light'), a cinema built on the location of the old Dangui Teahouse. Zhenguang featured foreign films of high artistic quality, distributed film plot sheets and projected Chinese subtitles during the show. Luo's weekend matinee discounts for students (at 0.1 yuan) (see Table 2.2, p. 16) made his theater a huge attraction for the young audience. Unfortunately, a fire destroyed the theater in late 1919.

With the help of his uncle Luo Wengan, who served as the Minister of Justice in the Beijing government, Luo Mingyou raised enough funds to construct a new Zhenguang Theater in 1921. It was a modern, three-storied, steel and cement structure boasting granite pillars and stairways, glass walls, a rooftop garden and over 800 cushioned seats. Luo reduced disturbance inside the theater by relocating the service of snacks and drinks to a separate area. The theater employed a band conducted by a former Russian professor to accompany every show and a *benshi* (screen narrator) to interpret the silent foreign film to the audience as the story unraveled on screen (ZDZ 1996a: 177–80). As manager, Luo raised the standards for film exhibition in China and continued to reject cheap pictures in his programs (Hou 1996: 199–218).

When his business had increased to ten cinemas in Beijing and Tianjin, Luo established Northern China Film (Huabei) in 1927 and recruited young talents such as Zhu Shilin, Fei Mu and Shen Fu. Luo's distribution and exhibition business prospered, and by 1929 he owned more than thirty cinemas in five provinces, including those in northeast China (Du 1988: 136–7). In 1929, Luo decided to invest in production, teaming up with Minxin to film *Memories of the Old Capital* (Gudu chunmeng) and *Wild Flower* (Yecao xianhua), both directed by Sun Yu in 1930. Luo's influence reached its peak in the early 1930s with his Lianhua, but during the 1920s he had proved himself to be a unique player in the foreign dominated exhibition sector.

In pursuit of a profession: film publications and film schools

The emergence of film criticism was evident by the mid-1920s, a time when the total number of film periodicals ranged from thirty to forty titles (Luo *et al.* 1992: 1: 3). Over the decade the conceptualization of film had shifted from film as play (hence, shadowplay or photoplay) through film as more than play to film as art. In 1921 Gu Kenfu argued that the shadowplay is the most 'realistic' of all plays; in 1928 Ouyang Yuqian declared that film is 'a synthetic art' and that 'photoplay' is only part of 'motion picture art' (Luo *et al.* 1992: 1: 4–5, 99). In general, critics of the time were more familiar with drama and more willing to advance the literary and dramatic arts than to explore film as a visual art.

In addition to regular film or entertainment columns in major newspapers, three groups of early film publications were most noteworthy. First, the promotional magazine issued irregularly by a major studio introduced a particular film and sometimes included the studio's policy, filmmakers' reflections as well as film criticism. Second, film periodicals, special issues and regular sections of literary and popular journals carried up-to-date film reviews and articles on domestic and foreign films. Third, film books contributed directly to the evolving industry and in many ways anticipated film as a legitimate subject of new knowledge. Among the major studios publishing numerous promotional magazines during this period were Great China-Lily, Great Wall, Mingxing and Tianyi, and filmmakers often participated in criticism.

In addition to magazine articles, a few film books helped establish film as a legitimate subject of new knowledge in the 1920s. Xu Zhuodai published *Film Studies* (Yingxi xue, 1924), the earliest Chinese book on film studies. Drawing on miscellaneous foreign sources, the book tackles topics ranging from the elements and types of film to screenwriting, directing, acting, cinematography, art design and special effects. Hou Yao's *Writing Scripts for Shadowplays* (Yingxi juben zuofa, 1926) covers a variety of topics on screenwriting, such as the functions, values and elements of shadowplays, special film terms (printed in English), as well as dramatic structure and techniques. Of particular importance in Hou's book is his list of thirty-two 'inappropriate' subjects for shadowplays. They include violence against women, juvenile delinquency, capital punishment, child abuse, ugly nude poses, incitement of mutual hatred, violent conflict between labor and capital, excessive gunshots, rape, prostitution, painful pregnancy and labor, incest, gambling and smoking (Luo *et al.* 1992: 1: 55–6). Albeit too restrictive and impractical, Hou's list, accompanied by another list of twenty-one 'appropriate' subjects, represents an early example of *self-censorship* by Chinese filmmakers.[9] Another publication, *The China Cinema Year Book 1927*, was the first of its kind in China, providing the most comprehensive information imaginable at the time (S. Cheng *et al.* 1927).

Indeed, Chinese filmmakers were working hard as they were fully cognizant of the urgent need to bring out a new generation more knowledgeable about film. As a result, a crop of film schools came into being in the 1920s, many of them under major sponsoring studios. Apart from Mingxing's school founded in 1922 (ZDZ 1996a: 32), 1924 saw the appearance of three film schools in Shanghai. China Motion Picture Company (Zhonghua) set up the China Film School with volunteer instructors who offered classes on acting, cinematography and screenwriting. Every week students could see two Western films free of charge at the Isis Theater owned by the studio's boss, Zeng Huantang. In nine months, the school brought out stars like Hu Die (ZDZ 1996a: 1604). The other two schools were the Great China Film School and the Changming Film Correspondence School founded by Wang Xuchang and Xu Hu. In its one-year operation, Changming taught students as far away as Japan and the Philippines, and it published the first Chinese film textbook, which covered topics ranging from the history, functions, genres and national characteristics of cinema, to directing, screenwriting and cinematography (Luo *et al.* 1992: 1: 11–46).

Altogether, fourteen Chinese-owned film schools operated in Shanghai at one time or another during the 1920s, in addition to three by foreigners (S. Cheng *et al.* 1927: chap. 40). These schools functioned principally as training programs for acting and did not produce famous directors or screenwriters. But at the very least, they represented early filmmakers' conscientious attempts to ensure that Chinese cinema would reach a higher level of professionalism in the near future.

CRITICAL ISSUES: ARTS, ARTISTS AND ARTISTIC THEORY

Before leaving the period of early cinema, we should consider the technical and artistic aspects of filmmaking and tackle the critical issues related to early 'artists' and their conceptions of film. This section also addresses such topics as 'films of theater people' and 'shadowplay theory', which did not surface in the period but are critical to our understanding of it.

Arts: learning the film basics

As Cheng Bugao recollects, when Zhang Shichuan started directing in the early 1910s, the fixed camera, exaggerated acting and a limited shooting range was the typical style. Zhang and his contemporaries relied on the 200-foot reel film, which lasted three minutes and twenty seconds.[10] While shooting, the cameraman had to crank the reel in the motor-less camera at approximately 120 rounds per minute in order to achieve the speed of sixty feet per minute, and his work was humorously compared to 'churning the ice cream'. A faster or slower speed would result in the distortion of facial expressions or bodily movements on screen. Before the introduction of the glass-wall studio, the crew used an open-air tent, and sometimes the painted backgrounds of pavilions and the like would move with the wind without being noticed by the filmmakers, and would create funny-looking scenes on screen (ZDZ 1996a: 1577–82).

Yet, such difficulties did not prevent Chinese filmmakers from experimenting with new film techniques. The Motion Picture Department inserted in *Dream of Immortality* (Qingxu meng, dir. Ren Pengnian, 1922; 3 reels) the following special effects: a broken water jar reappears in one piece, a man walks through a wall, and an inanimate object moves by itself. Such camera tricks were

Figure 2.5 Chinese filmmaking in the 1920s: fixed cameras and exaggerated acting

greatly welcomed by the audience (ZDZ 1996a: 1460). By 1924, Mingxing cinematographer Dong Keyi had figured out how to use double exposure to shoot an actor playing two roles. In 1926 Dong used miniature models to shoot the scene of colliding trains in *Lonely Orchid*. In the late 1920s he designed special effects, for example flying swordsmen, which further enchanted the audience. A martial arts film, *Four Heroes from the Wang Family* (Wangshi sixia, dir. Shi Dongshan, 1927; 10 reels), was reportedly the first to use a dolly shot in China (ZDZ 1996a: 1414).

In 1927 Dan Duyu had already experimented with underwater photography in *The Spider Cave*. Two years later, Zhang Shichuan and Hong Shen directed six cameras simultaneously shooting a soccer game on location for *A Patriotic Game* (Yijiao ti chuqu, 1929), a sports picture based on a real-life game between a Chinese team and one consisting of foreign expatriates in Shanghai (S. Li and Hu 1996: 251). In the late 1920s, the public fascination with film techniques was such that film periodicals published articles explaining camera tricks such as double exposure, stop motion, matte shot, glass shot, miniature and slow motion (ZDZ 1996a: 950–71).

A Chinese film aesthetic?

By the end of the 1920s, Zhang Shichuan had developed his style of directing and typically repeated sequences of frontal, eye-level shots from the long shot through the medium shot to the close-up (J. Li 1995: 40–1). Such 'three-step' presentations foregrounded acting and accustomed the audience to a conventional film language in close proximity to their experience with the Chinese stage (Hong Kong Arts Centre 1984).

Other artistic features characteristic of early Chinese cinema can be enumerated here. Influenced by traditional theater, early films did not use lavish sets and props, and painted backgrounds were usually simple, more symbolic than realistic. Influenced by traditional art, early films first relied on a single source of light and then preferred flat lighting to chiaroscuro lighting, paying more attention to black-and-white contrast than to varied shades and tones that embodied a three-dimensional or sculptural fullness. Spatial relations were also based on traditional aesthetics. As if on stage, the main characters usually stood up front, at or near the center, thus commanding the viewer's attention, while supporting characters were grouped around in accordance with their respective social positions. The preference for characters' left–right movements rather than forward–backward ones further enhanced the illusion of watching a stage play. In contrast to frequent subject movements, camera movements were kept at a minimum, so techniques such as panning, tilting, tracking and dolly shots were all rarities at the time (K. Hu 1996).

On the surface, minimal camera movements and monotonous shot sequences might suggest that early Chinese filmmakers were fearful of film techniques. However, apart from the technical and technological inadequacies hinted above, a more direct cause for such 'techno-phobia' was the entrenched preference for stable spatio-temporal frameworks in traditional Chinese art and theater. As with the traditional stage, a safe viewing distance – physical as well as psychological – was always appreciated, so that the spectator was less likely to identify actively with screen characters than to remain passively as an onlooker of screen actions.

This does not mean that early Chinese filmmakers were conscientious in exploring a 'Chinese' film aesthetic. As a matter of fact, many 'Chinese' practices resemble what Noël Burch calls a 'primitive mode of presentation' or PMR in the early cinema of the West. Among other unfamiliar structures, the PMR consisted of 'a spatial approach combining frontality with non-centered composition and distant camera placement to create a "primitive externality"; a lack of narrative coherence, linearity, and closure; and an underdevelopment of character' (Gunning 1998: 256). To say the least, early Chinese filmmakers' reliance on traditional art and theater was perfunctory, superficial and reactive to the audience's changing needs (K. Hu 1996: 58).

Artists: 'films by theater people'

Three features characterize early film artists in China. First, with a few exceptions, most leading directors and screenwriters were self-taught artists who did not receive formal training in film. Second, again with some exceptions, most were in one way or another affiliated with theater or drama of the time. In fact, Zheng Zhengqiu, Li Minwei, Hong Shen and Hou Yao had already been well-known drama figures before they embarked on their film careers. Third, except for studio founders, most artists were highly mobile and often moved between studios, a practice that would continue in the next two decades.

Appropriately, critics have referred to the products of this early generation as 'films by theater people' (*xiren dianying*). The term first surfaced at a forum held during the 1983 Hong Kong retrospective of early Chinese cinema. Huang Jichi used *xiren dianying* to describe films by Zheng Zhengqiu and others influenced by the civilized play. In contrast, *wenren dianying* (films by literature people) was coined to refer to the leftist artists who emerged first as fiction writers and playwrights in the 1930s and who emphasized film's literary quality (*wenxue xing*) and developed a new method of realism. A third alternative, that of *yingren dianying* (films by film people), was associated with directors like Sun Yu who received film training at Columbia and Wisconsin but who worked closely with literature people. Inasmuch as early cinema is concerned, 'films by theater people' obviously dominated the scene (Hong Kong Arts Centre 1984).

As Fei Mu observed in 1935 (ZDZ 1996a: iii), 'films by theater people' drew directly on the civilized play, a new form of non-operatic play that participated in spreading nationalist sentiments in the years leading to the Republican Revolution. After 1911, however, the public interest in political issues declined, and the civilized play faced a severe downturn. By switching attention away from the political arena toward the domestic sphere, theater people like Zheng Zhengqiu quickly revived the civilized play and produced several popular stage plays in the 1910s (Zhong *et al.* 1997). Although the latter-day civilized play was criticized for its abandonment of political intervention and its submission to con-servative ideologies (J. Cheng *et al.* 1981: 1: 21–3), as a whole the genre served an indispensable function by cultivating a staple of audiences for the emergent shadowplays.

In its own turn, the civilized play drew on traditional Chinese narratives, including various types of storytelling. Like traditional narratives, both the civilized play and 'films by theater people' are character-driven, focusing on a complex of relationships and interactions between characters, unraveled in a unilinear temporal development, marked by convoluted plots and coincidences. All these are narrative elements traceable to the literati's genre of 'romance' (*chuanqi*) from the Tang dynasty. It should not be a surprise to see the famous Tang story of Scholar Zhang and Beauty Yingying finds its cinematic representa-tion in *Romance of the West Chamber*. Interestingly, the Chinese emphasis on convoluted plots and incredible coincidences resembles that of the nineteenth-century European novel, which came to China via translation in the late Qing and exerted a considerable impact on butterfly fiction (ZDZ 1996a: 1511–13). It was only natural that 'films by theater people' would benefit from cooperation with butterfly writers as well (W. Chen 1992: 294).

Shadowplay theory: an indigenous brand?

The shadowplay theory as 'indigenous' invention starts with an exegesis of the term 'yingxi'. As Gu Kenfu reasoned in the 1920s, 'since it is called shadow-play, film ought to treat play as essential and shadow as supplementary; the priority of play necessitates the conveyance of play by means of shadows' (J. Li 1995: 40). Writing in 1986, Chen Xihe speculated that the prioritization of 'play' (with related elements such as drama, narrative, theme) over 'shadow' (image, technique, structure) has consolidated the centrality of the script in the Chinese conception of film. Indeed, the centrality was systematically formulated as early as 1926 in Hou Yao's *Writing Scripts for Shadowplays*.

As Chen claims, from script to set design, 'shadowplay' is saturated with dramatic elements, and this is a unique artistic phenomenon in early Chinese cinema. Nevertheless, Chen believes that, as 'an aesthetic concept', the shadow-play has transcended its historical boundary and has become a fundamental idea in the Chinese conception of film, which has persisted right to the mid-1980s. Chen abstracts from Hou's book 'a complete system of film theory based on the core idea of shadowplay' and contends that the shadowplay theory, as an independent entity 'endowed with strong Eastern colors', stands 'shoulder to shoulder with' and 'in diametric opposition to major systems of Western film theories' (Luo *et al.* 1992: 2: 291–2, 305).

To illustrate the shadowplay theory, Chen neatly charts the perceived differences between the Chinese and the Western conceptions of film. The Chinese regard 'play' as essential whereas Westerners regard 'shadow' as essential. The Chinese treat 'shadow' as an expressive means to complete the play whereas Westerners treat 'play' as an individual mode of 'shadow'. The Chinese are obsessed with debates on dramatic and literary qualities whereas Westerners are obsessed with differentiating montage and the long take. The Chinese only study montage and the long take so as better to present 'play', whereas Westerners approach dramatic theory only as pure techniques. All this reflects two different ways of thinking: the Chinese are holistic whereas Westerners are analytic (Luo *et al.* 1992: 2: 296).

In his 1986 exposition of the shadowplay theory, Zhong Dafeng observes the influence of the civilized play on early Chinese conceptions of film. Instead of a binary list of East–West differences, Zhong concentrates on the 'dual structures' of the shadowplay theory. On the surface is a theory of dramatic techniques, but 'beneath the cover of dramatization, the deep structure . . . of the shadowplay theory has produced an ontology of film narration based on film's functions and objectives' (Luo *et al.* 1992: 2: 315). Again, Hou's 1926 book is cited as example, and his neglect of film's technical aspects such as shots and editing is taken as the sign of early Chinese filmmakers' ignorance of the ontology of film.

A number of problems undermine if not invalidate the arguments for the shadowplay theory. First, its claim to being 'indigenous' is untenable because the evidence cited in support comes from a few Chinese who drew extensively on *Western* dramatic or literary theory in the 1920s. Indeed, in the same year when his book came out, Hou Yao published an article citing a British critic's theory of literature – an art that comprises elements such as emotion, imagination, thought and form. Since these four essential elements are crucial to film itself, Hou advanced a thesis that transcended national and cultural boundaries: 'Film is literature! Film is live literature!' (ZDZ 1996a: 500–1). Second, the kind of film theory differentiating between drama and film Chen and Zhong refer to either had not been formulated or had not been translated in the 1920s. Instead of their perceived fundamental differences, historically Western and Chinese filmmakers were equally occupied with the dramatic aspects of film arts in the silent period. Third, to the extent that the shadowplay theory privileges narration and the social function of narrative, it is not so much a distinguishing feature for Chinese film as it is for Chinese narrative in general. What is missing in the shadowplay theory, in this respect, is a critical distinction between Chinese and Western narrative theory. Given unsolved problems like these, the best way to appraise the conception of 'shadowplay' is not to abstract it as an indigenous theory, but to contextualize it in early Chinese cinema as a *convenient practice* through which filmmakers successfully reached out to the audience familiar with traditional theater and fiction.

CONCLUSION: A GROWING SENSE
OF NATIONALISM

The articulation of the national in early Chinese cinema was made at multiple levels, from the unconscious through the symbolic to the allegorical. At an unconscious level, the Chinese initially held onto the term 'shadowplay' in order to claim film as at least partially traceable to certain traditional Chinese cultural forms. At the symbolic level, they relied on women's sufferings to delineate a society in radical transformation and to express a pressing need for traditional virtues such as filiality, chastity and sincerity. At the allegorical level, while the message of 'rescuing grandfather' (or tradition) in family dramas was undoubtedly a reference to 'rescuing the nation', even martial arts films might have functioned as some kind of 'national allegory' whereby heroes would right the wrongs and justice would eventually triumph.

On a small scale, the concern with the national was evident in the naming of film studios. The enlightenment spirit and the discourse of nationalism prevalent in the late Qing and the May Fourth periods left a visible mark in names such as 'Xinmin' and 'Minxin', both pointing to a 'new people' of China. The Commercial Press gave its subsidiary studio Guoguang (literally, 'light of the nation') an equally striking English name, 'National Enlightenment' (S. Cheng *et al.* 1927: chap. 3).

However, in reality domestic films at the time rarely lived up to these expectations. An exclusive reliance on national traditions such as folk tales, myths and legends engendered a kind of mass culture catering to lowly tastes. A leading May Fourth writer, Yu Dafa, criticized in 1927 the tendency of some studios to lower the Chinese taste to suit the demand of distributors from colonies in Southeast Asia. While he was all in favor of turning the aristocratic to the plebeian, the metaphysical to the accessible and the dull to the lively, Yu contended that the plebeian was not vulgarity, the accessible was not monotony and that liveliness was not mere amusement (Luo *et al.* 1992: 1: 87–9).

Similarly, Chen Zhiqing contended in 1926 that a national cinema must preserve and promote the 'national spirit'. For Chen, the insufficient presence of the national spirit in Chinese cinema was a result of the filmmakers' preference for the upper classes over lower-class people, who alone preserved the national spirit. In a sense, Chen's argument anticipated the emergence of leftist film and its glorification of the working classes. To change the Western myths of Chinese long queues and bound feet, Chen thus urged Chinese screenwriters, 'when you hold your pen, bear in mind the national spirit innate in China. Do not forget this pen is at the hand of a Chinese, and do not forget from this pen a Chinese screenplay will come into being' (ZDZ 1996a: 711).

Chen's argument reflected a growing sense of nationalism in Chinese cinema, but it also indicated that people conceived the national largely at the level of filmic representation yet to be achieved by Chinese cinema. In any case, by the end of the 1920s film had become an acceptable form of entertainment, a new kind of art and an emergent cultural industry in China.

3

CINEMA AND THE NATION-PEOPLE, 1930–49

INTRODUCTION: A 'GOLDEN AGE' PERIOD

This chapter covers a period that includes what some historians see as two 'golden ages' in Chinese cinema – the prewar 1930s (Teo 1997: x) and the postwar 1940s (Lee 1991: 6).[1] The period started in 1930, a year in which Lianhua was launched with high expectations to 'revive national cinema'. The period ended in 1949, a year in which the Kuomingtang relocated its Republic of China government to Taiwan and the Chinese Communist Party founded the People's Republic of China in the mainland.

The fundamental changes in the film industry in this period were directly linked to social, political and military events of the times. First, Japan invaded northeastern China on 18 September 1931 and established a puppet Manchuria government. On 28 January 1932 the Shanghai battle erupted when Japanese troops took over part of Shanghai. The fighting lasted until May 1932 when a ceasefire was reached through mediation of the international powers anxious to protect their extra-territorial interests in China during the Great Depression. The surge of patriotism soon clashed with the KMT policy of non-provocation as Chiang Kai-shek's Nanjing government sought peace with Japan. The ideological fissure between the population and the government opened the door for a leftist film movement through the mid-1930s. The KMT policy proved a failure when Japanese troops came down through northern China and occupied Shanghai in August 1937. It was not until the outbreak of the Pacific War that Japan finally stormed *zujie* – the International Settlement and the French Concession – in Shanghai, thus making the years 1937 to 1941 a special interval of 'orphan island' (*gudao*) in Chinese film history when filmmakers inside non-occupied Shanghai were independent from direct Japanese interference. In 1941 Japan invaded Hong Kong, and from then to the end of the war Hong Kong's feature production dropped from an average of over eighty films a year in the late 1930s to zero (Fu 2000a: 205). Meanwhile, the KMT set up its wartime capital in Chongqing and kept the Japanese at bay from the mountainous hinterland, while the CCP organized guerilla warfare across China. After eight years of the resistance war Japan surrendered in 1945, and the KMT controlled much of the nation.

58

Four years of the large-scale civil war concluded with the triumph of the CCP over the KMT, and the political landscape of modern China had forever changed.

In terms of film history, this period can be further divided into three phases. First, in the *prewar* phase (1930–7), the emergence of Lianhua and its movement of reviving national cinema lent momentum to a fundamental restructuring of the film industry. The gradual transition to sound redrew the map of the exhibition sector,[2] and the establishments of new companies along with changing sentiments and tastes made leftist films an astonishing success. On the other hand, the centralized censorship operations under the Nanjing government attempted to score victories on several fronts, clashing with Hollywood imports, domestic martial arts productions and the leftists on countless occasions. Significantly, a new group emerged to claim a middle ground in politicized film circles, and the debate on 'soft film' angered leftist critics but suggested an alternative in film theory and practice in China.

Second, in the *wartime* phase (1937–45), commercial filmmaking returned to Shanghai in the 'orphan island' years and continued well into the occupation when the Japanese forces sought to restructure the Shanghai industry after their Manchurian model. Many veteran filmmakers relocated to Chongqing, where they helped with the KMT-run studios and with wartime drama activities. A few reached Yan'an, the CCP headquarters, where they started documentary filmmaking. Others briefly stayed in Hong Kong, where they promoted patriotic films, some released in Mandarin, thereby foreshadowing the rise of Mandarin cinema in postwar Hong Kong.

Third, in the *postwar* phase (1946–9), the KMT confiscated Japanese studio facilities in Shanghai and Manchuria and established a huge system of filmmaking and distribution. Veteran filmmakers either joined the KMT studios or started their own, producing films of high artistic quality, direct emotional impact and immense popular appeal. The ideological divide was particularly deep during this time, and the line-up of filmmakers according to their political affiliations anticipated their choices of geographic residence after 1949. The postwar phase also witnessed new developments in film production in Hong Kong and Taiwan, which will be treated separately in Chapters 4 and 5.

PREWAR CINEMA, 1930-7

If overriding *commercial interests* and intimate ties to *national traditions* characterize the period of early cinema, the first 'golden age' in the prewar 1930s is marked by incessant *ideological struggles* between the Nationalists and the leftists, between heroic glorification and humanistic exploration, between social realism and aesthetic modernism. Significantly, such struggles were often waged in the name of the *nation-people* and accompanied by such slogans as 'national defense' and 'national salvation', whereas the issue of tradition became rather suspect in theory, albeit not entirely absent in practice. Patriotism and nationalism thus characterized the rhetoric of such contenders as the Lianhua founders, the KMT censors and the leftists.

Lianhua and the movement of 'reviving national cinema'

The emergence of Lianhua (United Photoplay Service) could not have come at a more propitious moment. By the end of the 1920s the 'suicidal acceleration' in production had driven dozens of small studios to bankruptcy, and the drastic reduction of American silent imports and the impending transition to sound scared exhibitors nationwide. A business-savvy visionary, Luo Mingyou knew all too well that a restructuring of the film industry was imminent, but he decided to proceed step by step.

First, in 1929, he teamed up with Li Minwei and produced *Memories of the Old Capital* and *Wild Flower* (sound accompaniment). Contrary to previous urban titles, these two films represented an uncompromising attitude to social problems and in a sense connected filmmaking to the May Fourth spirit. Both films were released to critical acclaim in 1930 and broke box-office records in some cities (ZDZ 1996a: 1186–7, 1191–2). Second, Luo adopted a method of splitting the box-office returns with theaters rather than selling prints for a flat fee. As a result, he raked in 20 to 30 per cent more profits (M. Li 1993: 85). Third, Luo appealed to nationalist sentiments when announcing the establishment of Lianhua in 1930. Written in semi-literary Chinese, Lianhua's notice denounced 'the cultural and economic invasions in the form of imported films' and declared the company's aim to 'launch the movement of reviving national cinema, so as to save domestic theaters from a shortage of films and to meet the demand of domestic audiences' (ZDZ 1996a: 70–1). This notice also claimed that the new company had contacted over sixty major theaters nationwide and planned to raise 1 million yuan and set up studios in Hong Kong, Shanghai and Tianjin.[3] Listed among sixty Lianhua 'cofounders' were theater owners like He Tingran (T.J. Holt) and luminaries like Mei Lanfang (ZDZ 1996a: 779).

Lianhua's headquarters was in Hong Kong and registered with both the Nanjing and the Hong Kong governments on 25 October 1930. In March 1931 Lianhua opened a management branch in Shanghai to oversee the operations of Studio 1 (former Shanghai Minxin) and Studio 2 (former Great China-Lily). Initially, the Hong Kong studio was named Studio 3 and based in part on the early Minxin equipment managed by Li Beihai. Studio 4 was formerly Dan Duyu's Shanghai Photoplay, but it would soon be destroyed in the Shanghai battle. Due to the changing political and economic situation, neither a 1931 plan for Studio 5 in Beiping nor a 1932 plan for a new studio in Sichuan province materialized, but Studio 6 was established by Zhu Shilin in Shanghai in August 1932. In October 1932, Studio 6 was renamed Studio 3, and the original Studio 3 became Hong Kong Lianhua (ZDZ 1996a: 72–3).

Clearly, Lianhua was an early example of vertical and horizontal integration in the entertainment industry, a kind of synergy or 'cartel' that centralized operations of production, distribution, exhibition and more (ZDZ 1996a: 1424; Zhu 1998: 62–4). Apart from his merger of studios, Luo brought in over twenty theaters controlled by his Northern China Film. He also cooperated with other theater chains such as Ping'an and Yangtze in Shanghai, Mingda and China Entertainment in Hong Kong, Songhua in Haerbin and Cathay (Shenzhou) in Guangzhou. In 1932, Luo opened a Lianhua distribution office in Singapore after his trip to Southeast Asia. In addition, Luo made an incursion into the printing business by recruiting Huang Yicuo and aiming at the lucrative business in magazines, posters and advertisements (ZDZ 1996a: 68). All in all, Lianhua encouraged *healthy cooperation* – rather than the previous cut-throat competition – between various business sectors and sought to make itself a self-sufficient, all-powerful entertainment giant.

The names of the Lianhua cofounders reveal that Luo had cultivated a close connection with the political and financial establishments as well, and many prominent figures were elected to Lianhua's board of trustees in 1930 (ZDZ 1996a: 72). Luo himself served as Lianhua's general manager and benefited from his high-profile connections. He was elected an executive member of the official China Education Film Association in 1932, appointed an advisor to the planning committee for the KMT-run studio and was dispatched by the government on a tour to inspect film industries in Europe and the US in 1934. In May 1933, Luo signed a contract with the KMT central committee to produce newsreels for them. Luo also actively participated in the KMT-sponsored New Life Movement and co-directed, with Zhu Shilin, *National Customs* (Guofeng, 1935).

In comparison with other film projects of the late 1920s, Luo's allocation of budgets was fairly liberal: each film was given 40,000 yuan and a shooting time of four to five months (ZDZ 1996a: 1378) (see Table 2.4, p. 45). Lianhua released twelve titles between 1930 and 1931. Films like *Love and Responsibility* (Lianai yu yiwu, dir. Bu Wancang, 1931) soon won over patriotic audiences, especially urban intellectuals who had been put off by cheap martial arts pictures. Lianhua's patriotism, decent production values and strong financial support also enticed Cai Chusheng and Ma-Xu Weibang from Mingxing. In 1931 Lianhua established a film school in Beiping. Also in 1931 Lianhua merged Li Jinhui's famous Bright Moon Song and Dance Troupe to its newly formed Lianhua Song and Dance Troupe and helped Li's top students such as Li Lili and Wang Renmei to become leading actresses in the 1930s. Yet, in spite of Luo's affiliation with the KMT government, Lianhua still served as a significant leftist base, and several Lianhua directors had turned 'progressive' (*jinbu*) if not completely leftist.

Lianhua's size and stature might have concealed its financial difficulties. The Japanese occupation of northeastern China in 1931 took away a substantial part of Luo's theater chain. Tensions erupted inside Lianhua in 1932 over such problems as high salaries, colossal expenses in its Hong Kong Studio and its Shanghai office, insufficient number of new releases and low revenues from its Guanghua Theater in Shanghai (ZDZ 1996a: 1331). Lianhua's Hong Kong studio leased its site for HK$250 a month and offered a monthly salary of HK $60 to its top stars (M. Yu 1997: 19) (see Table 3.1). In 1933–4, Luo failed in two Lianhua stock offerings, and his Shanghai studios owed employees' salaries for over six months by the end of 1934 (S. Li and Hu 1996: 374). After the withdrawal of its partner Chiu Shu-sen (Zhao Shusen), Lianhua shut down its Hong Kong studio, where Moon Kwan and Leung Siu-po had directed six silent pictures (W. Guan 1976). In spite of his growing political reputation, Luo did not secure a stable financial basis for the sprawling Lianhua.

In August 1936 huge unpaid debts forced Luo to hand over Lianhua's management to Wu Xingzai's financial group Hua'an, which continued to use Lianhua's name for releases until July 1937. By this time Li Minwei had withdrawn from Lianhua and relocated to Hong Kong; Luo followed suit and later made a living as a Christian priest. Nevertheless, Luo's revival of national cinema had been judged to be 'an important revolution' as early as 1934 (ZDZ 1996a: 1351). Even though historical exigencies prevented him from accomplishing what he had envisioned in the late 1920s, Luo helped implement a new perception of national cinema in the 1930s.

State censorship: an evolving institution

The Nanjing government pushed its own agendas of nationalism in film circles by way of regulation and censorship. If censorship did not play a crucial role in early cinema, it became ubiquitous in the new period. Before the late 1920s, film censorship was implemented mostly by municipal and provincial governments but was enforced sporadically (ZDZ 1996a: 126–55). Yet, several critics had articulated the need for state censorship to protect domestic films and to publish regulations for companies to follow. A 1928 article complained about the 'foreign' tariffs leveled by the *zujie* customs authorities at domestic films 'exported' out of Shanghai and sighed: 'Oh! The Chinese . . . Such an inferior people lacking a fighting spirit!' (ZDZ 1996a: 119). Zhou Jianyun also blamed the Chinese lack of control over custom tariffs as a direct cause for the domination of Euro-American films in China, which would translate into an estimated annual loss of over 20 million yuan to the foreign entertainment industry (ZDZ 1996a: 116, 1045).

The resistance of the imperialist 'cultural invasion' often went hand in hand with the protest against offensive images of the Chinese in Hollywood films, as illustrated in Hong Shen's publicized case in February 1930. Enraged by the humiliating portrayal of the Chinese in Harold Lloyd's *Welcome Danger* (dir. Clyde Buckman, 1929; trans. *Bu pasi*), Hong took to the stage and instructed the audience to boycott the film when it was shown at the Grand Theater (Daguangming) in Shanghai. Hong was routed and arrested by the security guards but was released following public denouncement (Xiao 1997: 38–41).

After the establishment of the Nanjing government, the state censorship system evolved quickly. In September 1928 the Ministry of Interior issued thirteen regulations on film censorship, to take effect on 1 January 1929. In July 1929 the Ministries of Interior and of Education issued sixteen regulations on film censorship, and the KMT Shanghai Bureaus of Police, Society and Education formed their own film censorship board. From then on a domestic film had to go through *double censorship* in Shanghai: first to clear the KMT system and then the police department of the Shanghai Municipal Council (Gongbu ju) or the French Concession's film censorship office.

In 1930-1 the Nanjing government published the 'Film Censorship Laws' and other documents regarding the institutions and procedures of film censorship nationwide (J. Cheng *et al.* 1981: 1: 174-5; ZDYYZ 1993: 1089-1109). In March 1931 the National Film Censorship Committee (NFCC) was instituted under the joint administration of the Ministries of Interior and of Education, and it quickly issued a ban on all films featuring martial arts or immortals and demons (S. Li and Hu 1996: 196). In December 1933 it also announced that studios could submit screenplays for pre-production review in order to reduce unnecessary financial losses down the road. In March 1934 the NFCC was disbanded and its work transferred to the Central Film Censorship Committee (CFCC) under the jurisdiction of the KMT central propaganda committee, which also supervised the operations of the central screenplay review committee (ZDZ 1996a: 161-9, 1434-42). Among other matters, the CFCC confronted the emergent leftist film activities.

The emergence of the leftist film: critical interventions

Apart from Lianhua and state censorship, the leftist film movement was a significant force that fundamentally changed the landscape of national cinema in the 1930s. According to an official definition, 'leftist films' refer to those anti-imperialist, anti-feudal films produced between 1933 and 1935 by the leftist film movement engineered by the underground Communist film group under the leadership of the Cultural Alliances of Chinese Leftists. Additionally, 'patriotic films' produced in the name of national defense in 1936 are considered ideologically akin to leftist films (J. Zhang and Cheng 1995: 1411).[4] However, I believe that the term should be extended to include films released in 1937, and the movement's starting date be pushed back to account for film criticism that anticipated the emergence of leftist films.

With hindsight, it is apparent that the leftists were presented a unique opportunity in the early 1930s. The surging patriotism in the wake of the Japanese aggression had pushed to the top of the agenda the urgent question of national salvation. The publicity over Lianhua's revival of national cinema had cleared the way for films with new ideas and styles. Leading newspapers established regular film sections and thus opened the door to leftist film criticism. Domestic theaters were in dire need of new films after the government's ban of martial arts pictures

Table 3.1 Salary comparison in Hong Kong, 1930s–90s

Year	Pay (HK$)	Name	Job/film/language	Studio
1931–4	60/month	—	actor or actress	Lianhua
1938	500/month	—	actor or actress (C)	—
1938	1,000	Hu Die	Ronge Tears (C)	Nanyue
1938	5,000	Hu Die	Ronge Tears (M)	Xinhua
1939	500	Chen Yunshang	actress (C/M)	Xinhua
1948	300–500	—	screenwriter (C)	—
1948	1,000–1,500/month	—	director (C)	—
1948	2,500–4,000/month	—	actor or actress (C)	—
1948	10,000/month	—	lead actor (C)	—
1953	75,000	Li Lihua	lead actress (M)	Xinhua
1957	500–2,000	—	producer or screenwriter	—
1957	90–200/month	—	carpenter	—
1958	4,000–5,000	—	lead actress (Amoy)	—
1958	15,000	—	lead actor (Amoy)	—

Period	Name	Role / film	Salary	Studio
late 1950s	Li Hanxiang	new director (M)	8,000/month	Shaw Brothers
late 1950s	—	screenwriter (M)	2,000	Shaw Brothers
late 1950s	—	assistant director (M)	1,000	Shaw Brothers
late 1950s	Yue Feng	top director (M)	30,000	Shaw Brothers
1950s–60s	Yam Kim-fai	opera star (C)	17,500	—
1960s	Kwan Tak-hing	lead actor (C)	1,000	—
1960s	—	director (C)	1,500	—
1960s	Chor Chee	director (C)	7,000	—
1960s	—	cameraman (C)	800–1,200	—
mid-1960s	—	screenwriter (C)	1,500	—
1967	Josephine Siao	lead actress (C)	1,000	—
1969	Chan Wan	*Social Characters* (C)	8,000	—
1971	Bruce Lee	*Fist of Fury* (M)	US$7,500	Golden Harvest
1972	Li Hanxiang	*The Warlord* (M)	100,000	Shaw Brothers
early 1980s	Sam Hui	lead actor (C)	2,000,000	—
1992	Jet Li	lead actor	12,000,000	—
1992	Veronica Yip	lead porn actress	1,000,000	—

Sources: Bordwell 2000: 74; Chiao 1993: 192, 214; Davis and Yeh 2001: 14–18; Du 1988: 536; Gongsun 1977: 2: 128; HKIFF 1982a: 50, 94; HKIFF 1984: 139; HKIFF 1996: 109; M. Yu 1997: 19, 177; M. Yu 1998: 170; M. Yu 2001: 92–5, 165–6; Zhan and Lan 1996: 209.

Notes: Unless otherwise indicated, salary is per title; C = Cantonese; M = Mandarin.

and the decrease of imported silent films, while major studios desperately sought new screenplays to meet the new market demand.

In 1931 Jin Taipu posed this question in a film magazine: after the government's ban on films of immortals and demons, what direction should the industry take? While endorsing Lianhua's 'art films' as a laudable enterprise, Jin judged their taste to be 'too aristocratic' and advocated artistic films dealing with *plebeian life*, especially that of peasants and workers. In conclusion, Jin considered it a lacuna that at the height of revolutionary movements the industry had not promoted 'revolutionary films' (ZDZ 1996a: 667). There was no evidence that Jin belonged to the emergent leftist group, but his argument suggests that certain critical opinions were conducive to the kind of ideological criticism the leftists would embrace in a year or two.

Within the leftist circles, the China Leftist Dramatists Association approved an action plan in September 1931 that recommended adopting 'independence, cooperation and alliance' as three methods of organizing a popular drama movement, which aimed to expose conflicts between capitalism and the proletariat and to point out the inevitable downfall of the middle classes. The plan deemed it necessary to launch a 'leftist film movement' – a kind of 'proletarian cine' – and to criticize reactionary theory and the bourgeois and feudal tendencies in Chinese cinema (ZDYYZ 1993: 17–8). Newly created forums in newspapers and magazines provided a timely outlet for leftists and their affiliates (M. Yi 1993: 736–43).

In its first anniversary issue, 'Screen Daily' (ed. Yao Sufeng) of *Chenbao* (Morning news) announced that its film criticism would aim to expose 'poisonous' elements and promote educational titles and technical achievements. Fifteen critics signed the announcement, including such active leftists as Xia Yan (pen-name Cai Shusheng) and Ah Ying (pen-name Zhang Fengwu) (ZDYYZ 1993: 25, 127–34). Among other agendas, leftist film criticism engaged in reviewing current domestic and foreign films, discussing individual directors, debating ideological issues and introducing Soviet film theory (S. Lu 1962: 3–13). The impact of leftist film criticism was immediate, and its penetration to the heart of the KMT-controlled newspapers disturbed the Nanjing government, which had tried every means possible to curb the spread of pro-Communist or pro-socialist ideas.[5] As in film production, the crackdown on the leftists was relentless and even drove critics like Lu Si into exile in Japan, but leftist film criticism proved resilient and thrived beyond 1937.

In retrospect, a 1930s film criticism insider cited dogmatism, sectarianism and isolationism as among the leftists' chief strategic mistakes, which alienated many liberal critics and readers and which were responsible for losing key forums like 'Screen Daily' to 'reactionary' forces through confrontational politics (Y. Shu 1994: 91–2). While judging film criticism to be the most successful part of the leftist film movement, Xia Yan admitted in 1984 that the leftists had been influenced by 'leftist dogmatism' in their critical practice at the time. In their creative work, however, the leftists had much less control due to the censors' vigilant policing of ideological messages and the producers' constant demand for profit (Xia 1984: 24).

Leftist film production: studio affiliations

Leftist film production started in 1932 when Zhou Jianyun, troubled by Mingxing's shaky finance, instructed Hong Shen to contact Ah Ying and to seek screenplays from leftist writers. The oldest film establishment by this time, Mingxing was triply hurt in 1931 by the ban on martial arts pictures, its competition with Tianyi in sound film production and its heavy investment in a new studio. In what the press described as 'a desperate battle', the company poured 1.2 million yuan into an ambitious new series, *Fate in Tears and Laughter, I–VI* (Tixiao yinyuan, dir. Zhang Shichuan, 1932; partial sound) (see Table 2.4, p. 45). Adapted from an immensely popular butterfly novel by Zhang Henshui, which mixed urban romance with martial arts (Y. Zhang 1996: 105–12), Mingxing expected the film to attract the audience back to its tradition of family dramas. Yet a year-long lawsuit with Dahua over the adaptation rights had generated negative publicity for Mingxing. When the first episode was about to premiere at the Nanking Theater in June 1932, the censors ordered a ban to pressure for legal settlements. The case was dismissed months later after all parties involved had reached a compromise through the mediation of Du Yuesheng, a powerful Shanghai gangster, who oversaw the transfer of 100,000 yuan compensation from Mingxing to Dahua (Gongsun 1977: 146–57; ZDZ 1996a: 1331–2).

By 1932 Mingxing had incurred a deficit of 47,320 yuan (Y. Shu 1994: 74). Financial difficulties compelled Zhou Jianyun to recruit the leftists in producing new films that would compete with Lianhua. The underground CCP cultural committee under Qu Qiubai held a meeting in Shanghai, which tentatively approved the penetration of Xia Yan, Ah Ying and Zheng Boqi into Mingxing. Around the same time, Tian Han was asked to set up a studio for Yan Chuntang, a notorious opium dealer and a protégé of Huang Jinrong, another powerful Shanghai gangster. Tian immediately sought approval from the CCP leadership, which gave him the green light after a meeting in September 1932. With Yang Hansheng and two other Communists on board, Tian recruited Shi Dongshan and Bu Wancang and launched a new studio, Yihua (Chinese Arts Movie Company) in 1932 (X. Ding 1984: 12–13).

To coordinate the leftist film production, a CCP film group headed by Xia Yan was set up in March 1933.[6] As the inaugural issue of *Yihua Weekly* (ed. Wang Chenwu) announced in September 1933, Yihua aimed to produce movies that would deal with 'realities as experienced by the masses in the midst of public moaning over floods, droughts, epidemics and civil wars' (X. Ding 1984: 12). Some of these subjects were incorporated in the first group of leftist films Mingxing released in 1933, including two based on Xia Yan's scripts, *Wild Torrents* (Kuangliu) and *Spring Silkworms* (Chuncan), both directed by Cheng

Bugao. Yihua also produced leftist films in 1933. In retrospect, Communist historians call 1933 'the year of leftist films' because, by an official count, forty-three titles of the year (out of over seventy) are claimed to be either leftist or pro-leftist (ZDYYZ 1993: 1122).

It must be borne in mind that the leftist penetration came almost exclusively by means of screenwriting. Most of the leading leftists who worked in the film industry were noted playwrights at the time. This means that, in order to convey their ideological message, the leftists depended on their relations with the directors and actors, and it is likely that a gap might exist between the leftist script (i.e., words) and the finished film (i.e., images).[7] Through friendship and 'constructive' film criticism, the leftists were able to recruit otherwise unlikely candidates to their cause. Nonetheless, since some directors might not be fully committed to the leftist politics, it was not unusual that the leftists praised one film by a director and then criticized his next work. Such examples include Wu Yonggang's *Goddess* (Shennü, 1934), an acclaimed leftist classic, and his *Little Angel* (Xiao tianshi, 1935) and *The Desert Island* (Langtao sha, 1936), both judged to be 'pro-KMT' or 'reactionary' (J. Cheng *et al.* 1981: 1: 351, 461).

The leftists themselves learned along the way. For instance, Yang Hansheng, who did not know much about screenwriting, was instructed by Hong Shen to write like fiction. The result was *Heavy Taxes* (Tieban zhu), a story about a peasant who flees the village to avoid taxes but returns years later to lead the villagers in resistance against the landlord. A member of the landlord's militia kills the landlord who has taken away his sweetheart and beaten her to death. Although the leftists treated this script as their 'first gunshot' at the corrupt political establishment, Hong Shen was tactful enough to change the title to *A Tale of Red Tears* (Tieban honglei lu, dir. Hong Shen, 1933), which sounded like a typical butterfly story. After showing his synopsis, which was written in an ambiguous way, to Pan Gongzhan, a KMT cultural leader, who thought the story was about two men fighting over a woman, Hong met with Nanjing censors and hinted Pan's consent to them. The film was approved for shooting, but before its public release the censors cut numerous scenes of class conflict (X. Ding 1984: 5–6).

As more leftists joined the film cause, their influence expanded from Mingxing and Yihua to Lianhua and Diantong, the latter a company founded in 1934 with direct CCP supervision. Contrary to Mingxing and Lianhua, both of which continued producing silent pictures, Diantong relied on overseas-trained Chinese sound technicians and produced four sound films. *The Plunder of Peach and Plum* (Taoli jie, dir. Ying Yunwei, 1934), a story about the downfall of two honest intellectuals, Tao (Yuan Muzhi) and Li (Chen Boer), was the first Chinese film to make effective use of diegetic sound. *Children of Troubled Times* (Fengyun ernü, dir. Xu Xingzhi, 1935), a story – based on Tian Han's script – of a romantic poet's awakening to patriotism, included a theme song, 'The March of the Volunteers' (music by Nie Er), which was popular in this period

68

and was adopted as the national anthem of the PRC. In spite of its prominent contribution to Chinese sound films, Diantong was shut down in 1935 due to political and financial reasons.

Whereas the CCP historiography insists that leftist films were popular at the time, the pro-KMT accounts point to the opposite. Even though both sides failed to find contemporary box office to back their respective claims, the fact that Mingxing incurred a loss of 85,687.39 yuan in 1933 proves that leftist film productions did not help the company get out of the red (ZDZ 1996a: 1418). In 1934, under increasing KMT pressure, Mingxing terminated Xia Yan and other prominent leftists' appointments, and Zhou Jianyun's campaign to revive Mingxing drove the company deeper in debt, to the tune of 3 million yuan in November 1934. By July 1935, Mingxing owed its employees three months' back pay, and Zhou resorted to drastic measures, laying off 200 staff, cutting the salaries of the rest by between 15 and 34 per cent, and reducing production costs per film from 40-50,000 to 30,000 in June 1936 (S. Li and Hu 1996: 290-2, 374-5).

Figure 3.1 The Plunder of Peach and Plum (1934): the advent of sound and leftist ideology

Three areas of censorship confrontation

As to be expected, the leftists blamed the KMT regime for intervention in film production. In the 1930s state censorship vigilantly policed three large areas. First, it negotiated with Hollywood in reducing offensive portrayals of the Chinese in American films, which was the least successful of its operations. Second, it promoted nation-building by cracking down on sex and superstition in domestic films and by privileging Mandarin over Cantonese-dialect films, which were quite successful (Xiao 1999). Third, it reinforced the KMT policies by controlling the ideological content of domestic films and curtailing the leftist agendas, which produced mixed results. One immediate cause of the conflict between the censors and the leftists was the KMT decision to negotiate peace with Japan. At a time of rising patriotic sentiments, the Nanjing government opted to join ranks with the Hong Kong colonial government and the Shanghai Municipal Council, which under the pretext of 'neutrality' had censured films featuring anti-Japanese activities in 1932 (ZDZ 1996a: 1333, 1429–30). As late as 1937, before *Crossroads* (Shizi jietou, dir. Shen Xiling, 1937) was released in *zujie*, foreign censors cut the sequences featuring a map of northeastern China and the song 'Thinking of My Homeland', both of which had survived the KMT censors (S. Lu 1962: 46–7).

According to the 1934 Chinese film yearbook, in 1933 the censors approved ninety-two features and fourteen shorts for public release but banned twenty-one features, including ten martial arts films, eight social films, one romance, one comedy and one 'outlandish film'. The banned films represented 22.8 per cent of the total number of features or 15.6 per cent of the total lengths of films. Significantly, five martial arts films (or one-third in this genre) were approved for release. All major studios were affected by the ban: three titles were from Mingxing and two each from Lianhua and Tianyi (ZDZ 1996a: 1046–7). Among Mingxing's banned titles, *Twenty-Four Hours in Shanghai* (Shanghai ershisi xiaoshi, dir. Shen Xiling, 1933), a film contrasting the lives of the proletariat and the capitalists, was based on Xia Yan's script. After ordering the director to implement extended revisions, the censors kept the review print for a year and proceeded with cuts themselves before releasing the final version in December 1934 (X. Ding 1984: 9–11).

The fact that a film like *Twenty-Four Hours in Shanghai* could be released at all pointed to the censors' sympathy for or tolerance of some leftist agendas. For instance, *Wild Torrents* won second place in the first film awards sponsored in May 1933 by the China Education Film Association, whose members included prominent KMT leaders such as Chen Lifu, Chen Guofu and Wang Jingwei (ZDZ 1996a: 1341–2). Of course, the censors' sympathy also went to small companies, which had sustained huge losses from their banned films. The censors struck a deal with them in January 1933 and allowed for two possibilities. First, a banned film could be submitted for a second review and might be approved for release with certain cuts and revisions. Second, to partially recuperate investments, a banned film might be exhibited for a short duration even if it failed the second review (ZDZ 1996a: 1336). This deal was ironic in that if the censors would approve a banned film for public release, it was no longer 'banned' in the legal sense.

The censors' lack of power over Hollywood was evident in the case of *Shanghai Express* (dir. Josef von Sternberg, 1932). As a result of Chinese protest, Paramount agreed in July 1932 not to show the film in China but did not destroy all their prints as ordered. In August the censors retaliated by refusing to issue permits to other Paramount films, but Paramount ignored the 'ban' and showed a film at the Capitol Theater (Guanglu). When the censors protested, Paramount threatened to stop submitting films for review (ZDZ 1996a: 1334). Although KMT censors either banned or declined to review Hollywood titles like *The Bitter Tea of General Yen* (dir. Frank Capra, 1933), the extraterritorial protection in Shanghai's *zujie* rendered their authority over foreign venues dubious, if not outright ineffective (ZDZ 1996a: 1342–3).

Hollywood domination: facts and myths

According to a 1930 report by the US Department of Commerce, among American films imported into China, sound films accounted for 1,648,504 feet (50.2 per cent), whereas silent films totalled 1,610,225 feet (49.8 per cent). Among 823 American titles (1,655,640 feet) listed in a 1932 Chinese censorship document, 65.6 per cent were sound and 34.4 per cent were silent. In comparison, Chinese exhibitors managed to put in circulation a mere 428 Chinese titles (1,170,310 feet), 98.6 per cent of them silent films used to feed those theaters unable to convert to sound (ZDZ 1996a: 1423). A 1934 censorship publication displays a clearer picture of Hollywood domination. Compared with twenty-two pages of Chinese films approved for release and four pages of Chinese banned titles, the publication lists 259 pages of foreign films, mostly Hollywood, approved for exhibition between June 1931 and June 1933 (NFCC 1934). Without dubbing or subtitles, Hollywood products appealed to the educated Chinese, who relied on plot sheets and film reviews in their comprehension and appreciation (Lee 1999: 85–93). Indeed, even Lu Xun, the most prominent Chinese writer of the time, watched almost exclusively Hollywood films from 1928 until his death in 1936.[8]

The Hollywood domination was also noted in subsequent film historiography. For instance, 1933 saw 431 imported features, 355 or 82 per cent of them from Hollywood, compared with eighty-nine domestic features produced that year.[9] In 1934 there were 407 imported features, 345 or 84.8 per cent of them from Hollywood, compared with eighty-four domestic features produced that year. And in 1936, there were 367 imported films, 328 or 89 per cent of them from Hollywood (Z. Wang 1998: 62). Hollywood continued to dominate the Chinese market until 1941. Even when the Pacific War wiped out its operations in Shanghai, Hollywood was still a noticeable presence in the KMT-controlled hinterland.

Hollywood distributors relied on three methods of marketing in China: exclusive theater contracts, one-time purchase and split box-office proceeds. The first was exemplified by MGM's 1939 contract with the Roxy (Dahua), formerly Embassy, as its exclusive first-run venue for ten years. The second was exemplified by the hefty price of 80,000 yuan that He Tingran paid for a new Chaplin film in the 1930s. In comparison, as recently as 1928, rental prices (for three to four days of exhibition) ranged from 200 yuan for a mediocre foreign movie to as high as 1,200 yuan for an excellent one (ZDZ 1996a: 185–6) (see Table 2.5, p. 46). The third, which had been typical theater practice since the mid-1920s, was to divide the proceeds in certain percentages, usually 50 per cent but often more to Hollywood.

As stipulated in a contract, a film must run for a week, and after that a theater could pull the film but only one day after the attendance rate fell below 45 per cent. To maximize the returns, Hollywood usually put just one or two prints in circulation in China, beginning with the first-run theaters in Shanghai and subsequently traveling to Tianjin, Beiping and other large cities. Hollywood customarily sold films in a package deal, thus dumping mediocre products bundled with one or two good films. To guarantee their profits, Chinese exhibitors might schedule 'bad' films on weekends and holidays and 'good' ones on weekdays, for they had to shoulder all publicity expenses as well. Moreover, with dozens of good films, Hollywood would also force a Chinese theater to suspend or abandon showing Chinese films (Z. Wang 1998: 58).

In spite of its incredible overall number of titles, one must remember that Hollywood domination was most secure in the exhibition sector and for that matter mostly concentrated in Shanghai, which accounted for over 50 per cent of the nationwide box-office total. Nonetheless, myths of domination aside, geographical variations in Chinese cities were substantial. Even in the treaty-port city of Tianjin, Chinese audiences consistently showed much less interest in Hollywood, with a two- or three-day full-house run the average for a Hollywood film at a first-run theater there. A 1935 film yearbook indicated that audiences in hinterland cities like Kaifeng and Taiyuan preferred domestic films, and theaters in Chengdu had a hard time enticing audiences even when ticket prices for foreign films had dropped below those for domestic films (Z. Wang 1998: 60–1). Surely, apart from the language issue, which existed in coastal cities, questions of lifestyle and tastes came into play here.

One may further question why Hollywood never succeeded in penetrating in the production sector in China. As a matter of fact, buttressed by their domination in exhibition, foreign ventures had attempted production several times, two of them very noticeably. First, the British-American Tobacco Company, which started operations in China as early as 1903 and owned numerous factories of cigarettes, machinery, paper and printing over time, set up a motion picture department in 1923 with a budget of 50,000 yuan. In addition to documentaries, it produced comic shorts, purchased and built movie theaters (five in Shanghai by April 1925), and refused to exhibit Chinese features. However, the rising patriotism and the boycott of British products eventually drove the company into financial crisis in 1927. Its film operations were terminated, and its film equipment was sold to Tianyi. Second, China First Sound Pictures Company (Zhongguo diyi) and United Film (Lianhe dianying), both Sino-American joint ventures registered in the US, made high-profile debuts in July 1932. China First alone claimed an asset of US$500,000 and planned to build a 'Chinese Hollywood' that would earn 1 million yuan in annual profits. Again, the Chinese press criticized the plans and leading Chinese filmmakers refused to cooperate with these two companies, which ceased operations within a month (J. Cheng *et al.* 1981: 1: 121-7, 187-90).

Transition to sound: technological and linguistic implications

If Hollywood failed to make significant inroads in Chinese production as a whole, its contribution to the technical aspects of film production was crucial in this period, especially in China's transition to sound. According to Gu Jianchen, the earliest exhibition of partial sound films in China took place in the mid-1920s (ZDZ 1996a: 1373-4). In December 1926, four months after the premiere of the world's first feature with synchronized music, *Don Juan* (dir. Alan Crosland, 1926), the Pantheon Theater in Shanghai showed seventeen Phonofilms made by Lee de Forest's company. These shorts featured political speeches and musical performances (Yeh 2002: 83), and the tickets were sold at doubled prices. In 1928, the Shanghai YMCA invited an American, Dr Robertson, to lecture on sound technology while displaying the sound equipment.

The transition to sound in Chinese filmmaking went through three stages. The first was the production of films with *sound accompaniment* (*peiyin*) or partial sound, inaugurated by *Wild Flower*, in which phonographic records of theme songs were played to accompany silent screen performances. The second stage was the complete sound film using *sound-on-disk* technology (*lapan fayin*), also known as 'Vitaphone' (*witafeng*). Mingxing invested 120,000 yuan, leased a Pathé sound camera and spent six months making *Sing-song Girl Red Peony* (Genü Hong Mudan, dir. Zhang Shichuan), which opened at the Strand (Xinguang) on 15 March 1931 to enthusiastic crowds. The third stage was the complete sound film using synchronized *sound-on-film* technology (*pianshang fayin*), or 'Movietone' (*muweitong*), which produced better quality than sound on disk. The initial success in this category came from the newly established company Huaguang, which invested 50,000 yuan and sent its crew and cast to Japan to produce *Reconciliation* (Yuguo tianqing, dir. Xia Chifeng, 1931), with recording by an American, K. Henry. In the meantime, Tianyi spent over 200,000 yuan on sound-on-film technology, entered into partnership with a few Americans who had brought the sound-on-film equipment to China, and successfully produced *A Singer's Story* (Gechang chunse, dir. Li Pingqian, 1931) after a year's hard work (see Table 2.4, p. 45). Unsatisfied with its Pathé

73

equipment, Mingxing dispatched Hong Shen to the US and purchased the right – at a price of over 100,000 yuan – to use the Multicolor sound-on-film equipment in China, thus catching up with Tianyi. During this transition period, several Chinese were successful in their inventions of sound technology (Du 1988: 164–6; ZDZ 1996a: 54–5, 1374–5, 1425–6).

Apart from technological problems, Chinese filmmakers faced the language problem in their transition to sound. In the silent period, the important things were facial expressions and gestures, thus it was not unusual for the cast to speak a mixture of dialects while shooting (ZDZ 1996a: 1576). With sound films, however, what kind of language to speak became a pressing question, and in order to fall in line with the Nanjing government's policy, most studios adopted Mandarin (or *guoyu*, literally 'language of the nation'). Because China was divided by numerous local or regional dialects, many of which were mutually unintelligible, it was believed that a standard language across the nation would strengthen the sense of national solidarity and facilitate communication. However, given their primary markets in Southeast Asia, studios in Guangdong insisted on making Cantonese films and openly resisted the KMT censors' attempt to terminate their preferred linguistic practice. A compromise was in the works when the war broke out in 1937 (Xiao 1999).

The transition to sound equally presented new problems to screenwriters, actors and actresses. While the former had to balance between the Europeanized new vernacular and 'vulgar' everyday speech (ZDZ 1996a: 1352–3), the latter rushed to learn the Mandarin (i.e., Beiping) accent and correct dialect habits. Audiences, in turn, needed extra time to adjust to the new experience of sound on screen. These technological, economic, cultural and human factors enumerated here combined to make the Chinese transition to sound an unusually long process. Silent films continued to appear in 1936, when Lianhua released *A Lamb Astray* (Mitu de gaoyang, dir. Cai Chusheng; added soundtrack but no spoken dialogue).

Movie theaters: prestige, prices and pretensions

Approximately forty theaters in Shanghai were equipped with sound systems in 1933, compared with twenty-seven in 1931 (ZDZ 1996a: 1431). A 1932 guide to Shanghai theaters listed forty-nine venues, up from thirty-nine in 1927 (a 25.6 per cent increase in five years). Major theaters had signed agreements with Hollywood and Europe regarding first-run privileges by July 1932. The air-conditioned Capitol was devoted to Paramount's sound films and served mostly foreign audiences (1 yuan admission charge). Other venues showing first-run sound films from the rest of the eight Hollywood majors and the German Ufa included the Lanxin (formerly New Carlton), Nanking, Carlton, Grand, Cathay (Guotai) and Strand theaters. Some of these theaters occasionally showed first-run domestic sound films and they charged from 0.6 to 1 yuan. Those showing first-run domestic films and second- or third-run foreign films (sound as well as silent) included the Paris, Iris, Odeon, Peking, Palace, Embassy, Apollo (Aipulu) and Wiley (Weili, formerly People's or Guomin) theaters, all charging 0.4 yuan. And those showing second- to third-run domestic films and second- to fourth-run foreign films included the Star (Mingxing), Guanghua and New Palace (Xinzhongyang) theaters, all charging 0.3 yuan. It is interesting to note that theaters managed by Central Movie Company, a domestic theater chain established in 1926 by leasing Ramos's business, had lost much of their earlier prestige. While the Palace and New Palace theaters competed in the second or third tiers, the Empire, Carter and China (Wanguo) theaters were relegated to the lower ranks that offered little comfort and charged a mere 0.2 yuan (ZDZ 1996a: 191–8).

In the 1930s the audience for domestic films consisted largely of young students, shopkeepers, office clerks and other petty bourgeois, whereas the 'superior Chinese' favored Hollywood products (ZDZ 1996a: 1585). For the latter group, a new breed of Chinese cosmopolitans (e.g., businessmen, professionals and society ladies), going to the first-run theaters was a status symbol as well as an indispensable item in 'modern' (*modeng*) lifestyles. The architectural styles, interior design and decorations, the comfort of air-conditioning and even the hygiene of the restrooms in modern theaters were noted as features appealing to the fancy of the rising Chinese bourgeoisie (Lee 1999: 82–119).

Studio metamorphoses: Yihua and the 'three majors'

In addition to several theaters, the 1932 Shanghai battle destroyed numerous studios and left fewer than ten in operation, many surviving by shooting newsreels. By the end of 1932, the number of studios climbed up to thirty-four nationwide (ZDZ 1996a: 1431). Lianhua joined Mingxing and Tianyi as 'three majors' dominating the prewar phase. For instance, of 113 feature productions reviewed by the censors in 1933, Mingxing's output accounted for 22.5 per cent, Lianhua 14 per cent and Tianyi 12.5 per cent, and their combined output was nearly 50 per cent of the total (ZDZ 1996a: 1048).

Given its leading role in commercial filmmaking in the late 1920s, Tianyi had acquired a reputation for *opportunism*. However, among all the studios, Tianyi poured in the most money in the early 1930s on its transition to sound, and its subsequent leading edge in sound films ironically changed the focus away from its earlier tradition in costume dramas. Because sound theaters usually served middle- to upper-class audiences, Tianyi turned its attention to ordinary urbanites, and its films took on a different look. Announcing its intention to chart a new direction in the new cultural movement, Tianyi now was dedicated to 'propagating anti-imperialist resistance for the existence of the Chinese nation' (ZDZ 1996a: 55). *Two Orphan Girls on the Battlefield* (Zhandi er gunü, dir. Shao Zuiweng, 1932) was reportedly shot on location when the Shanghai battle was raging on, and its patriotic theme provoked the *zujie* censors to ban the film (ZDZ 1996a: 1429–30).

In the early 1930s, Tianyi had about 200 employees and produced around ten films each year, which covered diverse genres and included *White Gold Dragon* (Baijin long, dir. Tang Xiaodan, 1933; sound), the first Cantonese talkie. In addition to a second studio in Shanghai, Tianyi set up a branch office in Hong Kong in 1934 and built another sound studio there to produce Cantonese talkies and export them to Southeast Asia, where Tianyi independently owned fifteen theaters and jointly owned three others (ZDZ 1996a: 55–6). After producing close to 100 features (including thirty-five sound films), Tianyi terminated its Shanghai operation in early 1937 and shipped all its equipment to Hong Kong, where it established Nanyang and produced Cantonese films.

Contrary to Tianyi's politically neutral position, Yihua ran into trouble with the censors because its four patriotic films released in 1933 violated a new censorship ban on anti-Japanese films. On the morning of 12 November 1933, two truckloads of perpetrators clothed in blue stormed Yihua unexpectedly, setting fire to the studio and systematically vandalizing its facilities. They distributed pamphlets signed by 'The Association for Eradicating Communists in the Chinese Film Circles' and, according to newspaper reports, had sent warning letters to other Shanghai studios and major theaters. The CCP suspected that the perpetrators came from two groups, the KMT CC agents and Du Yuesheng's thugs, but most likely Pan Gongzhan had masterminded the event. As a result, Tian Han and Yang Hansheng were forced out of the studio, but they continued to advise on unfinished work through underground connections (X. Ding 1984: 14–15).

After the Nationalists arrested Tian and Yang in the spring of 1935 and the withdrawal of Shi Dongshan and Ying Yunwei, Yihua changed its ideological position and relied on a group of advocates for 'soft film' such as Huang Jiamo, Huang Tianshi and Liu Na'ou (X. Ding 1984: 15). Entertainment films ('soft' and artistic) replaced social films ('hard' and patriotic) in Yihua's productions. Huang Jiamo contributed all four scripts of *Girl in Disguise* (Huashen guniang, dir. Fang Peilin, I–II: 1936, III–IV: 1939), a cross-dressing, gender-bending urban comedy flaunting female sexuality and glamorizing bourgeois life in Shanghai and Singapore. The strong box-office returns of the first two episodes reportedly saved Yihua – previously US$600,000 in debt – from bankruptcy and 'cured' the Strand's owner of high blood pressure caused by market anxiety (Gongsun 1977: 2: 86–8). The press, on the other hand, denounced Yihua's switch to entertainment, and thirty-two film critics published two open letters in *Dawanbao* (Evening news) warning the studio in late 1936 (ZDYYZ 1993: 48–50). Yet, contrary to Mingxing, Yihua never reopened its doors to the leftists and continued its commercial film production until the war broke out.

Mingxing had its own share of ups and downs. After the Yihua vandalism in 1933, tightened censorship delayed many Mingxing films. The studio had deficits two years in a row and faced a new financial crisis. An American banking group sought to purchase Mingxing for 300,000 yuan and offered Zhou Jianyun a handsome salary, but Zhou refused to sign the contract and reportedly filed a lawsuit instead. It was not until after the spectacular success of *Twin Sisters* (Zimei hua, dir. Zheng Zhengqiu, 1933; sound) that Mingxing's business turned around. In 1935 Zhou Jianyun and Hu Die – the newly elected 'movie Queen' – represented Mingxing in a Chinese delegation on a tour through

Figure 3.2 Hu Die: movie queen of the 1930s

the Soviet Union and Europe, showing eight films along the way (D. Hu 1988: 111–205).[10]

The censors' systematic crackdown on leftist films drove Mingxing to another financial crisis in 1935. The hefty operating costs at 2,000 yuan a day placed the studio in a vulnerable situation (ZDZ 1996a: 1352). In June 1936, Mingxing attempted a desperate move: mortgaging all its assets and real estate holdings to acquire a loan of 160,000 yuan from the Jiaotong Bank in Nanjing. 100,000 yuan was used to pay its debts for the new studio while the remainder was ear-marked for production (Du 1988: 211). Mingxing issued a reform manifesto in July 1936 and declared that its films must 'serve the epoch': 'for our nation as well as for our own business, we are prepared immediately to start producing films of national defense' (ZDYYZ 1993: 28). The restructured Mingxing was divided into Studio 1, with Zhang Shichuan and the old Mingxing staff, and Studio 2, which recruited leftist artists. Mingxing planned to produce two films each month, and this round of reform pushed the leftist film movement to a new height, producing some of its best films like *Street Angel* (Malu tianshi, dir. Yuan Muzhi, 1937). The Japanese invasion of Shanghai in August 1937 terminated Mingxing's production. A fire destroyed its main studio in 1938, so Mingxing

Figure 3.3 Street Angel (1937): a classic leftist film featuring Zhou Xuan (right)

closed shop after an admirable leadership position in Chinese cinema for fifteen years, to its credit claiming 192 features, including fifty sound films.

Cinematic negotiations: *Twin Sisters* and *Song of the Fishermen*

From 1933 to 1937, leftist films displayed several distinct thematic features:

- the danger of imperialist invasion and the urgency of national salvation (disguised as fights against bandits and warlords or hinted by exiles from northeastern China);
- exposure of class exploitation and bourgeois lifestyles (disguised as moral battles of good and evil), as well as natural or human-made disasters;
- depiction of the working-class people and their miserable, often tragic life;
- encouragement to fight and to survive rather than to compromise with realities;
- replacement of private, individual concerns with a collective spirit;
- a final note of optimism or utopianism.

One crucial point is that none of these features was exclusively the leftists' property and many of them were actually shared by liberal and progressive directors, such as Zheng Zhengqiu, whose participation in reviving national cinema indirectly strengthened the leftist agenda. Another point is that the discrepancy between screen images and original scripts often resulted from either a director's distinct aesthetic or ideological orientation or the censors' cuts and revisions. In other words, ideological analysis alone does not suffice to exhaust the audio-visual and emotional impact of a given 'leftist' film.

A comparison of *Twin Sisters* (with sound but no music) and *Song of the Fishermen* (Yuguang qu, dir. Cai Chusheng, 1934; sound accompaniment) can help us flesh out the intricacies of cinematic negotiations (W. Chen 1992: 311–22). *Twin Sisters*, a Mingxing release, foregrounds the contrasting lives of twin sisters Dabao and Erbao (both played by Hu Die). Erbao's arms-smuggler father took her away with him thirteen years previously, leaving Dabao behind with her distressed mother (Xuan Jinglin). Set in 1924, the film opens with a happy family scene in which Dabao tells her husband Taoge (Zheng Xiaoqiu) that she is pregnant. The news worries Taoge's father since the family depends on Taoge as a hired farm worker. Taoge's father is shot dead by arms smugglers and the family run away from the bandits and move to Shandong province. The film cuts to a mansion where a warlord teases with his seventh mistress (Erbao). Taoge's poor health drives Dabao to become a nanny for the mistress. Bearing an uncanny resemblance to Dabao, the mistress, who is arrogant and cruel, slaps Dabao on the face when the latter begs for an advance on her wages after Taoge has been injured at a construction site and needs medical treatment. 'For the rich, playing mahjong is more important than saving the lives of the poor', complains Dabao. When she notices the baby's gold necklace pendant, a minute-long extreme close-up of her face indicates her moral struggle, and a montage of Taoge crying for help in the darkness motivates her to steal. The mistress's sister-in-law spots Dabao's desperate act, but the former is killed accidentally when a large porcelain vase falls on her head. Dabao is sent to jail. While pleading for a visit outside the jail, Dabao's mother meets her long-separated husband, who is now in charge of the court thanks to having married Erbao off to the warlord. A secret dinner meeting in the jail provides Dabao and her mother with a perfect opportunity to vent their frustrations against the rich and the powerful. In an unexpected twist, Erbao is reconciled with Dabao and her mother, and a family separated by fate and class is thus tearfully reunited.

On the one hand, as the most unlikely location for such bitter-sweet reconciliation, the jail betrays Zheng Zhengqiu's idealistic solution to pressing problems such as poverty, corruption and class conflict. On the other hand, such a compromising solution based on traditional family ethics was most likely what appealed to Shanghai audiences. After it premiered at the Strand around the Chinese New Year in January 1934, *Twin Sisters* had sold over 140,000 tickets by its fortieth day of release. It had a record of sixty days at the first-run theater, over forty days at the second-run and over ten days at the third-run, raking in a profit in excess of 240,000 yuan or US$100,000 (J. Gong 1967: 479). Film critics, however, were not as impressed. While praising the film for its 'realism' (*xieshi zhuyi*), they faulted its sentimentalism, its use of conventional genre (e.g., family drama) and its appeal to 'petty urbanites' (*xiao shimin*), particularly to those sympathetic ladies who normally did not frequent movie theaters (ZDYYZ 1993: 471–8). Nonetheless, Zheng was pleased with this latest success of his career-long dedication to 'venting frustrations for the weak' (Yi 1993: 37).

What is significant for our comparison is that *Song of the Fishermen*, a 1934 Lianhua release subsequently acclaimed as a 'leftist film' classic (J. Cheng *et al.* 1981: 1: 334), in many ways resembles *Twin Sisters*. First, both films sympathize with the downtrodden and promote human compassion; second, both stress class differences and dramatize social conflicts; third, both rely on unlikely coincidences and supply a dose of idealism in the end. No wonder that in 1934 Zheng Boqi described *Song of the Fishermen* as 'a typical film for petty urbanites' – a film combining Zheng Zhengqiu's ethical views with Sun Yu's poetic sensitivity (ZDYYZ 1993: 547–9).[11]

After an initial peaceful sequence of fishing boats on the sea, *Song of the Fishermen* conveys a sense of doom in an impressionistic fashion: the dark shadows of the midwife handling fisherman Xu's newborn twins (Kitty and Monkey) are repeatedly projected onto the wall. The shabby house of debt-ridden Xu is contrasted with the luxury of the rich merchant He Renzhai, who, after Xu has died on the stormy sea, forces Xu's wife to serve as a nanny for his son He Ziying. Years later, Xu's wife is kicked out of the He residence after breaking a precious antique and gradually turns blind. On the beach, her teenage daughter Kitty (Wang Renmei) sings the theme song to bid farewell to her childhood friend Ziying, who goes abroad to study the fishing business. When Ziying returns two years later, his father has relocated to Shanghai, started a fishing company and married a socialite named Xue (Tan Ying). Meanwhile, Kitty and her slow-witted twin brother Monkey (Han Lan'gen) have also migrated to the city. They join the long lines outside a factory but fail to find work; instead they first pick garbage and then make a living by performing on the street. A 100-yuan bill they receive from Ziying in a chance meeting gets them into trouble after a bank robbery. They are arrested as suspects but are released only to see their mother burned to death in a fire. Ziying brings them to Renzhai's mansion, but they are beaten and scared away by Renzhai, who by this time has lost all his money and his young wife to his partner Liang. In front of the multiple reflections of the dressing table mirror, Renzhai cannot stand his visions of Liang and Xue together, so he pulls out a pistol and commits suicide. The film then cuts to Kitty and Monkey working on a modern fishing ship, where Ziying serves as captain. Monkey soon collapses and, before his death, asks Kitty to sing the theme song for the last time. Ziying listens in tears as the peaceful scene of fishing boats on the sea is repeated. A net full of fish is poured on the ship's deck, but the poor appear no better off in spite of the technological advancement.

The idealism in *Song of the Fishermen* derives in part from Ziying's compassion for the poor and his vision of reform by way of science. Probably due to the unsettled labor dispute and the suicide of a capitalist in the film, the KMT censors did not like *Song of the Fishermen*. When they reluctantly approved it after pressure from theaters, they intentionally scheduled it in the summer to discourage attendance (X. Ding 1984: 16). Contrary to their expectation, from its opening on 14 June 1934, the film ran for eighty-four days in spite of record high temperatures of 103.8°F in Shanghai (J. Cheng *et al.* 1981: 1: 334). In 1935, the film was entered at an international film festival in Moscow and won an honorable prize, the first-ever international award for a Chinese film, which Lianhua considered an honor for all Chinese (ZDYYZ 1993: 406).

Undoubtedly, *Song of the Fishermen* articulated a leftist belief in the inevitable 'rural bankruptcy' in the age of imperialism (ZDYYZ 1993: 61). This belief undermined the utopian vision of an idyllic countryside as a safe haven from urban evils, which was evident in *Back Home from the City* and *Song of China* (Tianlun, dir. Luo Mingyou, Fei Mu, 1935). Nevertheless, the exposure of excessive poverty or the dramatization of human suffering alone did not automatically qualify a film as 'leftist'. In other words, in visual as well as narrative terms, leftist films did not occupy a clearly demarcated territory but were rather themselves cinematic negotiations open to varied interpretations and marking a *continuum* from the 1920s to the 1940s. As cinematic negotiations, leftist films thus shared moods, plots and tropes with family dramas characteristic of Chinese cinema. Frequently, what distinguished leftist films at the time was the ideological reading leftist critics imposed on given titles, whereby they assigned the directors to certain ideological camps.

Urban images: new women, prostitutes and sing-song girls

As in the 1920s, urban evils stood as major targets of criticism in the 1930s, and images of modern or new women continued to be focal points in urban landscapes. If *Wild Flower* criticizes traditional patriarchal ideology through the suffering of a career woman (Ruan Lingyu), it nonetheless betrays its fundamental *male* perspective in its tactful articulation of the female voice by an enlightened male artist (Jin Yan). The simplified May Fourth narrative of woman's liberation with male support becomes more complicated in *Three Modern Women* (San'ge modeng nüxing, dir. Bu Wancang, 1933), where the screenwriter Tian Han camouflages male agency and presents three choices to educated urban women. In Tian's class analysis (ZDYYZ 1993: 346–9), the self-indulgent bourgeois lady is written out of history, and the lovesick petit-bourgeois movie fan is disposed of as an embodiment of futility and death. Only the self-sacrificing worker (Ruan Lingyu), who is obsessed with the nation and the masses and who converts a movie star (Jin Yan) into a patriot, is pronounced as the 'truly modern woman' (Y. Zhang 1996: 190–4). Similarly, *New Woman* (Xin nüxing, dir. Cai Chusheng, 1934; sound accompaniment) contrasts the suicide of a lovesick woman writer (Ruan Lingyu) with the triumph of a factory woman worker (Harris 1997).[12] The latter emerges as the titular 'new woman', whose physical

Figure 3.4 Ruan Lingyu (left): a tragic silent movie star in *City Night* (1933)

strength enables her to defeat male representatives of urban evils (money and media) and who announces the arrival of the collective through her lyrics in the theme song (ZDZ 1996b: 2909):

New women, charge forward courageously!
New women, charge forward courageously!

As hinted in a scene in *New Woman* where the writer is almost forced to sell her body, prostitution was a recurring theme in the 1930s. Set in the beautiful West Lake in Hangzhou, an otherwise favorite romantic location for Shanghai films, *Boatman's Daughter* (Chuanjia nü, dir. Shen Xiling, 1935; sound) portrays the worsening conditions in which an innocent young woman is forced into prostitution and loses the memory of her identity. *Goddess* portrays a prostitute (Ruan Lingyu) with a heart of gold, a self-sacrificing mother whose only dream is her son's social advancement through education. Arguably, her imprisonment after killing the evil pimp near the end of the film indicates that no hope of personal salvation could be offered to the prostitute herself (Y. Zhang 1999b). Such pessimism is also articulated in *Street Angel*, where the murder of a miserable streetwalker conveys the pathos of overwhelming prewar anxiety. Like *Crossroads*, *Street Angel* features a collective of poor youths willing to fight urban evils; but unlike *Crossroads*, where four youths march triumphantly forward amidst city traffic, *Street Angel* offers no evidence of hope. Even the comedic form of acting and the romance between Xiao Chen (Zhao Dan) and Xiao Hong (Zhou Xuan, the 'golden voice'), a sing-song girl and the victim's younger sister, do nothing but make misery more pronounced. The concluding upward tilting shot of a high-rise building, a repeat of the opening shot in a reverse camera movement, suggests the sheer impossibility – at least for the time being – of those living in the subterranean to get out of the urban hell.

Significantly, the murdered prostitute in *Street Angel* is an exile from north-eastern China. Indeed, an image of woman violated by urban evils was often used to symbolize the nation violated by Japan. Such symbolism appeared in films like *Lianhua Symphony* (Lianhua jiaoxiang qu, dir. Situ Huimin *et al.*, 1937), but it was only after the war broke out that direct screen portrayal of the violation of women-cum-nation would be possible, as in Tian Han's *Three Women* (Liren xing, dir. Chen Liting, 1949).

WARTIME CINEMA, 1937–45

During the war, the film industries were geographically divided into east (Shanghai), south (Hong Kong), northeast (Manchuria), southwest (Chongqing) and northwest (Yan'an and Taiyuan). The KMT studios retreated to the hinterland and depended on limited film stock to produce documentary and feature films. Meanwhile, Zhang Shankun emerged as a central figure in Shanghai, and

Japanese-sponsored film companies attempted to infiltrate and control the Chinese market.

Manchuria: production and exhibition

Man'ei (Manying), or Manchurian Motion Picture Association (Manzhou yinhua xiehui), was established in Changchun (renamed Xinjing, literally 'new capital') in 1937 by the puppet Manchurian government and the Manchurian Railroad Corporation. The company established business relations with Japanese-controlled distribution networks and Japanese film studios (e.g., Toho and Shochiku), ran film schools from 1937 to 1944 that graduated hundreds of students, and in 1939 built a new studio with cutting-edge equipment. The company's size was immense, employing 900 people by December 1940 and 1,800 by November 1944. The company produced a large number of films in several categories: 108 'entertainment' (*yumin*) features, 189 'education' (*qimin*) features, 307 issues of newsreels in Japanese, 113 other issues in Chinese, and fifty-five issues of children's programs. In all, Man'ei aimed at propagating the Manchurian 'national policy' and spreading the ideology of the Great East Asia Co-Prosperity Sphere (X. Hu and Gu 1990). In reality, however, due to market and other factors, those films that strictly conformed to the Japanese 'national policy' accounted only for 16 per cent of the total Man'ei feature output, although this percentage was substantially higher than that (3 per cent) of similar titles from occupied Shanghai (D. Li 2000: 277).

Man'ei depended heavily on Japanese personnel in feature productions, which was regarded as a source of contradiction or even a 'fatal blow' to Man'ei. On the one hand, Japanese filmmakers did not know Manchuria well and were blamed for losing market shares to Shanghai films. On the other hand, it was too risky to entrust inexperienced Manchurian directors, even though the new rising star Zhou Xiaobo was praised for easing the situation (Manzhou zazhi she, July 1940: 23). Indeed, as reported by *Screen Pictorial* (Dianying huabao), formerly *Manchurian Screen* (Manzhou yinhua), the majority of Manchurian audiences preferred Shanghai films. A July 1940 poll of thirty-one Man'ei film school students yielded three Shanghai titles among the top five best Chinese films. Five votes went to *Yue Fei Defends the Nation* (Yue Fei jinzhong baoguo, dir. Wu Yonggang, 1940), four votes each to *Crossroads* and *Singing at Midnight* (Yeban gesheng, dir. Ma-Xu Weibang, 1937), compared with seven and five votes, respectively, to two Man'ei features (Manzhou zazhi she, July 1940: 42). Actually, the majority of films polled were Shanghai products, and *Screen Pictorial* itself contributed to Shanghai's popularity by regularly featuring the latest releases from Shanghai and news about Shanghai actresses.

Of course, *Screen Pictorial* carried news of Man'ei productions, too. Its August 1941 issue prominently featured the film stills and production photographs of *The Yellow River* (Huanghe, dir. Zhou Xiaobo, 1942), which had just completed its three-month location shooting near Kaifeng. The film deals with the aftermath of the KMT army's 1937 attempt to block the Japanese military advancement by blowing up the Yellow River dam, causing a severe flood and forcing tens of thousands of people to flee their villages. The film captures the reconstruction of the river dam by thousands of workers and endorses the project as the spectacular achievement of the Co-Prosperity Sphere. The same issue of *Screen Pictorial* also published a four-page report on a forum attended by the enigmatic star Li Xianglan (Yamaguchi Yoshiko), who had flown from Tokyo to play the female lead in the film (Manzhou zazhi she, Aug. 1941: 28–31). A Japanese actress who passed as Chinese but whose nationality remained a top secret guarded by the Japanese occupation forces, Li moved freely between Manchuria and Shanghai in the early 1940s. She enchanted audiences with her 'Chinese' look and her sweet voice in dozens of films (Stephenson 1999).

Star attraction notwithstanding, the Manchurian audience still favored Shanghai films. A survey of Changchun theaters listed Guodu, Guotai and Changchun showing mostly Man'ei and Shanghai films, Da'an, Guangming and Xinjing showing second- or third-run movies to shopkeepers and middle-school students. Xinjing was singled out as a 'miracle' because it had consistently shown reruns of 'low-taste' Shanghai martial arts flicks since 1924 to workers, women and children who happily chatted and laughed throughout the films. As Guodu's manager admitted, audiences now preferred detective films to costume drama, and Shanghai films fared much better than Man'ei titles (Manzhou zazhi she, Aug. 1941: 45–6). According to another survey, theaters in Manchuria had increased from less than eighty in 1937 to 150 in 1941, an average theater's yearly attendance could be as high as 105,000, and ticket prices ranged from 0.2 to 1.5 yuan (Manzhou zazhi she, March 1941: 21) (see Table 2.2, p. 16).

Shanghai as an 'orphan island', 1937–41

Unlike Manchuria, Japan occupied Shanghai only partially between November 1937 and December 1941, a period known as the 'orphan island' because *zujie* had managed to stay outside Japanese rule due to their claimed neutrality. In spite of the fact that numerous notable leftist filmmakers and KMT cultural workers had left for the hinterland, Shanghai witnessed the 'anomalous boom' in both its economy and its film industry (Fu 1998: 88). War refugees provided cheap labor to boost manufacture in Shanghai, and dislocated provincial landlords and merchants took advantage of their stay to pack the venues of cultural consumption.

The most famous producer to seize this unique wartime opportunity was Zhang Shankun, who had founded Xinhua (New China) in 1934 and had achieved a measure of a reputation with *Singing at Midnight*, a sensational horror film with a heightened revolutionary spirit. To test the market, Zhang brought part of his former Xinhua cast and crew to Hong Kong and completed *Sable Cicada* (Diao Chan, dir. Bu Wancang, 1938), which was 90 per cent finished before the war and which Zhang premiered to enthusiastic crowds at the Grand in Shanghai (Gongsun 1977: 2: 125). After producing four more Mandarin pictures in Hong Kong, Zhang returned to Shanghai, rented the former Mingxing Studio 2, recruited veteran directors stranded in Shanghai, and followed the prewar Tianyi tradition by launching politically neutral, ideologically conservative costume dramas. The result was the second wave of commercial films in Shanghai in 1939–41.

Several high-profile filmmakers played an active role in this second wave. Based on a script by Ouyang Yuqian, *Mulan Joins the Army* (Mulan congjun, dir. Bu Wancang, 1939), which featured the rising Cantonese star Chen Yunshang and preached Confucian ideas of loyalty and filiality, proved immensely popular with Shanghai audiences, who readily picked up its hidden patriotic theme (Ouyang 1984: 36–9). Costume dramas based on classical novels, legends and folk tales dominated the screen. Some historical films contained high production values, such as *Confucius* (Kong fuzi, dir. Fei Mu, 1940), adaptations of contemporary fiction and drama constituted a minor trend, and *Princess Iron Fan* (Tieshan gongzhu, 1941), the first Chinese feature-length cartoon from the Wan brothers, was a welcome event.

The initial rosy business outlook impelled Zhang Shankun to seek maximum distribution as early as 1938. Since Xinhua had signed the Jincheng Theater as its first-run venue, Zhang set up two additional film companies, Huaxin and Huacheng, respectively signing the Strand and the Astro (Huguang) as their first-run theaters. Claiming an asset of 500,000 yuan, Xinhua competed effectively with its two rivals: Yihua (with an asset of 300,000 yuan, now managed by Yan Youxiang, Yan Chuntang's son), and Guohua (partially owned by Zhang Shichuan). Altogether, twenty or so film companies, most of them funded with around 40,000 yuan, produced over 200 features between 1938 and 1941 (Fu 1998: 90). The emergence of Jinxing (Golden Star), a company cofounded by Zhou Jianyun in June 1940, was credited for initiating a trend of contemporary-themed films in wartime Shanghai (D. Li 2000: 173–89).

The Shanghai industry was plagued by persisting problems. Political terrorism on the part of both Japan and KMT, which resulted in the 1940 assassinations of Liu Na'ou and Mu Shiying, two advocates for soft film who had assumed positions in the pro-Japanese government, compelled filmmakers to keep a low political profile.[13] Since the hinterland market was no longer accessible by this time, Southeast Asia had once again emerged as a crucial market for Shanghai commercial films. Moreover, while ticket prices climbed to 3.2 yuan for first-run Hollywood titles, production costs had soared by 400 per cent in 1940. All these factors combined to drive studios desperately to cut costs, which averaged 30,000 yuan per feature in 1939 (see Tables 2.2 and 2.4, pp. 16 and 45).

As in the first commercial wave a decade before, studios competed in churning out features as fast as six days per title (Fu 1998: 91–9). For example, Yihua completed *Three Smiles* (Sanxiao, dir. Zhang Shichuan, Zheng Xiaoqiu, 1940) in seven days and released it on 3 June 1940. A week later, Guohua's film of

Figure 3.5 Confucius (1940): a historical film from the 'orphan island' period

the same title also opened, and both companies were satisfied as their films ran respectively for twenty-three and twenty-eight days in Shanghai (D. Li 2000: 168). As expected, Shanghai filmmakers' profiteering mindsets drew severe criticism in the press.

While Hollywood continued to dominate the 'orphan island' of Shanghai, the Japanese made repeated attempts to penetrate into the industry. Backed by Toho, Man'ei and the pro-Japanese Nanjing puppet government, Kawakita Nagamasa, a Beijing University graduate, launched China Movie Company (Zhonghua) in Shanghai in June 1939 with a budget of 1 million yuan. In addition to producing propagandist 'cultural films' and managing film projection units to tour battlefronts, Kawakita, aided by collaborators such as Liu Na'ou, increased his pressure on the Shanghai studios to distribute their products through his company. After meeting Kawakita in person, Zhang Shankun realized that the Japanese now controlled the film supplies and it would be to his advantage to voluntarily submit to Japanese censorship in exchange for the distribution of his films in Japanese-occupied areas (D. Li 2000: 262–3).

A sharply divided reception marked Zhang's controversial move. *Mulan Joins the Army* premiered in Nanjing in July 1939 to popular success amidst criticism from the Japanese censors,[14] but a print was burned in a public protest when the film opened in Chongqing in January 1940, triggering a heated debate in the hinterland (Fu 1998: 99–104). The accusation of Zhang Shankun as a 'traitor' had since followed this controversial producer, as he moved to a larger scale of collaboration with Japan in the subsequent years.

Shanghai occupation cinema, 1941–5

Japanese troops entered *zujie* and fully occupied Shanghai at the onset of the Pacific War. As instructed by Japan's Army Press Bureau, Kawakita took over the US-owned Asia Cinema Company and opened all Shanghai theaters in December 1941. In April 1942, Xinhua and eleven Shanghai studios were merged into China United Productions (Zhonglian). Serving as general manager, Zhang Shankun continued his earlier policy of pursuing *entertainment* genres, especially family dramas and tragic romances. Even though Zhang could expect only a quarter of the total income each film earned after paying taxes, distribution and exhibition, China United Productions was able to attract strong financial support when it went public in August 1942. Ironically, before Hollywood reruns had eventually disappeared by early 1943, Shanghai filmmakers often modeled their products on Hollywood melodramas, much to the displeasure of the Japanese censors. What is more, evidence suggests that Zhang Shankun had maintained a secret tie with underground KMT agents, through whom he reportedly sent some scripts to Chongqing for advice and approval (G. Zuo and Yao 2001: 66–7).

China United Productions produced twenty-four titles in 1942 and twenty-three in 1943 (Shimizu 1995: 301–4). *Eternity* (Wanshi liufang, dir. Bu Wancang *et al.*, 1943), a historical film produced under increased Japanese pressure, did not prevent a thorough restructuring of the Shanghai studios. Featuring Li Xianglan in a secondary storyline, whose sweet voice made her theme song an instant hit nationwide, *Eternity* relishes in a romantic triangle that projects Lin Zexu more as a lovesick scholar than a courageous official resisting British imperialism at the dawn of the Opium War. In May 1943, China United Productions merged with Kawakita's China Movie Company and Japanese-controlled Shanghai Movie Theaters Company to become United China Motion Picture Company (Huaying). In near-complete vertical and horizontal integration, United China thus presaged the nationalization of the entire film industry pursued by the KMT in the postwar era and accomplished by the CCP in the 1950s.

From 1943 to 1945 United China produced eighty features, most of them entertainment fare: twenty-four in 1943, thirty-two in 1944 and twenty-four in 1945 (Du 1988: 325). Zhang Shankun had lost much of his power by this time. Due to his dubious ties, he was arrested twice in early 1945, first by the Japanese and then by the KMT police (G. Zuo and Yao 2001: 79–85). He moved to Hong Kong where he continued his movie dream in the next decade (see Chapter 5).

Apart from the mercurial political situation, rampant inflation rendered wartime cinema a difficult business to run. The production costs per feature skyrocketed from 100,000 yuan in 1940 to at least 300,000 yuan in 1942, 1 million in 1943 and over 10 million yuan in January 1945. Correspondingly, a first-run theater ticket also soared from 8 yuan in 1942 to 60 yuan in 1945 (Fu 1997: 72–7) (see Tables 2.2 and 2.4, pp. 16 and 45). But the worst of the inflation had yet to come in the postwar era.

Prewar and wartime Hong Kong: between patriotism and commercialism

A production center of Cantonese talkies since the advent of sound, Hong Kong had produced its first patriotic film as early as 1934. To presage what was to come in wartime Shanghai, even historical films would take on patriotic themes in prewar Hong Kong cinema. Hong Kong's Tianyi, for instance, inserted this dialogue – 'we would rather die fighting than perish without resistance' – in its epic *Burning the E Pang Palace* (Huoshao E Pang gong, dir. Shao Zuiweng, 1935), which had a ten-day run when most films showed for three to five days. Tianyi invested HK$70,000 in the epic, compared with the typical production costs of HK$5,000 per film at the time (M. Yu 1997: 42, 84) (see Table 3.2). Unfortunately, two fires in May and August 1936 destroyed much of Tianyi's Hong Kong equipment and its film prints, and what remained was transferred to Nanyang under Runde Shaw's management in 1937.

By 1940 Hong Kong had over forty film companies. Major players included Nanyang, Grandview (Daguan), originally set up by Chiu Shu-sen and Moon

Table 3.2 Production costs per film in Hong Kong, 1920s–90s

Year	Film	Studio	Cost (HK$)
Average			
1924	silent (limit 1,000 feet)	—	1,000
mid-1930s	Cantonese	—	5,000
late 1930s	Cantonese	—	7,000–8,000
1950	Cantonese	—	30,000
1951	Cantonese	—	40,000
1952	Mandarin	—	80,000
1954	Amoy	—	40,000
1955	Cantonese	—	60,000–90,000
1960s	Cantonese	—	100,000–300,000
1960s	Mandarin	—	500,000–600,000
early 1980s	Cantonese	—	700,000–800,000
mid-1990s	Cantonese	—	10,000,000
mid-1990s	Cantonese blockbuster	—	50,000,000
late 1990s	Cantonese	—	4,000,000
Specific			
1925	*Rouge*	Minxin HK	9,000
1935	*Burning the E Pang Palace* (C)	Tianyi HK	70,000
1937	*Twelve Beauties in the Golden House* (C)	Grandview HK	100,000
1947	*An All-Consuming Love* (M)	Great China	175,000
1947	*Soul of China* (M)	Yonghua	1,000,000
1952	*Modern 'Red Chamber Dream'* (M)	Great Wall HK	1,000,000
1958	*Diau Charn* (M)	Shaw Brothers	300,000
1959	*The Kingdom and the Beauty* (M)	Shaw Brothers	500,000
1982	*Aces Go Places* (C)	Cinema City	8,000,000
1997	*Made in Hong Kong* (C)	Team Work	500,000
1998	*The Storm Riders* (C)	BoB	10,000,000

Sources: Bordwell 2000: 70, 119; Chiao 1993: 14; HKIFF 1982: 15, 50; HKFA 1997a: 15–18; S. Li and Hu 1996: 97; M. Yu 1996: 134; M. Yu 1997: 84, 157; M. Yu 1998: 118–19; M. Yu 2000: 71, 91, 200; M. Yu 2001: 30.

Note: C = Cantonese; M = Mandarin; HK = Hong Kong.

Kwan in San Francisco in 1933 and relocated to Hong Kong in 1935 (Law 2000: 50–4), and Nam Yuet (Nanyue), founded in 1935. These three companies teamed up with others and produced *The Critical Moment* (Zuihou guantou, dir. Su Yi *et al.*, 1937), which dramatizes college students' recruitment efforts among all ranks of life and concludes with the departure of a propaganda team to the war front. The film was funded by generous donations from local filmmakers, who volunteered their time, and the HK$23,900 proceeds from the exhibition rights were used to purchase the national salvation bonds.

Since 1935 patriotic films had consistently made up a large percentage of Hong Kong productions, and more titles followed in 1938, such as Grandview's *Behind the Shanghai Battlefront* (Shanghai huoxian hou, dir. Tang Xiaodan, 1938). But most studios, especially those one-picture companies, became reluctant after Guangzhou fell in December 1938. Meanwhile, Hong Kong audiences started to show more interest in spectacular Busby Berkeley-style musicals like *Stage Glamour* (Wutai chunse, dir. Tang Xiaodan, 1938).

Like Shanghai in the late 1920s, Hong Kong relied heavily on its local audiences and Southeast Asian markets, but the war rendered the latter increasingly unreliable. Consequently, the industry's profits plummeted 44.4 per cent from over HK$900,000 in 1938 to under HK$500,000 in 1939. Compared with Shanghai's standard of HK$30,000 per feature, the average production cost in Hong Kong was small, between HK$7,000 and 8,000 per feature. Like their Shanghai counterparts, Hong Kong producers rushed their already cheap productions to the market in as little as seven to ten days, and the industry sustained an average of more than eighty features a year between 1937 and 1941 (Fu 2000a: 201–5).

Similar to Shanghai of the late 1930s, most Hong Kong features were based on folk tales, costume dramas, legends and myths, many from the existing Cantonese opera versions and therefore familiar to local audiences (HKFA 1997b: 1). But unlike their Shanghai counterparts, quite a few Cantonese operas were actually adapted from foreign films (Y. Li 1994: 16). *White Gold Dragon*, for example, was based on Sit Kok-sin's (Xue Juexian) Cantonese opera of the same title, which was originally derived from *The Grand Duchess and the Waiter* (dir. Malcolm St. Clair, 1926) (Fonoroff 1997: 12). Cantonese opera fans quickly became movie fans and their favorite opera idols, such as Sit Kok-sin and Kwan Tak-hing (Guan Dexing), were instantly transformed into movie stars (Law 2000: 59–68). Although only 35.5 per cent of the thirty-one theaters in Hong Kong showed Cantonese features, some theaters would alternate between movies and operas. Eighteen theaters (58 per cent) were devoted to Hollywood, and two (6.5 per cent) screened Mandarin films shipped from Shanghai (Fu 2000a: 205). Japan's occupation of the city from 1941 to 1945, of course, ended Hollywood exhibition.

Prior to the war, Hong Kong did not produce any Mandarin films. Since the KMT ran a wartime office in Hong Kong to purchase equipment for its Chongqing studios, several Shanghai leftists seized the opportunity and founded two production companies, Dadi (Great Land) in 1938 and Xinsheng (New Life) in 1940. Although both ceased operation within a year due to a shortage of funding, together the two companies produced three Mandarin films in Hong Kong. *Paradise on Orphan Island* (Gudao tiantang, dir. Cai Chusheng, 1939) had a record twelve-day run in September in Hong Kong, reached over 50,000 viewers and was welcome in Southeast Asia and Chongqing. Either completed or distributed in Chongqing, *White Clouds of Home* (Baiyun guxiang, dir. Situ Huimin, 1940) and *The Boundless Future* (Qiancheng wanli, dir. Cai

Figure 3.6 Paradise on Orphan Island (1939): the emergence of Mandarin film in Hong Kong

Chusheng, 1941) were counted as KMT studio productions (J. Cheng *et al.*, 1981: 2: 80–6).

In addition to launching Mandarin cinema in Hong Kong, Cai Chusheng and Situ Huimin also assisted in the production of patriotic Cantonese features, most notably *The March of Guerrillas* (Youji jinxing qu, dir. Situ Huimin, 1938) from Qiming (Enlightenment). To keep its neutrality, the Hong Kong government banned the film in 1940 but approved its release in 1941 after numerous cuts (as long as 2,000 feet) and a new title, *Song of Righteousness* (Zhengqi ge). The censors' 1939 discouragement of 'anti-Japanese sentiments', however, did not prevent Hong Kong studios from making more patriotic Cantonese features. When the city fell to Japan on Christmas Day of 1941, many notable filmmakers left for the hinterland (M. Yu 1997: 142), and the entire industry refused to cooperate with Japan. No features were made until after the end of the war.

KMT wartime operations in the hinterland

The KMT owned two large filmmaking complexes in this period: Central Film Studio (Zhongdian) and China Motion Pictures Studio (Zhongzhi). A third branch, China Education Film Studio (Zhongjiao), was established by the

Ministry of Education in January 1942 but did not play a major role (Y. Yang 2001: 118).

The KMT central propaganda committee set up Central Film in Nanjing as early as 1934. After producing two features in 1936-7, Central Film was relocated to Wuhan and Chongqing in 1937-8 and shot documentaries along the way. From 1938 to 1945, Central Film employed veteran directors like Cheng Bugao and Shen Xiling and produced three features and numerous documentaries on limited film stock. Among them, *The Sky Rider* (Changkong wanli, dir. Sun Yu, 1940), a story of air combat, opened in December 1941 in Chongqing. By 1942, Central Film suffered from budget cuts and material shortage, and personnel changes further prevented the studio from more productions.

Instead of being party-owned, China Motion Pictures, established in 1937, was army-owned since it was based on a studio set up in 1935 by the Nanjing government's military affairs committee. Many Shanghai filmmakers joined the studio in Hankou. They produced patriotic features, propaganda cartoon shorts as well as newsreels. *Protect Our Land* (Baowei women de tudi, dir. Shi Dongshan, 1938) premiered in April 1938 at the Shanghai Theater in Wuhan and set the tone for the subsequent war films. In 1938 the studio relocated to Chongqing and employed leftists like Yang Hansheng and Xia Yan – a direct result of the wartime CCP–KMT united front. During the war, the studio benefited from increased military spending (as high as 87.3 per cent of the overall

Figure 3.7 The Sky Rider (1940): wartime filmmaking in Chongqing

government budget in 1945) and produced twelve features. Like Central Film, China Motion Pictures had to suspend all feature productions in 1941–3 due to supply problems. Many filmmakers turned to wartime drama activities and a few, such as Chen Liting, translated or wrote film books (Chongqing shi 1991: 199–203, 635–50).

Three China Motion Pictures releases are worthy of closer attention. First, *Storm on the Border* (Saishang fengyun, dir. Ying Yunwei, 1940), which premiered in Chongqing in February 1942, promoted the national solidarity of the Han and ethnic minorities. Second, *The Light of East Asia* (Dongya zhi guang, dir. He Feiguang, 1940) featured twenty-nine real-life Japanese POWs who had turned pacifist and had staged a play to spread an anti-war message (D. Li 2000: 119–21). The third film, *Japanese Spy* (Riben jiandie, dir. Yuan Congmei, 1943), a precursor of popular postwar espionage films, ran into censorship problems. In the middle of its Chongqing screenings, a ban was imposed after Chiang Kai-shek had found its images of the Northeastern Volunteer Army too much resembled Communist soldiers. Even though the film had already cleared the normal KMT censorship channels, new scenes were added with Volunteer soldiers wearing KMT army uniforms and saluting Chiang's portrait (X. Ding 1984: 29–32).[15]

In addition to production, the KMT also controlled distribution and exhibition channels. Films served an educational purpose, thus the KMT offices leased them at a nominal fee of 100 yuan per month or free of charge. By 1941 China Motion Pictures had 182 prints in circulation in ninety-two cities overseas. In addition, it set up ten projection teams to tour separate battle regions. In the first half of 1940 alone, approximately 2.6 million soldiers and villagers had watched 493 shows projected by Teams 1 to 7. These figures exclude audiences served by Teams 8 to 10, which toured in and around Chongqing, as well as those served by six projection teams organized by Central Film (Y. Yang 2001: 119–20). The KMT wartime projection activities are significant because they foretold the similar efforts of reaching out to the rural population by the CCP regime in the 1950s.

Filmmaking in the northwest: Northwest Film and Yan'an

Compared with Shanghai and Chongqing, filmmaking in the mountainous northwest was underdeveloped. Yan Xishan, a regional military power, established Northwest Film (Xibei) in Taiyuan as early as 1935. In addition to documentary shorts, it produced two features before the war. In 1937–8, the company was relocated to Xi'an and later to Chengdu and produced war documentaries. With the participation of patriotic filmmakers, it shot two more features, one of which was never completed due to the studio shutting down in 1940.

Yan'an film operation was on an even smaller scale than Northwest's. In 1938, Yuan Muzhi purchased 10,000 feet of film stock and other equipment in Hong

Kong and brought them, together with a 33mm camera donated by Dutch filmmaker Joris Ivens, to Yan'an. In September 1938, Yan'an Film Corp was established, and it started shooting the documentary *Yan'an and the Eighth Route Army* (Yan'an yu balu jun, 1938–40). Yuan was dispatched to the Soviet Union to work on its postproduction in 1940, although the ensuing Second World War prevented its completion. From this time to 1945, several more documentaries were made that chronicled important historical events in Yan'an, and several Soviet films were toured through the Communist regions with their original soundtracks (D. Li 2000: 29–30, 138–55). Importantly, the Yan'an operation trained the Communist film personnel, who would be instrumental in taking over the industry in a matter of a few years.

POSTWAR CINEMA, 1946–9

In August 1945 Soviet troops entered Changchun and shut down Man'ei. In May 1946 the CCP groups transported part of the studio equipment to Xingshan, Heilongjiang province. With the arrival of Yan'an Film Corp, North-east Studio (Dongbei) was established in October 1946, specializing in war documentary production (Y. Su 1986). The remaining Man'ei equipment was confiscated by the KMT central committee's Ministry of Propaganda and formed Changchun Studio (Changzhi) in July 1946, headed by Jin Shan, an active wartime dramatist and underground Communist. As the four-year civil war between the CCP and KMT waged on, the negotiations of political, social and sexual differences were conducted on and off screen, in film narratives as well as in the battles to control the industry and the market. Astronomical postwar inflation might have added to public resentment and helped accelerate the collapse of the KMT regime in the mainland, but against all odds Chinese cinema staged an unprecedented revival and produced a dozen classics in its second 'golden age'.

The postwar film market: Hollywood versus domestic films

After the war, Hollywood returned to China with a vengeance. From August 1945 to May 1949 when the CCP troops took control of the city, Shanghai had at its disposal a total of 1,896 American films, including the newly imported and those stuck in China following the Pacific War. In the same period, Shanghai's first-run theaters showed 1,083 Hollywood titles, most of them from the eight majors (e.g., 158 from MGM, 153 from Universal, over 120 each from Columbia, Warner Brothers and Twentieth-Century Fox). In 1946 alone, among 383 films screened in Shanghai's first-run theaters, only thirteen were Chinese titles, compared with 352 American films, fifteen British films and three Soviet titles (J. Cheng *et al.* 1981: 2: 161–2).

The situation soon changed due to a number of factors. First, beginning in 1947, more quality Chinese films entered the market. From four in 1946, Shanghai's film production rose to fifty-seven in 1948. In contrast to 1946, when all individual films with over 100,000 viewers belonged to Hollywood, in 1947 seven such films were American but six were Chinese – nearly equal in numbers. Second, given sky-rocketing inflation,[16] Hollywood had no guarantee of monetary values in its share of the proceeds and had started to reduce its releases in Shanghai. Compared with 881 American films imported to Shanghai in 1946, only 393 were shipped in 1947, and the number dropped to 272 in 1948. Third, the lower number of Hollywood features cleared the way for more screenings of domestic films. In 1946, 21 per cent of Shanghai theaters exhibited domestic films. In 1947, this figure tripled to 66.7 per cent, about the same rate as the prewar era. In 1948, it reached 84 per cent, roughly identical to those theaters showing American films.[17] Finally, a deciding factor is that a huge percentage of viewers now came from the lower social strata, including ordinary urbanites as well as factory workers, who took advantage of the relatively affordable ticket prices to increase their theater visits.[18] According to one calculation, whereas the average postwar production cost was three times that of the prewar, the total number of postwar viewers was four times that of prewar viewers.[19] In other words, even with higher expenses and lower ticket prices, producers could expect higher box-office revenues due to increased movie attendance (Z. Wang 2000: 26–9).

Hollywood blockbusters continued to fare well in postwar Shanghai. In 1947 *Gone with the Wind* (dir. Victor Fleming, 1939) sold 170,000 tickets, and *Arabian Nights* (dir. John Rawlins, 1942) 220,000 tickets, both figures from two Shanghai theaters alone. But several Chinese films did equally well or even better in 1947. *Code Name Heaven No. 1* (Tianzi diyihao, dir. Tu Guangqi, 1947) sold 150,000 tickets at the Empress (Huanghou) alone, and *Long Live the Mistress!* (Taitai wansui, dir. Sang Hu, 1947) achieved the same box office at the Empress and Jincheng. *Phony Phoenixes* (Jiafeng xuhuang, dir. Huang Zuolin, 1947) was the top performer at the Grand, selling 165,000 tickets. *Spring River Flows East* (Yijiang chunshui xiangdong liu, dir. Cai Chusheng, Zheng Junli, 1947) swept over several Shanghai theaters, selling 712,874 tickets between October 1947 and January 1948, and total audience figures might have exceeded 1 million if the rerun tickets were counted (Z. Wang 2000: 30–2).

By 1948 Hollywood was obviously losing its market share in China. This is confirmed by a comparative analysis of theater showings in Shanghai, Beiping, Tianjin and Guangzhou on a random date, 25 January, respectively in 1927, 1937 and 1948 (see Table 3.3, p. 99). Whereas Hollywood consistently dominated the Guangzhou market (over 60 per cent of the number of films screened), in Beiping its shares dropped from 60 per cent in 1937 to 22 per cent in 1948. Whereas Hollywood had always enjoyed the highest number of films exhibited in any given day in Shanghai (at least 44 per cent of the total), in 1948 the majority of first-run theaters in the city simultaneously showed Chinese features.

Figure 3.8 Long Live the Mistress! (1947): an entertaining comedy, with a script by Eileen Chang

The Hollywood dominance in other large cities became questionable by early 1948 as domestic films occupied all screens in the following days: on 25 January all four theaters in Fuzhou, 20 February all eight theaters in Nanjing, and 15 August all five theaters in Xi'an (Z. Wang 1998: 62–3).

Admittedly, this three-year random sampling cannot represent an overall trend, and the choice of 1933 and 1946 instead of 1937 and 1948 might drastically increase the percentages of Hollywood dominance. However, is it safe to conclude that Hollywood did not monopolize the later half of the postwar Chinese market as it had done in the prewar era, thus leaving room for successful Chinese productions.

The KMT studios: industry expansion and specialization

In 1946 the army-owned China Motion Pictures relocated to Nanjing and specialized in films for military education as well as newsreels and documentaries, and consequently it achieved nothing comparable to its early war feature production. By April 1946 Central Film had completed its confiscation of most film facilities owned by Japanese and pro-Japanese organizations and had restructured

Figure 3.9 Spring River Flows East (1947): a popular postwar epic tear-jerker

this Party-owned enterprise into a giant corporation with its headquarters in Shanghai, managing three studios and a business department. Located in Shanghai, Studio 1 specialized in newsreels and documentaries and produced six features. Also located in Shanghai, Studio 2 specialized in features and produced seventeen titles. Located in Beiping, Studio 3 also specialized in features and produced fourteen titles. Together these studios produced thirty-seven features by 1949, exclusive of three others released by Changchun, sometimes also called Central Film Studio 4. In April 1947, in order to disguise its Party-owned nature, Central Film renamed itself as a film enterprise corporation and went public, but that did not prevent Zhang Daofan, the propaganda minister of the KMT central committee, from serving as its nominal head.[20]

The KMT quickly moved to monopolize the film industry nationwide by controlling distribution and exhibition, tightening censorship and foreign currency exchanges, and prohibiting the opening of private film companies. For instance, between October 1945 and September 1948, the censors ordered cuts or revisions to forty-eight out of 162 films submitted for approval. The ending of *Dream in Paradise* (Tiantang chunmeng, dir. Tang Xiaodan, 1947), a sober reflection on postwar poverty, was completely changed by the censors. Originally the lead character, an unemployed architect, was to die falling from the dream house of his own design, but the release version ends with his family walking away from the house, which is built by a profiteering merchant for his mistress.

Table 3.3 Film exhibition in major cities in China, 1927–48

Date/city	Theaters	Total no. of films	Chinese	US	European
25 January 1927					
Shanghai	22	22	6 (27%)	14 (64%)	2 (9%)
Beiping	8	8	4 (50%)	4 (50%)	0
Tianjin	4	4	1 (25%)	3 (75%)	0
Guangzhou	3	3	1 (33%)	2 (67%)	0
25 January 1937					
Shanghai	34	30	14 (47%)	15 (50%)	1 (3%)
Beiping	5	5	2 (40%)	3 (60%)	0
Tianjin	9	9	4 (44%)	5 (56%)	0
Guangzhou[1]	7	8	3 (37.5%)	5 (62.5%)	0
25 January 1948					
Shanghai	46	35	14 (40%)	21 (60%)	0
Beiping[2]	15	9	6 (67%)	2 (22%)	1 (11%)
Tianjin	19	11	5 (45%)	6 (55%)	0
Guangzhou	12	10	4 (40%)	6 (60%)	0

Source: Z. Wang 1998: 62–5.

Notes: 1 The Guangzhou figures are from 1 June 1937.
2 The Beiping figures are from 25 December 1947.

The shooting of *Hope in the World* (Xiwang zai renjian, dir. Shen Fu, 1949) was delayed for a year because the director refused the censors' eighteen revision requests, including one that meant changing all Chinese collaborators to Japanese (Y. Ding 1998: 15, 47, 299).

Commercial filmmaking and genre experiments

Several former producers, who had refused to cooperate with Japan during the war, challenged the KMT prohibition on private studios and successfully revived or launched companies. In July 1946, brothers Liu Zhonghao and Liu Zhongliang, who had made a fortune managing such theaters as Jincheng and Jindu, founded Guotai in Shanghai, which branched into Datong in January 1948 and employed Zhang Shichuan as its production manager. Others soon followed, and around forty – about half of them one-picture companies – operated in postwar China (Y. Ding 1998: 110).

As in wartime Hong Kong and Shanghai, rampant inflation drove numerous private studios to churn out cheap flicks, and an average shoot took between ten and twenty days (Y. Ding 1998: 45). Without recourse to state subsidies like their KMT counterparts, private companies tended to cater to mainstream audiences and rushed out sensational genre films such as detective, gangster, horror, spy and soft-porn romance. Xu Xinfu directed two titles for Guotai, *Pink Bomb* (Fenhong se de zhadan, 1947) and *Shadows in an Ancient House* (Guwu moying, 1948), which were indicative of this commercial trend. Other favorite genres included comedy, martial arts and the musical. *Orioles among Willow Leaves* (Liulang wenying, dir. Wu Cun, 1948), for instance, was shot on request from a Philippines distributor and delivered eighteen songs – all pre-recorded by Pathé – by such stars as Bai Guang and Gong Qiuxia. The distributor's offer of US$10,000 (or HK$45,000) offset production costs, and thus any revenue from the domestic market was straight profit. Indeed, many of these genre films did well in the market, and some conveyed a new perspective on their subject matter (Y. Ding 1998: 105–24).

Lianhua veterans and Kunlun: political melodrama

In early 1946, several prewar Lianhua veterans arrived in Shanghai and helped the former Lianhua investors reclaim their studio site, which was used to shoot *Eight Thousand Li of Cloud and Moon* (Baqianli lu yun he yue, dir. Shi Dongshan, 1947) under the Lianhua Film Art Society. A eulogy of a wartime drama troupe, the film contrasts a poverty-stricken couple of war heroes, Gao Libin (Tao Jin) and Jiang Lingyu (Bai Yang), and a profiteering merchant turned KMT official. By the end of the film, Gao suffers from a lung disease and Jiang gives birth to a premature baby. Short of money for food and medical bills, they and their friends have no idea what to do next. The widespread postwar disillusionment was thus crystallized in the director's confession: 'It was more difficult for us to understand why, in the months after victory, we felt defeated' (Pickowicz 2000: 396).

In May 1947, the Lianhua Film Art Society merged with Kunlun, a private company founded in 1946, which employed a number of former leftist and progressive filmmakers, such as Chen Liting, Sun Yu and Yang Hansheng. Kunlun emphasized quality rather than quantity, and the immensely popular two-part *Spring River Flows East* testified to the success of this production strategy. By leading its viewers through an emotional roller-coaster ride, the film dramatizes the traumatic experience schoolteacher Zhang Zhongliang (Tao Jin), his mother (Wu Yin) and his wife Sufen (Bai Yang) undergo throughout the war. While his family suffers from lack of food and shelter in occupied Shanghai, Zhang escapes arrest by the Japanese and travels to Chongqing, where his fortune turns with the help of Wang Lizhen, a former Shanghai socialite and a rich businessman's adopted daughter. Zhang is soon corrupted and lives with Wang as a common-law couple. After the war, Zhang returns to Shanghai and stays with Wang's cousin He Wenyan (Shangguan Yunzhu), and the two become sexually involved. Sufen now works as a servant in He's mansion, where she is shocked to see Zhang and Wang dancing the tango amidst cheers at a house

Party. Zhang's mother hears this unexpected news and rushes to scold him as a faithless husband, but he remains undecided and powerless in front of Wang and He. The film ends with Sufen drowning herself in the Huangpu River, Zhang standing speechless by his moaning mother, and Wang waiting in her car for Zhang to return.

Film historian Ding Yaping rightly locates postwar 'progressive films' in a continuum that connects to films of the 1930s. Such leftist trademark features as the exposure of class conflict and a bourgeois lifestyle, the dramatization of the misery of the working classes and the endorsement of collectivity at the expense of individuality were carried over in the Kunlun releases. What distinguished the postwar films, nonetheless, was their urgent sense of political intervention, their emphasis on realistic representation (instead of idealistic in the 1930s) and their willingness to reach out to the masses. Just as before, the family was staged as a microcosm of the society in radical transformation, women were projected as the embodiment of conflicting values, and the intellectuals' perspectives were favored in exploring social, political, sexual and psychological issues (Y. Ding 1998: 73–91).

Indeed, many Kunlun films functioned as *political melodrama*. This is 'an expression of a mode of injustice whose mise-en-scene is precisely the nexus between public and private life, a mode in which gender as a mark of difference is a limited, mobile term activated by distinctive social powers and historical circumstances' (Browne 1994: 43). Two other such examples from Kunlun were *Myriad of Lights* (Wanjia denghuo, dir. Shen Fu, 1948) and *Crows and Sparrows* (Wuya yu maque, dir. Zheng Junli, 1949). Contrary to the previous Kunlun titles that dwelled excessively on postwar disillusionment and concluded in an ambivalent light, these two films pointed to a hopeful future. The end scene of solidarity in *Myriad of Lights*, in which a factory worker denounces the current era as 'incorrect', endorses the collective effort for change. The final celebration of the Chinese New Year in *Crows and Sparrows*, which was completed after the founding of the PRC, doubles as the celebration of the beginning of a new era in Chinese history.

Wenhua: humanistic values and artistic visions

Another eminent postwar private studio, Wenhua was established in 1946 by Wu Xingzai, who had taken control of Lianhua's assets in the mid-1930s but had refused to work with the Japanese regime in occupied Shanghai. Dedicated to sponsoring small or no profit art films, Wu also founded Huayi, specifically to shoot the first Chinese color feature, *Remorse at Death* (Shengsi hen, dir. Fei Mu, 1948), an opera movie starring Mei Lanfang. Immediately following this film, Fei Mu turned to the post-production of *Spring in a Small Town* (Xiaocheng zhichun, 1948), a film that took him eight months to complete.

Set in a secluded, run-down house, *Spring in a Small Town* is a psychological exploration of the female protagonist Zhou Yuwen and her intricate relationships

Figure 3.10 Crows and Sparrows (1949): on the eve of a new society, with Zhao Dan (right)

with her sickly husband, Dai Liyan, and her former lover Zhang Zhichen, a doctor who unexpectedly comes for a visit. The innocence of her sister-in-law Dai Xiu further complicates Zhou's emotions, and the presence of Old Huang, a longtime family servant, reminds Zhou of this changeless, hopeless household. Zhou's and Zhang's passion is rekindled, but a sense of moral duty prevents Zhang from yielding to Zhou's advance. Following an aborted suicide by Liyan, Zhang leaves the family, as Zhou, speechless, watches his departure from the top of a city wall.

To enhance the melancholy ambience, Fei Mu preferred the use of long takes and medium shots, supplemented by the slow rhythm created by panning, tilting and tracking shots that capture the nuances of the characters' gestures, eye contacts, facial expressions and bodily movements. The silent scenes in the film are often the most effective and create an unbearable sense of tension. Fei Mu's alternation of narrative points of view between the third person and Zhou's voice-over commentary proceeds seamlessly and adds extra layers of meaning to the evolving psychological drama.

Never intended as a crowd-pleaser, *Spring in a Small Town* garnered enthusiastic reviews that compared the film to a lyrical poem, a tender flower and a delicious wine (Y. Ding 1998: 469–78). Unfortunately, Communist

Figure 3.11 Spring in a Small Town (1948): a critically acclaimed art film classic, directed by Fei Mu

historiography censured the film for its petit-bourgeois 'decadence', its ideological 'backwardness' and its alleged 'narcotic effect' on the audience at a time of war (J. Cheng *et al.* 1981: 2: 271–2). Since the 1980s, however, it has been critically acclaimed as the best Chinese film of all time and a classic example of 'Eastern cinema' (Ying 1993).[21] In particular, the film is praised for legitimating female subjectivity and exemplifying the cinematic art of dissent vis-à-vis patriarchy and the logocentric tradition of Chinese fiction and film.

In the late 1940s Wenhua was not alone in addressing female subjectivity, but its films in particular excelled in their humanistic values, best reflected in the seamless collaboration between director Sang Hu and screenwriter Eileen Chang (Zhang Ailing). The box-office success of *Phony Phoenixes* owed less to the public protests by the Shanghai Barbers' Association than the film's re-enactment of bitter-sweet everyday struggles, as well as outstanding performances by Shi Hui and Li Lihua. *Long Live the Mistress!* continued Sang Hu and Eileen Chang's collaboration, and *Sorrows and Joys of a Middle-Aged Man* (Aile zhongnian, dir. Sang Hu, 1949), also featuring Shi Hui, remains one of very few Chinese films to acknowledge the necessity of pursuing happiness by the older generation.

Finally, Wenhua's *Night Inn* (Yedian, dir. Huang Zuolin, 1947), an adaptation of Ke Ling's stage play based on Maxim Gorky's *The Lower Depths*, represented another trend in postwar filmmaking, that is the adaptation of Chinese and

Western literary and dramatic works. Authors whose work was adapted include Lu Xun and Tian Han, Theodore Dreiser (USA), Anatole France (France) and Ivan Turgenev (Russia). *Night Inn* premiered in five Shanghai theaters, and the 520 showings between February and April 1948 illustrated the audience's appreciation of a higher standard of art. The wide circulation of translated Western literary classics in the postwar Chinese market further strengthened this appreciation (Y. Ding 1998: 262–3).

CRITICAL ISSUES: CINEMA AND MODERNITY

The cross-fertilization between cinema, drama and literature in postwar China brings us to critical issues regarding the characteristics of the second generation of filmmakers, alternative cinematic visions and the conceptualization of film as a synthetic art in two reputed 'golden ages' of Chinese filmmaking. Such issues revolve around the relationship between cinema and modernity in China.

'Films by literature people': didacticism and melodrama

As mentioned in Chapter 2, 'films by literature people' characterized the 1930s and 1940s as the leftist playwrights entered the film industry and emphasized film's *literary quality*. Just as the civilized play had served its transition role in the silent period, the concept of 'film literature' helped elevate film to a *mature narrative art*. As Fei Mu asserted in 1948, screenwriters were at the forefront of filmmaking and, as such, the screenplay should take priority over financial investment (Y. Ding 1998: 432). This emphasis on the screenplay might explain why the screenwriter's name always precedes that of the director in standard Chinese references (J. Cheng *et al.* 1981; J. Zhang and Cheng 1995).

However, the importance of film's literary quality did not reduce the value of drama itself, for both film and drama now aspired to a higher form of *language art* than that of their predecessors – silent film and the civilized play. In fact, many important film directors of this period (e.g., Fei Mu, Li Pingqian and Shen Fu) – also known as the 'second generation' – were themselves noted playwrights and directors of stage dramas. Moreover, leading film actors and actresses (e.g., Zhao Dan and Bai Yang) were deeply immersed in the dramatic arts as well. For example, Wenhua employed many members of the Hard Work (Kugan) Troupe (e.g., Ke Ling and Shi Hui) headed by Huang Zuolin in the orphan island of Shanghai. Similarly, Kunlun employed members of Central Film's wartime drama troupes headed by Zhang Junxiang. Both Huang and Zhang had studied theater abroad and earned their master's degrees at Cambridge and Yale universities respectively.

As explicated by the shadowplay theory, *didacticism* persisted in the films by literature people, and their preferred mode of cinematic expression during this period was *melodrama*, which was characterized by 'moral polarization, excessive emotionalism, exaggerated expression, unusual human suffering, and extreme suspense' (Pickowicz 1993). Rather than opposing itself to realism and romanticism favored by May Fourth literature, melodrama combined elements from both and provided leftists and the non-leftists alike with an effective form in which to address social problems while articulating versions of idealism, be they Marxist or conservative in nature. Through tropes such as sadistic evils, masochistic virtues, male effeminacy, drastic simplification and stereotyping, what Paul Pickowicz (1993) labels the 'May Fourth melodrama' became a new cinematic tradition that would be carried on and practiced up to the 1980s and beyond.

Realism, romanticism and modernism

Ke Ling believes that *realism*, the excellent tradition of May Fourth literature, scored a complete victory in this period (W. Chen 1992: 301). Theoretically a loose concept, realism in Chinese cinema can be further differentiated into different variations, such as social realism of the 1930s, critical realism of the late 1940s and socialist realism of the 1950s and 1960s. For Chinese filmmakers of the two 'golden ages', one way to intensify realism was to include documentary footage of disasters and wars, as in *Big Road* (Dalu, dir. Sun Yu, 1935; sound accompaniment) and *Spring River Flows East*, the purpose of which was to invite the spectator's immediate identification. Another method was to use a cast whose real-life experience approximated that of the main characters, as in the case of Bai Yang and Tao Jin in *Eight Thousand Li of Cloud and Moon*. A third way was to cast non-professional actors, as in *The Watch* (Biao, dir. Huang Zuolin, 1949), where the combined use of real orphans and a hidden camera create artistic effects that bear a close resemblance to those of postwar Italian neo-realism. As in neo-realism, Chinese cinematic realism dwelled excessively on poverty and suffering but insisted on human dignity and compassion. It is no wonder, then, that decades later Georges Sadoul, an eminent historian of world cinema, was surprised to discover a resemblance between *The Watch* and Italian neo-realism (Y. Ding 1998: 319).

As Fei Mu correctly pointed out in 1948, realism itself might pose a problem because its mandate in pursuing the real would clash with a director's subjective input and *romantic* or *idealistic* tendency (Y. Ding 1998: 429–30). A case in point is Sun Yu the 'poet director' whose take on reality was colored by his unique subjectivism (Y. Sun 1990: 244). As early as 1936, Ling He described Sun Yu as an 'optimistic, emotionally pure, romantic, upward looking and revolutionary poet' and distinguished Sun's 'revolutionary romanticism' from the older, antisocial, escapist and decadent romanticism (ZDZ 1996a: 1279–85).[22] Typically, Sun's romanticism is evident in his films' endings. For instance, Lingling (Li Lili) enchants the viewer with her radiant smile in front of her executioners in *Daybreak* (Tianming, 1932), and Dingxiang (Chen Yanyan) envisions the resurrection of her friends killed by the Japanese air raid in *Big*

Road. Although Sun's films were criticized for being too utopian and idealistic, Xia Yan defended Sun in 1933 by arguing that sometimes exaggeration might be necessary (ZDYYZ 1993: 516).

Theoretically films which have been labeled as realism, romanticism and the May Fourth melodrama may all be regarded as Chinese filmmakers' different approaches to modernity by way of cinema. Of the films by Sun Yu and his contemporaries, Miriam Hansen observes: 'What makes these films modern or, more precisely, modernist, is that they dramatize conflicts and contradictions that may be *phrased* in traditional terms but cannot be *resolved* with recourse to or by restoring a traditional social order, regardless of whether or not the films end up espousing the revolution' (2000: 15). Here, Hansen theorizes modernity as something in excess of traditional ideologies and cinematic conventions, something that demands new *visual* representation.

Hansen's term 'modernist' brings us to alternative practices in Chinese filmmaking that do not fit nicely in mainstream realism, nor perhaps even in romanticism. Some critics identify the signs of German expressionism in Wu Yonggang's use of camera positions and lighting, as well as in He Mengfu's *A Scene Under the Moon* (Yuexia xiaojing) and Fei Mu's *Spring Boudoir's Dreams* (Chungui duanmeng), two episodes from *Lianhua Symphony* (Hong Kong Art Center 1984). Indeed, with his abstract concept of humanity and his avant-garde techniques, Wu Yonggang had made a courageous excursion in *The Desert Island* but had to admit his failure in reaching out to the audience (ZDYYZ 1993: 393). By contrast, an equally rich text in psychoanalysis and visual experimentation, Ma-Xu Weibang's *Singing at Midnight* proved a box-office sensation due primarily to Zhang Shankun's shrewd strategy of marketing it as China's first horror film. As is evident in *Singing at Midnight*, a Chinese director could creatively integrate impressionist techniques and the romantic spirit in pursuit of cinematic realism, and the result could still be a legitimately *modern* – if not strictly modernist – film of ideological and emotional impact.

Soft film: alternative aesthetics and the modernist sensibility

Unlike the directors experimenting with modernist techniques without theorizing their rationales, a group of young critics – some themselves rising stars of modernist writers in Shanghai – made a radical move in promoting cinematic techniques during the early 1930s. Their first target was the kind of ideologically coded realism promoted by the leftists, who had just embarked on film criticism at that time. But the modernists' immediate goal was to advance a new film aesthetic based on the nature of film as a new artistic medium – a goal unfortunately sidetracked by their polemical debate with the leftists.

From July to October 1932, Liu Na'ou, who had introduced 'new perceptionism' or 'new sensationism' (*xin ganjue pai*) to China from Japan and had cultivated a literary following since the late 1920s, published an extended treatise

Figure 3.12 Mise-en-scene of urban modernity: interior design in *Heng Niang* (1931)

on film art in eight installments in *Cinema Weekly*. Liu first defines film as an art appealing to human emotions and demanding visual cultivation, specifically the elevation of techniques of 'watching', thus linking the camera eye to the human eye. Citing Russian director Vsevolod Pudovkin, Liu regards *montage* as an artistic process whereby a new 'filmed reality' is created that bears no relation with the real-world time and space. Liu distinguishes the *cinegraphique* (created images) from the *photographique* (raw material) – customarily punctuating his original with French and English words – and attributes Ruan Lingyu's screen eroticism to the former and Hu Die's lack of it to the latter. He further discusses the 'Cine-Eye' (or Kino-Eye) expounded by Russian 'mechanistic' theorist Dziga Vertov, as well as 'absolute film' pursued by Viking Eggeling, a Swedish avant-garde filmmaker who accentuated visual rhythms and produced such landmarks in abstract cinema as *Diagonal Symphony, Parallel* and *Horizontal*.

In conclusion, Liu argues that the notion of the *cinegraphique* implies *resistance* to literature, theater and painting, because the motion picture is the *art of motion* and must resort to expression in and through motion. From this perspective Liu criticizes Chinese cinema for relying too much on literature (i.e., literary or verbal expression). *Fate in Tears and Laughter, II*, for example, consists of 40 per cent titles (35 per cent subtitles and 5 per cent spoken titles), a fact that should qualify it as a work of literature rather than cinema. Liu locates in this film the typical weaknesses of Chinese cinema, such as the habit of watching a film as if reading a book, the sense of flatness without tension and suspension, and the fixed frontal viewing without motion to and from various directions (ZDZ 1996a: 489–97).

Ostensibly, from the outset, Liu's passion resided in the theoretical, visual and formal aspects of filmmaking. To promote new film aesthetics, Liu launched *Modern Screen* (Xiandai dianying) in March 1933 with a group of friends. In April 1933, the magazine carried his article on the problem of depth in Chinese cinema, in which he compares *Fate in Tears and Laughter, II* with *Sunrise* (dir. F. W. Murnau, 1927) and finds the latter's ratio of titles to images a much smaller figure of 1:18. For Liu, the most serious problem in Chinese cinema is the supremacy of content, which has produced a 'deformed' baby with a giant head and a tiny body. In fairness, Liu's criticism that 'Chinese cinema is abundant in words but famished in images' (*ziduo yingshao*) was directed at the majority of Chinese filmmakers, not exclusively at the emergent leftists (Luo *et al.* 1992: 1: 256–61).

What started as a theoretical investigation soon turned polemical after *Modern Screen* published two articles by Huang Jiamo. 'Film's Color Ingredients and Poisonous Ingredients' (October 1933) rejects the use of film as propaganda and charges that the indoctrination of 'red ingredients' without the viewer's prior consent amounts to an act of poisoning. 'Hard Film and Soft Film' (December 1933) further charges that innocent Chinese producers have been 'raped' by 'Mr Ideology' and that modern viewers detest hypocritical sermons in 'hard films'. In opposition to the leftist 'revolutionary slogans', Huang offers this metaphorical definition: 'Film is the ice cream for the eye to taste, the sofa chair for the heart to sit on'. He concludes that since film is made of soft celluloid, it should be 'soft in nature' (*ruanxing*), hence the term 'soft film' (M. Yi 1993: 840–5).

Modern Screen ceased publication in June 1934, but *Chenbao*'s 'Screen Daily' provided an outlet for heated exchanges between the leftists and the soft film advocates. The belligerence of the leftists' vitriol was apparent in their article titles, such as 'Liquidating the Theory of Soft Film' (by Tang Na, June 1934) and 'Liquidating Liu Na'ou's Theory' (by Chen Wu, August 1934). Writing in a generally more sophisticated language, the leftists condemned these soft film positions: prioritization of form over content, pure aesthetic meditation at times of national crisis, pleasurable experience of sensuality and sexuality, and concern for entertainment tastes and commercial values. At stake were dozens of more fundamental issues, such as the nature of art, the functions of aesthetics and ideology, the validity of class analysis, the mission of a film critic and the assessment of leftist films. By March 1935, the debate had turned ugly, as *Minbao*'s 'Film Forum' (edited by Lu Si) was packed with retaliatory personal attacks on Mu Shiying and Ye Lingfeng (M. Yi 1993: 744–836).

Personal attacks notwithstanding, the soft film debate must be re-examined in its specific historical context. On the one hand, the leftists' initiation into Marxist ideology was part of an international phenomenon of the 'left turn' in art and literature. On the other hand, the soft film advocates represented an ongoing Chinese effort to learn from and participate in the international avant-garde movement. In this respect, they found an early kindred spirit in Yu Dafu, who had announced in 1927 that 'ice cream and cinema are the crystallization of the twentieth-century culture', for both provide a gratifying experience at an affordable price to a large majority (Luo *et al.* 1992: 1: 84). Another kindred spirit was Tian Han, whose 'Silver Dream' (1927) contains a lengthy quotation from Tanizaki Jun'ichiro, who describes film as a dream that humankind manufactures with machines, and who goes on to join film to wine and music as three human masterpieces (ZDZ 1996a: 442). What distinguishes Tian Han from the soft film advocates, however, is that Tian 'awakened' from his silver dream in the face of Japanese aggression and realized in 1930 that film could work equally as imperialist propaganda (ZDZ 1996a: 472–5). In a matter of three years, Tian had changed completely from an aesthete to a leftist, renouncing his previous indulgence in film's mesmerizing capacity, something Liu Na'ou and his associates decided to advocate in the 1930s.

Another factor to consider is the connection between cinema and the modern city. As a quintessential symbol of modern civilization, the city offers an array of entirely new experiences that traditional literary means have difficulties in articulating. It is in this connection that cinema emerges as a vehicle for expressing new urban experiences by way of manipulating time, space, light, speed and the like. Itself a technological invention, cinema thus underscores the city as the embodiment of mechanical civilization. In an article bearing the French title 'Escranesque' (April 1933), Liu Na'ou insists that 'the art form that most characteristically depicts the social environment of this mechanical civilization is the cinema' (Lee 1999: 92). Although Liu vehemently denounced film's dependence on literature, in his fictional work he creatively drew from cinematic techniques and, together with his new perceptionist friends, considerably enriched the expressive potential of modern Chinese literature (J. Li 1997). Ironically, whereas the soft film debate inevitably 'incriminated' the new perceptionists in official history, their literary works have remained a prime example of the fruitful cross-fertilization of film and literature in China.

Film as a synthetic art

In 1934 Shi Zhecun noted Liu Na'ou's habit of watching a film twice, the first time concentrating on the story and acting, and the second time on shot composition and editing (J. Li 1997: 36). Indeed, like their predecessors, the second generation of filmmakers also mastered basic film techniques by frequenting theaters. Xia Yan recalled bringing a stopwatch and a flashlight to the theater and taking notes of the types, lengths and functions of individual shots (M. Yi 1993: 14). Shen Xiling and Tang Xiaodan used to spend whole days in a theater watching the same titles again and again and memorizing such details as frame composition and mise-en-scene. Zhu Shilin watched Hollywood and German films and could recount exact sequences of shots. Sang Hu viewed both Chinese and Hollywood films and could remember names like Yang Naimei and Yin Mingzhu as well as Mary Pickford, Douglas Fairbanks and Greta Garbo. As early as 1934, Fei Mu had reportedly watched over 1,000 films (Y. Ding 1998: 267–8, 293).

During this period, the Chinese film language continued to favor the medium shot and the long take as the structuring principle (A. Huang 1983). But the mise-en-scene revealing the depth of field was employed to enhance a film's ambience, parallel and sound-image montages were structured to highlight contrasts, point-of-view shots were used to convey subjective feelings, and close-ups were implemented to produce a strong psychological impact. For instance, *Spring in a Small Town* features three sequences of close-ups of the female protagonist's feet when she visits her ex-lover at night, but each close-up conveys a different impression. In the first sequence, she hesitates under psychological pressure; in the second, she walks briskly with a blanket; and in the third, she stumbles while intoxicated after the birthday dinner. In order to fully explore the intricate relationships between characters as well as between them and their environments, *Spring in a Small Town* frequently resorts to long takes, some as long as 2 minutes and 15 seconds (Y. Ding 1998: 354–62).

While Western – especially Hollywood – influence was all too obvious in this period,[23] Chinese filmmakers also drew extensively on traditional art and aesthetics. Acclaimed as a 'cinema poet' and a master stylist (Gao 1996), Fei Mu believed that 'Chinese cinema cannot but express its own national style'; thus in *Remorse at Death* he sought to create a unique style poised between 'realism' (*xieshi*) and 'abstractionism' (*xieyi*). Like Fei Mu, Zhu Shilin also used the concepts of 'emptiness' (*xu*) and 'substance' (*shi*) from traditional aesthetics to illustrate film language, repeatedly referencing the unique features of Chinese painting and theater (Y. Ding 1998: 370–3). Even Sun Yu, an 'exceptional' auteur who had studied at the New York Photography Academy and Columbia University and who was the first Chinese director to use a crane, tapped into Chinese literary sources in *Big Road*, at least in two instances. First, the film's 'cyclical form' of narrative structure resembles the traditional Chinese novel, which consists of episodes loosely connected by characters. Second, the 'flower drum song' sequence performed by Moli (Li Lili) is said to exemplify 'the folk spirit of Chinese poetry' and endows the film 'with a strong sense of national identity' (C. Li 1991: 61). According to Ke Ling, both Zheng Zhengqiu and Cai Chusheng engaged in the nationalization of cinematic expressions, and their popular films resorted to a contrastive structure similar to that of classical Chinese literature. Similarly, although each has his own artistic character, the above-mentioned directors as well as Shi Dongshan, Shen Xiling and Yuan Muzhi all shared certain Chinese styles (W. Chen 1992: 317).

CONCLUSION: IN THE NAME OF THE
NATION-PEOPLE

The 'golden age' period witnessed a series of radical – and 'memorable' as Zheng Zhengqiu put it (ZDYYZ 1993: 85) – transformations of Chinese cinema on many fronts – artistic, conceptual, ideological and political. Artistically, the participation of 'literature people' elevated the screenplay to the level of literary art. The concentration of actors and actresses trained in spoken drama brought about a gradual maturation in the areas of dialogue and acting. And prominent filmmakers were self-confident enough to develop film as a synthetic art, drawing inspiration from literary, visual, musical and performing arts from both China and abroad.[24] In spite of his dissatisfaction with the filmmaking situation in China, Fei Mu contended in 1948 that the best Chinese directors had already exceeded their American counterparts in terms of self-cultivation and capability (Y. Ding 1998: 429).

Conceptually, film was no longer confined by Chinese cultural traditions as it had been in early cinema. Except for the cases of prewar Hong Kong and wartime Shanghai, the majority of the audience was no longer obsessed with legends, myths and classic novels. Instead, audiences learned to appreciate film as a vehicle for confronting existential problems and articulating popular sentiments, especially in times of national defense and psychological recovery. As Shen Fu aptly put it in the postwar context, film had assumed the sacred mission of providing comfort, confidence and light to the people who had suffered hunger, death and endless misery and who were still struggling in the dark (Y. Ding 1998: 80). In other words, film performed a *therapeutic* function as well as being educational and entertaining.

Ideologically, except for the soft film advocates who moved in the opposite direction, most filmmakers turned progressive. Even the moralist Zheng Zhengqiu could sound as radical as his leftist counterparts. In a 1933 article punctuated with such phrases as 'bourgeois,' 'capitalist', 'imperialism' and 'sub-colony', Zheng referred to 'the great May Fourth movement' and Soviet films as sources of inspiration and emulation, and proposed to Chinese film circles the slogans of 'anti-imperialism, anti-capitalism and anti-feudalism'. He urged his fellow filmmakers to unite and resist double censorship and ended his article with this battle call: 'Comrades, march on and on! Fight hard and march on!' (ZDYYZ 1993: 84–6). Otherwise a moderate reformist, Zheng here sounded as belligerent as his leftist counterparts.[25]

Politically, film was increasingly subjected to censorship and other forms of government interference, and the acknowledgment of film's educational function only made the medium a more fiercely contested battleground. The exigency of national salvation, however, had driven both the KMT regime and the leftist–CCP forces to compromise on numerous occasions, thereby leaving room for filmmakers to maneuver. For instance, in 1933, Luo Mingyou issued this slogan for Lianhua: 'save national cinema (*guopian*), propagate national essences (*guocui*), promote national causes (*guoye*) and serve the nation-state (*guojia*)'. Within a year, the employees in Lianhua Studios 1 and 2 negotiated with Luo and convinced him to change the slogan to 'advocate art, promote culture, enlighten people and save the film industry', which was then adopted as part of Lianhua's objectives (ZDZ 1996a: 73–4, 1338). Such a political struggle as this one over debatable conservative-sounding words versus more neutral terms demonstrated a high degree of popular distrust of the KMT regime and its claim to want to preserve traditional cultural essences (e.g., Confucianism). The preference of 'people' (*min*) over 'state' (*guo*) further highlighted a thorny issue that would continue to resurface in subsequent decades.

Finally, it must be admitted that the 'golden age' period appears 'golden' only in retrospect and that its achievements can be fully assessed only with historical hindsight. After decades of political repression and ideological brainwashing in mainland China and Taiwan during the 1950s and 1960s, the period looks attractive because it was marked by the flexibility of multiple political affiliations and the possibility of alternative aesthetics and artistic models. In short, the golden age period is attractive because everything was as yet unsettled, and opportunities, albeit often short-lived, were still obtainable.

4

CINEMATIC REINVENTION OF THE NATIONAL IN TAIWAN, 1896–1978

INTRODUCTION: A MATURING INDUSTRY

This chapter contains a brief section on Taiwan's colonial era (1896–1945) and concentrates on Taiwan cinema from the KMT takeover in 1945 to the eve of New Taiwan Cinema in 1978. Japan's defeat in the Second World War resulted in the return of Taiwan to China's sovereignty in 1945, thus terminating fifty years of Japanese rule in the island. But the postwar transition was not peaceful. The KMT military forces cracked down on the popular revolts against government corruption and hefty taxes, best exemplified in the 28 February Incident of 1947, which claimed tens of thousands of Taiwanese lives and remained a taboo subject in Taiwan history until the late 1980s. Due to its large-scale military setbacks in the mainland, the KMT relocated its ROC regime to Taiwan in 1949 and brought in a large population of mainlanders. In the 1950s, the KMT mobilized its propaganda machinery in support of the campaign to reclaim the mainland, but as time went by the government switched its attention to developing the economy and building Taiwan as a legitimate site of the Chinese nation and culture. A police state under martial law was gradually transformed into a modernizing society, eventually to become an economic power in the Asia-Pacific region.

Compared with the mainland and Hong Kong, Taiwan did not have a film production history of its own until the 1950s, although distribution and exhibition had been operative for a long time. In terms of film history, Taiwan cinema between 1945 and 1978 can be divided into three phases. First, in the phase of *postwar transition* (1945 to 1954), distributors imported movies made in Shanghai, Hong Kong and Hollywood as well as Japan when legally permitted, and the ROC government reorganized its studios on the island, producing documentaries and newsreels and sometimes anti-Communist features.

Second, in the phase of *two competing cinemas* (1955 to 1969), private companies vied with one another to produce popular Taiwanese-dialect films, tapping into local cultural sources and exploring alternative ideological, linguistic and psychological realms. Yet, overproduction, changing demographics and the rise of Mandarin cinema propelled the inevitable decline of dialect films in the 1970s. In the early 1960s Mandarin cinema asserted itself with 'healthy realism' promoted by state studios, which broke away from cold-war ideology and represented socioeconomic changes taking place in the island. The arrival of two leading Hong Kong directors, Li Hanxiang and King Hu (Hu Jinquan, 1931–97), in the mid-1960s further stimulated the growth of Mandarin cinema in private studios. Genre films, especially costume dramas, new-styled martial arts pictures and romances featuring 'youth idols', attracted an increasing number of urban audiences.

Third, in the phase of *political and industrial restructuring* (1970 to 1978), the government and filmmakers alike learned to cope with the deteriorating political situation in the wake of Taiwan's loss of its United Nations membership and the normalization of the PRC diplomatic relations with Japan and the US in the 1970s. State studios turned to historical and anti-Japanese war films, which articulated unsettled political anxiety and reasserted Taiwan's claim to Chinese nationhood, while private studios churned out escapist genre films of romance, martial arts, gangster and even soft porn in an effort to compete with the rapidly developing television industry on the island and films from Hong Kong.

By the late 1960s Taiwan cinema had securely established itself in the domestic as well as overseas markets. Mandarin films regularly won major awards at the annual Asian film festival, and from the mid-1960s onward consistently outperformed Hong Kong cinema at Taiwan's own respectable Golden Horse Awards (*Jinma jiang*). However, when the Taiwan film industry finally matured with medium-sized studios and distribution systems, it faced new challenges posed by the restructuring of media industries in general and a growing sense of Taiwanese identity among the population.

DIFFICULT POSTWAR TRANSITION, 1945–54

The postwar decade was a difficult transition phase in Taiwan film history since, as under Japanese colonial rule, film was subject to strict state regulation, instituted this time by the KMT regime. But unlike the CCP regime in the mainland, the KMT government did not invest a great amount in its studios,[1] although film was utilized as an ideological weapon in its anti-Communist campaign. Characterized by fundamental instability, this was a time when investors and filmmakers experimented in various ways with the aim of developing film as a viable industry in Taiwan. To place their experiments in a proper historical context, we must revisit Taiwan film activities in the colonial era.

Film activities in the colonial era, 1896–45

In August 1896, a year after Japan's colonization of the island, a Japanese merchant showed Edison's 'Kinetoscope' (*xiyangjing*) in a coastal town near

114

Taipei, the earliest such practice recorded in Asia. Approximatly ten Edison movies – each around one-minute long – were shown to one person at a time (Ye 1998: 21, 52). In June 1900, a Japanese showman used Lumières' 'cinéma-tographe' to project a dozen shorts to a mostly female Japanese audience in Taipei's Ximending area, where a complex of theaters gradually took shape (Ye 1997). In January 1904, Liao Huang, the first Taiwanese showman, began touring the island with twenty-six documentary and comic shorts, charging fees from 0.1 to 0.3 Japanese yen – a quite exorbitant sum for the time in Taiwan. Apparently, film exhibition was not profitable in Taiwan until 1908, when Taipei's Rising Sun Theater (Chaori zuo) showed a number of hand-colored films to the amazement of the audience, who paid 0.2 yen per ticket and packed the theater. In July 1911, the Fragrance Theater (Fangnai guan), Taiwan's first exclusive movie theater, opened in Ximending, charging three-tiered admissions at 0.2, 0.1 and 0.05 yen (see Table 4.1). As in the mainland at the time, men and women were required to sit separately, but this rule was relaxed in February 1916 (Ye 1998: 59–86).

In October 1921, a group of Taiwanese intellectuals organized the Taiwan Culture Association and declared their intention to 'elevate Taiwan culture, awaken the Han national consciousness and resist national oppression by the Japanese' (F. Chen 1988: 8). One of its members, Zhang Xiuguang, had met Tian Han and Ouyang Yuqian while studying in Japan in 1919. After engaging in

Table 4.1 Sample ticket prices in Taiwan, 1900s–90s

Year	Theater	Type of film	Price
1904	touring shows	short documentaries and comics	0.1–0.3 yen
1908	Rising Sun	hand-colored shorts	0.2 yen
1914	Fragrance	general	0.05, 0.1, 0.2 yen
1926	touring shows	educational	0.05–0.1 yen
1926	Taipei theaters	feature	0.2–0.5 yen
early 1946	—	—	20 yuan
late 1947	—	—	120 yuan
late 1948	—	—	3,000 yuan
April 1949	—	—	10,000 yuan
May 1949	—	—	40,000 yuan
June 1949	outside Taipei	—	NT$1.5
June 1949	Taipei theaters	—	NT$2.3
Feb 1950	Taipei first-run	—	NT$3.7–5
1963	—	—	NT$11.6
1971	—	—	NT$19
1998	Taipei average	—	NT$260–80
1998	Warner Village	—	NT$280–300

Sources: Guojia dianying 1999: 63–4; Z. Wei 1993: 98; L. Ye 1995: 75–6; L. Ye 1998: 59–86, 136–8.

Note: In June 1949, the Taiwan currency reform converted 40,000 yuan to NT$1.

new drama in Taiwan, Zhang left for Shanghai in 1923 and began his three-year film study there. He subsequently brought back four Shanghai features, *Orphan Rescues Grandfather*, *The Revival of an Old Well*, *The Migration Act* and *Visiting City Relatives* (Tan qinjia, dir. Wang Yuanlong, 1926), which toured the island to enthusiastic crowds. In the meantime, the Taiwan Culture Association had expanded its film activities and dispatched three projection teams on tours showing educational titles upon popular demand. For instance, in April 1926, over 2,000 people crowded their two shows in Tainan (a southern city), forcing them to schedule an extra evening. Apart from low admission charges of 0.05 to 0.10 yen (compared with 0.20 to 0.50 yen in major theaters), the growing sense of Taiwanese identity was cited as a reason for the popularity of these tours. Although the association was dissolved in January 1927 due to factional conflicts, its film activities helped to encourage Taiwanese audiences to movie theaters (Ye 1998: 136–8).

The first feature-length film shot in Taiwan was a Japanese production, *Eyes of the Buddha* (Dafo de tongkong, dir. Tanaka King, 1922), which cast a few Taiwanese actors. One actor, Liu Xiyang, was discharged from his bank position because acting was considered a disgraceful career. In May 1925 Liu and a group of film fans set up the Taiwan Cinema Research Association and produced the first Taiwanese feature, *Whose Fault is This?* (Shui zhi guo, dir. Liu Xiyang, 1925; 8 reels). Because of its poor quality, this triangular romance turned out a box-office flop. The association was disbanded soon after, but some members teamed up with a local *gezaixi* troupe in 1928 and produced eight small reels (three minutes total) for a series of chained-sequence plays. The cinematic tricks projected between the acts of the stage plays piqued the audience's curiosity and saved the financially troubled troupe. Energized by their experiment, the team produced *Bloodstains* (Xuehen, dir. Zhang Yunhe, 1929), a martial arts picture similar to its Shanghai counterparts but set in Taiwan's tribal mountains. With a production cost of 3,000 yen, the film had an unexpected three-day run in March 1930 at the Lasting Pleasure Theater (Yongle zuo), which returned over 950 yen. Nevertheless, compared with Shanghai and Hong Kong, Taiwanese feature production in the silent era was underdeveloped, and a local newspaper article in February 1932 listed three principal reasons: lack of government support, shortage of quality screenplays and rigid censorship (F. Chen 1988: 13–14).

Between 1931 and 1937 only six or seven features were produced in Taiwan, and most of these were co-productions between Japan and Taiwan, typically with the Taiwanese providing the initial funding and the Japanese serving as directors, cameramen and leading casts.[2] *Wu Feng the Righteous Man* (Yiren Wu Feng, dir. Ando Talo, Jiba Hiroki, 1932; 8 reels, silent), a biography of a Han official of the mid-eighteenth century, dealt with the sensitive issue of ethnic violence in Taiwan's indigenous tribes. To propagate the myth of peaceful coexistence, the colonial government promoted Wu Feng as an example of devotion to duty, honesty and self-sacrifice through literature, drama, song and dance in the 1930s. According to the folk legend, which contradicted historical records, Wu Feng had sacrificed his life in exchange for the tribe's consent to terminate their practice of decapitating the innocent Han and using their heads in tribal rituals. The film showed for three days at the Fragrance Theater and went on to tour schools with government support.

Another co-production, *Map of the Seven-Star Cave* (Qixing dong ditu, dir. Jiba Hiroki, 1933; 7 reels, silent), a detective–martial arts film that cost 3,000 yen to produce, had a decent three-day run at the Lasting Pleasure and sold briskly elsewhere (see Table 4.2). The first sound picture, funded in part by 6,000 yen raised by a group of Taiwanese investors, was *Laments by Zhishan Cliff* (Zhishan yan, dir. Shizuka Hachirou, 1936), a film glorifying six Japanese teachers killed by the local Taiwanese for imposing Japanese-language education. A tearjerker about a singing courtesan's unrequited love and her tragic suicide, *Waiting for the Spring Wind* (Wang chunfeng, dir. Ando Talo, 1937) was based on a popular Taiwanese folk song and funded exclusively by Taiwan money. The Japanese soundtracks for these two talkies were dubbed in Japan, for a Taiwanese soundtrack was inconceivable because the colonial government had increasingly limited the use of Taiwanese dialect in public. After the Pacific War broke out in 1941, the Taiwanese were required to take Japanese names, and the Japanese language was reinforced in schools.

Taiwan adopted the Japanese method of *benshi* or *katsuben* (*bianshi*) in film exhibition. In the silent era, a *benshi* was a man who appeared before the movie started, sat or stood behind a desk by the left side of the screen, announced his name and narrated the story from a script. More like a storyteller than a screen artist, the *benshi* invented different accents and tones for various characters, adding jokes and comments from time to time. An the experienced *benshi* could controlled the viewers' emotional responses, making them in high demand. But because of their subversive potential, especially when commenting in idiomatic dialect, they were placed under surveillance by a policeman (and sometimes also a firefighter just in case) and were required to pass annual examinations. In 1930 forty-one Japanese and nineteen Taiwanese worked as *benshi* in Taiwan. But in 1932 Taiwanese *benshi* increased to forty-six, compared with fifty-six Japanese *benshi*. By 1937, there were no Japanese *benshi* in Taiwan because the colonial government dictated that all sound films produced in Taiwan use Japanese dialogue. Taiwanese *benshi* survived the wartime, however, because local audiences relied on them to narrate Japanese and Mandarin soundtracks – the latter from both Shanghai and Man'ei productions (F. Chen 1988: 5–6).

During the 1920s and 1930s there were sixteen registered Taiwanese-owned companies which specialized in film exhibition tours. These companies either purchased distribution rights directly from Shanghai film companies or obtained old Chinese prints from Xiamen (aka Amoy, a coastal city in Fujian province across the Taiwan Strait) or Southeast Asia. Over 300 Chinese titles had been shipped to Taiwan by 1945. Most of them were ethical family dramas, romantic stories and martial arts pictures, but progressive films like *Wild Flower* also made their way to the island (Ye 1998: 131–5). Some Taiwanese (He Feiguang, Lin

Table 4.2 Production costs and revenues per film in Taiwan, 1929–2002

Year	Film	Studio	Costs	Grosses
Average				
1950s	average dialect film	—	250,000–300,000	—
1950s	average Mandarin film	—	600,000	—
1960s	average film	—	3,000,000	100,000
1960s	average martial arts film	—	150,000	—
Specific				
1929	*Bloodstains*	Cinema Research Association	3,000 yen	950 yen
1933	*Map of the Seven-Star Cave*	Japan-Taiwan	3,000 yen	—
1961	*Storm Over Jinmen Bay*	Nikkatsu/CMPC	US$200,000	—
1956	*Xue Pinggui and Wang Baochuan*	Huaxing	250,000	300,000
1965	*Hsi Shih: Beauty of Beauties*	Guolian/Taiwan Studio	23,000,000	5,600,000
1979	*The Pioneers*	CMPC	60,000,000	—
1985	*The Heroic Pioneers*	Taiwan Studio	50,000,000	—
1986	*The Battle of 23 August 1958*	CMPC/Yinfeng	200,000,000	—
1994	*Vive l'amour*	CMPC/Xiongfa	11,000,000	—
2000	*Hidden Whisper*	CMPC	16,000,000	—
2000	*Legend of the Sacred Stone*	Dapili	300,000,000	—
2002	*Double Vision*	Nan Fang/Columbia Asia	US$5,000,000	US$2,000,000 in 3 weeks

Sources: F. Chen 1988: 13–14; H. Chiao 1993: 118; Du 1988: 614; Guojia dianying 1996: 112; R. Huang 1994b: 35, 141; F. Lu 1998: 74–8; S. Lü 1961: 41–2; Rosen 2002a; Yeh *et al*. 1999: 46.

Note: All currencies in NT$ unless otherwise indicated.

Na'ou and Luo Peng, for example) were inspired by mainland productions and joined the Shanghai film circles.

As the world's leading film-producing country by 1925, Japan consistently dominated the Taiwan market, pouring in over 1,000 titles every year after 1927. Between 1926 and 1928, Japanese films accounted for 70 per cent of annual film imports, and the figure rose to 80 per cent in 1929–30, compared with 10 per cent each for Hollywood and China (Ye 1998: 123, 208). Although the figure declined to 63 per cent in 1935, it was far better than Hollywood (18 per cent) and China (6 per cent). In 1940, among the 2,760 titles which were submitted to the Japanese censors, 2,234 came from Japan (89.9 per cent), 422 from the US (15.3 per cent), 53 from Germany (1.9 per cent), 31 from France (1.1 per cent), six from Manchuria (0.2 per cent) and two from China (0.07 per cent) (Ye 1998: 292). The dismal figure from China was the result of the government's ban on mainland imports starting in 1937, but upon petitions a few Shanghai releases, such as *Mulan Joins the Army* and *Princess Iron Fan*, were screened in 1942 (F. Chen 1988: 23–4; Ye 1998: 284). Replacing Shanghai films, the Man'ei products were regularly imported, and many of them showcased the popular star Li Xianglan, who visited Taiwan in 1941 and 1943.[3]

In 1941 there were forty-nine movie theaters in Taiwan, sixteen of them in Taipei alone. The Japanese and the Taiwanese owned nineteen theaters each, and the rest were owned by film companies (nine) and a municipality (one). There were, of course, more theaters that showed both stage plays and films, and the figure for such venues in the island was 168 in 1944, with twenty-eight movie theaters and sixty stage theaters (see Table 4.3). In the early 1940s, 70 per cent of movie audiences were Japanese and 30 per cent Taiwanese. This was partly because of the dominance of Japanese films and partly because of increasing Japanese immigration to Taiwan due to the Pacific War. In 1938, for instance, 308,845 Japanese lived in the island, when the population was estimated at 5.7 million (Du 1988: 454; Ye 1998: 209, 295). After the war, 480,000 Japanese soldiers, officials and their families were shipped from Taiwan to Japan in 1945 (F. Chen 1988: 32).

In 1941 the colonial governor's office set up the Taiwan Cinema Association in charge of all distribution on the island. The Association also produced newsreels and assisted the Japanese studios in shooting feature films in Taiwan. Not surprisingly, these wartime productions were propagandist in nature and exhorted the Japanese colonial efforts in the Asia-Pacific region. Significantly, very few Han Taiwanese participated in these productions, which cast indigenous peoples as extras instead. Overall, during the colonial era, the Japanese controlled production, and a true Taiwan film industry was not established until the 1950s.

The chaotic postwar market, 1945–54

As on the mainland, the KMT officials confiscated Japanese-owned film facilities and about twenty theaters in Taiwan and founded Taiwan Studio in Taipei

Table 4.3 Movie theaters and annual attendance in Taiwan, 1941–94

Year	Theaters	Seats	Attendance (million)	Approved films	Visits per capita
1941	49	—	—	—	—
—	—	—	—	—	—
1944	30	—	—	—	—
1945	40	—	—	—	—
1946	17	—	—	—	—
1947	—	—	—	—	—
1948	20	—	—	—	—
1949	39	—	—	—	—
1950	—	—	—	597	4
1951	71	—	—	766	—
1952	—	—	—	—	—
1953	347	173,500	—	—	—
—	—	—	—	—	—
1959	—	410,000	67	—	7
1960	—	—	—	—	—
1961	474	—	94	—	8.6
1962	508	251,000	95	—	8.4
1963	574	297,000	96	—	8.2
1964	617	330,000	110	—	9.1
1965	638	343,000	119	—	9.6
1966	693	372,000	127	—	9.9
1967	730	402,000	133	—	10.1
1968	759	422,000	152	—	11.3
1969	799	440,000	164	—	11.7
1970	826	441,000	180	—	12.4
1971	700	367,000	156	—	10.5
1972	645	330,000	134	—	8.9
1973	554	314,000	135	—	8.7
1974	499	312,000	135	—	8.6
1975	478	312,000	134	—	8.4
1976	475	359,000	156	409	9.6
1977	481	355,000	175	—	10.5
1978	483	416,000	164	—	9.4
1979	594	548,000	216	—	12.5
1980	551	482,000	229	—	13
1981	602	516,000	250	578	13.9
1982	704	528,000	192	579	10.5
1983	736	553,000	135	579	8.1
1984	717	543,000	—	523	—
1985	602	516,000	—	457	—
1986	577	486,000	—	464	—
1987	568	480,000	—	533	—
1988	534	447,000	—	637	—
1989	456	406,000	—	791	—
1990	370	—	—	506	—
1991	343	—	—	500	—
1992	282	—	—	514	—

Table 4.3—Continued

Year	Theaters	Seats	Attendance (million)	Approved films	Visits per capita
1993	247	—	—	437	—
1994	255	—	—	377	—

Sources: F. Chen 1988: 29, 37–8, 47–9; F. Lu 1998: 42, Table 20e.

in 1945 and a distribution–exhibition company in 1948. Immediately after the war, the KMT censors banned all Japanese films as well as Japanese dialogue and subtitles in films. Consequently, exhibitors dug out their stock of old Chinese silent features banned during the war, and also hastily arranged the shipment of over 100 Shanghai films to Taiwan. Many of these were genre films from postwar Shanghai and Hong Kong studios such as Guotai and Great China (Da Zhonghua), but some were Man'ei and Shanghai occupation-period titles then banned in the mainland. Others, still, recycled the prewar Mingxing and Yihua releases. As these commercial pictures flooded the market, the audience was overwhelmed and soon turned to the more exotic Hollywood imports, many of them color features. In 1948 KMT's Central Film and Changchun studios teamed up with Wenhua and Kunlun and set up a distribution office in Taiwan, and a number of quality Shanghai titles, such as *Spring River Flows East* and *Spring in a Small Town*, were exhibited to enthusiastic Taiwan audiences. Even so, Chinese films made up a mere 20 per cent of the market, whereas Hollywood and Europe claimed over 70 per cent of the market share.

The number of distribution companies in Taiwan grew from four in 1948 to over thirty in 1951, but a lack of communication sometimes led to two different distributors acquiring the same print and thus created a chaotic exhibition situation. Even worse, the KMT retreat to Taiwan in 1949 meant the end of the exhibition of most mainland movies because filmmakers who stayed in the mainland were automatically classified as Communist supporters and their films were therefore banned (Ye 1995: 145–8). Many Mandarin films produced in Hong Kong were also banned in Taiwan because of the studios' or the filmmakers' affiliations with the PRC. Seizing this opportunity, Hong Kong distributors started to dub politically neutral Cantonese films with Mandarin soundtracks, while making new prints of whatever old films they could find from the mainland and Southeast Asia and dumping them in Taiwan. According to an official estimate, among the 236 Mandarin films in exhibition in 1951, only forty-one were new features (17.4 per cent), compared with 121 new features (24 per cent) out of 505 Hollywood films exhibited in the same year (F. Chen 1988: 47). Since Taiwan produced just three features in 1952, the majority of 'domestic' films came from Hong Kong. Thus, hidden behind the Hollywood dominance in Taiwan was the ascendance of Hong Kong films.

In August 1950, once-banned Japanese films began to make an appearance in Taiwan. Since over half of the seven million people in Taiwan understood Japanese at the time, the exhibition of Japanese films was a highly profitable business. Ticket prices were higher for Japanese films than for Western films, and the estimated attendance rate for the former was twice that of the latter. No wonder, then, that distribution companies of Japanese films rapidly grew to ten in 1951. However, Japanese films were banned again in Taiwan in 1952, and this on again off again banning of Japanese imports, which would occur in the following decades, reveals a fundamental difference in the perception of Japan between the KMT government and the Taiwan population. The chief beneficiary of the resumed ban of Japanese films was Hollywood, which claimed over half of the market share in 1954, compared with 23.4 per cent for other foreign countries. In particular, Hollywood technological break-throughs such as 3-D and widescreen met with considerable public interest in 1954.

Some film historians consider the immediate postwar years a time of 'decay' or even 'destruction' for Taiwan cinema.[4] To prevent public demonstrations like the 28 February Incident, the KMT government declared martial law in Taiwan and its neighboring islands in May 1949, which would remain in effect until July 1987. Additional regulations soon followed, and 7.5 million Taiwan people were denied freedom of speech, freedom of press and freedom of public demonstration (Du 1988: 455; R. Huang 1994b: 5). The exhibition sector was hit hard in the wake of the 28 February Incident and the once-bustling evening shows disappeared due to a government curfew. As in postwar Shanghai, rising inflation drove ticket prices in Taiwan from 20 yuan in early 1946 to 120 yuan in late 1947, 3,000 yuan in late 1948, 10,000 yuan in April 1949 and 40,000 in May 1949. The situation was stabilized slightly with the new Taiwan currency (NT$) reform in June 1949, which converted old Taiwan currency, 40,000 yuan to NT$1. Nonetheless, ticket prices still rose from NT$2.3 in Taipei (compared with the average NT$1.5 elsewhere) in June 1949 to NT$3.7–NT$5 at the first-run theaters in February 1950 (see Table 4.1, p. 115). This is because the prices now had absorbed the newly imposed defense tax of 100–200 per cent, in addition to other miscellaneous taxes (Ye 1995: 75–6).[5]

In 1951 there were 122 theaters in Taiwan (down from 168 in 1944), seventy-one of them exclusively for movies. Out of these seventy-one theaters, only seven specialized in Chinese films, while thirty-eight showed Western films, and the remainder showed both Western and Chinese. In 1950, film-related spending in Taiwan was NT$35.6 million, and movie attendance per capita was four times per year (see Table 4.3, pp. 120–1), much higher than any mainland province. The number of theaters reached 347 in 1953 (F. Chen 1988: 37–8, 49).

The prolonged postwar economic and political instability prevented private investors in Taiwan from venturing into film production. Apart from a few mainland studios that came to Taiwan for location shooting in 1947–8 (F. Lu

1998: 33), the only exception was *Wind and Cloud on Ali Mountain* (Alishan fengyun, dir. Zhang Ying, Zhang Che, 1949). Shanghai's Guotai had sent the directors of the film to Taiwan for location shooting earlier in 1949, but the KMT debacle in the mainland had left them stranded. By this time, Guotai's former studio head Xu Xinfu had also relocated to Taiwan. He quickly set up the Wanxiang Company and helped the directors complete the film, which became the first Mandarin sound picture in Taiwan.

As in the 1932 silent movie about Wu Feng, *Wind and Cloud on Ali Mountain* portrayed the aboriginal people as 'savages' and Wu Feng as a self-sacrificing hero. The historical parallels between Wu Feng 'enlightening' the aboriginal people and the KMT 'educating' the Taiwanese about peaceful coexistence thus adds extra significance to *Wind and Cloud on Ali Mountain*. Indeed, this parallel between the KMT and the Japanese colonial government can also be seen in that both used Wu Feng as a legendary 'peacemaker' in times of political instability. Little wonder that, when the Taiwan Studio produced *Wu Feng* (Wu Feng, dir. Bu Wancang, 1962), its leader argued that Wu's story proved that the Taiwanese had originated from the mainland and that the spirit of self-sacrifice was crucial to the anti-Communist cause (R. Huang 1994b: 208).

State-run studios and 'policy films'

By the end of 1949, the KMT had shipped to Taiwan what they could from their mainland studios – Central Film, China Motion Pictures, as well as China Agricultural Education Studio (Nongjiao) founded in Nanjing in 1946. By one estimate, the KMT now claimed a small 5 per cent of the total film facilities and personnel in China, Hong Kong 15 per cent, and the PRC 80 per cent (Du 1988: 460). In addition to Taiwan Studio (under the provincial government), which had been producing newsreels and documentaries, the KMT reopened China Motion Pictures in Taipei (under the Ministry of Defense) and established Agricultural Education Film Company (under the KMT central committee).

Given its special circumstance, the relocation of the KMT film facilities to Taiwan meant several consequences (F. Lu 1998: 35–7). First, like never before, the KMT had complete control over film without any formidable industrial or political opposition, and its studios assumed a leading role in Taiwan because the private studios that had dominated the prewar and postwar productions now either stayed in Shanghai or moved to Hong Kong. Second, since the relocated KMT personnel came from the administrative, documentary and technical departments of filmmaking rather than directing and screenwriting, the Shanghai tradition of humanist – not to mention leftist – films was suspended in Taiwan. Third, the predominance of KMT ideology in the relocated film personnel spelled the end of political tension characterizing the Shanghai era and thus implied the loss of another Shanghai film tradition, that of liberal and radical critiques of the sociopolitical status quo. Finally, since there was no tradition of film production in Taiwan, Taiwan cinema had to develop its own strategies in attracting domestic as well as overseas audiences, strategies that involved political interference (vis-à-vis Taiwanese-dialect cinema), ideological persuasion (vis-à-vis Hong Kong) and state subsidy (vis-à-vis Mandarin cinema).

Nominally headed by Chiang Ching-kuo (Jiang Jingguo), Chiang Kai-shek's elder son and a future ROC president, Agricultural Education Film was lucky to receive a shipment of new film equipment (valued at US$2 million) from the US and was best positioned to launch feature production among all the state studios. To alleviate the anxiety of the newly arrived mainland population of up to 1.5 million (F. Lu 1998: 39), as well as to redirect the pent-up anger of the Taiwanese population under martial law, the KMT promoted anti-Communist literature and art in Taiwan. Agricultural Education Film utilized its cutting-edge equipment and borrowed personnel from other studios to start feature production. The immediate result was *Awakening from a Nightmare* (Emeng chuxing, dir. Zong You, 1950), the first anti-Communist picture, co-produced with China Motion Pictures, which depicts the suffering of a patriotic woman and her family during the Communist revolution.

In early 1951 the KMT government offered subsidies to any film promoting its new agricultural policy of reduced tax rates (down to 37.5 per cent of the harvest). In response, Wu Shuxun, the former head of China Motion Pictures, organized Dahua and traveled to Hong Kong to recruit a cast and borrow equipment. Unwilling to offend the PRC, many Hong Kong stars declined Wu's invitation. But Wu managed to produce *Spring in the Countryside* (Chunman renjian, dir. Tang Shaohua, 1951), which showed the mutually beneficial relationship between the landlord and the tenant farmers but did poorly at the box office (R. Huang 1994b: 302).

Awakening from a Nightmare and *Spring in the Countryside* represented the KMT policy of 'resisting Communism and recovering the nation', which translated into film narratives exposing CCP brutality on the one hand and applauding the KMT accomplishments in Taiwan on the other. From 1951 to 1954, Agricultural Education produced seven such 'policy films' as well as numerous documentaries, some shot for and subsidized by other government agencies. Because propaganda films rarely sold well, Agricultural Education had to lease its equipment to other studios, for instance to a Hong Kong company shooting a feature in May 1954. In September 1954, under Chiang Kai-shek's instructions, Agricultural Education and a state-owned distribution–exhibition company merged to become the Central Motion Picture Company (CMPC), a 'party-owned' enterprise that would emerge as a major player in Taiwan cinema in the subsequent decades.[6]

China Motion Pictures had lost much of its personnel to the financially more stable Agricultural Education after their co-production in 1950. The separation of its personnel in Taipei, its technology office in Taichung (a central city) and the majority of its equipment in Kaohsiung (a southern city) put China Motion

Pictures at a disadvantage. After its 1951 release of an anti-Japanese spy movie shot in Shanghai before the retreat, the studio did not make any feature films until 1954. In comparison, Taiwan Studio was in better shape because at least it had a studio and had purchased equipment for making 35mm films. To compete with its counterparts, the studio head Yuan Congmei, a wartime veteran, directed *Poppy* (Yingsu hua, 1954), an anti-Communist spy film set in Macao, which portrays the female lead as a seductive Communist and uses her subsequent 'awakening' as a testimony to the danger of Communist brainwashing.

TWO COMPETING CINEMAS, 1955–69

While the state studios continued to produce policy films in the 1950s, private studios discovered a gold mine in Taiwanese-dialect films. From 1955 to 1969, 1,052 Taiwanese-dialect films were produced, whereas only 373 Mandarin films were released during the same period. For the first time in Taiwan history, a viable industry came into being, which also stimulated the growth of Mandarin cinema in the mid-1960s. In the late 1960s, genre films further strengthened the market links between production, distribution and exhibition, and the annual movie attendance rates were at an all-time high (see Table 4.3, p. 120–1).

The KMT film administration: operations and problems

In 1955 the KMT regime issued film censorship regulations and stipulated the legal consequences of various forms of violations. Among the topics that were censored were 'poisonous' Communist ideology and anything that would benefit the Soviet bloc, erode Taiwanese morale, insult KMT leaders, misrepresent current situations, or expose Taiwan's backwardness (F. Lu 1998: 71). The ambiguity of these terms left ample room for contradictory interpretations, and the increase in political and financial instability thus drove Taiwan cinema away from the realist tradition of Chinese cinema and spawned widespread escapism and stereotypes for at least two decades.

In response to Chiang Kai-shek's idea of 'a belligerent kind of literature and art' (*zhandou wenyi*), the KMT central committee launched a campaign in 1956 to promote such literature and art, and subcommittees were formed at county and city levels to mobilize artists. However, except for a limited number of anti-Communist features, some co-produced by 'overseas Chinese', the campaign produced no substantial result.

The KMT film administration was more effective in its implementation of regulations, subsidies and taxation measures. In terms of regulation, the state set quotas for Japanese imports in 1956 and in return imposed a ratio of Taiwan films to be exported to Japan. In the meantime, quotas were set for all foreign films, restricting the numbers of theaters approved for screening specific foreign films as well as the numbers of foreign prints in circulation.[7] To promote the production of policy films, the state not only provided cash awards and subsidies to studios but also set export ratios, which could be transferred at a high margin of profit.[8] In order to convince Hong Kong investors to produce anti-Communist films, the state treated Hong Kong cinema as 'domestic' and excluded it from restrictions on foreign films, thus keeping the door wide open for Hong Kong's domination in Taiwan's exhibition market over a long period of time. In terms of taxation, the state also sidestepped its high taxes on imported material by arranging a special deal for film equipment. Instead of paying taxes at 100 per cent, the investors could leave their tax deposits at the customs office and reclaim them when shipping out the completed films. Originally designed to attract Hong Kong investors like Huang Zhuohan, this arrangement became an unforeseen incentive to producers of Taiwanese-dialect films, who could actually benefit from importing negatives alone due to tax advantages.[9]

One film critic has pointed out several fundamental problems with the KMT film administration from the 1950s to the 1980s: self-contradictory regulations, inconsistency in administration policy, incompetent administrators, intractable ideological positions and excessive taboos (R. Huang 1994b: 15–24). The KMT central committee defined film as a 'cultural enterprise', but in reality film was treated as 'special entertainment' and was subject to between 30 and 40 per cent sales taxes, a source of constant dispute between the central, provincial and local governments, and which was not removed until 1980. The special entertainment status also required that waitresses at theaters undergo annual health examinations, causing humiliation and a dispute that was not resolved until 1992. The inconsistencies in the administration's policy translated into periodic reassignments of film under different jurisdictions. Film was first placed under the police bureau of the Ministry of Interior, and in 1956 the responsibility was split between a film advisory committee under the Ministry of Education in charge of production and the Government Information Office (GIO, Xinwen ju) in charge of censorship. Because several films recommended by the advisory committee did not clear the GIO censors, film advisory work was transferred to the GIO in 1958. In 1967 film administration was returned to a culture bureau under the Ministry of Education. In 1973, the culture bureau was disbanded and film was turned over to the GIO once again.

Similarly, appointments of 'incompetent' administrators necessitated a frequent turnover of state studio leaderships. For example, after a China Motion Picture release was slighted at the 1956 Asian Film Festival held in Japan, its studio head immediately resigned. In 1959 CMPC's Taichung studios were leased to three private studios shooting three films at the same time, which caused a fire that destroyed two studios and much of the equipment. Under investigation and restructuring, CMPC was hit by two other disasters in 1960: a flood besieged its Taichung facilities in August and another fire erupted in its warehouse and burned 1,507 reels of film. In 1961 alone CMPC changed its leadership twice.

Censorship, however, was the most conspicuous among all the problems. At one point, censorship involved the joint operation of seven branches of the government, such as the bureaux of police and investigation, as well as the Ministries of Defense, Foreign Affairs and Education. Representatives from these branches competed with one another in finding potential fault with films under review. Some 'faults' were understandable in the cold war situation, such as images of Mao Zedong and CCP insignia or scenes of major railroad stations and airports in Taiwan (Ye 1999: 133). However, intractable positions sometimes led to embarrassing 'diplomatic' situations. For instance, *The Chairman* (dir. J. Lee Thompson, 1969), an American anti-Communist espionage film featuring Gregory Peck, was banned in Taiwan simply because it contains Mao's portrait. The same reason was cited for the ban placed on *China Behind* (Zaijian Zhongguo, dir. Tang Shuxuan, 1974), a Hong Kong production that exposes the brutality of the Cultural Revolution. An even more strange case was *Storm Over Jinmen Bay* (Jinmen wan fengyun, dir. Matsuo Akinori, 1963). Co-produced by CMPC (US$20,000) and Nikkatsu (US$180,000), the film is a triangular love story set against the backdrop of the prolonged artillery shelling between the KMT-controlled Jinmen Islands and the PRC coast. The film was exhibited at 150 theaters in Tokyo for eighteen days in 1961, but it was banned in Taiwan for two years because the censors disliked the ending where the Chinese woman is killed on her way to find her Japanese lover. The film was released only after a new ending had been added where her Japanese lover dies instead. The controversy surrounding this film occasioned another turnover in the CMPC leadership in 1963.

Obviously, censorship problems led to financial problems. The majority of 'policy films' did badly at the box office in Taiwan, and because of their anti-Communist message, these films could not be exported to Hong Kong, Singapore and Malaysia – all crucial overseas markets without which the Mandarin film studios in Taiwan would fail to recoup their investments. An average feature production cost NT$600,000, but the total Taiwan box-office returns for a film were estimated at NT$100,000 (S. Lü 1961: 41–2). Financial problems such as these were not restricted to state studios, for numerous private studios, some funded by noted Hong Kong producers like Li Zuyong, either went heavily into debt or closed shop for good after making anti-Communist films (R. Huang 1994b: 25–31).

The ups and downs of Taiwanese-dialect films

One consequence of the martial law rule – also described as 'white terror' – in Taiwan was the silence of Taiwanese intellectuals in film circles, who were never as confrontational as their counterparts in journalism and literature.[10] The successful land reform measures in the early 1950s (such as selling public land to tenant farmers) had significantly improved the economic situation in rural areas and propelled a rapid growth of folk entertainment. A native theater form, *gezaixi*, thus flourished, the number of troupes grew from 160 in 1956 to 235 in 1958. Over the same two years, Taiwanese spoken drama troupes increased from twenty to forty-two (F. Chen 1988: 96–7). In one estimate, 367 theaters were solely devoted to *gezaixi*, exclusive of countless open-air stages in villages and townships (F. Lu 1998: 60). The KMT central committee attempted to ban *gezaixi* in 1950, but the ensuing government 'advice' on *gezaixi* reform was apparently fruitless. With familiar narratives, experienced casts, ready-made costumes and props, and above all devoted audiences, *gezaixi* was a perfect source for an indigenous cinema to explore.

The first Taiwanese-dialect film to emerge was *Six Talents' Romance of the West Chamber* (Liu caizi xixiang ji, dir. Ye Fusheng, 1955), which was shot in 16mm and contained one dream sequence in Eastmancolor. The cast came from the famous Duma Troupe, which originated from the Fujian province across the Taiwan Strait during the colonial era. The director Ye Fusheng had planned to make an opera movie five years before, and the recently successful exhibition in Taiwan of Hong Kong films in Amoy dialect (*Xiayu*, also known as *Minnanhua* or Hokkienese, which is the same as Taiwanese dialect except for tonal differences) but marketed as 'authentic' Taiwanese-dialect films finally convinced him to proceed.[11] Unfortunately, due to inferior techniques and incompatibility of the projection equipment, Ye's film had a depressing three-day run in Taipei in June 1955 (Guojia dianying 1994: 54). It was not until six months later, when *Xue Pinggui and Wang Baochuan* (Xue Pinggui and Wang Baochuan, dir. He Jiming, 1956) showed for twenty-four days in Taipei and grossed over NT$300,000 (with a production cost of NT$250,000, excluding cast and costumes), that the Taiwanese-dialect film became a recognized cultural force (F. Chen 1988: 75).

He Jimin's success energized dialect film production, and, as if overnight, dialect production companies mushroomed, with sixty-four in existence in 1958. Notable among them was Gaohe, which teamed up with He Jimin and produced opera movies and slapstick comedies. For his own Huaxing Studio, He Jimin directed two rare dialect films that dramatize historical anti-Japanese events in Taiwan and pay tribute to Taiwanese resistance heroes (Guojia dianying 1994: 78–108). Another company, Hanxing, used its Jinshan Studio in Taichung to produce numerous popular films awash in 'bitter pathos' (*kuqing*, sentiments characteristic of the *gezaixi* tradition). In five years, Taiwanese-dialect films had regained their 'authentic dialect' status and won the race against the Hong Kong-produced Amoy-dialect films exhibited in Taiwan.[12]

During its first wave (1955–9), Taiwanese-dialect cinema produced 178 titles, four times that of the total Mandarin productions (forty-one) in the same period (see Table 4.4). As with the first wave of Shanghai commercial filmmaking of the mid-1920s, a large proportion of Taiwanese-dialect films were adapted from stage plays – both local operas and spoken dramas (*xinju*) – as well as myths, legends and folk tales, and its artists were deeply immersed in theater traditions. However, unlike the Shanghai example, dialect films also drew from folk ballads,

Table 4.4 Annual feature production in Taiwan, 1949–2002

Year	Total Taiwan-produced	Mandarin films	Taiwanese dialect films	Special film	Total non-Taiwan-produced	Co-productions
1949	1	1	—	—	—	—
1950	1	1	—	—	—	—
1951	3	3	—	—	—	1
1952	3	3	—	—	—	—
1953	5	5	—	—	—	—
1954	1	1	—	—	—	—
1955	8	6	2	—	—	—
1956	18	6	12	—	—	2
1957	66	4	62	—	—	17
1958	76	13	62	1 silent	—	13
1959	52	12	40	—	—	5
1960	26	5	21	—	—	1
1961	44	7	37	—	—	1
1962	128	7	120	1 silent	—	1
1963	97	8	89	—	—	1
1964	120	22	97	1 silent	—	4
1965	138	24	114	—	—	3
1966	151	45	106	—	—	4
1967	142	49	93	—	—	1
1968	189	76	113	—	169	2
1969	173	89	84	—	179	3
1970	117	99	18	—	123	3
1971	114	101	13	—	113	5
1972	81	59	21	1 Hakka	135	1
1973	45	36	8	—	186	—
1974	66	65	1	—	227	2
1975	49	48	1	—	169	2
1976	51	51	—	—	152	—
1977	49	49	—	—	230	5
1978	95	95	—	—	197	—
1979	121	120	1	—	184	7
1980	133	133	—	—	187	1
1981	138	138	—	—	179	5
1982	144	144	—	—	174	1
1983	79	78	—	—	232	5
1984	58	57	1	—	208	2
1985	65	65	—	—	183	1
1986	71	70	1	—	164	4
1987	86	85	1	—	166	5
1988	158	157	1	—	181	4
1989	101	99	2	—	202	9
1990	76	76	—	—	172	6
1991	47	46	1	—	168	5
1992	43	42	1	—	195	5
1993	48	47	—	—	—	13
1994	24	—	—	—	—	5

Table 4.4—Continued

Year	Total Taiwan-produced	Mandarin films	Taiwanese dialect films	Special film	Total non-Taiwan-produced	Co-productions
1995	28	—	—	—	—	—
1996	18	—	—	—	—	—
1997	23	—	—	—	—	1
1998	22	—	—	—	—	—
1999	16	—	—	—	—	—
2000	35	—	—	—	—	—
2001	17	—	—	—	—	—
2002	20	—	—	—	—	—

Sources: GIO 1997: 286; GIO 2001: 285; GIO 2003: 280; T. Li 1997: 251; F. Lu 1998: Tables 5, 11a, 12; Rosen 2002a.

Notes: Non-Taiwan productions are mostly Hong Kong titles but also include those titles resubmitted to the censors.

Since the mid-1990s a number of productions have each year failed to obtain theatrical release; some have waited for a couple of years before commercial exhibition while others have gone straight to video or television.

popular songs, news reports, and sometimes even Japanese sources (Du 1988: 501; R. Huang 1994a). *Madwoman's Eighteen Years* (Fengnü shibanian, dir. Bai Ke, 1957) is a tearjerker about a suffering woman who fakes madness to escape prostitution and who endures eighteen years of confinement in an outdoor wooden cage until she is rescued by welfare workers. Based on a real-life story and a script by Du Yunzhi, the film had over 160 screenings and made the female lead Xiao Yanqiu an instant star (F. Chen 1988: 76–7).

Lacking real directing talents, the dialect film producers actively recruited people from Mandarin cinema, such as Bai Ke, Xu Xingfu and Zhang Yi. Not surprisingly, dialect productions provided a much needed training ground for future Mandarin directors. For instance, Li Xing's directorial debut was a dialect comedy, *Brothers Wang and Liu Tour Taiwan* (Wang ge Liu ge you Taiwan, 1959), which unraveled Taiwan's cultural and natural scenery so as to ease the tension between the mainlanders and the Taiwanese, something he continued in his subsequent Mandarin projects.

In 1960 dialect productions fell to twenty-one (down 90.5 per cent from forty in 1959), due to a combination of factors. A flood in August 1959 had devastated the economy in central and southern Taiwan, the added flood relief taxes and complimentary screenings for soldiers had placed extra burdens on the exhibitors, and the smuggled Japanese films had posed a serious threat to dialect producers. Yet, dialect production regained momentum in 1961 (thirty-seven titles) and surged to a record high in 1962 (120 titles), altogether adding up to 874 in its second wave (1960–9) (see Table 4.4). This second wave benefited from several government measures. The 10 to 20 per cent reduction in import taxes helped the purchase of film material, and a crackdown on smuggled Japanese films and the suspension of Japanese films beyond the first runs added market competitiveness to domestic productions.[13] The incremental decrease of imported films, which fell from over 400 in the 1960s to around 275 per year in the 1970s, and lower ticket prices due to the elimination of defense taxes, further boosted the filmmakers' confidence (F. Lu 1998: 109–14).

Reflecting contemporary socioeconomic changes in Taiwan, the second wave saw dialect releases that addressed issues of social problems in comic and melo-dramatic forms, and many films began to exhibit a fresh upbeat ambience. In terms of cultural values, dialect films now increasingly addressed contemporary issues, as the migration of the rural population to urban areas and the aging dialect audiences gradually chipped away the foundation of dialect cinema. *The Last Train from Kaohsiung* (Gaoxiong fade weiban che, 1963; b/w) and *Early Train from Taipei* (Taibei fade zaoban che, 1964; b/w), two melodramas about moral and sexual degradation in evil cities directed by Liang Zhefu, were representative of the new thematic reorientation in dialect films. Occasionally, directors also ventured into historical films, as in *The Opium War* (Yapian zhanzheng, dir. Li Quanxi, 1963; b/w), partially to please the censors. In the late 1960s, dialect films participated in genre experiments concurrent in Mandarin cinema, expanding from costume drama and ethical melodrama to urban romance, martial arts, fantasy, science fiction, detective, gangster and espionage (J. Liao 2001: 94–5; Ye 1999: 200–3). In the process of genre expansion, dialect films had acquired certain transnational or transregional characteristics, and their new themes and styles reinforced connections between Taiwan and Hong Kong, Japan, Hollywood as well as Southeast Asia (Liao 2001: 94–5; Ye 1999: 200–3). In addition to securing overseas markets in the Philippines, Vietnam, Singapore, Malaysia and South Korea, dialect films also entered co-productions with Japan with mixed casts from Japan and Taiwan (R. Huang 1994a: 19–20).

Nonetheless, the nature of speculation restricted the artistic and thematic reorientation in the Taiwanese-dialect film, and speedy production and low pro-duction values severely hurt its competitiveness. Whereas Mandarin cinema had turned to color, widescreen big-budget productions since the mid-1960s, the majority of dialect films remained black and white. Lin Fudi, a leading dialect director, admitted that it was not unusual for him to complete a film in seven days, and the average dialect production schedule was twelve to thirteen days. Like him, directors in demand were pushed to the limits, routinely sleeping only two or three hours a day (Chiao 1993: 242).[14]

As Mandarin cinema gained momentum, and even though they would earn less (see Table 4.5), Lin and other directors left dialect production and joined the former. By the late 1960s, dialect films had lost the race with Mandarin cinema. In 1969 Mandarin productions (eighty-nine) exceeded dialect films (eight-four)

Table 4.5 Salary comparison in Taiwan, 1950s–80s

Year	Pay (NT$)	Name	Job	Studio
mid-1950s	5,000/title	—	director	—
mid-1950s	1,000/title	—	scriptwriter	—
early 1960s	35,000/title	Lin Fudi	dialect film director	—
mid-1960s	30,000/month	Lin Fudi	Mandarin film director	Guolian
mid-1960s	5,000–10,000/month	—	dialect film star	—
mid-1960s	1,400/month	Zhen Zhen	new Mandarin actress	Guolian
mid-1960s	70,000/month	Song Cunshou	Mandarin film director	Guolian
1965	2,000–3,000/month	Yang Qun	new Mandarin actor	Guolian
1967	8,000/month	Yang Qun	Mandarin star	Guolian
late 1960s	100,000/title	—	star on loan to others	Guolian
early 1980s	60,000/title	Chu Yen-ping	new director	—
mid-1980s	2,600,000/title	Hsu Pu-liao	star comedian	—

Sources: Chiao 1993: 238, 252, 260; L. Ye 1999: 71.

for the first time in history, although the latter were still impressive in total numbers. But such numbers were deceptive because hundreds of completed dialect films did not get exhibited in theaters due to overproduction (F. Lu 1998: 161). From 1970 on, Mandarin titles consistently outnumbered dialect films: while the former increased to 101 in 1971, the latter dropped to one in 1974 and none in 1976 (see Table 4.4, pp. 129–30).

Taiwanese-dialect films have received increasing scholarly attention in Taiwan since the mid-1990s (J. Liao 2001: 29–32). Ye Longyan believes that dialect films are particularly significant in terms of cultural history. First, through work-shops, they trained film and future television talents. Second, they promoted indigenous culture and produced cross-media ventures in dialect radio shows and records of dialect songs. Third, by their very popularity, they increased the ethnic, regional and linguistic integration among the diverse Taiwan population. Moreover, the dialect production produced women directors, such as Chen Wenmin and Wang Manjiao, the first such group in Taiwan's film history (Ye 1999: 114–15, 237–55), which parallels the emergence of women directors in socialist China.

Healthy realism: a turning point in Mandarin cinema

In March 1963 Gong Hong left the GIO and assumed leadership of the troubled CMPC. Turning away from his predecessor's policy of co-production with Japan, Gong promoted 'healthy realism' as a way out for Mandarin cin-ema. From the start, Gong specifically envisioned healthy realism as something different from European realist films that expose darkness, poverty and social evils. In general, healthy realism was in agreement with the KMT cultural pol-icy as defined by Zhang Daofan's 'six no's': 'no privileging of social darkness, no instigation of class hatred, no pessimistic tones, no romantic sentiments, no meaningless creation and no erroneous ideology' (F. Lu 1998: 103–4). Healthy realism in essence thus differs from postwar Italian neo-realism and comes closer to the Soviet version of socialist realism, with emphasis more on *idealism* perceived as 'healthy' (*jiankang*) than on 'realism' (*xieshi*) that tends to be critical of the status quo. Envisioned as such, healthy realism marks a decisive departure from both the private studios' commercial operations and the state studios' anti-Communist stereotypes. But ironically, in terms of pro-jecting a utopian future, healthy realism inadvertently aligns itself with the kind of socialist realism that the CCP promoted in mainland films in the 1950s and 1960s.[15]

Reputedly the 'first realistic work' in Taiwan was *Head of the Street, End of the Lane* (Jietou xiangwei, 1963; b/w), which Li Xing directed for the private com-pany Independence (Zili). Following the daily life of a poverty-stricken group of displaced mainlanders and destitute Taiwanese in a slum courtyard, the film exhorts their virtues of simplicity, honesty, altruism, solidarity, perseverance and optimism. Little girl Zhu's father died in a mining accident years ago and her sick mother struggles to raise her. Neighbors help in whatever way they can. Granny provides meals from time to time. Garbage-picking Shi brings home medicine for Zhu's mother, who refuses to sell Zhu when conversing with her prostitute neighbor Lili in Taiwanese dialect. Zhu's mother dies one rainy evening while Zhu is doing homework. A series of shots of a hillside grave, withered trees, and the sunset are followed by those of Shi and Zhu cheerfully picking garbage and eating noodles by a street, as well as Shi restlessly sleeping in a single bed he uses in turn with tricyclist Chen.

Zhu's teacher visits Shi and persuades him to send Zhu to school again. One day, Zhu returns home crying because her schoolmates have ridiculed her for being dependent on a garbage-picker. Shi tries to learn other trades – riding tricycles, selling newspapers, polishing shoes and carrying advertisement boards – but soon exhausts himself. To help Shi to recover, Zhu skips classes and sells lottery tickets and apples on the streets; she even sells her pet dog. Zhu's teacher visits Shi to complain about Zhu's lack of concentration. Shi blames Zhu but embraces her in tears once he learns the truth. Shi decides to work as a miner but breaks his leg. Again, his neighbors chip in – Chen sells his tricycle and Granny offers jewelry (her funeral savings) – and pay for the surgery. In the meantime, Lili's husband, a hooligan who has lived off the money she has earned through prostitution, is arrested for dealing in drugs, and Lili is all too happy to rejoin the 'big family' in the courtyard. The film ends with the beginning of another day, with Lili washing clothes, Chen going out in his tricycle, and Zhu following Shi to pick garbage.

Announced at the film's outset as 'a story of the poor set in an urban corner, with love but without hatred' , *Head of the Street, End of the Lane* is imprinted with contemporary politics. In one scene, Granny weeps when she fails to find her long lost son among the newly rescued mainland refugees. To ease her worries that the mainland people can barely survive the widespread famine, Shi reasons that they will all return home once the mainland is recovered. Nonetheless, the film concentrates on the immediate problem of survival in Taiwan and subtly suggests the integration of mainlanders and Taiwanese. Chen and Lili have apparently fallen in love, and Shi has assumed his new role as the surrogate father of an orphaned Taiwanese girl. In terms of its sympathetic portrayal of the lower classes and their impoverished but dignified lives, *Head of the Street, End of the Lane* not only conveys the bitter pathos characteristic of Taiwanese-dialect films but is also reminiscent of the social realism of 1930s Shanghai films like *Goddess* and *Song of the Fishermen*.

Since *Head of the Street, End of the Lane* exemplified the idea of healthy realism, CMPC recruited Li Xing, who co-directed with Li Jia *Oyster Girl* (Kenü, 1964), the first widescreen color feature completed entirely in Taiwan, and directed *Beautiful Duckling* (Yangya renjia, 1964), an equally successful follow-up. To enhance the 'healthy' appearance, these two films reduce realistic images of poverty and foreground uplifting scenes of collective labor, modern reconstruction and bountiful harvests in rural settings, thus presenting a completely new look for the otherwise formulaic state products. Similar to the humanist tradition of the pre-1950 mainland cinema, Li's films concentrate on family values, dramatize separation and suffering, and represent women as the embodiment of both traditional virtues and a modern outlook. Such cinematic integration of tradition and modernity continued in subsequent CMPC productions and reflected a more *positive* vision of the future than the one outlined in the majority of dialect films set in contemporary times.

In one of its posters, CMPC presented *Oyster Girl* as 'a giant work that signifies the take-off of domestic productions, a challenge to the stage of international cinema and a march toward overseas markets' (F. Lu 1998: 105). Amid great anticipation, *Oyster Girl* won the best picture award at the Asian Film Festival held in Taipei in 1964 – at the time, the highest honor for a Taiwan film – and *Beautiful Duckling* won a few awards at the same festival held in Tokyo in 1965. From then on, Taiwan productions claimed all Golden Horse best picture awards until 1988, when Hong Kong productions regained their prestige as they had done at the first two Golden Horse Awards. *Oyster Girl* had two separate runs (72 days) in 1964, grossed NT$2 million and made it to the year's Chinese top ten list, a rare honor for a Taiwan production. *Oyster Girl* and *Beautiful Duckling* also sold well in Hong Kong, Singapore and Malaysia and set a high standard of expectation of Taiwan cinema in these countries (F. Lu 1998: 107).

By the early 1970s, Mandarin cinema had developed a stable overseas market in Southeast Asia and North America, a market capable of returning the upwards of 60 per cent of the investment on a given film (F. Chen 1988: 113). But this impressive success took more than healthy realism or CMPC itself to achieve, as the rise of genre films engineered by Hong Kong and Taiwan artists by the mid-1960s had made a definitive contribution to the rebirth of Mandarin cinema.

The rise of genre films in the 'golden age'

The period between 1964 and 1969 has been referred to as a 'golden age' in Taiwan cinema not only because of the rise of Mandarin cinema but also because of the number of consistent releases, from 84 to 114 titles each year in the second wave of Taiwanese-dialect films (F. Chen 1988; F. Lu 1998). While the combined annual Mandarin and dialect productions remained steadily between 120 and 189 from 1964 to 1969, Mandarin cinema climbed from eight in 1963 to twenty-two in 1964 and soared to eighty-nine in 1969 (see Table 4.4, pp. 129–30). Apart from the benefits enumerated above in the account of the second dialect wave, the growing student population and their familiarity with Mandarin as a result of its legitimization as the standard 'national language' also played a role in the increasing popularity of Mandarin cinema (F. Lu 1998: 116).

In the golden age, the number of private production companies surged from forty-one in 1963 to 129 in 1969. The number of movie theaters rose from

Figure 4.1 A poster for *Oyster Girl* (1964): an example of Taiwan's healthy realism in film

617 in 1964 to 826 in 1970. Correspondingly, movie attendance increased from 110 million in 1964 to 180 million in 1970, and the average attendance rates per person rose from 9.1 times in 1964 to 12.4 times in 1970 (see Table 4.3, pp. 120–1). The steady increase of entertainment spending was consistent with economic growth in Taiwan from 1963 to 1972 at an average annual rate of 18.5 per cent, including five years each over 20 per cent (F. Chen 1988: 123–5).

In retrospect, 1963 was indeed an eventful year for film. First, the publicity surrounding healthy realism signaled an impending breakthrough in state studio productions. Second, Qiong Yao published 'Outside the Window' – a sentimental love story that soon spawned a new type of film romance. Third, the success of *The Love Eterne* (Liang Shanboyu Zhu Yingtai, dir. Li Hanxiang), a Shaw Brothers opera movie, exerted an enormous impact in Taiwan, and the subsequent operation of Li Hanxiang's Guolian (Grand Film Company) fundamentally changed Mandarin cinema in the island. To say the least, what came out of this eventful year was the popularity of genre films that launched the 'take-off' of Mandarin cinema and sustained its spectacular rise in the golden age.

Li Hanxiang, Guolian and the emergent studio system

In May 1963, *The Love Eterne* had a huge success in Taiwan and set records for the longest theater run (186 days), screenings (930), tickets sold (721,929,

Figure 4.2 The Love Eterne (1963): a popular Hong Kong opera movie in Taiwan

approximately 90 per cent of the Taipei population at the time) and box office (NT$8.4 million) (F. Chen 1988: 116; Chiao 1993: 17).[16] Fans went to see the film repeatedly, some reportedly up to 100 times. After the movie won several major prizes at the second Golden Horse Awards, 200,000 fans crowded the airport and its adjacent streets when the actress Ling Bo, who was given a special acting prize for her cross-dressing role as Liang Shanbo, arrived for the award ceremony. For safety reasons, Ling Bo was secretly escorted out of the airport in a police vehicle, but to satisfy her fans, she was paraded in a car the next day to 180,000 people lining the streets and Taipei was turned into a 'frenzied city' (F. Chen 1988: 118).

As an immediate result of such frenzy, theater chains specializing in Chinese films expanded from one to six in Taiwan, and 80 per cent of Taipei theaters now regularly showed Mandarin films (F. Lu 1998: 114). Another, far more significant, result was Li Hanxiang's decision to cut short his contract with Shaw Brothers' and set up Guolian in Taiwan in December 1963. Li had been instrumental in making Shaw Brothers a dominant force in Hong Kong cinema (see Chapter 5) but believed that his boss and colleagues had treated him unfairly (Chiao 1993: 191–200). In the meantime, Union Film (Lianbang), a leading distributor–exhibitor in Taiwan, also felt slighted because they had recently given up Shaw Brothers' distribution rights in Taiwan because of the latter's outrageous prices and the first big hit they had missed was *The Love Eterne*. In retaliation, Union Film turned to Cathay (Guotai) based in Singapore, which operated MP&GI (Motion Picture & General Investment, Dianmao or Dianying maoye) in Hong Kong and had been the biggest rival of Shaw Brothers for years. Together, Union Film and Cathay successfully attracted Li Hanxiang to Taiwan (HKFA 2002: 142–9).

Guolian took its name from Cathay (Guo[tai]) and Union Film (Lian[bang]), which promised to fund Li Hanxiang HK$400,000 (or NT$2.8–3.2 million) per film, at four films per year. Early Guolian releases, which used the production facilities of Taiwan Studio, fall largely in the genre of costume drama, some on an epic scale. For instance, *Hsi Shih: Beauty of Beauties* (Xi Shi, dir. Li Hanxiang, 1965) was a two-part, 220-minute blockbuster that cost Guolian and Taiwan Studio between NT$23 and 26 million and fifteen months to produce. Evidently influenced by Hollywood epics such as *Cleopatra* (dir. Joseph Mankiewicz, 1963), Li thus set an unprecedented example at a time when average production costs were merely a few million (Chiao 1993: 30, 117–18, 199).

Unfortunately, five days before *Hsi Shih* began shooting, Guolian suffered a fatal blow. In June 1964 Li's chief supporters, Loke Wan Tho (Lu Yuntao, 1915–64) of Cathay, Xia Weitang of Union Film and Long Fang of Taiwan Studio, died in a plane crash in Taichung. The tragedy derailed a plan that could have brought to Taiwan an investment of US$5 million from overseas (F. Lu 1998: 109). Nevertheless, following Guolian's earlier successes, *Hsi Shih* was number one of the 1965 top ten Chinese films, reaching 30 million viewers and raking in over NT$5.6 million at the box office (Chiao 1993: 118; R. Huang 2001: 53).

However, Li Hanxiang's procrastination in production, extravagant expenditure in non-production areas and incompetent financial management soon left Guolian in a shaky position. For instance, his glossy promotional magazines alone incurred a deficit of NT$4–5 million (Chiao 1993: 247). By 1966 Taiwan Studio refused to lease its facilities to Guolian because of reputed overdue payments, but Li Hanxiang still forged ahead and borrowed more money to build his dream studio. In 1967 Li owed his employees eight months of salaries and was unable to pay his mounting bills. Worse yet, by insisting on using a former drug-addict to direct an anti-Japanese espionage film (which had been delayed many times and was never released), Li offended his new bosses at Cathay and Union Film, who refused to bail him out. Later in 1967 Li was forced out of the leadership, and to manage Guolian's debts the government appointed a financial group, which raised NT$6 million and purchased the studio, renamed it 'Tongyi', and produced a few more films as Guolian releases until 1970, with or without Li's actual involvement.

A bitter Li nonetheless continued his creative work for Guolian and CMPC, consolidating his reputation as a unique director whose films most frequently made it to the annual top ten lists in Taipei. Li's career stalled again when he was investigated as a CCP suspect and prohibited from leaving the island. This was the last straw; in 1971 Li managed to escape to Hong Kong via Tokyo (Chiao 1993: 217). In 1972 he rejoined Shaw Brothers and invented new genres in Hong Kong cinema.

In its five-year stint, Guolian had made a tremendous impact on Taiwan cinema. First, it encouraged private companies to produce Mandarin cinema and thus aborted Shaw Brothers' plan to monopolize the Taiwan market. Second, it challenged the state studios and through co-productions raised their standards and helped them become competitive in the market. Third, it fostered the concept of an emergent studio system with emphasis on actors' training, production teamwork (regular roundtable discussions), high artistic values, effective publicity and overseas marketing. Fourth, it trained new talents in acting and production, such as Qin Han and Song Cunshou, and intentionally de-emphasized the star system then widely practiced in Hong Kong. Fifth, a number of Guolian's releases, like *The Winter* (Dongnuan, dir. Li Hanxiang, 1969), constituted rare examples of cinematic realism, which resembled the 1930s Shanghai tradition and foreshadowed similar attempts in New Taiwan Cinema. Finally, Guolian's eight adaptations of Qiong Yao's fiction contributed to the craze for this new sub-genre of romance in the subsequent decade (F. Chen 1988: 120–3; Chiao 1993: 69–70).

Qiong Yao's romance and King Hu's swordplay

The craze for Qiong Yao's romance stories started when three films adapted from her work were released in 1965. Among them was *The Silent Wife* (Yanü qingshen, dir. Li Xing, 1965), a story about a virtuous mute wife abandoned by her husband but still dedicated to serving her husband's parents without complaint, which became a box-office hit. *The Silent Wife* and two other Qiong Yao adaptations made it to the annual top ten lists during the decade (F. Lu 1998: 135).

Qiong Yao's romances have a unique formula. Her stories involve love triangles and dramatize the differences between genders, generations, geographical regions and social classes, thus they construct a fictional world overwhelmed by emotions. Time and again, incessant tribulations, constant misunderstanding and unrelenting social prejudice keep the romantic couples from consummating their love. In particular, female characters are forced to suffer mistreatment, endure hardship and frequently sacrifice their happiness in order to embody the patriarchal virtues of chastity and filiality.

Qiong Yao's romances have been criticized as 'escapist', but the popularity of her brand of escapism points to a deeper layer of meaning untouched by moral criticism. At a time of fundamental socioeconomic change that undermined the patriarchal hierarchy in traditional Chinese society, her romance appealed to male and female audiences alike because it addressed their needs for imaginary security and gratification through narratives of upward mobility and multiple identifications. Although men might continue to indulge in the illusion of male dominance, women could find pleasure in moments of free imagination unhindered by household chores or heavy work shifts. As Lu Feiyi suggests, Qiong Yao's romances 'eased social anxieties, nurtured the alienated female souls, intensified nostalgic sentiments and identification with the Chinese nation, and thereby strengthened the patriarchal system and the traditional moral order' (1998: 135).

Insomuch as they are family-oriented, Qiong Yao's romances are thematically linked to Zheng Zhengqiu's family drama of the 1920s and Eileen Chang's comedy of manners in 1940s Shanghai and 1950s and 1960s Hong Kong, all three offering interest to the female audience while endorsing patriarchal ideology. In terms of industry restructuring, the suspension of the MP&GI production of family melodramas in Hong Kong might have helped the emergence of romance in Taiwan. As filmmakers fought over her movie rights, Qiong Yao set up Firebird (Huoniao) in 1966 and produced two adaptations to her own liking before closing the company in 1971. The craze for Qiong Yao's romance stories in the second half of the 1960s evidently contributed to the ascendance of film romance in Mandarin cinema, and even Cathay and Shaw Brothers were compelled to 'romance' the genre in Hong Kong. By 1968, romance became the second most popular genre and thus further consolidated the overseas market for Taiwan cinema (F. Lu 1998: 135–6)

The most popular genre of the time was martial arts, sometimes also known as 'swordplay' films. By 1963 Hong Kong had produced sixty-one martial arts pictures, while Taiwanese-dialect films claimed only four to their credit, including *Jade Carp in a Gold Pot* (Jinhu yuli, dir. Chen Chensan, 1958), a pioneering 16mm silent color release. The new-styled swordplay trend started in Hong Kong when King Hu, who had co-directed with Li Hanxiang for Shaw Brothers in 1962, surprised the film world with his *Come Drink with Me* (Da zuixia, 1966). By this time Union Film wanted to venture into production but had terminated its relations with Li Hanxiang's Guolian. So it repeated its earlier strategy and attracted King Hu from Shaw Brothers to Taiwan in 1967. Hu served as Union Film's production manager and directed a series of stylistically refreshing swordplay films. *Dragon Gate Inn* (Longmen kezhan, 1967) showed for 105 days in Taipei and beat all Hong Kong and foreign films at the box office (F. Lu 1998: 136–7).[17] Much later, *A Touch of Zen* (Xianü, 1970) received the Technical Superiority Prize at the 1975 Cannes Film Festival.

Both King Hu and Li Hanxiang had had formal training in the fine arts and paid meticulous attention to mise-en-scene, set design, camera movement and frame composition. But Hu was more of a perfectionist than Li: on average Hu directed only one film every three years, whereas Li directed one or two films a year while in Taiwan, but as many as seven a year in Hong Kong. More so than Li's opera movies, Hu's swordplay films exhibit powerful Chinese *national* characteristics, not only in their beautifully choreographed martial arts fights but also in their theatrical ambience and poetic landscape scenes (Bordwell 2000: 254–60; Rodriguez 1998). Through a dramatic tension between easily recognized heroes and villains, Hu's swordplay films often feature the triumph of the morally upright and politically marginal knights-errant over the powerful, abusive, corrupt and treacherous. Set in remote historical times, Hu's films thus invited an *allegorical* reading. As Lu Feiyi suggests, Hu's lonely, often misunderstood heroes commanded identification from the male viewers frustrated by the current socioeconomic changes of the 1960s and solicited sympathy from the female viewers eager for compassion towards legendary heroism on screen. Specifically for male viewers 'repressed by patriarchal culture', the swordplay film provided an occasion for self-indulgence, self-pity, and even narcissism as well as an outlet for imaginary sadistic violence, thus achieving the same kind of 'escapism' as film romance, albeit in the opposite direction (F. Lu 1998: 141–2).

As in Shanghai of the late 1920s, martial arts pictures flooded the Taiwan market; for example, Hong Kong and Taiwan produced 128 martial arts titles in 1968. Violence and allegorical subtexts in martial arts pictures alarmed the KMT regime. In June 1968 the culture bureau issued regulations on excessive or inexcusable on-screen violence and consequently violent martial arts pictures were banned at some theaters. But unlike the early 1930s in China, martial arts pictures seemed unstoppable this time, and much to the disappointment of the KMT regime, 150 films were produced between May and July 1973 alone (F. Lu 1998: 137–43).

POLITICAL AND INDUSTRIAL RESTRUCTURING, 1970–8

The KMT regime was hit by even greater disappointments in the political and diplomatic arenas. In October 1971 the United Nations granted membership to the PRC and terminated Taiwan's right to represent China officially. In February 1972 President Nixon visited the PRC and acknowledged Taiwan to be an inseparable part of China. In 1972 Taiwan lost diplomatic relations with twenty nations, including Japan. In April 1975 Chiang Kai-shek passed away and in January 1979 the US and the PRC established diplomatic relations. Amidst political setbacks and public anxieties, state studios sought legitimacy and recognition in the fictional world by staging anti-Japanese war films and historical dramas. Many private studios, on the other hand, continued to make escapist romance and martial arts films, but these two genres failed to arrest the precipitous decline in feature production.

The restructuring of the media industries

Apart from political uncertainties, the restructuring of the media industries greatly impacted upon the film market in the 1970s. The demise of Taiwanese-dialect films was intimately tied to the rise of the television industry in Taiwan. The establishment of Taiwan TV (Taishi) in April 1962 ushered in a new era, and the attendance rates for dialect films dropped 30 per cent in southern Taiwan in the wake of the island-wide television network coverage in November 1965. After Taiwan TV extended its broadcast to 62.5 hours a week in March 1969, Central TV (Zhongshi) began broadcasting in October 1969 and in February 1970 aired a Hong Kong Mandarin feature, *Long Alley* (Changxiang, dir. Bu Wancang, 1956), despite protest from film circles. Serial television dramas in Mandarin and Taiwanese dialect had driven thousands of employees of local theater troupes out of work, and the government's efforts to regulate dialect programs did not prevent the television stations from attracting more audiences with a variety of new programs in sports and entertainment.

The impact of the media restructuring was both immediate and profound. When China TV (Huashi) was instituted in August 1970, the household owner-ship of television sets was 32.2 per cent, compared with 826 movie theaters in business and 117 features produced in the year (down 32.4 per cent from 173 in 1969, mainly due to the decline of dialect films). When television ownership reached 86.22 per cent (with 13.3 per cent of color sets) in 1975, the numbers of theaters dropped to 478 (down 42.1 per cent) and feature productions to forty-nine (down 58.1 per cent) (see Table 4.4, pp. 129–30). Furthermore, when

ENG was introduced in television news reporting in April 1976, the era of showing newsreels in theaters was definitely declared over (F. Lu 1998: 148–51).

As if the impact of television itself was not severe enough, the advent of video recording technology dealt another blow to the shrinking film industry. In 1974, despite the critical reputation that *A Touch of Zen* earned, Union Film abandoned film production due to the sluggish film market doubly plagued by television and pirated videotapes (R. Huang 2001: 83). The video rental business was enormously profitable, and pirated recordings penetrated the market. Instead of going to theaters, an ever-increasing number of viewers preferred to stay at home and watch videos. Worse, the government did not regulate the video market until 1979 and thus it had no legal means of cracking down on piracy until the mid-1980s (F. Lu 1998: 243).

A new significance for policy and genre films

In October 1972, Gong Hong retired from CMPC and was succeeded by Mei Changling, who had produced *Storms Over the Yangtze River* (Yangzijiang fengyun, dir. Li Hanxiang, 1969), an anti-Japanese detective film from China Motion Picture that had topped the Taiwan box office that year.[18] Actually, long before his retirement, Gong Hong had changed his policy of 'healthy realism' to that of 'a healthy variety of arts' (*jiankang zongyi*), so that CMPC could embrace genre films in the 1960s and eventually expand beyond film production and distribution.[19]

Given the political exigency, Mei Changling promoted a new type of policy films in CMPC, reminiscent of the KMT productions in wartime China. Both directed by Ding Shanxi, *The Everlasting Glory* (Yinglie qianqiu, 1974), an anti-Japanese war film, proved surprisingly popular, and *Eight Hundred Heroes* (Babai zhuangshi, 1975) was in some sense a remake of a 1938 film of the same title that glorifies a KMT battle against Japan in Shanghai. Popular enthusiasm over CMPC's war films was apparent when *Plum Blossoms* (Meihua, dir. Liu Jiachang, 1975) topped the 1976 Taiwan box office. As private and state studios followed this trend of anti-Japanese historical and war films (R. Huang 1994b: 174–87), filmmakers attempted to retrieve the memory of 'victories' so as to fortify a defense mechanism vis-à-vis the present-day political setbacks (F. Lu 1998: 182). Ironically, by emphasizing nationalistic pride and heroic martyrdom, Taiwan's 'policy films' resemble similar genres in the PRC, and the two opposing ideological state apparatuses left similar marks on film productions on both sides of the Taiwan Strait.

To reinforce its leadership at a time of crisis, in 1973 the KMT regime started a 'moral purification' campaign in Taiwan's film circles and targeted violence and sex in commercial features. Actors were warned not to wear their hair too long and actresses not to star in soft-porn features in Hong Kong. In the meantime, the government avenged its loss of diplomatic relations with Japan by banning Japanese productions and co-productions altogether, forbidding the use of

Japanese cast members in domestic films and the 'Japanization' of film music. Other than these measures, state regulations had little effect on the film market, as martial arts and romance pictures continued to dominate.

There was, of course, a new significance to genre films of the 1970s. Popular gongfu films from Bruce Lee (Li Xiaolong) buttressed the image of a morally upright Chinese hero but underscored his sadomasochistic tendencies at the same time. Audience identification differed widely in various geopolitical locales and created what Lu Feiyi sees as 'an absurd phenomenon'. Whereas Hong Kong audiences located *nationalistic pride* in Lee's 'China image' because of the PRC membership in the United Nations, Taiwan audiences experienced 'a peculiar pleasure–pain complex' through identification with Lee's fight scenes and thus alleviated their 'castration anxiety' by way of an 'aesthetic of violence' (F. Lu 1998: 186–7).

The other option for psychological alleviation was the ever-popular film romance, in particular the sub-genre perfected by adaptations of Qiong Yao's fiction. A unique star grouping was developed, in which two Lin's – actresses Brigitte Lin (Lin Qingxia) and Lin Fengjiao – and two Qin's – actors Qin Han and Qin Xianglin – were paired to guarantee box-office appeal. As youth idols, these and other stars helped perfect the Qiong Yao formula known as the 'three-room film' – living room, ballroom, and café – and commanded a sizable loyal following (F. Chen 1988: 242–63). In August 1976 Qiong Yao stopped granting film rights to other companies, and established Superstar (Juxing) to standardize her film adaptations, producing thirteen titles and further consolidating a 'Qiong Yao kingdom' in Taiwan cinema. From August 1965 to March 1983, forty-nine films based on her works were produced (T. Li 1997: 150–3), thirteen of which (26 per cent) entered the annual top ten lists from the mid-1960s to the mid-1970s. The staying power of her brand of romance was evident when two films based on her work were ranked first and second on the 1975 top ten list.[20]

Leading directors of the 1970s

The popularity of Qiong Yao's romance stories owed much to the involvement of leading Taiwan directors of the time. Li Xing, for instance, started the 1970s with his meticulously crafted *Execution in Autumn* (Qiujue, 1971), a costume drama released by Dazhong, which he had cofounded with Bai Jingrui and others in 1969. Turning abruptly away from his former auteur style, Li directed two romance pictures that were ranked second and fourth in the 1973 top ten, losing only to two Bruce Lee films. Li's successful casting of actress Zhen Zhen and actor Alan Tang (Deng Guangrong) was believed to have cultivated a 'trademark value' (i.e., star appeal) that guaranteed distribution to overseas markets such as Southeast Asia and South Korea (F. Lu 1998: 190–1).

Like Li Xing, Song Cunshou set up Eighties (Bashi niandai) with two friends in 1972. His adaptation of Qiong Yao's *You Don't Tell Him* (Tingyuan shenshen,

1970) had come second in the 1971 top ten list, and his *Story of a Mother* (Muqin sanshi sui, 1972), a rare study of female sexuality produced by Li's Dazhong, had been acclaimed as a masterpiece in Taiwan. Song's next adaptation, *Outside the Window* (Chuanwai, 1973), featured the rising star Brigitte Lin and was critically acclaimed as the best Qiong Yao adaptation. Unfortunately, *Outside the Window* failed to secure Qiong Yao's permission and was not shown in Taiwan. As Song continued with his 'melancholy' pictures (F. Chen 1988: 214–24), Liu Jiachang, an ingenious director-actor-composer-singer working for CMPC, invented a subgenre of 'singing romance' and brought three of his films – all narratively loose, but with charming songs – to the top ten lists through 1973 to 1975.

A number of directors who had studied overseas and had returned to Taiwan in the 1960s, such as Bai Jinrui (from Italy) and Chen Yaoxin (from UCLA), were also swept up by the romance trend. Bai had joined CMPC in 1964 and had distinguished himself with two best director prizes and a best picture prize for *Home, Sweet Home* (Jiazai Taibei, 1970), all from the Golden Horse Awards. A CMPC release, *Home, Sweet Home* reflects the state ideology in its call for overseas students to return to Taiwan and embrace it as home again. To forge a new cinematic look of Taiwan, Bai showcases as the icons of homeland and modernity an idyllic farm in the mountains, the Sun-and-Moon Lake as a tourist attraction, a rooftop hotel restaurant and a luxury apartment with modernist furniture. But Bai's skillful handling of the romantic feelings of four main characters, three of whom decide to stay in Taiwan at the film's end, betrays his preference for the sentimental over the ideological.

Indeed, Bai soon competed with Li Xing and others in filming romance with less ideological baggage attached and brought three such films to the top ten lists in 1974–5, among them, *Girl Friend* (Nü pengyou, 1975) and *Dreams* (Yilian youmeng, 1975) produced by Huang Zhuohan's First Film (Diyi).[21] In 1977, Bai went on an extended trip to Europe funded by First Film and shot three films with the same stars at the same time. A high-profile director, he directed twenty films between 1970 and 1978, but his later films were not as remarkable as his earlier ones.

By the late 1970s, First Film, which was founded in Hong Kong in 1967 but based its production in Taiwan, had evolved into the fourth largest Chinese studio outside the mainland, trailing after Shaw Brothers, Golden Harvest (Jiahe) and CMPC. A trend follower rather than a trendsetter, First Film had ventured into various genre films, from romance and swordplay to comedy and policy. It reportedly invested NT$10 million in King Hu's *Legend of the Mountain* (Shanzhong chuanqi, 1979) and *Raining in the Mountain* (Kongshan lingyu, 1979), which were shot on location in South Korea and took two years to complete (F. Chen 1988: 191–4).

Compared with his contemporaries, Li Xing was clearly a trendsetter. After his award-winning *Our Land, Our People* (Wutu wumin, 1975), Li returned to the realist tradition of the 'native soil' (*xiangtu*) that had brought him distinction a decade before. *A Boat in the Ocean* (Wangyang zhongde yitiao chuan, 1978) is based on a popular autobiographical novel of Zheng Fengxi, a physically disabled man who overcame enormous difficulties to graduate from college with a law degree and returned to teach in his hometown. Zheng was named one of Taiwan's ten outstanding youths, and before Zheng died of cancer at age 32, Li bought the film rights and focused his adaptation on Zheng's romantic life with flashbacks to his childhood years. Produced by CMPC, the film set a box-office record of NT$40 million and functioned as a 'national allegory' for Taiwan at a time of crisis (F. Chen 1988: 199–201; F. Lu 1998: 222).

Li followed this success immediately with two award-winning films for his company Dazhong: *Story of a Small Town* (Xiaocheng gushi, 1979) and *Good Morning, Taipei* (Zao an Taibei, 1980), both exhibiting strong flavors of Taiwan culture. With his unusual talent, Li secured an unprecedented honor of three consecutive best picture prizes from the Golden Horse Awards. Indeed, Li's realist films of the late 1970s represent the apex of his career, foreground a growing sense of national identity in the wake of political setbacks and socio-economic changes in Taiwan, and point to different strategies of imagining Taiwan in the 1980s.

Signs of diversification and recovery

Contrary to an emergent studio system of the 1960s, the 1970s saw the trend of business diversification after the devastating oil crisis. One consequence of such diversification was the disappearance of the large studios. The expansion of the television and video markets had convinced the big players like Union Film, Shaw Brothers and First Film either to terminate their production or scale down their investments. Small companies were formed to fill the void. From thirty-seven in 1975, the number of production companies jumped to eighty-seven in 1979.

Another consequence of diversification was the emergence of theaters with multiple screens. The practice started as early as March 1973 and attracted more attention with the opening of three cinemas inside the Shizilin Department Store in March 1979 (F. Lu 1998: 241). Perhaps as a result, from 1975 to 1979, the number of theaters increased moderately from 478 to 594 (up 24.3 per cent), which indicates the restructuring of exhibition in progress. In the same period, movie attendance rose from 134 to 216 million (up 61.2 per cent), with an annual per person viewing up from 8.4 to 12.5 times (up 48.8 per cent), and feature productions from forty-nine to 121 (up 146.9 per cent) (see Tables 4.3 and 4.4, pp. 120–1 and 129–30). The signs of recovery are unmistakable, but exactly what fueled this recovery awaits further investigation.

CONCLUSION: CINEMATIC REINVENTION OF
THE NATIONAL

From 1945 to 1978, the articulation of the national in Taiwan cinema took different forms and carried different consequences: politically through administrative regulation and monetary awards, economically through industry restructuring and adaptation to market forces, culturally through audience participation and linguistic inter-penetration, and artistically through genre innovation and auteur styles.

Politically, like its arch-enemy in the mainland, the KMT regime implemented authoritarian rule in Taiwan, suppressed dissident voices and utilized film as part of the propaganda machine. The consistent investment in state-produced and assisted policy films testifies to the government's relentless efforts at nation-building and state-building in Taiwan. As part of the state ideological apparatuses, the three state studios produced films that spread anti-Communist messages, glorified the KMT achievements in Taiwan and re-imagined Taiwan as an inseparable part of the unified Chinese nation through historical and anti-Japanese war films. By policing ideological content through censorship and soliciting political allegiance through subsidies, the state film administrative agencies promoted Mandarin cinema at the expense of dialect production and fostered the image of a persevering nation in spite of Taiwan's contemporary setbacks in international politics.

However, there is a conspicuous difference between the KMT regime in Taiwan and the CCP regime in the mainland insomuch as their film operations are concerned. As Huang Ren argues, Taiwan cinema was neither the 'state apparatus' under the Communist regime nor a pure 'cash machine' in the capitalist system (2001: 44). What makes Taiwan cinema different from both the PRC and Hong Kong is its combination of state administration and market self-regulation. The profit factor was always significant in Taiwan since the KMT regime owned a substantial interest in exhibition and production. Apart from its own CMPC income, the state benefited tremendously from tax revenues from the exhibition sector, which explains its on-and-off romance with Japanese imports and its tolerance of Taiwanese-dialect productions, both sitting uneasily with nationalistic sentiments and the state policy on the standard language. Yet, it is precisely this market factor that prevented the KMT from overspending in film production as its mainland counterpart did in the 1950s and 1960s.

Economically, the Taiwan film industry went through a 'twisted development' from 1945 to 1975 due to the dominance of exhibition over production, which had resulted in part from the *market-influenced* state film policy (Z. Wei 1993). The cinematic invention of the national was thus compromised by what the market perceived as viable and sustainable at a given moment, from dialect opera movies to romance and swordplay genres. No wonder 'healthy realism' had quickly turned into a 'healthy variety of arts' within state studios. In the

147

shifting configurations of nationhood in Taiwan, Hong Kong and Japan played a peculiar role. Hong Kong was granted dual status as an indispensable overseas 'anti-Communist' partner and a predominant 'domestic' force in exhibition, which inevitably resulted in the dominance of Hong Kong productions in Taiwan. Japan, on the other hand, did not have the privilege of such consistent treatment and underwent a cycle of love–hate relationships from outright prohibition, quota regulations, controversial co-production, to illegal smuggling and vengeful prohibition again. The presence of Hong Kong and Japan in Taiwan also underscores a striking difference between the ideologically rigid PRC and the market-oriented KMT, for the latter had successfully secured an overseas market through its inclusion of the overseas Chinese in a reinvented Chinese nation centered in Taiwan.

Culturally, no equivalent of a bourgeois public sphere or civil society was conceivable in a police state under martial law, but cinema as a *public space* existed and indeed flourished in Taiwan, especially during the heyday of Taiwanese-dialect films. In a fashion similar to county fairs, going to see a dialect movie was a routine family event, a kind of communal celebration that resembles, when considered on a large scale, a grassroots folk arts movement in Taiwan. The experience of a communal gathering at a dialect screening thus approximated that of the *carnival*, where the sacred becomes profane, the dignified is ridiculed, and – incredibly and therefore more gratifyingly – even the emperor speaks Taiwanese dialect on screen (Ye 1999). A rare sense of pride was projected onto the Taiwanese population, who had remained powerless in political and symbolic representation under both the Japanese and the KMT rule for decades. In this sense, the prevailing bitter pathos in early dialect films was doubly significant because it constituted a popular outlet for repressed feelings and an *alternative* expression of the national (alternative to the heroic, for example). Nevertheless, the state control of historical representation was so effective that the dialect film movement, like the 28 February Incident, was unknown until recently to a new generation growing up in the 1960s.[22]

Artistically, Taiwan cinema bears close resemblance to pre–1950 Chinese productions. Leading Taiwan directors did not depart from typical 'national' characteristics and styles, such as the opera influence in exaggerated acting and contrastive characterization, linear plots punctuated by coincidences, conventional stage-like mise-en-scene and traditional aesthetic tastes in symbolism and landscape composition. Similar cinematic articulation of the national is found in Taiwan cinema's emphasis on Confucian ethics (filial piety and female chastity) and human dignity (especially in lower-class people), both illustrated in Li Xing's works. But a few directors, such as Bai Jingrui and King Hu, sometimes resorted to modern film language and ventured into the realm of directorial subjectivity, thus cultivating distinctive auteur styles (F. Chen 1994). It must be remembered that, although Taiwan cinema has been frequently criticized as 'escapist' in nature, it is just as escapist as its commercial counterparts in 1920s Shanghai and yet might be more 'realistic' than contemporary Hong Kong cinema (Eberhard

1972: 15). In short, the 'escapist' should be regarded as a *strategic* articulation of the national in Taiwan cinema of the martial law period.

Ru-shou Robert Chen describes 'dispersion', 'ambivalence' and 'hybridity' as three distinguishing features of Taiwan cultural experiences (1993: 3). Due to the combined effects of colonial legacy (Japanese language and culture), massive migration (displaced mainlanders, under-represented Taiwanese and scattered aboriginal peoples), political uncertainty (diplomatic crisis) and competing production modes (the state and the private), the national as reinvented in Taiwan cinema cannot but be multicultural, multi-ethnic, multiregional and multivalent. As we shall see in Chapter 7, dispersion, ambivalence and hybridity will find a more pronounced articulation in the era of New Taiwan Cinema.

5

CINEMATIC REVIVAL OF THE REGIONAL IN HONG KONG, 1945–78

INTRODUCTION

This chapter concerns itself with Hong Kong cinema from its postwar recovery in 1945 to the eve of the Hong Kong new wave in 1978. Two waves of massive migration occurred in 1945–6 and 1949–50, as Hong Kong residents who had left for the hinterland during the Japanese occupation returned home and new immigrants and refugees poured into the territory to escape political and economic problems resulting from the intensifying civil war in the mainland. The founding of the PRC signaled the advent of a new era of the cold war between the CCP and the KMT, the latter now with its headquarters in Taiwan. Although the British colonial government attempted to maintain political neutrality, Hong Kong studios and artists were inevitably classified as 'left wing' and 'right wing' as they struggled in the postwar market. The colony's moderate diplomacy and relative insulation had shielded Hong Kong from major international events, such as the Vietnam War and the normalization of the US–China relationships. As time went by, the pursuit of affluence and amusement in the 1960s and 1970s replaced the memory of poverty and separation in the 1940s and 1950s. Hong Kong became one of the world's largest movie production sites in the 1960s; by the late 1970s, after two decades of over or near double-digit growth, the territory consolidated its position as an economic power in Asia.[1]

In terms of film history, Hong Kong cinema between 1945 and 1978 can be divided into three phases. First, during the phase of transition *from Shanghai to Hong Kong* (1945 to 1955), a huge number of Shanghai producers and artists of various ideological persuasions migrated to Hong Kong, many of whom expected their sojourn to be temporary. They initiated a trend of Mandarin cinema in postwar Hong Kong that rivaled its Shanghai counterparts in both critical realism and genre innovations while exhibiting a strong nostalgic ambience. Meanwhile, Cantonese cinema was revived with popular enthusiasm and restructured along the lines of realism. By the mid-1950s, another transition from Shanghai to Hong Kong – this time psychological rather than physical – had been accomplished so that Hong Kong had replaced Shanghai and unnamed mainland locations as the focus of cinematic representation.

150

Second, in the phase of *competing studios* (1956 to 1965), the two largest companies in Hong Kong – Cathay-owned MP&GI and Shaw Brothers – had evolved into arch-enemies engaging in fierce competition to dominate the Hong Kong and Southeast Asian markets. In addition to cultivating their own stars and production personnel, they invested in modern musicals, opera movies and youth romances that appealed to a wide spectrum of audiences. Female stars prevailed in the era of singing and dancing known as 'Mandarin pop' (*shidai qu*), and screen fashions became a major attraction for a society that gradually moved from poverty and scarcity to sufficiency and affluence. Meanwhile, Cantonese cinema enjoyed its 'golden age', its opera movies as popular as ever and its urban melodramas attaining a new level of sophistication.

Third, in the phase of *reinventing genres* (1966 to 1978), the Cultural Revolution in the PRC spelled box-office disaster for the pro-PRC companies, while the termination of Cathay's feature production and the emergence of Golden Harvest in the early 1970s heralded a time of reinvention in studios and genres. The new-style martial arts film represented by Zhang Che's visceral swordplay and Bruce Lee's heroic gongfu fights dominated the screen, and masculinity and violence replaced femininity and romance as male stars eclipsed their female counterparts. By the mid-1970s the Hui brothers' comedy became a serious contender to martial arts pictures, and Cantonese cinema was revived after a dreadful decline in the early 1970s. The inauguration of the Hong Kong International Film Festival in 1977 declared the significance of Hong Kong cinema in the world, and the thriving television industry cultivated a group of young artists who would soon make a major impact with Hong Kong new wave cinema. 'Since the 1970s, [Hong Kong] has been arguably the world's most energetic, imaginative popular cinema' (Bordwell 2000: 1).

FROM SHANGHAI TO HONG KONG, 1945–55

The postwar transition from Shanghai to Hong Kong involved not just two waves of migration into the territory but also the new immigrants' psychological adjustment to make Hong Kong their new home as well as the new focus of their cinematic experience. Inasmuch as film history is concerned, the relationship between Hong Kong and Shanghai has long been a fruitful one and can be traced to the early twentieth century (HKIFF 1990: 102–15).

Highlights of early Hong Kong cinema, 1896–45

Hong Kong's film history started in 1896 when the Lumières sent its staff to shoot documentaries in this exotic British colony. As mentioned in Chapter 2, Brodsky's Shanghai-based Yaxiya managed to produce short features in Hong Kong, thus making *Stealing a Roast Duck*, directed by Leung Siu-po (Liang Shaopo) in 1909, the first feature in Chinese film history. In 1913 Brodsky established Huamei in Hong Kong and produced its only release, *Zhuangzi Tests His Wife*, with the assistance of Li Minwei and Li Beihai. In 1923 the Li brothers founded Minxin in Hong Kong but had to relocate its operations to Shanghai due to a prolonged labor strike in 1925–6, which involved 250,000 out of 600,000 Hong Kong residents.[2] From then until 1930 no film was produced in Hong Kong, whereas about a dozen came out in Guangzhou (Fonoroff 1997: xiv).

The revival of filmmaking in Hong Kong began in 1930, but the real driving force was the founding of Lianhua in Hong Kong and the opening of its Hong Kong studio (headed by Li Beihai in 1931), which produced six features. Interestingly, the first two full-sound Cantonese talkies were made outside Hong Kong in 1933: *White Gold Dragon* came from Tianyi in Shanghai and *Romance of the Songsters* (Gelü qingchao, dir. Chiu Shu-sen) from Grandview in San Francisco (Fonoroff 1997: xiv–v).[3] Hong Kong ceased silent film production in 1935 and the era of Cantonese sound cinema came into being.

The success of the two talkies in Hong Kong and the overseas Chinese communities convinced Tianyi to set up a sound studio in Hong Kong, and

Figure 5.1 Zhuangzi Tests His Wife (1913): a Hong Kong short feature, with Li Minwei

152

Grandview to relocate its production to Hong Kong, both in 1934. Chiu Shu-sen originally agreed with Luo Mingyou to operate under the name 'Overseas Lianhua', but he resumed the name 'Grandview' when Lianhua closed its Hong Kong studio in 1934 due to financial problems. A significant player in Hong Kong, Grandview was innovative and projected new images on the Hong Kong screen. *Life Line* (Shengming xian, dir. Moon Kwan, 1935) was a 'national defense' picture produced ahead of its Shanghai counterparts, which was temporarily banned by the Hong Kong censors (Law 2000: 53).[4] After leading patriotic film productions in the late 1930s, Grandview completed the construction of its Hong Kong studio in Diamond Hill in 1940, which was unfortunately destroyed in the 1941 Japanese bombing. During the war Grandview relocated its production to San Francisco and produced twenty-one films in black and white and four in 16mm, color.

Hong Kong filmmakers refused to cooperate with the Japanese invaders and no Chinese-funded feature was produced inside Hong Kong from the end of 1941 to the beginning of 1946.[5] Local movie theaters, estimated at twenty-eight in 1938, had no access to Hollywood films and had to show Cantonese features produced prior to the occupation as well as a limited number of Japanese films and Shanghai Mandarin titles whenever available (Fonoroff 1997: xvi).

The postwar revival, 1946–9

Large-scale migration occurred during and after the war. The onset of the resistance war brought an influx of refugees to Hong Kong, where the population swelled from 0.98 million in 1936 to 1.64 million in 1941. A reverse trend started in December 1941 when Japan occupied the city and Hong Kong residents headed for China's hinterland or overseas. By the time of Japan's surrender in 1945, Hong Kong had a population of 0.6 million. A second wave of migration to Hong Kong followed and the city's population increased to 1.75 million by 1947. A third wave of refugees poured into the territory in 1949, and by 1 May 1950 when the PRC officially closed its border, Hong Kong's population exceeded 2.23 million (Jarvie 1977: 58) (see Table 5.1).

A film production boom matched the postwar population boom: 419 titles were produced between June 1946 and December 1949, compared with 571 titles between March 1930 and December 1941.[6] Unlike the 1930s, the postwar period was characterized by a significant increase in both Cantonese and Mandarin cinema. From five in 1946, the number of Cantonese features jumped to 154 in 1949, while Mandarin features grew from four in 1946 to twenty-five in 1949. Indeed, in 1948 Cantonese cinema already broke its 1939 record of 120 titles (see Table 5.2). Most postwar Cantonese films were Cantonese opera movies; they accounted for 30 per cent of all Cantonese titles produced in the 1940s, with fifty-eight released in 1949 alone. Obviously, such production

153

Table 5.1 Theaters, attendance and population in Hong Kong, 1926–96

Year	Theaters	Attendance (million)	Visits per capita	Population (million)
1926	—	—	—	0.6
1936	—	—	—	0.98
1938	28	—	—	—
late 1930s	31	—	—	—
1941	—	—	—	1.64
1945	—	—	—	0.6
1947	—	—	—	1.75
1948	33	—	—	—
1950	—	—	—	2.23
1955	64	—	—	2.5
1959	—	66	22	3
1960	67	—	—	—
1961	72	—	—	3.1
1965	—	90.54	—	—
1967	—	100	27	3.7
1971	—	—	21	4
1975	—	54	—	—
1977	75	60	—	—
1979	80	65	—	—
1982	89	66	—	—
1985	104	58	—	—
1988	133	66	12	5.5
1993	—	44	—	—
1995	—	28	—	—
1996	—	22	—	—

Sources: Bordwell 2000: 34, 66, 75; Chan 2000: 69; Cheuk 1999: 11–20; Fu 2000a: 205; HKIFF 1982: 18; HKIFF 1991: 72; Jarvie 1977: 58; M. Yu 2001: 41.

capacity had surpassed the pre-occupation era when Cantonese opera movies constituted 24 per cent of all Cantonese titles produced in the 1930s, with thirty-three released in 1939 (HKIFF 1987: 18–19). As in the 1930s, leading male stars Sit Kok-sin and Ma Sze-tsang (Ma Shizeng) returned to the screen, accompanied by their protégés and younger colleagues from the opera world. Significantly, several postwar Cantonese dramas resembled their Shanghai counterparts in that both reenacted wartime traumas and re-staged family separation and female suffering.

On the other hand, the increased Mandarin-speaking population and new film talents from Shanghai ushered in a new era in Hong Kong cinema. Not surprisingly, when the first postwar Hong Kong film was released in December 1946, it was a Mandarin title because many producers believed that, with access to mainland cities now, Mandarin cinema commanded a larger market than Cantonese cinema (M. Yu 1998: 87–9). Like most postwar Mandarin companies,

Table 5.2 Annual number of feature productions in Hong Kong, 1913–2002

Year	Total films released	Cantonese films	Mandarin films	Amoy-dialect films	Other
1913	1	—	—	—	1 silent short
1914	2	—	—	—	2 silent shorts
—	—	—	—	—	—
1925	6	—	—	—	6 silent
1926	1	—	—	—	1 silent
—	—	—	—	—	—
1931	3	—	—	—	3 silent
1932	2	—	—	—	2 silent
1933	5	5	—	—	—
1934	15	15	—	—	—
1935	32	32	—	—	—
1936	49	49	—	—	—
1937	85	85	—	—	—
1938	87	83	4	—	—
1939	125	120	5	—	—
1940	89	84	5	—	—
1941	80	74	6	—	—
1942	3	3	—	—	—
1943	6	5	1	—	—
1944	2	2	—	—	—
1945	1	1	—	—	—
1946	9	5	4	—	—
1947	89	72	16	1	—
1948	141	123	18	—	—
1949	179	154	25	—	—
1950	187	169	17	1	—
1951	169	141	17	11	—
1952	217	163	44	10	—
1953	183	132	42	6	3 3-D films
1954	159	116	28	14	1 widescreen
1955	210	169	22	18	1 Chaozhou
1956	252	167	64	20	1 Chaozhou
1957	240	142	58	39	1 Chaozhou
1958	286	156	57	70	3 Chaozhou
1959	343	169	76	89	9 Chaozhou
1960	276	202	71	—	2 Chaozhou, 1 Shanghainese
1961	257	211	45	—	1 Chaozhou
1962	233	200	31	—	1 Chaozhou, 1 Shanghainese
1963	251	203	38	—	8 Chaozhou, 2 others
1964	224	175	43	—	5 Chaozhou, 1 Shanghainese
1965	205	169	32	—	4 Chaozhou
1966	166	125	40	—	1 Shanghainese
1967	172	105	67	—	—
1968	149	87	61	—	1 Chaozhou
1969	135	71	64	—	—
1970	118	35	83	—	—

Table 5.2—Continued

Year	Total films released	Cantonese films	Mandarin films	Amoy-dialect films	Other
1971	86	1	85	—	—
1972	87	—	87	—	—
1973	94	1	93	—	—
1974	101	—	—	—	—
1975	97	—	—	—	—
1976	95	—	—	—	—
1977	87	—	—	—	—
1978	99	—	—	—	—
1979	109	—	—	—	—
1980	116	—	—	—	—
1981	110	—	—	—	—
1982	106	—	—	—	—
1983	87	—	—	—	—
1984	86	—	—	—	—
1985	88	—	—	—	—
1986	87	—	—	—	—
1987	76	—	—	—	—
1988	115	—	—	—	—
1989	117	—	—	—	—
1990	120	—	—	—	—
1991	125	—	—	—	—
1992	215	—	—	—	—
1993	242	—	—	—	—
1994	181	—	—	—	—
1995	150	—	—	—	—
1996	116	—	—	—	—
1997	84	—	—	—	—
1998	89	—	—	—	—
1999	100	—	—	—	—
2000	133	—	—	—	—
2001	133	—	—	—	—
2002	92	—	—	—	—

Sources: Chan 2000: 547; HKFA 1997b; HKFA 1998; HKFA 2000; HKIFF 1984; HKIFF 1986; HKIFF 1987; HKIFF 1989; Z. Qi 2002: 84; Shackleton 2003; M. Yu 2000; M. Yu 2001.

Notes: The figures here exclude those features produced but not exhibited in the given year or those exhibited for the second time. The 1926 film was produced before the labor strike in 1925–6 and films released between 1942 and 1944 were produced before the fall of Hong Kong in December 1941.

Great China, established in 1946, appointed on its board such illustrious Shanghai producers as Yan Youxiang, Zhang Shichuan and Zhou Jianyun. Its production staff included leading Shanghai artists like Zhu Shilin and Dan Duyu. Great China leased Nanyang's facilities and produced thirty-four Mandarin titles before it ceased operation in 1949 (HKIFF 1995: 92–104). *An All-Consuming Love* (Chang xiangsi, dir. He Zhaozhang, 1947; Mandarin), set in wartime Shanghai, articulates the postwar pathos of separation and lost love, and Zhou Xuan's famous song 'Shanghai at Night' (Ye Shanghai) intensified the emotional ties between Hong Kong and Shanghai. Also set in Shanghai, two other Zhou Xuan vehicles from Great China, *Orioles Banished from the Flowers* (Huawai liuying, 1947) and *Song of a Songstress* (Genü zhi ge, 1948), both directed by Fang Peilin in Mandarin, further underscored the obsession with Shanghai. Most of Great China's Mandarin productions were exhibited in Hong Kong with separate Cantonese soundtracks and sold better than their Mandarin prints. As a result, Great China also ventured into Cantonese cinema and produced nine such titles.

A lesser-known company was Longma (Dragon-Horse), which Fei Mu founded in 1949 with support from Wu Xingzai, another powerful Shanghai producer. After Fei Mu died in 1951 at age 45, Zhu Shilin took charge of production and directed seven Longma releases celebrated for their distinct realist style. With his focus on ordinary urbanites in films like *Spoiling the Wedding Day* (Wu jiaqi, 1951; Mandarin), an acclaimed comedy, Zhu gradually directed the attention of postwar Mandarin cinema from its 'mainland complex' – especially its Shanghai obsession – to a humane examination of social realities in contemporary Hong Kong. For film scholars like Lin Niantong, Zhu surpassed Italian neo-realism and took the tradition of 1930s and 1940s Chinese film comedy to new heights (ZDZ 1998: 54).

Another noteworthy postwar company was Grandview, which reopened its business in Hong Kong in 1947 and released *All That Glitters* (Jinfen nishang, dir. Huang Hesheng, 1942), a 16mm color feature produced in San Francisco. Under Chiu Shu-sen, Grandview made remarkable technical advancement, producing the first 35mm full-color Cantonese feature in 1948, the first 3-D feature in 1953 and the first widescreen format film in 1954. Like most Cantonese companies of the time, Grandview stayed out of postwar politics in Hong Kong.

Of business and politics, 1949–55

The postwar battles between the KMT and the CCP were carried far beyond the military fronts and lasted long after the division of China into the PRC and Taiwan in 1949. For political reasons, numerous former leftist filmmakers, such as Cai Chusheng, Ouyang Yuqian, Shi Dongshan, Yang Hansheng and Yu Ling, had moved to Hong Kong and were active in film production and criticism there in 1948. In 1949, while most of these leading leftists had returned to the PRC to assume leadership positions, a group of remaining Shanghai artists organized the Fifties Company (Wushi niandai) in Hong Kong and collectively produced two films. Wang Weiyi had already directed an acclaimed Cantonese feature for Nanguo, *Tears Over the Pearl River* (Zhujiang lei, 1949), which dramatizes class conflict and female oppression in the tradition of postwar Shanghai critical realism. For Fifties Wang directed *Fiery Phoenix* (Huo fenghuang, 1950; Mandarin), a title that might have inspired the name for Phoenix (Fenghuang), a company founded in 1952, the year when Fifties was disbanded after most of its members had departed for the PRC. Phoenix also recruited several Longma personnel and appointed Zhu Shilin as head of production, a post he held for the next fifteen years. Known in particular for its Mandarin comedies poking fun at the petit-bourgeois mentality, Phoenix served as a left-wing base in Hong Kong in the following decades.

The ideological battle between the KMT and the CCP was best illustrated in the postwar career of Zhang Shankun, a controversial industry leader in occupied Shanghai. In 1947 Zhang cooperated with Li Zuyong, a Shanghai–Hong Kong industrialist who had a master's degree in literature from the US, and together they set up Yonghua (Yung Hwa Motion Picture Industries – 'Yong' from Li's given name and 'hua' from Zhang's former Xinhua). Li poured in US$3 million, built two studios in Kowloon Chai and purchased up-to-date equipment. He was ambitious and, with Zhang's help, enlisted first-rank artists from Shanghai. Produced on a budget of over HK$1 million, *Soul of China* (Guohun, dir. Bu Wancang, 1948; Mandarin) was an acclaimed patriotic historical film. Its success was followed by *Sorrows of the Forbidden City* (Qinggong mishi, dir. Zhu Shilin, 1948), a drama of imperial court intrigues that was shown in China and exported to Japan, Europe and the Middle East (M. Yu 2000: 66). Remarkably, Yonghua also released films by noted leftist or progressive artists that dramatize class conflict in a more radical way than its contemporary mainland counterparts. Evidently, postwar Hong Kong was a place where clearly demarcated political camps had yet to emerge and where filmmaking was primarily a business.

A market-savvy businessman, Zhang withdrew from Yonghua in 1948 because he was worried that, with extravagant production standards and the uncertainty of the mainland market, the company would soon encounter financial problems. Zhang accepted the invitation of Yuan Yang'an, a former president of the Shanghai Attorneys Association, who raised money and established Great Wall Pictures (Changcheng) in 1949. With Zhang serving as production manager, Great Wall released two Mandarin features directed by Yue Feng in 1949. Even with Great Wall's early box-office success, Zhang was immediately plagued by financial problems and was forced to quit Great Wall on account that he owed the company HK$3 million. According to his wife Tong Yuejuan, the real reason was Zhang's refusal to accept the CCP's invitation – conveyed by his Shanghai acquaintances like Xia Yan – to return to the PRC, but nonetheless Zhang borrowed cash and settled his debts (G. Zuo and Yao 2001: 90–5).[7]

After Zhang's departure, the company was restructured as Great Wall Movie Enterprises in 1950. In spite of its alleged PRC affiliation, Great Wall ran a successful business in the 1950s, promoting directors like Tao Qin and cultivating

Figure 5.2 Sorrows of the Forbidden City (1948): postwar Mandarin cinema in Hong Kong

new stars like Xia Meng. In fact, Lin Dai (Linda Lin), four-time winner of the best actress award at the Asian Film Festival, first signed with Great Wall in 1950. Great Wall's releases were consistently popular and topped the annual Mandarin box-office in 1951–2. *A Night Time Wife* (Jinhun ji, dir. Li Pingqian, 1951; Mandarin), a light urban comedy, brought in HK$133,000 in first-run revenues and sold briskly overseas, although it was banned in the PRC for its alleged bourgeois ideology. *Modern 'Red Chamber Dream'* (Xin honglou meng, dir. Yue Feng, 1952; Mandarin), a reinvention of the classic novel set in a present-day city, featured Yan Jun and Li Lihua and grossed HK$214,000. Nonetheless, it is not certain whether this film made a profit since the production lasted almost a year and cost HK$1 million (M. Yu 2000: 44–7, 90–3) (see Table 3.2, p. 90).

By 1951, Yonghua was short on cash and owed its employees salaries for as much as three and a half months, which resulted in a strike organized by Shanghai artists. In December 1951 Yonghua fired fourteen employees. In a radical move in January 1952, the Hong Kong government expelled more than twenty left-wing film people to the PRC, including Bai Chen, Liu Qiong, Shen Ji, Shu Shi and Sima Wensen, without giving them an adequate reason or advance notice (M. Yu 2000: 66–7, 98–9).

The expulsion was radical because the colonial government had not imposed film censorship as strictly as the KMT had in postwar China. Due to relative freedom, postwar Hong Kong had become a perfect site for the former leftists to create their idealistic works of art with financial support from capitalists. A significant number of postwar Mandarin titles exposed official corruption (set in the early Republican era or during the resistance war), class oppression (disguised as sexual exploitation or forbidden love) and the collapse of the feudal family. In spirit, these postwar Hong Kong productions continued the leftist film movement of the 1930s and resembled their postwar Shanghai counterparts. A May 1950 Hong Kong news report claimed that, 'almost without exception, all Hong Kong film producers were manipulated by the Communists'. Since then, the Hong Kong government had formally instituted its censorship operations and stepped up pressure on 'Communist' films. In any case, the 1952 expulsions were meant as a warning signal to Hong Kong producers and artists alike. Ironically, exactly around this time, even 'left-wing' companies had begun to lose their mainland market as their releases, such as *Fiery Phoenix*, were criticized by the new socialist regime as spreading petit-bourgeois ideology and containing poisonous ingredients (M. Yu 2000: 24–5, 63).

Meanwhile, Zhang Shankun had resumed filmmaking with his Hong Kong Xinhua (Hsin Hwa) in 1951. *Little Phoenix* (Xiao Fengxian, dir. Tu Guangqi, 1953; Mandarin), a romance set in the early Republican revolution, was one of ten Xinhua films in which Zhang cast Li Lihua, who was paid HK$75,000 per film or half of the film's budget (see Table 3.1, pp. 64–5). Li's high fee was considered the beginning of the expensive star system in Hong Kong and its effect was debated in the media (Du 1988: 535–6).

To strengthen their political ties, Zhang and his wife twice joined the Hong Kong film delegation to visit Taiwan and met with Chiang Kai-shek in 1953 and 1954. Zhang also cooperated with his wartime friend Kawakita Nagamasa in producing an Eastmancolor film. Traveling between Taiwan and Japan while making several films at the same time, Zhang was exhausted and died in Tokyo in January 1957 at age 52.

After Zhang's death, his wife Tong Yuejuan continued Xinhua's productions until 1962. She had managed an anti-PRC association in Hong Kong following her 1953 visit to Taiwan and in 1957 renamed it 'Hong Kong and Kowloon Cinema and Theatrical Enterprise Free General Association' (Ziyou zonghui, 'Free Association' hereafter). At the height of the cold war, Free Association had demarcated artists and film companies into 'left-wing' and 'right-wing' groups. Since the pro-KMT businessmen controlled the overseas markets, Free Association had considerable influence on Hong Kong film productions, and many artists were forced to declare their political allegiance publicly. The size of the Hong Kong film and theater delegations to Taiwan grew from eighteen in 1953, to sixty-four in 1954 and 110 in 1956, and their members included Chen Hou, Hu Die and Li Lihua. An ideologically opposite case, however, was the decision of Hung-hsin Nui (Hongxian Nü), a leading actress of Cantonese opera and a rising film star, to return to Guangzhou with her husband Ma Sze-tsang in 1955, preceded by Sit Kok-sin's similar move to the PRC a year before.

Film historian Law Kar (Luo Ka) questions the validity of political labeling. He cites the fact that Li Zuyong turned to the KMT regime in 1955 only after Yonghua was financially insolvent. Unfortunately for Li, Taiwan's loan of HK$500,000 through CMPC accelerated Yonghua's demise because an ensuing anti-Communist film made in 1957 could not sell in Hong Kong and major Southeast Asian cities for political reasons. Li died in 1959 at age 56, far from realizing his initial dream of building a Chinese movie empire. The inadequacy of political labeling is further evident in the releases from Asia Pictures (Yazhou), founded in 1953 with the support of the US-based Free Asia Association. Reputedly an 'anti-Communist' operation, Asia Pictures produced *Half Way Down* (Ban xialiu shehui, dir. Tu Guangqi, 1955; Mandarin), which promotes solidarity among a group of poverty-stricken mainland intellectuals stranded in a Hong Kong slum and criticizes the corrupting forces of money and the bourgeois lifestyle. Ironically, by portraying individual dignity, traditional ethics and alienation in Hong Kong society, *Half Way Down* resembles many contemporary 'left-wing' releases from Great Wall (HKIFF 1990: 10–20).

Between Cantonese and Mandarin cinemas, 1950–5

In 1950 Cantonese film production reached an all-time high of 169 titles, out of which 109 films were produced by the same number of one-picture companies – an indicator of a speculative trend in filmmaking at the time. One reason for such a surge in production was the addition of a new theater chain dedicated to Cantonese cinema, which translated into an increase of five to six theaters and a new demand for fifty more films per year in order to feed the theaters. In comparison, Mandarin-spoken productions dropped to seventeen titles in 1950, in part because Great China had folded due to the closure of the mainland market, but also because Yonghua's production was suspended due to the loss of its key staff to the PRC. But a lack of exhibition venues continued to plague Mandarin cinema. In 1951 only six theaters showed Mandarin films, and out of forty-two Mandarin titles released in 1953, twenty-four of them were actually produced in 1952. Nonetheless, Mandarin production could sustain itself because the advances from overseas sales alone were nearly sufficient to fund the production costs of HK$80,000 per title. In 1953 and 1954, Cantonese productions declined to 132 and 116 respectively, and the United Nations' economic sanctions imposed on the PRC and Hong Kong in the wake of the Korean War were cited as a direct cause. For film critics, however, the decrease in Cantonese productions was a good thing because it was matched by an increase in production values and artistic quality (M. Yu 2000: 5–127).

Despite its popularity, postwar Cantonese cinema had a rather poor critical reputation, mainly due to its fast pace of production – seven to ten days for an opera movie or a martial arts picture and twelve to twenty days for a drama

(Fonoroff 1997: xviii). To change the situation, 164 film artists signed a public manifesto in April 1949 and declared their intention to stop making films detrimental to the national interest and social morale, to unite and stand firm in their position and to bring glory to Cantonese cinema (M. Yu 1998: 211). The result was the third 'film purification' campaign in Hong Kong, which, more than the previous two, successfully brought new images to Cantonese cinema.[8] In July 1949 Ng Cho-fan (Wu Chufan) and several other Cantonese film artists organized the Southern China Film Industry Workers Union (Hua'nan yinglian, 'Workers Union' hereafter) and dedicated themselves to raising artistic standards and promoting social welfare for filmmakers in the region.

In 1952, following a much publicized separation of Cantonese opera and film stars in Hong Kong, a collective of twenty-one Cantonese film artists founded Union Film Enterprises (Zhonglian), which best exemplified the spirit of 'film purification'. In spite of a sluggish market, in which more than sixty Cantonese movies had been abandoned in mid-production during 1952–3, Union Film Enterprises released five features in 1953 to critical and popular acclaim. One of their strategies in elevating artistic standards was adapting well-respected literary works in Cantonese, most eminently Ba Jin's triology. *Family* (Jia, dir. Ng Wui [Wu Hui], 1953) reached a quarter of the Hong Kong population, *Spring* (Chun, dir. Lee Sun-fung [Li Chenfeng], 1953) won an honorary prize from the PRC government in 1957 and *Autumn* (Qiu, dir. Chun Kim [Qin Jian], 1954) topped the box office, making HK$250,000. With his additional Cantonese adaptations of modern Chinese literature, Lee Sun-fung emerged as a master of the melodrama in the 1950s (HKIFF 1986: 67–83). Another strategy of Union Film Enterprises was to expose social problems, in particular those of unemployment and housing shortages. *In the Face of Demolition* (Weilou chunxiao, dir. Lee Tit [Li Tie], 1953), which cast teenager Bruce Lee, encouraged the urban poor to help each other and influenced a great many subsequent films.

As members of a collective, Union Film Enterprises' artists received one-half to one-third of the income they normally did when working for other companies. In order to make ends meet, they also formed several branch groups, each of which raised production money on its own and distributed its products under the name of Union Film Enterprises. Due in part to its ideological position and also in part to its members' active role in the Workers Union, Union Film Enterprises was classified by Free Association as 'left wing', its name was blacklisted by Taiwan and its access to overseas markets was limited (HKIFF 1982: 39).[9] However, the artists learned to evade the political labeling by establishing their own companies in subsequent years and carrying on Union Film Enterprises tradition.

The *divergence* of Cantonese and Mandarin cinemas in Hong Kong was conspicuous in the early 1950s since their respective production staff rarely mixed, they served two separate audiences in Hong Kong and overseas, and their characteristics could be contrasted in opposite terms. Indeed, a scholar furnishes this list of opposing terms: for Cantonese cinema, cheap, simple, unpretentious, folk roots, southern, energetic, whereas for Mandarin cinema, expensive, arty, pretentious, urban roots, northern and stiff (Jarvie 1977: 86). The two-track industry practice was evident in 1952 when Huang Zhuohan founded two companies in Hong Kong. His Lingguang Company specialized in distribution in the 1950s and would venture into Cantonese production in the 1960s. His Liberty Company (Ziyou) was dedicated to Mandarin productions and later was renamed First Film and based in Taiwan, where it rose to prominence as the fourth largest Chinese production company in the 1970s. A boss of two companies, Huang thus envisioned Hong Kong as a city of two cinemas for many years.

If divergence characterized the film industry in Hong Kong, *convergence* was sometimes found in genres and themes shared by Cantonese and Mandarin cinemas. Like Union Film Enterprises, several Mandarin companies also emphasized literary adaptations. Union Film Enterprises' 1953 success might also explain the predominance of twenty-one literary adaptations and nineteen ethical dramas in Cantonese productions of 1954. Previously in Cantonese cinema, martial arts pictures dominated in 1950, comedies in 1951 and 1953, and singing films (*gechang pian*) in 1952. Another point of convergence between Cantonese and Mandarin cinemas was the attention to serious – and often tragic – social issues. *A Mother's Tears* (Cimu lei, dir. Chun Kim, 1953), a Cantonese release based on an 'airwave novel' (*tiankong xiaoshuo*) or radio storytelling and featuring Hung-hsin Nui,[10] explored ethical questions and set a box-office record of 450,000 tickets and HK$400,000 in revenue. In March 1954, a newspaper report indicated that Cantonese cinema had made great progress and films of immortals and demons had disappeared from the screen (M. Yu 2000: 5–158).

The impact of the new Cantonese cinema represented by Union Film Enterprises was both immediate and profound. In 1954 Cathay's International Films Distribution Agency (Guoji) in Hong Kong set up a Cantonese production team. Active in Mandarin productions since the early 1950s, Shaw and Sons quickly followed suit with their own Cantonese production group in 1955. Also in 1955, Kong Ngee (Guangyi), the third largest film enterprise in Singapore, established Kong Ngee in Hong Kong. In addition to working for Kong Ngee, members of Union Film Enterprises also participated in Sun Luen Films (Xinlian, founded in 1952) and Overseas Chinese Film (Huaqiao, founded in 1956), and together these 'four major' Cantonese companies contributed to the golden age of Cantonese cinema.

COMPETING STUDIOS, 1956–65

Unlike the precarious postwar market that was crowded with small one-picture companies, Hong Kong cinema entered its studio era between 1956 and 1965, marked by cut-throat competition between Cathay and Shaw Brothers, which kept luring each other's top artists and outpacing each other's production plans.

Genres were reinvented and repackaged, and melodious songs, exuberant dances and beautiful actresses enriched the screen experience.

Cathay and MP&GI: urban modernity and youth culture

As head of Singapore-based Cathay, Loke Wan Tho managed more than 100 theaters in Malaysia and Singapore and had for many years distributed Yonghua's films. But Yonghua incurred a debt of HK$500,000 after a fire destroyed its film warehouse and a few unreleased prints in 1954. A generous loan from Taiwan in 1955 helped Yonghua temporarily when the land which Yonghua leased for its studio was reclaimed by the Hong Kong government. To build a new studio in Hammer Hill and relocate its facilities, Yonghua agreed to a restructuring plan and accepted Cathay's additional investment of HK$2 million. From this time, Yonghua existed merely in name. In 1956 Cathay's International Films (Guoji), which managed Yonghua's facilities and had co-produced features with Yan Jun, was merged into MP&GI, Cathay's fully-fledged Hong Kong production company, which quickly emerged as a Mandarin cinema stronghold in the late 1950s (HKFA 2002).

The early MP&GI production staff preferred urban comedy and emphasized the integration of Chinese and Western cultures. Their films transformed Shanghai's opposing 'conservative' and critical traditions and transformed Mandarin cinema (R. Huang 2001: 29–33). Directed by Tao Qin, whom MP&GI recruited from Shaw Brothers, *Our Sister Hedy* (Si qianjin, 1957; Mandarin) won the best picture award at the 1957 Asian Film Festival and established MP&GI's rising reputation. The film follows four very different sisters living with their wealthy widowed father (Wang Yuanlong). The eldest sister Hilda is virtuous but traditional, and one by one her boyfriends fall for her second sister Helen, a gorgeous temptress. The third sister (Lin Cui) is pretty but mischievous and frequently intervenes on Hilda's behalf, and her youngest sister Hazel is simply naïve. While disparaging towards both outdated Confucian morality and outlandish Western behavior, the film simultaneously encourages the preservation of family values and the pursuit of individual happiness. The upbeat mood, energetic soundtrack, funny situations and fashionable parties all highlight a new attitude toward *urban modernity* in Hong Kong.

The celebration of urban modernity and its attendant *youth culture* is even more evident in *Mambo Girl* (Manbo nülang, dir. Yi Wen, 1957), an MP&GI Mandarin release that established Ge Lan as 'the number one screen musical personality of the era' (Fonoroff 1997: 188). The film opens with a close-up of two dancing feet, and the camera pulls back to show Kailing (Ge Lan), a cheerful high school student, dancing to the applause of her swinging hipster friends. After a few rounds of songs and dances, Kailing suddenly turns sorrowful when she discovers that she is adopted. She searches the urban labyrinth and finds her birth mother working as a nightclub janitor, but her mother refuses to confirm their relationship. Kailing is profoundly touched by her adoptive parents, who organize a birthday party and turn Kailing back into a cheerful 'mambo girl'.

Hailed by Stephen Teo (Zhang Jiande) as Hong Kong's 'first musical master-piece', *Mambo Girl* also reveals the persistent question of *identity* in Hong Kong cinema. 'For the Chinese population of Hong Kong, torn between living in the colony and wishing to return to the mainland, this [question of identity] is a familiar predicament on the symbolic level'. Nonetheless, in its preferred solution to the birth puzzle, *Mambo Girl* ends with the birth mother secretly watching a happy family reunion with Kailing from outside the house, and then shows her slowly walking away, a dark shadow in the background. The film thus embraces the modern bourgeois lifestyle at the expense of a painful memory of the unspeakable haunting past, and the attitude of 'fun, rhythm, innocence and youthfulness' prevails in the new generation (HKIFF 1993: 35, 40, 64).

Corresponding to changes in screen attitudes and moods, MP&GI's new urban films also illustrate changes in the representation of the female body as a cinematic attraction. If *Calendar Girl* (Longxiang fengwu, dir. Tao Qin, 1959; Mandarin), the first MP&GI release in Eastmancolor, is still conservative in its classic Broadway-style costumes, then *Mad About Music* (Yingge yanwu, dir. Yi Wen, 1963; Mandarin) takes a new direction, with its two female leads dancing in revealing dresses. Even *Air Hostesses* (Kongzhong xiaojie, dir. Yi Wen, 1959; color, Mandarin), a romance shot on location in Taiwan, features a scene in which the would-be air hostesses line up for a physical examination wrapped in bath towels, radiant with identical smiles on their faces. As well us displaying youthful idols with charming faces and healthy bodies, *Air Hostesses* is further graced by Ge Lan's big hit, 'I Want to Fly Up to the Blue Sky' (Fonoroff 1997: 127, 189–91).

In addition to cultivating its contract directors and stars from Hong Kong and Taiwan, MP&GI also enlisted talent from overseas. One screenwriter who contributed to the popularity of MP&GI family dramas during this time was Eileen Chang. Her comedies of manners, which ridicule old-fashioned ideas but typically conclude in a compromise, were popular in Hong Kong and Taiwan. In Taipei's Chinese rankings, for example, *The Battle of Love* (Qingchang ru zhanchang, 1957) and *The Wayward Husband* (Taohua yun, 1958), both directed by Yue Feng, were placed second in 1957 and ninth in 1958, respectively.

Among other similar films, Chang's sequels to *The Greatest Civil War on Earth* (Nanbei he, dir. Wang Tianlin, 1961), which topped Hong Kong's Mandarin cinema box office in 1961, are worth mentioning.[11] The tongue-in-cheek exaggeration of the 'greatest' is matched by the reversed meaning of 'civil war' in the Chinese title, which denotes 'integration' and 'compromise' between *nanbei* – the 'south' (Hong Kong) and the 'north' (the mainland) – the nuance missing in the English title. Indeed, it is this missing nuance that constitutes the focus of the comedy series: the 'mixing' (*he*) of Cantonese and Mandarin cultures in Hong Kong society. Both directed by Wang Tianlin, Chang's Mandarin sequels *The Greatest Wedding on Earth* (Nanbei yijia qin, 1962; b/w) and *The Greatest*

Love Affair on Earth (Nanbei xi xiangfeng, 1964; b/w) continue to present 'mixed' couples but emphasize 'happiness' (*xi*), 'affection' (*qin*) and 'family unity' (*yijia*). In a sense, MP&GI's 'south–north' dramas represent yet another example of *convergence* in Hong Kong cinema – the mixing of Cantonese- and Mandarin-speaking casts in the same films. Interpreted at a symbolic level, this points to a self-confidence which Hong Kong filmmakers had obtained by the early 1960s: that by confronting rather than evading the *hybridity* of their cultural identity they could expect nothing but 'happy' endings.

The contemporary orientation in its musicals and family dramas does not mean that MP&GI disregarded history. In fact, drawing on MP&GI's favorite plot of two or three women romantically involved with the same man, *Sun, Moon and Star* (Xingxing, yueliang, taiyang, dir. Yi Wen, 1962; Mandarin) achieves an epic scope in its dramatic rendition of the resistance war and its devastating effects on Chinese people. With the location shoot done partly in Taiwan, this two-part film won the best picture prize at the inaugural Golden Horse Awards in 1962 and ranked second in the 1962 Taipei box office with NT$1,755,185.

As reflected in the annual Taipei top ten listing of the time (R. Huang 2001: 50–6), MP&GI dominated the Mandarin cinema market in the late 1950s, although Shaw Brothers caught up quickly and gained an upper hand after 1962. Various personnel changes affected MP&GI operations in 1962. After the untimely death of Loke Wan Tho in 1964 and after producing 110 Mandarin features, MP&GI changed its name to 'Cathay Hong Kong' but gradually lost out to Shaw Brothers.

Shaw Brothers: costume dramas and Li Hanxiang

When the Great China folded and returned its leased studio to Nanyang, Shao Cunren established Shaw and Sons (Shaoshi fuzi, its logos including SS) in 1950 and embarked on Mandarin productions, because a Mandarin title could be sold at a higher price than a Cantonese one. Shaw and Sons employed such directors as Tu Guangqi, Tao Qin and Wang Yin and produced seventy features, none of which achieved much distinction. By 1957, Run Run Shaw, who had up until this time given HK$250,000 per film to Shaw and Sons, was extremely upset by the popularity of recent MP&GI releases in Southeast Asia. He brought HK$5 million to Hong Kong, founded Shaw Brothers Hong Kong (Shaoshi xiongdi, its logos including SB) with his brother Runme, and relegated Shaw and Sons to the business of distribution and exhibition in Hong Kong. Run Run recruited Raymond Chow (Zou Wenhuai) as Shaw Brothers' head of publicity, and the studio's international outlook resulted in prominent US news coverage of Shaw Brothers enterprises. Located in Clear Water Bay, Shaw Brothers 'Movietown' opened in 1961 with brand new studios, standing sets, processing and recording facilities and even staff apartments. Operating twenty-four hours a day, Movietown enabled Shaw Brothers to work its 1,200 employees in ten-hour

Figure 5.3 Sun, Moon and Star (1962): female stars dominating the Hong Kong screen

shifts and to produce up to forty-five films a year, with an average budget of HK$800,000 per title (Bordwell 2000: 63) (see Table 3.2, p. 90).

What distinguishes Shaw Brothers from MP&GI initially, however, was that the former followed the Tianyi tradition and invested in big-budget costume dramas. Li Hanxiang boasted that he had been instrumental in making Shaw Brothers the foremost player in Mandarin cinema. Li had studied art in Beijing and moved to Hong Kong in 1948, working on art design at the Great China, Great Wall and Grandview companies before joining Yonghua as an actor and assistant director. He proceeded to Shaw and Sons in 1954 and initiated the trend of the yellow-plum opera movies with *Diau Charn* (Diao Chan, 1958; color), which broke Hong Kong Mandarin cinema box-office records and earned him the best director award at the 1958 Asian Film Festival. Li's production budgets jumped from HK$300,000 to $500,000 for *The Kingdom and the Beauty* (Jiangshan meiren, 1959; color). This opera movie, which set the Mandarin box office at HK$403,000 (M. Yu 2001: 202), together with Li's *Rear Entrance* (Houmen, 1960; b/w), a Mandarin literary adaptation set in contemporary Macao, won two consecutive best picture awards at the Asian Film Festivals and further consolidated Li's status.

Given his spectacular performance, Li was not pleased with Shaw Brothers due to the fact that his monthly salary of HK$8,000 was minuscule compared with the HK$20,000–30,000 which Yue Feng earned for directing one Shaw Brothers film. As a 'third-rank director', Li had no access to new Shaw Brothers studios and instead had to use studios leased from Asia Film and Grandview (Chiao 1993: 14–15, 192). Although Li's salary was raised to HK$40,000 in the early 1960s (see Table 3.1, pp. 64–5), his feelings of being slighted contributed to his decision to quit Shaw Brothers in 1963 (see Chapter 4).

Fierce competition: from Hong Kong to Taiwan

From the start, Shaw Brothers specifically targeted MP&GI and rushed to produce films that had been scheduled by their rival. Run Run ruled Shaw Brothers in Hong Kong, whereas MP&GI often had to wait for a decision from its Cathay headquarters in Singapore. This meant that MP&GI was forced to abandon a few projects which Shaw Brothers had already got to first, as in the case of *Yang Kuei-fei* (Yang Guifei, dir. Li Hanxiang, 1962; Mandarin). In other cases, Shaw Brothers was able to release its version first and defeated MP&GI at the box office. For instance, *The Love Eterne*, which Shaw Brothers produced with location shooting in Japan, was a big hit in Taiwan in 1963 and grossed NT$8.4 million in Taipei alone. MP&GI's version, *Liang Shanbo and Zhu Yingtai*, featured Li Lihua in male drag, but it earned only NT$1.7 million in Taipei two years later.

Ironically, once Li Hanxiang went it alone in Taiwan, he found himself competing with Shaw Brothers. *Seven Fairies* (Qi xiannü, 1963; Mandarin), which Li completed in seventeen days, and *A Maid from Heaven* (Qi xiannü, 1963;

Mandarin), which involved four Shaw Brothers directors, opened simultaneously in Taipei in 1964. Although both sold about 270,000 tickets and earned NT$2.7 million, Li lost a lawsuit brought by Shaw Brothers and his version was banned in Hong Kong (F. Chen 1988: 119).

Shaw Brothers' primary rival, however, remained MP&GI, which enlisted its five directors and almost all its stars to rush out *The Magic Lamp* (Baolian deng, dir. Wang Tianlin *et al.*, 1963; Mandarin) ahead of a Shaw Brothers' version. Delayed by Lin Dai's suicide in 1964, the Shaw Brothers' version was not released until 1965. Nonetheless, Shaw Brothers had its revenge in the next round with its adaptation of Zhang Henshui's 'butterfly' novel, *Fate in Tears and Laughter* (Tixiao yinyuan). Shaw Brothers employed its entire roster of directors and stars and completed *Between Tears and Laughter* (Gudu chunmeng, 1964; Mandarin) four weeks before MP&GI's *A Story of Three Loves* (Jinghua chunmeng, dir. Wang Tianlin, 1964; Mandarin). Competition continued between the two, but Shaw Brothers' market advantage became definitive after Loke Wan Tho's death in 1964. By this time, MP&GI's leading ladies, Ge Lan and You Min, had withdrawn from the screen world after their respective marriages. Ye Feng left MP&GI for Shaw Brothers in 1962 and Le Di the other way around in 1964, ending a period when female stars reigned supreme and ushering in a new era which looked towards the male star.

Market factors: Hong Kong and overseas

Before 1953, Cantonese films generally did well in Southeast Asia, where a title could generate between HK$50,000 and 80,000 in exhibition. Hong Kong producers thus relied on overseas presales to cover 50 to 60 per cent of production costs, which averaged about HK$80,000 per title. After 1953, however, decreasing revenues changed the practice of overseas distributors, who preferred to purchase the completed films or reluctantly paid in two or three installments amidst a film's production, which lasted fifteen to twenty-five days. In 1955, a Cantonese feature's production costs could be broken down as follows: HK$14,000 for studio leases, HK$6,000 for costumes, sets and props, HK$15,000 for film stock, HK$10,000 for staff and crew, HK$5,000 for meals, transportation and other expenses, and the rest went to the cast. Since combined overseas sales could reach HK$30,000, these became the main source of profits for a Hong Kong producer. Even when a film grossed the break-even HK$120,000 in Hong Kong theaters, a producer would receive only HK$51,000 after paying 18 per cent entertainment taxes and going halves with the theaters (M. Yu 2001: 30–1, 93). Besides, theater ticket prices (HK$0.7–3.0) in 1957 were much higher than those of 1948 (HK$0.2–3.5) (see Table 5.3).

Compared with a Cantonese title, overseas sales of an Amoy-dialect feature during this same period would gross substantially more, up to HK$50,000.

Table 5.3 Sample ticket prices in Hong Kong, 1904–99

Year	Theater	Type of film	Price (HK$)
1904	—	silent shorts	0.25–1
1913	—	Edison's sound Kingtonphone	0.5–2.5
1948	front row-balcony	—	0.2–3.5
1957	first run	—	1.5–3
1957	second run	—	0.7–2.4
1969	front row-balcony	—	1.5–3.5
1972	front row-balcony	—	2–3.5
1976	front row-balcony	—	3.2–6.3
1978	front row-balcony	—	4–8
1980	front row-balcony	—	6–13
1982	front row-balcony	—	10–15
1986	front row-balcony	—	17–20
1988	front row-balcony	Hong Kong-foreign	23–30
1991	—	Hong Kong-foreign	30–36
1994	—	Hong Kong-foreign	40–45
1996	—	Hong Kong	40–55
1998	—	Hollywood blockbuster	60
1999	—	Hong Kong-foreign	45–60

Sources: Chan 2000: 65; S. Chang 2002: 87; Curtin 1999: 39; HKIFF 1987: 19–20; HKIFF 1991: 73; M. Yu 1996: 81; M. Yu 1998: 170; M. Yu 2001: 96.

In 1958 an Amoy-dialect film rarely exceeded HK$38,000 in production costs, but its presales could generate up to HK$21,000 from Singapore, HK$9,000 from the Philippines and HK$13,000 from Taiwan (M. Yu 2001: 166) (see Table 2.5, p. 46). Profit margins and a sizable Amoy-dialect audience in Southeast Asia – second only to the Cantonese-speaking population among overseas Chinese – resulted in a dramatic increase in Amoy-dialect film production in Hong Kong, from one in 1950 to eighty-nine in 1959. Indeed, 1959 was the second year in a row when Amoy-dialect productions outnumbered Mandarin films (see Table 5.2, pp. 155–6). Although most Amoy-dialect films did not have their premiere in Hong Kong, their impact in Taiwan inspired local competition there and inadvertently spawned Taiwanese-dialect filmmaking.

In 1955 there were sixty-four theaters in Hong Kong, with an estimated population of 2.5 million, and there were on average 1,000 seats per theater. In 1957 movie tickets ranged from HK$1.5 to $3 at a first-run theater and HK$0.7 to $2.4 at a second-run theater. Most theaters showed Cantonese titles, but around twenty theaters were devoted to Western features. Out of 211 Hollywood films exhibited in 1957, the first runs generated HK$14,936,315. In comparison, Cantonese films grossed more even though their total number in exhibition in 1957 was much lower. In 1958 Cantonese films continued to out-perform Hollywood, the former on average earning HK$120,000 per title. By contrast, Hollywood had seen a steady decline in Hong Kong from 1953 to

1958 in all categories: films in exhibition dropped from 407 to 266, box office from HK$16.5 million to HK$14.2 million, and attendance from 8.2 million to 7.1 million. By 1958 the gross amount for a Hollywood title was HK$53,000, less than half that of an average Cantonese film (M. Yu 2001: 41, 96–8, 134). As in the case of Cantonese opera movies illustrated below, audience composition and local tastes were among the principal reasons for the dominance of Hong Kong over Hollywood products.

Mandarin and Cantonese film fashion: musicals, adaptations and operas

To return to Hong Kong's Mandarin productions, musicals – as exemplified by *Mambo Girl* and other MP&GI releases – took hold in the mid-1950s through to the mid-1960s. The fashion started with Xinhua's *Peach Blossom River* (Taohua jiang, dir. Wang Tianlin, Zhang Shankun, 1956), which features an innocent country girl (Zhong Qing) whose singing talent is discovered by a visiting artist from the city (Lo Wei [Luo Wei]). Singer Yao Li's back-stage voice, her brother Yao Min's music and Chen Dieyi's lyrics combined to make Xinhua's singing pictures instant hits and helped make Mandarin pop an influential musical genre in Hong Kong. Film historian Yu Muyun identifies five sources of Hong Kong musicals: Shanghai popular songs, Chinese folk songs, Chinese regional operas, Chinese composers and popular foreign songs. Despite their non-Hong Kong origins, however, Law Kar argues that Hong Kong musicals gradually abandoned Chinese 'central plain culture' and embraced cosmopolitan cultures elsewhere. Progressing from the Shanghai songstress (Zhou Xuan) through the country maiden (Zhong Qing) to the Hong Kong modern girl (Ge Lan), a new kind of *cosmopolitanism* grounded in Hong Kong began to take shape. Subsequent musicals, such as *Hong Kong Nocturne* (Xiangjiang huayue ye, dir. Inoue Umetsugu, 1967; Mandarin), contributed to a construction of Hong Kong identity as unabashedly hybrid (HKIFF 1993: 75–7).

As in the case of musicals, the trend for literary adaptations betrayed the influence of mainland Chinese culture, albeit not what Law Kar narrowly conceived of as a 'central plain culture'. Parallel to a strategy adopted by Union Film Enterprises, the Great Wall also invested in adapting modern literary classics; its version of *The True Story of Ah Q* (A Q zhengzhuan, dir. Yuan Yang'an, 1958; Mandarin), based on Lu Xun's famous work, predated its mainland counterpart by twenty-three years. In Cantonese productions, Cho Kei (Zuo Ji) followed Union Film Enterprises' lead and adapted Ba Jin's works for MP&GI in 1955–6 and those of Zhang Henshui for Overseas Chinese Film in the 1960s.

Cho Kei's work reminds us that MP&GI and Shaw Brothers continued to produce Cantonese films during the studio era. Both companies established Cantonese divisions in 1957. MP&GI's Cantonese division produced over seventy features before it ceased production in 1965, while Shaw Brothers' Cantonese division released about twenty titles and closed in 1966. As in the 1940s, Cantonese opera movies dominated Cantonese cinema, representing one-third of 1,500 Cantonese titles produced in the 1950s. In 1958 alone, eighty-one Cantonese opera movies were released, a record in Hong Kong film history.

According to Lee Tit, there were several reasons for the enduring popularity of Cantonese opera movies. First, it was easy to fix exhibition schedules because opera movies were routinely shot in a week – hence the term 'seven day wonders' (*qiri xian*) (Fonoroff 1997: xvi–xviii) – and there were few production delays. Second, leading opera artists were offered high compensation in return for two-year contracts, and Yam Kim-fai (Ren Jianhui), who starred in around 290 films, reportedly earned HK$17,500 per title and HK$50,000 per month. Third, for the majority of opera fans, opera movies were still affordable. If one wanted to see Yam Kim-fai perform, a theater ticket could cost as much as HK$25, whereas a movie ticket was between HK$1.7 and $2.4. Nonetheless, after fifteen years of domination, Cantonese opera movies dropped to less than 13 per cent of a total of over 1,500 Cantonese films produced in the 1960s. From forty-nine in 1962, Cantonese opera movies plunged to two in 1965 and none in 1969 (HKIFF 1987: 19–20, 68–73).

As in the case of Taiwanese-dialect films, the decline of Cantonese opera movies had as much to do with demographic changes as it did with over-production and poor artistic quality. Of Hong Kong's population of 3.1 million in 1961, 80 per cent spoke Cantonese and over 1.2 million (or 38.7 per cent) were below the age of 15 (Jarvie 1977: 54–8). The first figure explains the continued popularity of Cantonese cinema. As to be expected, fifty-five out of sixty-seven movie theaters were devoted to Cantonese films in 1960. The percentage changed to 77.7 in 1961 after the number of Cantonese movie theaters grew to fifty-six while the total number of theaters increased to seventy-two (HKIFF 1982: 18) (see Table 5.1, p. 154). On the other hand, the pre-dominance of those below the age of 15, which decreased only slightly in 1971 (35.8 per cent) and in 1976 (30.1 per cent), indicates an unavoidable change in audience's tastes.[12] Capable of reading if not speaking Mandarin, the younger generation of Cantonese audiences were less devoted to traditional Cantonese culture than the previous generations, and their tastes in movies and lifestyles gradually moved closer to those depicted in Mandarin and foreign cinemas.

Changes in demographics and education levels engendered a shift in younger Cantonese directors and new Cantonese stars. Production companies also adjusted their orientations. Kong Ngee's releases, for instance, tended to favor white-collar workers and addressed their career concerns, whereas Lingguang's products targeted a growing number of women workers and offered modern Cinderella stories which defied class barriers (HKIFF 1982: 20–9). Similarly, fans were divided into those who supported Chan Po-chu (Chen Baozhu) in her screen image as an independent but filial factory worker and those who admired Josephine Siao (Xiao Fangfang) as a modern but often rebellious girl from a wealthy family. As discussed below, new Cantonese genre films – from musicals to martial arts – also displayed a greater degree of convergence or similarity with Mandarin cinema of the time.

REINVENTING GENRES, 1966–78

In the mid-1960s, Hong Kong cinema experienced an abrupt change, both audio-visually as well as conceptually, from enticing femininity to revengeful masculinity, from melodious music to graphic violence, from upbeat idealism to bitter cynicism, from moral preaching to immoral cheating. A slower but more fundamental restructuring of the film industry in the incipient television era paralleled a quick succession of genre inventions. Whereas Cantonese cinema experienced a complete cycle of boom to bust to boom again, Mandarin cinema seemed to enjoy its heyday without realizing its imminent collapse in the 1980s.

The Cultural Revolution and its repercussions

The frenetic Cultural Revolution launched by the CCP ultra-leftists in the mainland in 1966 had immediate repercussions in an otherwise peaceful Hong Kong. Between 1961 and 1965, the Hong Kong government carried an annual budget surplus of HK$77.3 to 139.8 million, but suddenly – and for once only in the 1960s – it incurred a deficit of HK$137.4 million in 1965–6 (Cheuk 1999: 11). People took to the streets in 1966 to protest about the increased fares of the Star Ferry (the passenger ferry between Hong Kong island and Kowloon), and violent confrontations with the police ensued. But worse was to come in 1967, a year marked by workers' strikes, student demonstrations and bomb scares. Riots erupted as the police rounded up protesters and imposed curfews. In May 1967, as students stormed the front entrance of Government House (HKIFF 1988: 77–82), left-wing film workers stormed Shaw Brothers with 'big-character wall posters' denouncing capitalist exploitation. Shaw Brothers fired over 140 striking workers and organized vigilante supporters to guard the studio facilities (C. Wu 1979: 359). Leftist fanaticism was such that, when mainland feature productions came to a halt, the Phoenix produced *The Battle of Sha Chia Bund* (Shajiabang jiandi ji, 1968; Mandarin), an adaptation of a 'revolutionary model play' that predated its mainland counterpart by three years.

Overall, the Cultural Revolution had an extremely negative impact on Hong Kong cinema. Due to left-wing agitation, major Cantonese companies suspended production for more than a year, and two companies, Union Film Enterprises and Kong Ngee, shut down entirely in 1967 and 1969 respectively. In 1979 Sun Luen Films also folded. Since 1966, left-wing strongholds Great Wall and Phoenix had suffered enormous box-office losses in Hong Kong and overseas, thus in 1982 they merged with the former Sun Luen Films and established Sil-Metropole Organization (Yindu).[13]

Taiwan seized upon the widespread sense of disillusion with the Cultural

Revolution, and saw it as a perfect opportunity to pressure former PRC sympathizers, such as Gong Qiuxia, to denounce the CCP. Shaw Brothers, Cathay, Kong Ngee and other regional distribution companies signed an agreement with the KMT regime and refused to distribute PRC films, and such films thus disappeared from Malaysia and Singapore for a while (R. Huang 2001: 36). Political pressure was also applied to Cantonese filmmakers. Chan Wan (Chen Yun), a notable Cantonese film director who had promoted Chan Po-chu and Josephine Siao but who had contributed screenplays to left-wing companies, was blacklisted by Free Association and had to visit Taipei in 1969 before Hong Kong producers offered him three more projects. Chan refused to pay his Free Association membership fees, killing his film directing career and forcing him to switch instead to television in 1970 (HKIFF 1996: 113).

Cantonese cinema: radical transformation and dismal decline

In the late 1960s Cantonese cinema came to depend disproportionately on two of its leading actresses, Chan Po-chu and Josephine Siao, to sustain box-office appeal. In 1967, when Chan was eighteen and Siao twenty, they starred either together or separately in fifty-eight out of 105 Cantonese features released in that year (Fonoroff 1997: xx). *Colorful Youth* (Caise qingchun, dir. Wong Yiu [Huang Yao], 1966; b/w) featured both Chan and Siao in a series of songs and dances and broke Cantonese box-office records with HK$600,000. This film started the vogue for youth musicals in Cantonese cinema, reminiscent of their Mandarin counterparts almost a decade earlier.

Since by this time young Cantonese audiences also watched Mandarin and foreign films, their expectations of Cantonese cinema were raised and they preferred films closer to their experiences. Contemporary urban cinema thus replaced Cantonese opera movies, and new Cantonese directors began to explore social issues from new perspectives and in new cinematic ways. *I Love Violet* (Wo ai zi luolan, dir. Chor Yuen [Chu Yuan], 1966), for example, combines comedy, romance and detective story in a psychological drama. David (Lui Kei [Lü Qi]) frequently receives phone calls from a strange woman named Jenny, but each time he tries to meet her he is beaten up. When they finally meet, Jenny seems to have known David for a long time. David and his friend suspect that Jenny might have gangster connections. One evening, after a dinner with Jenny's 'parents', David accompanies Jenny to the beach, but she becomes hysterical when a boy runs out from nowhere. At this point David is informed that Jenny has suffered from amnesia after her little brother was drowned the night she dated her fiancé, also named David. The reenactment set up by the psychiatrist was meant to recover Jenny's memory but it failed miserably.

If *I Love Violet* revisits failures in a sentimental setting, *Story of a Discharged Prisoner* (Yingxiong bense, dir. Lung Kong [Long Gang], 1967) examines similar themes but in a violent way. Li Zuoxiong is discharged from prison and is determined to restart his life, but the police and gangsters both want to use him to their advantage and make sure he stays unemployed. Without knowing what is going on, Li's brother is implicated in a burglary and Li has to kill his former gangster boss, for which he assumes all responsibility. After a court scene that features a confrontation between a detective and a social worker, Li is back in prison again.

By this time, director Lung Kong had acquired a visual style characterized by montage and a variety of camera angles, a fast rhythm and a sense of realism enhanced by location shooting. Lung experimented with multilinear narratives in his subsequent investigation of rebellious youth, *Teddy Girls* (Feinü zhengzhuan, 1969), which grossed HK$0.7 million. By casting Josephine Siao as a rebel from a wealthy household – reminiscent of James Dean in *Rebel Without a Cause* (dir. Nicholas Ray, 1955; trans. as A Fei zhengzhuan) – *Teddy Girls* explores issues of female juvenile delinquency and highlights the loss of faith in the justice system. Contrary to *The Orphan* (Renhai guhong, dir. Lee Sun-fung, 1960), which optimistically ends with a trouble-making orphan (Bruce Lee) returning to the care of his long-separated father (Ng Cho-fan), Lung Kong's films articulated anxiety and pessimism prevalent in post-riot Hong Kong.

As if already wearied of its charming youth idols and exhausted by its imaginative resources, Cantonese cinema turned to soft porn (*fengyue*, literally 'wind and moon', a Chinese euphemism for sex) in the early 1970s, which sustained its box office for a while but further damaged its reputation. Its dismal decline seemed destined: from seventy-one titles in 1969, the number of annual productions nose-dived to thirty-five in 1970, one in 1971 and none in 1972 – a far cry from the heyday of 211 titles in 1961 (see Table 5.2, pp. 155–6).

Suffering versus paranoia, or idealism versus fantasy

The apparent demise of Cantonese cinema compelled critics to reassess the 1950s and 1960s. As Lin Niantong contends, Cantonese films of the early 1960s, such as *All These Pitiable Parents* (Kelian tianxia fumu xin, dir. Chor Yuen, 1961), still exemplified the 'notion of suffering' and the 'plebeian ideals' of solidarity and perseverance and thus carried on the 1950s tradition of Hong Kong cinema. But 'a sense of paranoia' crept into Cantonese films of the late 1960s, in particular Lung Kong's works. Contrary to the observance of the time-honored realist tradition as in the 1950s, 'Cantonese films in the late 1960s failed to achieve a stylistic metamorphosis ... [and] this was perhaps one of the reasons for the waning of this dialect cinema's popularity at the end of the decade' (HKIFF 1982: 30–3).

Shu Kei (Shu Qi) modifies Lin's thesis of *suffering versus paranoia* with his own thesis of *idealism versus fantasy* – the former dominated the 1950s whereas the latter the 1960s. In addition to the disappearance of the sanctity of collective power in the 1960s, Shu Kei notices an augmenting emphasis on individual failures and an overwhelming sense of futility in the face of society or fate in Cantonese films of the 1960s. Unity as strength became a myth, family as sanctuary now an unrealized dream, and *nihilism* a prevailing attitude in the wake of the 1967 riots. The pathos of defeats thus authorized corresponding stylistic changes, such as a transition from medium and long shots (denoting security and harmony) characteristic of the 1950s to close-ups (isolation in space, time and psychology) and montages (disorientation and fragmentation) in the 1960s. Yet Shu Kei asserts that, as represented by Lung Kong, Cantonese films of the late 1960s 'came even closer to "realism"', although 'the best tradition' of Cantonese cinema – 'its concern for people and their emotions' – had been irretrievably lost (HKIFF 1982: 108–21).

The displacement of idealism by fantasy thus characterized what Stephen Teo regards as 'the restless years' of 'the paranoid sixties' (HKIFF 1996). Seen in this context, Cantonese soft-porn pictures of the 1970s functioned as a *symptom* of disillusionment and paranoia at the same time as they provided a fantastic – albeit sometimes freakish – route of escape. Exploitative rather than appreciative in nature, these pictures exhibited sex symbols like Tina Ti (Di Na, aka TNT) in such suggestive titles as *Magic Feeding* (Mantian xingdou, literally 'stars all over the sky'), aka *Breast from Outer Space* (Taikong nai, 1970). Lui Kei, who had played a handsome gentleman caught between rivaling loves Chan Po-chu and Josephine Siao, assumed an ironic role in the early 1970s when he transformed himself into a soft-porn producer and subcontracted work from Shaw Brothers. While the unprecedented attention to sexuality produced certain notable titles in mixed-genre films, like *Intimate Confessions of a Chinese Courtesan* (Ai nu, dir. Chor Yuen, 1976; Mandarin), where homoeroticism is mixed with martial arts, soft-porn pictures in general reflected a transition toward a sense of disillusion, nihilism and paranoia.

Characteristic of his ingenuity, Li Hanxiang played a decisive part in this transition. Produced for his New Guolian Company, Li's Mandarin 'cheating triology' (1971–3) was thoroughly decadent and populated by a variety of scandalous imposters. Mixing sex, horror and singing as well as folk wisdom and popular gags, Li's trilogy consisted of short segments which creatively combined comedians from Hong Kong and Taiwan and offered lowbrow entertainment – not without certain local color – to a mass audience (HKIFF 1984: 145). Li proceeded next with a series of soft-porn pictures for Shaw Brothers, combining his specialty in visually stunning costume dramas with a new attitude of unapologetic decadence.

With their erotic obsession and anti-romantic thrust, Li's films of the 1970s were symptomatic of the collapsed confidence in the arts and humanity and constituted what Stephen Teo calls 'aesthetics of the cynical' (HKIFF 1984: 90–8). Replete with excess, vulgarity and mimicry, Li's decadent Mandarin films, together with his Cantonese counterparts, represented a departure from – if not a protest against – moderation, decency and mimesis valued so much in the previous ethical drama films, which had been a tradition of not just Hong Kong cinema but Chinese cinema in general. Extended to purely visual spectacle, Li's decadent films also ridiculed the dream of affluence and romance manufactured by both Mandarin and Cantonese musicals. When one compares the beauty and idealism in the Hong Kong musicals of the 1950s and 1960s with the nihilism and paranoia in Li's decadent films of the 1970s, it is astonishing to see how much Hong Kong cinema had changed in two decades.

Mandarin cinema: from romance to new-style martial arts

In the mid-1960s, the import of Taiwan romances and the emergence of new-style martial arts pictures challenged and quickly eclipsed Hong Kong musicals and opera movies. Shaw Brothers confronted the Taiwan challenge with its own versions of the Qiong Yao-type of romance. Earlier, in competition with MP&GI, Shaw Brothers had produced such romances as *Love Without End* (Buliao qing, dir. Tao Qin, 1961; b/w), which featured Lin Dai as a self-sacrificing lover and was re-released several times after Lin's suicide in 1964. In 1967 Shaw Brothers scored an unprecedented victory with *One-Armed Swordsman* (Dubi dao, dir. Zhang Che), which set a record of HK$1 million in its first week of release and was ranked number one in the 1968 Taipei box-office listings. Subsequently, Shaw Brothers consolidated its market dominance by concentrating on martial arts pictures, steadily increasing its annual output from thirty-one in 1966 to thirty-seven in 1969 and releasing around forty-five martial arts films between 1973 and 1984 (Zhan and Lan 1996: 166–79).

Martial arts films had long been an established genre in Hong Kong cinema. *The True Story of Wong Fei-hung* (Huang Feihong zhuan, dir. Wu Pang [Hu Peng], 1949) featured Kwan Tak-hing and set a box-office record of 100,000 tickets (Rodriguez 1997). Between then and 1998, 101 films featuring Huang Feihong (Wong Fei-hung) were produced, exclusive of television episodes (M. Yu 1998: 193–5). Nevertheless, opera movies and musicals, both of which promoted female stars at the expense of their male counterparts, overwhelmed the martial arts genre in the 1950s and the early 1960s, and it was not until post-riot Hong Kong that martial arts pictures became a dominant genre.

With his role in Taiwan's first Mandarin film, *Wind and Cloud on Ali Mountain*, Zhang Che was not new to the film world. Zhang arrived in Hong Kong in 1957 and worked as a screenwriter for MP&GI and Shaw Brothers. His career took off, however, with the martial arts genre. From 1967 to 1974, Zhang followed the success of *One-Armed Swordsman* with a series of popular Shaw Brothers releases. He discovered such actors as Wang Yu, David Chiang (Jiang Dawei) and Ti Lung (Di Long) and led the trend of new-style martial arts pictures in the late 1960s and the vogue for Shaolin tales in the mid-1970s. In 1974 Zhang went to Taiwan to set up his own company but, like his predecessor Li Hanxiang, returned to Shaw Brothers in 1977 after it failed (C. Zhang 1989).

Zhang's martial arts pictures are known for their sadomasochistic male heroes. A proud wandering loner misunderstood by people around him, Zhang's hero displays male honor in its most idealized and hence most destructive form. Set in the warring states, *The Assassin* (Da cike, 1967) concludes with a heroic scene of self-defacement and suicide shot in darkness, a scene that glorifies death as the last means of self-fulfillment. Zhang's films foreground injured male bodies, in particular severed arms and bellies plunged with daggers. Through such gory images, Zhang simultaneously projects castration anxiety and intensifies male bonding to such a degree as to invite homoerotic interpretations. It is true that Zhang has injected masculine heroism into the blood of Hong Kong cinema, but his nurturing of male egotism at the expense of female characters often results in irrational fears and unwarranted violence (HKIFF 1984: 41–6).

For some critics, by overcoming his castration anxiety (his right arm chopped off by his master's daughter in a duel), the hero in *One-Armed Swordsman* represents a new breed of individual, unfettered by patriarchal obligations, which characterize their counterparts in the Huang Feihong series (HKIFF 1996: 27). For others, the over-indulgence in male narcissism and preposterous violence meant that Zhang did not achieve the same auteur status as that of his contemporary, King Hu (Bordwell 2000: 248–60). Using martial arts as a means rather than an end in itself, King Hu developed a unique style of motion and a film aesthetic grounded in traditional Chinese painting, literature and theater (HKIFF 1998b: 12–125). In many ways, it is King Hu who brought visual sophistication and international reputation to the new-style martial arts pictures, while it is Bruce Lee who best embodies masculine heroism on screen.

Golden Harvest and its two dragons

The rise of actor Bruce Lee owes much to Raymond Chow, who left Shaw Brothers to found Golden Harvest with Leonard Ho (He Guanchang) in May 1970, at the height of Shaw Brothers' monopoly of the Hong Kong and Southeast Asian markets. When Cathay ceased production in 1971, Chow purchased its Yonghua studio in Diamond Hill and invited Bruce Lee to star in *The Big Boss*, aka *Fists of Fury* (Tangshan daxiong, 1971), and *The Chinese Connection* (Jingwu men, 1972), both directed by Lo Wei in Mandarin. The public response to Bruce Lee, who had resumed his Chinese name Li Xiaolong (literally 'small dragon'), was phenomenal in Hong Kong: *The Big Boss* earned nearly HK$3.2 million and *The Chinese Connection* grossed HK$4.4 million. Bruce Lee not only swept Asia but he also became a star in Africa, Australia, Europe, and North and South America (Desser 2000). Lee directed *The Way of the Dragon*, aka *Return of the Dragon* (Menglong guojiang, 1973; Mandarin), a co-production with Golden Harvest, which grossed HK$5.3 million (Yeh *et al.* 1999: 19). The fascination with Bruce Lee became even greater with his untimely death in 1973 at age 33 while shooting *Game of Death* (Siwang youxi, dir. Robert Clouse), which was released in 1978 with a double playing Lee in some scenes (Chan 2000: 28; M. Chen 1996: 378–400).

Run Run Shaw was upset by Lee's success, especially since Lee had reportedly

Figure 5.4 Fist of Fury (1972): Bruce Lee and the worldwide gongfu craze

approached him first with a demand of US$10,000 per title. Shaw Brothers' counter-offer of a maximum HK$9,000 per title had convinced Lee to accept Golden Harvest's offer of US$7,500 per title (Zhan and Lan 1996: 206–9). In retaliation, as it had done to Li Hanxiang a decade earlier, Shaw Brothers brought a lawsuit against Golden Harvest accusing it of imitating Shaw's one-armed martial arts formula. But as the court proceedings dragged on with appeals made to England, Golden Harvest became established, especially when it signed its second 'dragon' Jackie Chan (Cheng Long, 'long' meaning 'dragon'). A superstar since his performance in *Drunken Master* (Zuiquan, dir. Yuen Wo-ping [Yuan Heping], 1978), Chan, together with Sammo Hung (Hong Jinbao), invented the subgenre of gongfu comedy.

Jackie Chan was on loan to Seasonal Film (Siyuan, founded by Wu Siyuan [Ng See-yuen] in 1975) when shooting *Drunken Master*. Golden Harvest's respective cooperation with Bruce Lee, Seasonal Film and others in the industry illustrates a new strategy. Contrary to Shaw Brothers' emphasis on huge scale and absolute control, which was typical of the studio system, Golden Harvest preferred 'an independent production system where stars and directors could agree to mutually profitable deals with the studio' (Teo 1997: 80). This quasi-independent system proved effective. By 1975 Golden Harvest controlled the largest theater chain in Hong Kong and had acquired dozens more screens overseas (Bordwell 2000: 68). An even more spectacular period of success came when it cooperated with the Hui brothers and helped revive Cantonese cinema.

Television and Cantonese cinema: the Hui brothers and comedy

In spite of the Mandarin box-office boom, the early 1970s was an unsettling time of double-digit inflation, economic recession, stock market crash, rampant crime and corruption – all of which, together with new mainland immigrants (legal and illegal), provided fertile subjects for Hong Kong cinema and television news coverage. According to one estimate, news and weather forecasts reached 1.7 million viewers daily and were the two most popular television programs in 1974 (HKIFF 1984: 12). The household ownership of television sets in Hong Kong had grown from 12.3 per cent in 1968 to 41.2 per cent in 1970, 72 per cent in 1972 and 90 per cent in 1976 (Cheuk 1999: 26). Unlike in Taiwan, however, television did not drastically affect movie attendance in Hong Kong. But the rapid growth of the television industry still had an impact on Hong Kong cinema, not just in personnel flow but also in subject matter and modes of representation. During the decline of Cantonese cinema in the early 1970s, many film artists migrated to the television industry, where they were able to experiment with new subjects and styles (Teo 2000). The establishment of the Independent Commission Against Corruption (ICAC) in 1974 and its high-profile arrests, as covered by the media, prompted public interest. And this explains the popularity of new crime films like *Anti-Corruption* (Lianzheng fengbao, dir. Wu Siyuan, 1975), with its fast-paced documentary-style presentation.

A more prominent Cantonese feature was *The House of Seventy-two Tenants* (Qishier jia fangke, dir. Chor Yuen, 1973), which set a new box-office record of over HK$5.6 million and single-handedly revived Cantonese cinema (HKIFF 1984: 149). Based on a hilarious Shanghai stage play about a housing shortage, this comedy remake of a Wang Weiyi film directed in Guangzhou a decade earlier is distinguished by its all-star cast, which included many top names in film and television of the time. Co-produced by Shaw Brothers and HK-TVB (Hong Kong Television Broadcast, TVB for short, Gangshi, aka Wuxian, established in November 1967), this ingenious work anticipated what was to come in Cantonese cinema from the *cross-fertilization* between film and television: loose episodic structure, smart punchlines, outrageous humor and exaggerated acting.

Under these circumstances, the Hui brothers' rise to fame in cinema was only natural. In 1971 Michael Hui (Xu Guanwen) and Sam Hui (Xu Guanjie) co-hosted a popular TVB variety show. In 1972 Michael Hui proceeded to play the lead in *The Warlord* (Da junfa, dir. Li Hanxiang, 1972; Mandarin), a Shaw Brothers production that established him as Hong Kong's leading comedian.

After a few more films Michael and his brother Ricky (Xu Guangying) both left Shaw Brothers, and together with Sam they established the Hui Brothers Company in 1974. From the start, the comedies directed by Michael Hui frequently ranked among the top ten – a trend that continued until the early 1990s (Chan 2000: 40). For example, co-produced with Golden Harvest, *Games Gamblers Play* (Guima shuangxing, dir. Michael Hui, 1974) outperformed Bruce Lee's films, taking HK$6.2 million at the box office. By the time *The Private Eyes* (Banjin baliang, dir. Michael Hui, 1976) grossed HK$8.5 million, the drawing power of Cantonese cinema had more than doubled that of *Colorful Youth* a decade earlier. The earlier temporary demise of Cantonese cinema now seemed very distant.

Owing much to the Hui brothers' ingenuity, satirical comedy – characterized by verbal gags, humorous situations, insignificant urbanites and their incon-sequential acts – had become an effective competitor to martial arts pictures by the mid-1970s. Neither a lone hero of the martial arts films nor a decadent philanderer of the soft-porn pictures, the Hui brothers' pathetic anti-heroes always work in a comic pair (*paidang*) – a Cantonese tradition of comedy that would be exploited to the fullest in subsequent decades. With all his pretensions, frustrations and complaints, the Hui brothers' anti-hero stood for what Law Kar describes as 'Hong Kong's Everyman, a screen persona which arouses audience identification' (HKIFF 1984: 65).

In Jackie Chan's case, a subgenre of comedy would integrate martial arts into gongfu or action comedy in the years to come. Thanks to the outstanding per-formances of the Hui brothers and Jackie Chan, by 1977 the annual Cantonese production output had once again surpassed Mandarin cinema. But contrary to the postwar revival, the Cantonese opera movie did not come back this time and virtually disappeared as a genre after three swan-song releases in the mid-1970s (HKIFF 1987: 21).

Of cinema and television: new talents, new styles and new competitions

A group of new talent emerged from cinema and television circles during the 1970s, and among them Tang Shuxuan (Shu Shuen, Cecille Tang), a visionary woman director educated at the University of Southern California, stood out at a time when martial arts and comedies inundated the market. Supported by American money, Tang brought a breath of fresh air to the Hong Kong screen with her debut, *The Arch* (Dong furen, 1970; b/w, Mandarin).

Set in the Ming dynasty, the film opens with a series of alternating panning and zooming shots of mountains, pine trees, clouds, woods, fields and a village, where soldiers arrive to protect the harvest from bandits. Madame Dong (Lu Yan) is a model widow living with her teenage daughter Weiling and her mother-in-law, and the villagers have petitioned the emperor for an arch of chastity in her honor. Captain Yang stays with the Dong family, and Weiling admires Yang's martial figure from behind a window. A series of shots detail Dong's household chores and a door dividing the inner and the outer compounds is highlighted several times, with Dong standing by silently after Yang has left or Weiling has gone through to pay Yang a visit. Yang leaves a love poem for Dong in the study and accompanies Weiling to the woods. Under the light of a shining moon, Yang watches Dong applying make-up from outside the window. A cricket surprises them, and while chasing it they touch each other's hands. In the wine party that follows, shots of Yang's hands carrying the dishes are repeated, and later in the night Dong in her bed hears Yang reciting a love poem outside.

As is typical of traditional widow tales, *The Arch* proceeds to show Dong repressing her emotions and marrying Weiling to Yang. A short shot-reverse-shot sequence foregrounds Yang and Dong speechless in the courtyard. Upon seeing the newlyweds off, Dong resumes her household routines. After her mother-in-law's death, Dong becomes even lonelier when the family's male servant prepares to leave. The news of the emperor's approval of the arch does not change her life. Dong shuts the window, sits by the spinning wheel, and the sorrow on her face is intensified by the overlapping images of hands – Yang's hand writing the love poem, her hands applying make-up, their hands together over a cricket, and a worker's hands chipping away at the arch stone. Dong stands up and paces around the room. She suddenly opens the door, grabs a knife, rushes out and kills a rooster, its blood spilling on her dress. The servant is stunned and, after a moment of facing each other, Dong runs away into the darkness. A cut to the firecrackers launched in celebration of the completion of the arch returns Dong to her usual demeanor. She lowers her head and silently stands alone under the arch dedicated to her name, while the camera pulls back and pans across the distant mountains and clouds, thus framing the story as an inconsequential drama in human history.

In many ways, *The Arch* is unique in Hong Kong cinema. First, it is a sympathetic exploration of female experience from a feminist perspective. Critic Liu Chenghan (Lau Shing-hon) has pointed out the inadequate portrayal of male characters in the film, but this proves Tang's strategy of privileging female subjectivity at the expense of a balanced treatment of the genders. Second, Tang's sophisticated use of cinematic techniques, such as dissolves, jump-cuts, deep focus and freeze-frame, has produced a psychological text which is rich in traditional symbolism and psychoanalytic implications. The shots of Weiling stroking an ear of corn and of Yang eating a peach, for instance, symbolically express their sexual desires, although such symbols of the male and the female sexual organs might appear all too obvious by present-day standards. The symbolic enactment of castration in the killing of a rooster also reveals Tang's reliance on Freudian psychoanalysis: it is only through such an act of bloody violence that Dong can give vent to her frustrations and resume her semblance of peace (HKIFF 1984: 103–9). Third, the film's critical and popular reception was sharply divided. Even though *The Arch* had a discouraging three-day run in Hong Kong theaters, Tang's talent was immediately recognized at the 1971

Golden Horse Awards, which honored her with a special prize for superlative imagination in film and Lu Yan with the best actress award.

Shot on location in Taiwan in 1974, Tang's second Mandarin feature, *China Behind*, further confirmed her exceptional talent. In this first Hong Kong feature to confront the Cultural Revolution at a time when it was going on, Tang dramatizes the physical and emotional traumas four mainland students endure in their illegal border crossing to Hong Kong. Ironies abound in Tang's drama. In the anti-climatic ending, the illegal immigrants who have reached the land of their dreams find Hong Kong an alienating city, as frenetic with capitalism as China is with Maoism. Even more unfortunate than *The Arch*, *China Behind* was banned in Taiwan for containing images of the CCP leaders and in Hong Kong on the premise that it would 'damage good relations with other territories' (Law 2001: 36).[14] Although its Hong Kong ban was lifted in 1981, the film has never been released commercially, although its significance – especially its daring investigation of sensitive geopolitical issues – has been belatedly recognized.

Tang Shuxuan was ahead of her time with her avant-garde spirit and vision. She made two more features in 1975 and 1979 and, after both failed miserably, quit filmmaking altogether. Her sponsorship of the film magazine *Close Up* (Da texie) between 1976 and 1979, however, brought together a group of young writers who would launch *Film Biweekly* (Dianying shuangzhou kan) in 1979 and promote a new wave of cinema in Hong Kong.

Apart from Tang's work, signs of a new wave were also present in *Jumping Ash* (Tiaohui, 1976) co-directed by Josephine Siao and Leong Po-chi (Liang Puzhi), a gangster film that created a new visual style in Hong Kong cinema. Skilled at filming commercials, Leong was credited for his realistic use of the hand-held camera, his location shooting in places like Kowloon's Walled City, and his fast-paced, free-moving documentary style. With the opening scenes shot in Amsterdam and two pleasing theme songs, the film was nicely packaged and did well at the box office, indicative of the potential commercial value of avant-garde techniques.

Although new to the film world, Leong Po-chi was a pioneer of Hong Kong television, having started with TVB as early as 1967. By the time *Jumping Ash* was produced, television had become a training ground for future film artists. Between 1975 and 1977, when Selina Chow (Leong Suk-yi, Zhou-Liang Shuyi) was in charge of programming and production, TVB gradually shifted its emphasis from variety shows to 30- and 60-minute programs shot in 16mm film. With his distinctive style, Patrick Tam (Tan Jiaming) contributed to such TVB series as *CID* (1976) and *Seven Women* (Qi nüxing, 1977), the latter courting controversy with its daring exploration of female sexuality (HKIFF 1999a: 94–105). A pioneer in television dramas, TVB was able to attract several overseas-trained talents, including Tsui Hark (Xu Ke) from Texas, and Ann Hui (Xu Anhua) and Yim Ho (Yan Hao) from London.

Meanwhile, Hong Kong's oldest station RTV (Rediffusion Television, Lidi), which had begun operating in cable in May 1957 and had switched to color and non-cable in December 1973,[15] employed talents like Johnny Mak (Mai Dangxiong). Mak soon earned recognition with the RTV series *Ten Assassinations* (Shida cike, 1976) and *Operation Manhunt* (Da zhangfu, 1976). In September 1975, a third station, CTV (Commercial Television, Jiashi), was launched. In 1976 CTV also launched a martial arts series, which reached a million viewers, and it competed with RTV for second place in the television market. By early 1978 CTV had consolidated its position with the high-profile defection of Selina Chow along with around 200 former TVB personnel, including Tsui Hark, Patrick Tam, Ringo Lam (Lin Lingdong) and Eddie Fong (Fang Lingzheng). A bidding war for television talent ensued, but TVB was able to win back many of its defectors because it was the only station that generated profits. By late 1978 CTV had ceased production after having spent HK$50 million on production in merely three years (Cheuk 1999: 16).

In the midst of the unprecedented competition, RTHK (Radio-Television Hong Kong, Xianggang dianshi), the only public station in Hong Kong, produced *Below the Lion Rock* (Shizishan xia, 1975). Shot on film, this series benefited from young artists such as Allen Fong (Fang Yuping) and Ann Hui, the latter also shooting episodes for the ICAC (Law 2001). Not owning its own channel, RTHK broadcast its programs on commercial channels during government-allocated time (HKIFF 1999a: 167–94).

A number of characteristics distinguish this group of television talent from previous filmmakers or their contemporaries like the Hui brothers. First, their sense of television professionalism compelled them to capture the reality of Hong Kong using candid camera techniques, confronting taboo subjects and exposing government bureaucracy in an earnest rather than in a cynical way. Second, their profound sympathy for the underprivileged continued the humanist tradition of Cantonese cinema, but without the former's didacticism. Further, the limited time per television episode prevented lengthy moral preaching and resulted in a realist documentary style. Third, their command of new film techniques further enhanced the visual quality and emotional impact of their dramas, which appealed in particular to younger audiences. By the time TVB canceled its film unit after the closure of CTV, most of these new television program-makers were on their way to feature filmmaking. *Extras* (Qielifei, dir. Yim Ho, 1978), the first feature film from this group, heralded the advent of a new wave in Hong Kong cinema.

The death of Mandarin cinema

Even though it had monopolized the Mandarin market, Shaw Brothers had no idea when it co-produced *The House of Seventy-two Tenants* a year after Cantonese cinema's temporary demise that the boom in Mandarin cinema would face an even worse fate. As Teo states: 'By 1979, Mandarin-language cinema was dead' (Teo 2000: 90). Teo attributes several factors to Mandarin cinema's demise, a situation that was unimaginable at its peak in the early 1970s. First, when Shaw

Brothers and Golden Harvest raised their distribution fees in the boom years, Southeast Asian exhibitors changed their strategy by seeking partnership with Taiwan and co-producing Mandarin films there. Second, the profitable partnership with Taiwan inevitably caused overproduction, which resulted in a backlog of Mandarin titles waiting for release in Southeast Asia. Third, Indonesia imposed an import quota on Mandarin films, which dropped from 300 in 1972 to 100 in 1973, ninety in 1974 and fifty-six in 1977. Malaysia, Singapore and Thailand raised their import duties on films, and the South Vietnam market was closed at the end of the Vietnam War in 1975. Finally, unlike Cantonese cinema, where new talent simply migrated from film to television and back, Mandarin cinema in Hong Kong suffered from the drain of its talent pool. Therefore, as the new wave pushed Cantonese cinema into the international spotlight, Mandarin cinema suddenly disappeared, and the history of Hong Kong cinema began an entirely new chapter.

CONCLUSION: TOWARD REGIONAL IMAGINATION

In April 1977 the Hong Kong Urban Council inaugurated the annual Hong Kong International Film Festival (HKIFF), which exhibited films from various countries and regions and organized special retrospectives and forums on Hong Kong cinema. Apart from its political significance in promoting Hong Kong as a cosmopolitan city and its artistic significance in discovering new talent, themes and techniques, the HKIFF has carried cultural significance in reconstructing Hong Kong film history. Since 1978, the annual retrospectives and the accompanying bilingual publications have placed Hong Kong cinema on research agendas. Given the involvement of a new generation of critics and scholars, Cantonese cinema has received special attention.

A manifesto-like introduction by Li Cheuk-to (Li Zhuotao), a veteran HKIFF program coordinator, to the 1988 retrospective, *Changes in Hong Kong Society Through Cinema*, states that:

> Hong Kong is a city commonly thought of as having no history . . . Where the last generation is concerned, Hong Kong was a place of refuge but whose time and locality was borrowed. Hence, a sense of belonging was lacking. To the newer generations, the sense of belonging is stronger but their perspective of history (especially that of China) is sadly limited . . . Hong Kong's history has been subdued and a new historical consciousness was never nurtured.

When Li announces the intention of the 1988 retrospective as 'a beginning towards understanding Hong Kong's history', his ultimate goal is not history per se but culture – 'Without a local history, there is no local culture. Without a local culture, the meeting of minds from both east and west would essentially come to naught' (HKIFF 1988: 9). The Chinese phrase Li uses for 'local culture' is *wenhua benwei*, literally 'culture's original locale', which foregrounds both the *locality* of Hong Kong culture and the *historicity* of this culture's transformation. In this sense, cinema furnishes a means of retrieving collective memory and experience as well as reconstructing local history and culture.

Li Cheuk-to's overview of Hong Kong cinema of the 1970s represents an attempt at such historical reconstruction of a 'local culture' through cinema. On the one hand, Li locates in Cantonese television programs and comedies such as *The House of Seventy-two Tenants* a sign of renewed interest in 'the strong oral tradition of the Cantonese culture', which added to local color and fostered a 'genuine Hong Kong consciousness'. On the other hand, insatiable desires permeated the screen, as exemplified by Zhang Che's swordsmen fighting for personal gain rather than moral principles or by Li Hanxiang's women seeking emotional and sexual fulfillment while volunteering themselves as objects of the male gaze. As affection and morality became objects of distrust or ridicule, *cynicism* spread across all genres and furnished an outlet for discontented Hong Kong audiences: while submitting to the status quo, they at least could deride authority, injustice and decency. Such cynicism, nonetheless, betrayed a fundamental contradiction in Hong Kong culture and engendered an intensifying identity crisis that sometimes verged on schizophrenia (as in soft-porn pictures produced by Lui Kei). For Li Cheuk-to, the cinematic search for Hong Kong's 'original locale' (*benwei*) or local culture failed to go beyond native legends and folk wisdom, and the apathy to contemporary politics and marginality in history continued to characterize Hong Kong identity in the 1970s (HKIFF 1984: 123–31).

It is evident from Li Cheuk-to's overview that an uneasy relationship exists between 'Cantonese culture' and Hong Kong's 'local culture'. Significantly, in a 1966 review Law Kar chose to describe Chan Po-chu as a 'Cantonese woman' rather than a 'Hong Kong woman', and as someone who represented 'a progressive new woman' entirely independent in a male-centered society and thus distinguished herself from previous Cantonese female stars. Law detected in Chan's screen images such 'traditional Cantonese qualities' as compassion, filiality, perseverance, reticence and righteousness. Already 'modernized but not completely Hong Kong-ized' as were some of her counterparts in Mandarin cinema, Chan's was an outstanding image of 'a new generation of Hong Kong's Cantonese women' (HKIFF 1982: 88–90).

For both Law Kar and Li Cheuk-to, Cantonese culture extends beyond Hong Kong's borders, and Hong Kong's *local culture* is therefore intimately related to Cantonese culture as a *regional culture*, at least up to the late 1960s. This intimate relationship is illustrated in the case of Li Wo's radio storytelling, which reached a large number of listeners in the region of Guangzhou (originally designated as Canton), Hong Kong and Macao in the 1950s. Nevertheless, upon closer scrutiny, Law Kar and Li Cheuk-to differ in their concept of Hong Kong culture. Law's term 'Hong Kong-ized' (*Xianggang hua*) reveals his suspicion of the 'contaminating' effects of a Westernized Hong Kong culture of the 1960s, which as a *cosmopolitan culture* (represented by Mandarin musicals) was not 'local' to Hong Kong but was originally imported from Shanghai in the postwar period. Li's insistence on a 'local culture' in Hong Kong is therefore problematic, for what was 'local' to Li (Cantonese orality) was part of a regional culture and what was 'Hong Kong' to Law (Westernization) was, in Stephen Teo's terms, the 'Shanghai hangover' or 'Shanghai redone' (1997: 14–39).

The historicity of Hong Kong culture is accentuated by the locality of its *multiple origins*, and what Leo Lee describes as the 'Shanghainization' of Hong Kong in the 1950s (1999: 330) is itself only part of a larger and longer process of translocal, transregional, transnational cultural integration in Hong Kong. With her multiple ties to Shanghai, Hong Kong and the US from the early 1940s to the mid-1960s, Eileen Chang's Mandarin screenplays for MP&GI contributed to the formation of a cosmopolitan culture in Hong Kong that recognizes its multiregional origins (hence the popular theme of *nanbei he* – 'south–north integration'). By the time Cantonese cinema reinvented itself with *The House of Seventy-two Tenants*, even characters from other regional backgrounds (Shanghai, Shandong and Chaozhou) spoke Cantonese, albeit with regional accents. In Teo's opinion, *The House of Seventy-two Tenants* is 'one of the first instances in Hong Kong cinema to show the territory as a Cantonese society able to assimilate Chinese people from different regions' (1997: 145).

Grounded in such *regional imagination*, by the late 1970s Hong Kong cinema had gained the flexibility of crossing national and regional borders and the advantage of assimilating east and west as well as north and south. The grounding in regional imagination also enabled Hong Kong filmmakers to approach Chinese culture not as a single entity but as one consisting of multiple regional cultures characterized by many regional dialects. The awareness of southern Fujian thus accounts for a large number of Hong Kong productions of Amoy-dialect features intended predominantly for Southeast Asia and Taiwan. The cinematic negotiation with northern Chinese culture in martial arts pictures further confirms the advantage of regional imagination. It is interesting to note that in all three cases of Bruce Lee, King Hu and Zhang Che, a haunting sense of rootlessness accompanies the physical journeys of these artists and their screen heroes. Traveling between the US, Hong Kong and Taiwan, these martial artists presented uprooted knights-errant whose claims to certain origins – specific schools of martial arts connected to certain mountains or temples – remain at best nominal and must be tested through countless duels. The kind of Chinese 'nationalism' projected by these martial arts pictures, consequently, cannot help but be abstract: 'China' exists as an abstract 'cultural ideal' that does not impose any obligation on the part of Hong Kong filmmakers to support 'a particular regime or political ideology' (Teo 1997: 112).

Herein lies another definitive advantage of regional imagination. Hong Kong cinema can effectively evoke *cultural nationalism* – a sense of cultural pride and national belonging – without endorsing or identifying with competing representatives of the Chinese nation (either CCP or KMT).[16] Bypassing the question of authenticity and legitimacy, Hong Kong's cinematic productions of 'China' and 'Chineseness' are intended for mass consumption in Taiwan and overseas Chinese communities and at times have met with critical acclaim. The fact that Hong Kong has served as the site of such a large-scale production of *signs* of China and Chineseness – not just in martial arts films but also in opera movies originated from numerous localities – has further confirmed the advantage of regional imagination. Compared with Taiwan and the PRC, Hong Kong cinema may have been denied the status of a national cinema (see Chapter 1), but Hong Kong's marginality in history and politics has fostered a distinctive type of regional imagination that transcends the national by assimilating both the local and the international. As evidenced by the multilocal operations of Minxin and Tianyi between Hong Kong and Shanghai, Grandview between Hong Kong and San Francisco, Cathay and Shaw Brothers between Hong Kong, Singapore and Taiwan, Hong Kong cinema has always been 'borderless' (Yau 2001) in its transregional and transnational imagination. Simply put, 'Hong Kong's is the regional cinema par excellence' (Bordwell 2000: 61).

6

CINEMA AND THE NATION-STATE IN THE PRC, 1949–78

INTRODUCTION: SOCIALIST CINEMA OF THE PRC

This chapter covers the period of socialist cinema in the People's Republic of China. The period started on 1 October 1949, when the Chinese Communist Party founded the PRC after defeating the Nationalist troops and driving the Republic of China government to Taiwan. The period reached its end in 1978, when filmmakers were gradually recovering from the Cultural Revolution and a new CCP policy paved the way for a rapid growth of cinema in the subsequent decades.

More than any other period in film history, cinema was under complete control of the Party, which acted autocratically in the name of the *nation-state*, and the fate of filmmakers and, to a lesser degree, film administrators was subject to the unpredictable whims of the CCP leadership. Nationwide campaigns against artists and filmmakers were launched every few years, and the internal CCP conflicts translated into years – or even months – of relative relaxation and resumed tightening and thus produced a pattern of zigzag development, elevating cinema to a new altitude and then capriciously plunging it to a new abyss. In the international context, the outbreak of the Korean War in 1950 immediately severed China from the US and its allies, and the persistence of the cold war firmly secured China in the Communist camp. Nevertheless, the growing tension with the Soviet Union from the early 1960s further isolated China from the First and the Second World and pushed China down the road of self-reliance, self-sufficiency and self-importance.

In terms of film history, this period can be divided into three phases. First, during *nationalization* (*guoyouhua*, 1949–52) the CCP confiscated what remained of the KMT's film facilities and turned them into three state-run studios, Northeast, Beijing and Shanghai. Although initially private studios out-performed state studios by continuing their humanist pursuits, the CCP under Mao Zedong's leadership was suspicious of the filmmakers' ideological stance and implemented unrelenting political interference that hastily forced all private studios to be nationalized by January 1952.

Second, in the phase of *socialist realism* (1953–65), the CCP deployed film as an effective weapon of propaganda and expanded its film operations, setting up new studios in key geographic locations, sending projection teams to remote areas, and training new personnel in workshops and film schools. Working within the ideological state apparatuses, filmmakers did their best to cultivate national styles and explore acceptable genres – particularly war, ethnic minority and opera movies – without offending the CCP leadership, but they failed miserably from time to time.

Third, in the phase of the *Cultural Revolution* and beyond (1966–78), the CCP ultra-leftist fraction headed by Mao's wife Jiang Qing suspended all feature production and condemned the achievements of socialist cinema of the previous seventeen years. As the nation was submerged in factional fighting and political persecution, production restarted with the filming of the 'revolutionary model plays' and those features which conformed to the ultra-leftist ideology. In 1977–8, the two years that immediately followed the Cultural Revolution, cinema became a popular means of venting frustrations and filmmakers were too busy condemning political persecution to bring their films out of rigid ideological confinement and formulaic representation.

In all, socialist cinema marks an unusual period in Chinese film history, in which film art was intimately wedded to revolutionary politics and cinema functioned all too effectively in propagating the socialist spirit and consolidating the power of the nation-state at the expense of the nation-people.

THE NATIONALIZATION OF CINEMA, 1949–52

The Korean War broke out in June 1950, and four months later Chinese soldiers entered Korea and fought alongside North Korean troops against the US-led United Nations forces until a cease-fire was declared in July 1953. Shanghai theaters began to suspend all screenings of US films in November 1950, and within a short time a nationwide boycott had terminated the long-time Hollywood domination in China.[1] Through the combined measures of ideological coercion and administrative control, the CCP accomplished the nationalization of the entire film industry by January 1952, and the zigzag development characterizing this transition phase set the pattern for what was to come in socialist cinema.

The ideological state apparatuses: cinema as sprawling bureaucracy

The CCP control of Chinese cinema proceeded quickly in the areas of administration, distribution and exhibition, production and criticism. First, administratively, as early as December 1949, Yuan Muzhi was appointed the director of the Central Film Bureau, an office under the Ministry of Culture, supervising Northeast, Beijing and Shanghai studios as well as all film-related business. In April 1950 the Film Bureau issued regulations, requiring that all film scripts, including those of animation and documentary, were cleared by the Bureau prior to production. A month later, a censorship committee was set up with Yuan Muzhi, Cai Chusheng and Shi Dongshan in charge. In July 1950 the Ministry of Culture established a film advisory committee headed by Shen Yanbing (Mao Dun) and appointed thirty-plus members, and a branch committee headed by Xia Yan was formed in Shanghai in 1951. Before it was disbanded in early 1952, the advisory committee had convened ten meetings and censured more than forty screenplays (Y. Luo 1995: 158–61; ZDYYZ 1995: 203–4). Through all this, the CCP sent the signal to filmmakers that cinema was no longer a simple matter of business or art, but rather a serious political operation subject to strict censorship from start to finish.

Second, in the area of distribution and exhibition, China Film Corporation (Zhongying gongsi) was founded in February 1951; together with its branches in major regions, the corporation managed all film distribution domestically and overseas. Within a short time, 596 theaters from the 'old China' were either nationalized or strictly supervised by the state. Meanwhile, new projection teams were organized to bring 16mm films to factories, mines, villages and military camps, thus maximizing the effects of cinema as a propaganda weapon in socialist China while bringing art and entertainment to a previously underprivileged section of society. From 100 such projection teams in 1949, the number jumped to 600 in 1950, and by 1955 a total of 2,300 teams were in operation (Clark 1987a: 36). According to one official count, exhibition outlets (including projection teams) increased from 646 in 1949 to 2,285 in 1952. Movie attendance grew correspondingly: 47 million in 1949, 146 million in 1950, 560 million in 1952, 752 million in 1953 and 822 million in 1954 (Clark 1987a: 36; ZDYYZ 1995: 202) (see Table 6.1). Certainly, not all moviegoers paid for a ticket under the new regime, an important change when considering official statistics. Thus the term 'film market' is perhaps misleading since film operations in socialist China were characterized by their *administrative* rather than economic nature.

Third, in the area of production, the CCP gradually finalized management appointments in the state studios. In 1949, Wu Yinxian was appointed as head of Northeast (replacing Yuan Muzhi), Tian Fang as head of Beijing Studio and Yu Ling as head of Shanghai Studio. In 1952 Chen Bo headed the newly instituted PLA Studio. In the same way that Northeast was renamed Changchun Studio in 1955 (X. Hu 1986), PLA Studio became August First (Bayi) Studio in 1956. Personnel matters notwithstanding, what invites closer attention is the kind of thematic reorientation with which socialist cinema experimented in this transition phase.

Table 6.1 Select exhibition statistics in the PRC, 1949–2002

Year	Projection teams	Exhibition outlets[1]	Attendance (million)	Revenue (RMB million)[2]
1949	100	646	47	—
1950	600	—	146	—
1952	—	2,285	560	—
1953	—	—	752	—
1954	—	—	822	—
1955	2,300	—	—	—
1957	6,700	9,900	1,700	60
1959	10,109	14,808	4,170	—
1974–6	—	—	—	(20)
1979	—	—	27,900	
1984	—	180,000	25,000	1,300
1991	—	—	14,400	2,360
1992	—	—	10,500	1,990
1994	—	—	3,000	—
1998	—	—	—	1,440
1999	—	—	460	850
2000	—	—	—	960
2001	—	—	220	840
2002	—	—	—	900

Sources: H. Chen 1989: 2: 263–9, 277–9; Clark 1987a: 36; S. Huang 2003; J. Liu 2003: 1; Yeh *et al.* 1999: 180; ZDYYZ 1995: 202, 222.

Note: 1   Exhibition outlets include theaters, film clubs and projection teams.
      2   A large percentage of box-office revenue after 1994 came from exhibiting Hollywood blockbusters.

Thematic reorientation: revolutionary war and class struggle

In April 1949 Northeast Studio released the first socialist feature, *Bridge* (Qiao, dir. Wang Bin; b/w).[2] Set during the liberation war, the film tells how against the odds workers complete the construction of a bridge in time for PLA soldiers to move across the Sungari River. At the same time as glorifying the *collective wisdom* of the proletariat, the film also shows the transformation of the chief engineer, whose initial lack of confidence in the strengths of the working classes is in the end proved wrong. Although the film lacks credible psychological details, its tripartite attention to the revolutionary war, the wisdom of the proletariat and the transformation of the intellectuals, points to three recurring themes in socialist cinema. In earnest, the film was meant to reflect the studio's intention of making films for and about workers, peasants and soldiers.

Considering the fact that many filmmakers as well as military and rural audiences had lived through years of battles and that the Korean War was raging on, it is not surprising to see the immense popularity of the war or military genre during this period. A glorification of the eight female martyrs who fought Japanese invaders in northeastern China, *Daughters of China* (Zhonghua nüer, dir. Ling Zifeng, 1949; b/w) is shot largely on location in forests and establishes a rugged look of cinematic realism and a fresh *documentary aesthetic.* *From Victory to Victory* (Nanzheng beizhan, dir. Cheng Yin, Tang Xiaodan, 1952; b/w) re-stages a large-scale battle between the PLA and KMT troops and effectively uses mise-en-scene and group images to intensify the visual power of the film. The film was praised as a model of 'epic scope', a new category desired by the CCP leadership, and was screened many times over a period of twenty years.

In general, war films portrayed exemplary Communist heroes as larger-than-life. Rather than seeing it as propaganda, the audience tended to identify with the heroes and marvel at their courageous deeds and unrelenting revolutionary spirit. Communist martyrs and war heroes would continue to populate the socialist screen. Indeed, war films functioned also as historical films due to the fact that the CCP, now securely in power, had resorted to cinema to *rewrite the history* of modern China as a teleological process in which the Communists led the Chinese people 'from victory to victory'.

In the meantime, *class struggle* was repeatedly depicted in feature productions, in part to assist the CCP land reform movement and in part to remind its audience of the 'permanent' threat of class enemies. *The White-Haired Girl* (Baimao nü, dir. Wang Bin, Shui Hua, 1950; b/w) is a popular adaptation of a 1944 CCP-sanctioned village opera from the Yan'an era (H. Chen 1989: 1: 91). The film dramatizes the miserable life of Xi'er (Tian Hua), whose debt-ridden father commits suicide one snowy Chinese New Year's eve, after unwillingly sealing a contract letting Xi'er serve in the landlord's household. Dachun, Xi'er's fiancé, is driven out of the village. Xi'er is raped and becomes pregnant. She escapes into the wild mountains, where she lives for years, and her hair turns white. The villagers perceive her as a 'white-haired fairy', and Dachun, now a Communist soldier returning to mobilize people to fight the Japanese, chases the ghostly creature to a cave.

In the opera version, Dachun shoots and injures Xi'er before realizing her identity and bringing her and her child back to the village. In the film version, the baby is dead soon after the birth. Back in the village, Xi'er's hair turns black again and she is happily married to Dachun. As in the opera version where a 'fair' trial is mentioned for the sake of Communist policy on land reform, the evil landlord is arrested after a public meeting. The film ends with Dachun and Xi'er harvesting in the field, a scene evocative of romance that would become increasingly problematic in socialist cinema.

Clearly, the film presents the villagers as less superstitious and more responsive to Communist mobilization than in the opera version. But the cinematic fore-grounding of female oppression still bears visible evidence of *female sexuality* in the scenes of rape (in a few suggestive shots) and childbirth (in five close-ups

Figure 6.1 The White-Haired Girl (1950): staging class struggle and sexual oppression

of Xi'er's face and hands) (X. Shu 1996: 18–19). Such scenes would be gradually eliminated in subsequent years. When *The White-Haired Girl* (dir. Sang Hu, 1972) was remade as a filmed revolutionary ballet, the rape of Xi'er was scaled down to an aborted attempt. The fact that Xi'er could get pregnant and give birth to a landlord's child was unthinkable to a new generation of audiences. In the ballet version, Xi'er and the rest of the villagers – or 'peasants' (*nongmin*) as preferred in the Communist rhetoric – are endowed with an instant revolutionary spirit and wholeheartedly participate in the CCP-led movement, shouting slogans and singing to the rising sun, the symbol of Mao the great savior.

The toll on the private studios: *The Life of Wu Xun*

The necessity of thematic reorientation created unforeseen difficulties for twelve private studios still in operation in Shanghai. True, Kunlun and Wenhua had released titles critical of the KMT regime, and the wartime exigency had made censorship an inconsistent practice at best. But under the new regime, in spite of pledging allegiance to the CCP, no one – not even such veteran Communists as Xia Yan and Yu Ling – was sure of where to draw the line of *political correctness.*

194

Figure 6.2 The White-Haired Girl (1972): revolutionary ballet performance on celluloid

Initially, the private studios welcomed the CCP policy of assistance or co-management (*gongsi heying*) by way of loans, subsidies and screenplays. In 1950 they released thirty-one features, compared with eight in 1949. New releases included *This Life of Mine* (Wo zhe yibeizi, dir. Shi Hui, 1950; b/w) from Wenhua, an acclaimed adaptation of Lao She's story about the suffering of a Beijing policeman in the 'old society'. The state studios' feature productions numbered twenty-nine in 1950, only a short title in 1951 and four features in the second half of 1952. In comparison, the private studios did quite well and released sixteen in 1951 (down from sixty-seven originally planned) and six in 1952 (H. Chen 1989: 1: 93, 2: 424–5, 2: 459) (see Table 6.2). But these declining numbers barely hint at what actually happened at the time, which is best illustrated in *The Life of Wu Xun* (Wu Xun zhuan, dir. Sun Yu, 1950; b/w), a controversial Kunlun release.

The production and reception of *The Life of Wu Xun* became symptomatic of the absolute supremacy of politics over art in Chinese cinema. As early as 1944, Sun Yu had conceived the idea of making a film eulogizing Wu Xu, a poverty-stricken villager in the Qing dynasty dedicated to raising money and offering free education to poor kids. The idea did not materialize until 1947, when Sun had returned from a two-year sojourn in the US for medical reasons. Following

195

Table 6.2 Annual feature production[1] in the PRC, 1949–2002

Year	Total films	Beijing	Changchun (Northeast)	Shanghai (Haiyan + Tianma + Jiangnan)	Other state studios (% of total)	Private companies (% of total)
1949	14	—	(6)	—	—	8 (57.1%)
1950	60	8	(13)	8	—	31 (51.7%)
1951	17	—	(1)	—	—	16 (94.1%)
1952	10	1	(2)	1	—	6 (60%)
1953	13	4	(4)	5	—	—
1954	20	1	(8)	10	1 (5%)	—
1955	23	1	10	11	1 (4.3%)	—
1956	42	3	15	19	5 (11.9%)	—
1957	42	4	14	19 (6+3+10)	5 (11.9%)	—
1958	105	8	31	50 (16+19+15)	16 (15.2%)	—
1959	80	8	26	27 (15+11+1)	19 (23.8%)	—
1960	66	9	19	14 (8+6)	24 (36.4%)	—
1961	28	5	6	8 (4+4)	9 (32.1%)	—
1962	35	6	5	9 (4+5)	15 (42.9%)	—
1963	36	3	9	14 (7+7)	10 (27.8%)	—
1964	31	8	8	9 (5+4)	6 (19.4%)	—
1965	42	8	11	10 (7+3)	13 (31%)	—
1966	13	3	1	—	9 (69.2%)	—
1967	—	—	—	—	—	—
1968	—	—	—	—	—	—
1969	—	—	—	—	—	—
1970	2	1	—	—	1 (50%)	—
1971	2	1	1	—	—	—
1972	5	1	1	2	1 (20%)	—
1973	4	—	3	1	—	—
1974	17	4	5	4	4 (23.5%)	—
1975	24	6	5	6	7 (29.2%)	—
1976	39	8	7	13	11 (28.2%)	—
1977	20	3	6	4	7 (35%)	—
1978	44	8	9	11	16 (36.4%)	—
1979	67	11	15	14	27 (40.3%)	—
1980	84	11	16	19	38 (45.2%)	—
1981	106	11	16	19	60 (56.6%)	—
1982	117	10	19	21	67 (57.3%)	—
1983	133	12	19	20	82 (61.7%)	—
1984	144	18	21	20	85 (59%)	—
1985	126	16	21	14	75 (59.5%)	—
1986	151	16	20	18	97 (64.2%)	—
1987	144	21	23	17	83 (57.6%)	—
1988	153	21	21	15	96 (62.7%)	—
1989	129	17	22	15	75 (58.1%)	—
1990	133	18	23	17	75 (56.4%)	—

Table 6.2—Continued

Year	Total films	Beijing	Changchun (Northeast)	Shanghai (Haiyan + Tianma + Jiangnan)	Other state studios (% of total)	Private companies (% of total)
1991	124	18	21	17	68 (54.8%)	—
1992	166	23	30	19	94 (56.6%)	—
1993[2]	154	24	24	19	84 (54.5%)	3 (1.9%)
1994	148	23	22	20	80 (54.1%)	3 (2%)
1995	146	18	21	17	87 (59.6%)	3 (2.1%)
1996	110	11	9	10	78 (70.9%)	2 (1.8%)
1997	85	13	5	9	56 (65.9%)	2 (2.4%)
1998[3]	82 (37)	12	6	4	—	3
1999	99 (40)	12	7	7	—	3
2000	83	—	—	—	—	—
2001	80	—	—	—	—	—
2002	100	—	—	—	—	48

Sources: H. Chen 1989: 2: 424–59; S. Huang 2003; W. Huang 1999: 133–4; J. Liu 2003: 1; Yin 1999: 23; ZDX 1996; ZDX 1997; ZDX 1998–9; ZDX 2000; ZDYYZ and ZDZ 1995.

Note: 1 Features include opera movies but exclude animation films.
2 Private company figures from 1993 to 1998 are exclusive of Sil-Metropole in Hong Kong.
3 Total films in parentheses in 1998–9 indicate the number of exhibited films as estimated by scholars.

Yang Hansheng's instructions, Sun started shooting in 1948 with the KMT China Motion Pictures so as to divert its resources from making additional anti-Communist films. However, China Motion Pictures abandoned the project in 1949 and sold the film's rights and rushes to Kunlun for 1.5 million yuan (one-sixth of the money spent).

By late 1949, Sun had no interest in the film because its theme was 'insufficiently progressive' and Chiang Kai-shek had reportedly praised Wu Xun during the war. Due to a lack of screenplays, Kunlun resumed the project in 1950 and collectively revised the script, adding subplots (e.g., a peasant uprising), changing the original eulogy of Wu to a tragedy of his failed ambition, and expanding the film into two parts, regardless of Sun's objection (Y. Sun 2000: 60). 'The result was that the "Kunlun" style (critical realism of the progressive left) overshadowed the style of the "auteur" ', and the released film lacks the trademarks of Sun's 1930s films, such as 'brilliance' (or brightness), sensuality and good-natured humor (C. Li 1991: 62).

In fact, in 1950 Sun cared less about *auteur* status than about the political correctness of his films. To accommodate a critical assessment from a post-liberation perspective, *The Life of Wu Xun* ends with a female teacher lecturing to children in front of Wu Xun's tomb in December 1949:

Wu Xun had established three schools, but the landlords eventually took all of them away. So learning from books alone could not liberate the poor . . . After toiling and struggling for thousands of years, the Chinese people finally toppled the three mountains [i.e., imperialism, feudalism and capitalism] and achieved complete liberation under the correct leadership of the Chinese Communist Party!

As she speaks, the teacher's image dissolves and shots of Wu Xun (Zhao Dan) are cross-cut with footage of the Tiananmen ceremony of the founding of the PRC and cheering crowds in Beijing (Y. Luo 1988: 1: 48).

The Life of Wu Xun premiered in Shanghai and Nanjing in February 1951, showing the two parts consecutively and charging the doubled price. Sun was delighted because the film drew enthusiastic crowds and rave reviews. Later that month he brought a print to Beijing, where he cut a one-part version of less than three hours and screened it to a special audience including Premier Zhou Enlai, Yuan Muzhi and about a hundred other CCP leaders. Chairman Mao Zedong was not present at the screening but obviously watched the film soon afterwards and detected serious problems. The continued positive reviews following the Beijing release might have further angered Mao, who wrote an editorial and had *People's Daily* (Renmin ribao) publish it on 20 May 1951. The editorial criticized the film for 'insanely promoting feudal culture', 'distorting peasants' revolutionary struggles and misrepresenting Chinese history' (Y. Sun 1990: 193–5, 261). Among some of the issues at stake were such questions as who had the right to historical representation (the Party, not filmmakers) and what form images of peasants could take on screen (fighters, not reformists).

Since Mao's editorial diagnosed the initial media praise of the film as a symptom of ideological confusion in the cultural realm and the infiltration of bourgeois thought into the CCP, a nationwide campaign was rashly launched and spread to all levels of the ideological state apparatuses. From November 1951 to January 1952, entire film circles were forced to go through 'rectification', a process of brainwashing Mao had successfully implemented in Yan'an to suppress dissident voices among the intellectuals in 1942. Not only did Sun Yu and Xia Yan admit their errors in newspapers, but Premier Zhou himself told Sun that he had also apologized for his oversight to the CCP central committee. Yuan Muzhi, a filmmaker experienced in both Shanghai and Yan'an, was removed from the Film Bureau leadership in 1952 and disappeared from the public eye due to 'health reasons' (J. Zhang and Cheng 1995: 1265). The campaign halted feature production in the state studios for a year and a half, while the leading newspapers continued to pick new targets from the private studio releases, accusing them of spreading humanism and petit-bourgeois sentiment.

The private studios faced mounting deficits as official criticism quickly scared audiences away. Unable to survive separately, Kunlun and Changjiang merged into a semi-private, semi-state studio in September 1951. After releasing three features in 1952, the new Changjiang–Kunlun Studio joined Wenhua – which also released its last three titles in the year – and five other private studios and formed Shanghai United Studio under state management in January 1952. The nationalization of the film industry closed its final chapter when Shanghai United, which did not make a single feature, merged into Shanghai Studio in February 1953.

Implications of the *Wu Xun* campaign

In 1990 Shu Kei asked the question that had puzzled many observers for decades: Why did Mao himself start a campaign against a 'poisonous' film so early on in the PRC's history? And why was *The Life of Wu Xun* chosen? Rereading Xia Yan's self-criticism, published in *People's Daily* in August 1951, Shu argues that Xia was speaking on behalf of all Shanghai artists. Admitting that Shanghai had been a city plagued by the reactionary propaganda of imperialism, feudalism and capitalism and a place influenced by bourgeois and petit-bourgeois ideas, Xia now urged Shanghai artists to study the thoughts of Mao Zedong (Y. Sun 1990: 264). Xia's self-criticism, therefore, symbolized the voluntary, albeit somewhat belated, acknowledgment of the *authority* of the Yan'an-trained, rural-educated cadres by the Shanghai-affiliated, urban-centered artists. Through the *Wu Xun* campaign, Mao thus consolidated his power position within the CCP leadership and crushed the naïve dream of creative freedom held by all artists, no matter what credentials they might possess.

Shu's argument is corroborated by Paul Clark's thesis that the transition to socialist cinema was most obviously one 'from Yan'an to Shanghai', for the CCP 'cultural purposes superseded, and largely dismissed, the heritage of filmmaking epitomized by the Shanghai achievement of the late 1940s'. Although Clark also detects a less obvious movement 'from Shanghai to Yan'an' in terms of implementing managerial and artistic standards (1987a: 55), his metaphorical use of Shanghai and Yan'an is stretched. For him, Yan'an (influenced by Moscow) is equated to the Party and politics, whereas 'Shanghai' (influenced by Hollywood and the May Fourth tradition) is equated to filmmakers (not necessarily those based in Shanghai alone) and their artistic creation. However, as time went by, the initial sharp divisions became blurred, and the Shanghai and Yan'an models were compromised and transformed into what may be broadly termed 'socialist realism'.

TOWARD SOCIALIST REALISM, 1953–65

The road toward socialist realism was tortuous and at times perilous. The conflicts between the radicals and the moderates in the CCP leadership translated into constant shifts in Party policy, which further heightened the zigzag development of film production. The Anti-Rightist Campaign in 1957, which inflicted heavy casualties in film circles, cut short the hopeful Hundred Flowers movement in 1956. Yet, in spite of the mercurial political climate, filmmakers built on their socialist experience and cultivated new genres, forms and styles, producing a series of excellent films that simultaneously appealed to the general audience and at least partially reflected their artistic aspirations.

The expansion of state film enterprises

The rapid growth of the film industry dictated that feature production must press forward in spite of the perceived ideological problems. Shanghai Studio had about 1,700 employees by 1953 and Northeast Studio 1,000 by 1954, not to mention those at Beijing Studio. The beginning of the first five-year plan in 1953 again pushed for more economic development. The appointment of five Soviet experts by the Ministry of Culture to help with film planning in January 1953 signaled the increasing importance of Soviet and East European cinemas, which had gradually filled the gap created by the absence of Hollywood in Chinese exhibition. By early 1953 there were 200 employees working full-time at the dubbing facilities at Northeast and Shanghai studios, and by mid-1952 more than 300 million people had reportedly watched over 180 dubbed foreign films since 1949 (Clark 1987a: 40, 53).

To spur economic growth, Shanghai Studio was restructured in April 1957 to become the Shanghai Film Corporation. In addition to Tianma (Sky Horse), Haiyan (Petrel) and Jiangnan (Southern China) – three studios specializing in feature production and headed respectively by Ying Yunwei, Shen Fu and Chen Liting – the corporation managed an animation studio, a dubbing studio, a technology studio, a symphony orchestra and an acting troupe. A science and education studio was put under the corporation's management a month later. In October 1958, the corporation changed to the Shanghai Film Bureau, and Jiangnan was disbanded to aid smaller studios that were mushrooming in the wake of the Great Leap Forward, an over-enthused movement designed to catch up with the developed countries, particularly the UK and the US. As a result, several regional studios were established in 1958: Pearl River (Zhujiang) in Guangzhou (in the south), Emei in Chengdu (in the southwest), Xi'an (in the mid-west), and Xinjiang (renamed 'Tianshan' in 1979) in Ürümqi (in the north-west). From 1959 to 1966, feature productions from these small studios and August First Studio accounted for nearly 20 per cent or more of the annual total (see Table 6.2, pp. 196–7). In early 1953, Central Newsreels and Documentary Studio, which would also shoot opera movies, was founded in Beijing, the PRC capital where several film technology and research facilities were clustered. By the end of the 1950s, a network of sprawling state enterprises seemed to have covered all aspects of filmmaking.

The 1950s also witnessed developments in other areas. First, of note was the technological advancement. Of eighty features released in 1959, color films comprised 45 per cent, and the widescreen, stereo-sound format was successfully introduced. Second, the exhibition networks continued to expand.

By the end of 1957 (which concluded the first five-year plan), there were 9,900 exhibition outlets nationwide (1,000 theaters, 2,200 film clubs and 6,700 projection teams). Movie attendance for 1957 was 1.7 billion and exhibition revenues were RMB60 million (H. Chen 1989: 2: 269). In 1959 exhibition outlets increased to 14,808 (4,699 theaters and clubs as well as 10,109 projection teams), and movie attendance reached 4.17 billion (ZDYYZ 1995: 222) (see Table 6.1, p. 192).

Third, film education was given high priority. Based on the Beijing Film School, which opened in 1951, the Beijing Film Academy was founded in 1956, offering a four-year education in three departments (directing, acting and photography). Departments of film arts, film engineering and film literature were subsequently added, as well as an experimental film studio in 1958, which became Youth Studio (Qingnian) in 1979 when the academy reopened after the Cultural Revolution. Other smaller film schools also opened in major cities such as Beijing (under Beijing Studio, 1960–2), Changchun (1960–4) and Shanghai (1959–63). Education-related projects included the introduction of Italian neo-realist films in 1954 and a series of film weeks in 1956 showcasing Japanese, French, Soviet and Yugoslavian cinemas. Indian and Mexican films were also shown, and film-culture exchanges with foreign countries were active in the 1950s (X. Shu 1996: 34–5).

Fourth, to encourage film research, the Chinese Film Press (Zhongguo dianying chubanshe or ZDC) and *China Film* (Zhongguo dianying) were launched in Beijing in 1956. The latter was renamed *Film Art* (Dianying yishu) in 1959 and has remained one of the very few journals which deals with film theory and history. In 1958 another research facility, the China Film Archive, was established in Beijing. To classify its collections of foreign prints, the archive employed foreign experts like Jay Leyda, an American scholar of film studies (including Russian-Soviet cinema), who worked there between 1959 and 1963 and later published the first history of Chinese cinema in English (in 1972). In 1961–2 the archive sponsored two early American cinema retrospectives in Beijing, showcasing twenty films by, among others, Charlie Chaplin. In 1963 it organized a rare retrospective of thirteen outstanding Chinese films from the 1930s, including *Goddess* and *Twin Sisters* (ZDX 1985: 394).

Finally, film awards and screenplay competitions were held at the national level. In April 1957 the Ministry of Culture issued 'excellent film awards' to films made between 1949 and 1955, which included in the feature categories: first (five titles), second (five) and third (nine) prizes, and an honorary prize to five Hong Kong titles. Significantly, three releases from the private studios were awarded, among which *Crows and Sparrows* was added to the first prize list with an official apology at a press conference in May 1957 (ZDYYZ 1995: 232).

In comparison, the Hundred Flowers Awards (*Baihua jiang*), inaugurated in 1962, was an unofficial competition, majority votes cast by mail from the readers of *Popular Cinema* (Dazhong dianying) decided the winners. Two features from the Shanghai studios garnered most honors in the first two Hundred Flowers Awards: in 1962, *Red Detachment of Women* (Hongse niangzi jun, dir. Xie Jin, 1960), a Tianma war film; in 1963, *Li Shuangshuang* (Li Shuangshuang, dir. Lu Ren, 1962; b/w), a Haiyan comedy. The Hundred Flowers Awards were to be held annually, but from 1964 to 1979 all activities were suspended for political reasons, a disheartening fact that underscores the ceaseless political interference in the socialist era.

Socialist realism: concepts, characteristics and critiques

In March 1953 the Film Bureau convened two meetings urging artists to pursue socialist realism as the highest standard in their creative work. The concept originally came from a literary slogan propagated by Soviet writers such as Gorky in the 1930s, but in their efforts to safeguard political correctness, Chinese leaders, filmmakers and critics seemed to agree that socialist realism was a way out of the dreadful Wu Xun crisis.

However, as with the majority of critical concepts circulated in socialist China, socialist realism remained an abstract – indeed slippery – concept, as illustrated in Zhou Enlai's two official definitions. First, in 1953, Zhou explained, 'socialist realism is the combination of revolutionary realism and revolutionary idealism' (H. Chen 1989: 1: 116). Second, in 1959, he praised socialist cinema for creating 'new styles that combined revolutionary realism and revolutionary romanticism' (ZDYYZ 1995: 234). What is problematic is not just the facile interchangeability of 'idealism' and 'romanticism', two terms best characterizing the *utopian* and uplifting moods of the socialist screen, but also the blind refusal to acknowledge the incompatibility between 'realism' and 'romanticism', two radically different modes of artistic representation. More than 'socialist', 'revolutionary' then appeared to be a magic word that glossed over differences and guaranteed political correctness. Unfortunately, the slippage of 'socialist realism' as a guiding concept thus left leeway for an outrageous reformulation of 'revolutionary romanticism' during the Cultural Revolution.

A discussion of contrastive characteristics of pre-socialist and socialist cinemas can help delineate the radical process whereby the latter replaced the former in a matter of years.

Aspect	*Socialist cinema*	*Pre-socialist cinema*
Ideology	class consciousness	Confucian or bourgeois virtues
Heroes	workers, peasants, soldiers	petit-bourgeois intellectuals
Setting	factories, mines, villages, camps	domestic, private, personal spaces
Action	violent struggle	sentimental persuasion
Concern	public welfare, collective interest	personal frustration
Process	identification with the masses	individual fulfillment
Method	typification (good and bad)	ambivalence (middle characters)
Goal	political correctness (Party-state)	humanism (nation-people)

Ideologically, CCP-codified class consciousness displaces Confucian and bourgeois virtues (e.g., filial piety, paternal responsibility, heterosexual love), and the new screen heroes are predominantly workers, peasants and soldiers rather than 'petit-bourgeois' intellectuals, who now function as foils to the revolutionary masses and to the ultimately rectified Party leadership. Correspondingly, factories, mines, villages and military camps – all public, political spaces – become the preferred settings, drastically reducing the number of domestic, private and personal spaces (newly judged to be 'bourgeois' or 'backward'). The typical plot usually ends with the triumph of the public over the private: just as verbally and physically violent struggles substitute sentimental persuasion and rational negotiation, public welfare and collective interest become the governing concerns, leaving little or no room for addressing personal frustrations. The mandated identification with the masses is internalized as a process in which any feeling of individual fulfillment must be sublimated to a more glorious sense of contributing directly to the revolutionary war or socialist construction. 'Typification' (*dianxing hua*), a concept in socialist realism that emphasizes 'typical characters' and a 'typical setting', emerges as the principal method of idealization that transforms individuals to certain 'types' (i.e., embodiments of ideas) and gradually purges the screen of potential ambivalence (e.g., mixed emotions, uncertain motivations). The black-and-white dramatization of ideological conflicts with purely good and bad characters thus makes 'middle characters' – most often intellectuals neither positive enough to qualify as agents of revolution nor reactionary enough to represent the villainous force – superfluous in the politicized narrative. The ultimate goal of socialist realism is no longer education for the nation-people's sake, for a humanist version of such education might repeat the mistake of *The Life of Wu Xun*. Rather, the goal is the 'interpellation' – by politically correct methods – of the audience (as potential subjects of history) into voluntary subjection to the socialist nation-state, in the name of which the CCP has legitimated its rule.

The negation of humanism and the sublimation of the private by the public in socialist realism might entail a lack of appeal to the audience's psychological needs. Nonetheless, as Xiaobing Tang argues, socialist *utopianism* commanded a broadly based following in the 1950s and 1960s, particularly among the young generation eager to sublimate everyday life into an artistic experience teeming with theatricality and ecstasy (2000: 163–95). Ban Wang uses *Song of Youth* (Qingchun zhige, dir. Cui Wei, Chen Huaiai, 1959) and *Nie Er* (Nie Er, dir. Zheng Junli, 1959) as examples to demonstrate that Communist culture was attractive precisely because it recognized 'the importance of the individual's libidinal pleasure' and successfully constructed a new psychological process. Revolutionary films worked to seduce the viewer into 'imaginary identification' with the mother (the homeland, the nation) and then to 'orient the released psychic energy' to 'the sublime order of the symbolic' – the law of the father (the Party), embodied by the supreme leader Mao Zedong (B. Wang 1997: 154).

Figure 6.3 Song of Youth (1959): intellectuals and Communist revolution

For Meng Fanhua, socialist film culture transformed the discourse of nationalism prevalent in the previous decades by infusing it with a sense of national pride ('we Chinese') and a realization of the superiority of the socialist nation-state ('our new China'). A kind of 'romantic political thinking' ordained that cinema must achieve a broader range of historical representation and elevate ordinary people to historical heroes. Repeated criticism of humanism and sentimentalism, as in the year-long assault on *Daji and Her Fathers* (Daji he tade fuqin, dir. Wang Jiayi, 1961), an ethnic minority film eulogizing the new, all-inclusive socialist family, ruthlessly severed socialist cinema from the human compassion that had characterized pre-socialist cinema. After politicizing everyday life (the material) and repressing individual desires (the libidinal), socialist cinema overcompensated by investing exclusively in the revolutionary 'will' (the rational) and projecting a mirage of absolute confidence in the Communist future, thereby sowing the seeds for the post-Mao ideological crisis (F. Meng 2001).

In the 1950s, the audience might at first find the new rhetoric of socialist realism alienating, but they had few other alternatives in entertainment. Indeed, filmmakers and cultural leaders were already aware of the shortcomings of socialist cinema. In 1953, Cheng Yin and two other directors singled out 'abstraction' and 'simplification' as serious problems, which resulted in 'formulaic' plots and flat characters. Chen Huangmei likewise pointed out in 1955 the importance of delving into the heroes' psychological states so as to make them 'humans' rather than 'machines' (Y. Luo *et al.* 1992: 1: 334–47, 370–2). But the most incisive criticism came from Zhong Dianfei in December 1956, who published an article in *Literary Gazette* (Wenyi bao) in response to a Shanghai newspaper forum entitled 'Why Are There So Few Good Domestic Films?' From November 1956 to January 1957, this forum published about fifty letters from readers, including famous artists like Sun Yu and Lao She, the latter issuing the plea – 'Save our cinema' (H. Chen 1989: 1: 130).

Zhong Dianfei's article reveals dismal statistics. A Beijing newspaper reported that 70 per cent of the 100 plus films released between 1953 and June 1956 did not recoup their production costs, with some returning merely 10 per cent of the costs, and one documentary failing even to recover its promotion fees. As for four recent films in Shanghai, attendance rates were a small 9 to 23 per cent of the seating capacity. Zhong finds it ironic that films dedicated to serving workers, peasants and soldiers did not reach the targeted audiences. Attributing the cause to dogmatism and factionalism, Zhong specifically chastizes arbitrary administrative interference (from scriptwriting to material supplies), widespread disregard of individual styles and the lack of artistic freedom for filmmakers. At one point, Zhong feels obliged to remind his readers (Y. Luo *et al.* 1992: 1: 426):

> Never oppose the film audience to the policy that literature and art must serve workers, peasants and soldiers. Never oppose a film's box-office values to its social and artistic values. Never take the truism that films serve workers, peasants and soldiers to mean exclusively 'films about workers, peasants and soldiers'.

The Hundred Flowers harvest and the Anti-Rightist casualties

Zhong Dianfei's criticism, which exposed certain fundamental problems in socialist cinema, would not have been published if not for the CCP policy of 'letting one hundred flowers bloom and one hundred schools of thought contend'. In May 1956 Mao himself announced the new policy, and soon across the nation the general public was encouraged to air constructive criticism. Like Zhong, many critics targeted political interference, bureaucracy, dogmatism and factionalism, and called for reform (Clark 1987a: 70–6).

Numerous reform measures were introduced in this liberal environment. For example, folk tales with 'national characteristics', documentaries of a variety of regional operas, theaters and ethnic minority music and dance, as well as comedy and satire, were added at the bottom of the official list of acceptable subjects. At the top were socialist constructions, revolutionary history, historical figures and adaptations of classical and modern literature. In March 1956 the Film Bureau decided to terminate the centralized control of screenplay production implemented since 1953 and allow individual studios to recruit writers and develop their own screenplays. Previously, professional writers assigned to the only two national screenplay institutes would take administrative orders, produce screenplays to strict specifications and distribute them to studios in accordance with set quotas. Under the new system, however, the studios were responsible for literary scripts, script continuities (*fenjingtou juben*) and synopsis, which until 1956 had been subject to a system of three-tiered censorship by the Ministry of Culture, the Film Bureau and the studios or the screenplay institutes (H. Chen 1989: 1: 121–3).

The effects of these reform measures were immediate: annual feature production almost doubled, rising from twenty-three in 1955 to forty-two in 1956 and again in 1957. Several breakthroughs are easy to identify in this new harvest. First, May Fourth literature returned to the screen with *New Year's Sacrifice* (Zhufu, dir. Sang Hu, 1957), an adaptation – based on Xia Yan's script – of Lu Xun's celebrated story of a poverty-stricken woman (Bai Yang). Second, heterosexual love, otherwise a controversial subject in rigid military films, was integrated seamlessly in a poetic ambience – heightened by picturesque scenery and sweet folk songs – in *Story of Liubao Village* (Liubao de gushi, 1957; b/w), the solo debut of Wang Ping, the first woman director in socialist China. Third, sport was utilized as a vehicle of nationalism and the collective spirit in *Woman Basketball Player No. 5* (Nülan wuhao, 1957), which presented real-life athletes and established the director Xie Jin as an emergent auteur. Fourth, intellectuals, especially the younger generation educated in socialist China, received more affectionate portrayals, as in *Girls from Shanghai* (Shanghai guniang, dir. Cheng Yin, 1958).

But the breakthrough most fitting the Hundred Flowers harvest was the satirical comedy, as illustrated by Lü Ban's three films. An actor who had appeared in *Crossroads* and had studied in Yan'an, Lü was put in charge of a comedy research unit created by the Film Bureau in 1955. His first film, *Before the New Director Arrives* (Xin juzhang daolai zhiqian, 1956; b/w), ridicules a petty bureaucrat who tries to ingratiate himself with his new boss even before his arrival by over-spending public funds for office renovation and disregarding the wellbeing of the workers. *A Man with Bad Manners* (Buju xiaojie de ren, 1956), his second film, exposes a hypocritical writer who promotes civilized manners in his writing but behaves badly in public, throwing litter and taking advantage of others. Finally, in an unusual move to re-establish connections with early cinema and the leftist tradition, Lü presented a pair of famed comedians from the 1930s, the skinny Han Lan'gen and the overweight Yin Xiucen, in three slapstick episodes of *The Unfinished Comedies* (Wei wancheng de xiju, 1957; b/w). Films within a film, the episodes poke fun at hypocrisy, bragging and unfiliality and do not please the celebrity critic named Yi Bangzi (a pun on the Chinese expression 'a single blow'), who subsequently kills off all three comic shorts. With such an obvious punning device, Lü targeted dogmatic Party critics who specialized in finding fault in every single feature film.

Figure 6.4 New Year's Sacrifice (1957): Xia Yan's adaptation of a story by Lu Xun, featuring Bai Yang

By June 1957 it was evident that Mao had allowed the Hundred Flowers harvest as a means only to lure dissidents out in the open so as to crack down on them. The Anti-Rightist Campaign, another nationwide political operation, dealt more than 'a single blow' to film circles. In August and September alone, fifteen meetings were held in Beijing to criticize Zhong Dianfei. The Ministry of Culture judged *The Unfinished Comedies* to be a 'poisonous weed' (X. Shu 1996: 43), and numerous other films were identified as 'white flags' (or non-revolutionary) to be plugged. Due to the non-negotiable quota assigned to each work unit, Zhong Dianfei, Guo Wei, Lü Ban, Sha Meng, Shi Hui, Wu Yin and Wu Yonggang, in addition to an unspecified number of other filmmakers, were classified as 'Rightists' and banished from the public eye, some for over two decades.[3] Significantly, while the last three mentioned above were renowned Shanghai artists, the first four had a Yan'an background, although Sha Meng, like Lü Ban, had the additional experience of playing in *Crossroads*. The signal from the Anti-Rightist Campaign was crystal-clear: the CCP now *indiscriminately* persecuted dissenters, regardless of their background, affiliations and achievements.

In rapid succession, the Great Leap Forward in 1958 and an anti-right-wing campaign in 1959 followed the Anti-Rightist Campaign. As before, film leaders like Chen Huangmei and Xia Yan – the latter appointed in 1954 as Vice Minister of Culture in charge of film, a post he would hold until 1965 – had to admit 'errors' in order to survive politically. However, this time, the urgent task of making 'tributary films' for the tenth anniversary of the PRC had somehow protected feature productions, and the artists' skillful negotiations and creative output scored an unprecedented success. In 1958 annual feature production reached 105, which remained a record until 1981. The Anti-Rightist Campaign, which delayed numerous films in mid-production, partially explains the 1958 record. Another factor was the predominance of opera movies and the 'documentary art film', the latter a new genre occasioned by the Great Leap Forward. The figures for 1959 (eighty features) and 1960 (sixty-six features) were still impressive, but the momentum ran out in the first half of the 1960s, the average then being thirty-five films a year, although the quality of these films more than made up for the loss in quantity.

Genre experiments and stylistic innovations

Luo Yijun published an article in 1961 calling for films to include more of a variety of subjects, styles and genres (*yangshi*). While acknowledging existing genres such as drama or 'serious film', comedy, 'thriller' (*jingxian pian*), biography, children's film, myth, musical, as well the opera movie and docu-drama as two special Chinese genres, Luo identified three problems. First, genre films of the non-serious kind were few in number; second, the distribution of genre films in a given year was uneven; third, genre features were far from distinctive among non-serious films. For instance, based on a folk tale, *Third Sister Liu* (Liu sanjie, dir. Su Li, 1960; b/w) abandoned numerous original episodes of strong romantic colors and transported the protagonist from a poetic setting to a realistic one, thus 'modernizing' her but losing much of her folkloric charm. Thus, the closer one gets to reality, the farther away one might depart from the artistic truth (Luo *et al.* 1992: 1: 559–70).

Compared with pre-socialist cinema, the ethnic minority film is a relatively new genre that routinely features picturesque landscape, melodious music and songs, beautiful costumes, exotic customs and romantic love – creating an audio-visual treat unthinkable in a politicized Han-majority setting (Clark 1987b). The entertainment value of this genre is obvious. Like *Third Sister Liu*, which ends with several long shots of the lovers boating down the beautiful Li River and disappearing into a misty setting, *Five Golden Flowers* (Wuduo jinhua, dir. Wang Jiayi, 1959) concludes with an enchanting love song celebrating the reunion of the lovers by the camellia decorated Butterfly Pond. Glorifying socialist construction in contemporary China, *Five Golden Flowers* achieves a measure of realism by casting Yang Likun, of Yi nationality, as the female protagonist. Set in the Xingjiang Uygur region, *Visitor on Ice Mountain* (Bingshan shangde laike, dir. Zhao Xinshui, 1963) incorporates the elements of intrigue and suspense typical of the spy film and stages the solidarity of the Han (represented by the PLA army) and the minorities in defeating schemes of sabotage instigated by foreign perpetrators. The themes of class exploitation and ethnic solidarity combine to make *Serfs* (Nongnu, dir. Li Jun, 1963; b/w), with a predominantly Tibetan cast, another example of cinematic legitimization of the Han centrality in its constant surveillance of ethnic border regions (Y. Zhang 2002: 151–67).

The ethnic minority films provided urban (and mostly Han) filmmakers with a rare opportunity to pursue certain cinematic arts theoretically justifiable as *national styles*. For example, influences of the symbolic (*xieyi*) ink-and-wash (*shuimo*) landscape and the refined (*gongbi*) rich-color (*nongcai*) flowers genres of traditional Chinese painting are, respectively, traceable in *Third Sister Liu* and *Five Golden Flowers*.[4] Another fertile source of 'national forms' was traditional opera and theater, which had been turned into an equally spectacular genre in socialist cinema. Although opera movies were as old as Chinese features, this genre attracted many veteran filmmakers, arguably in part due to its time-honored, safe subject matter, remote from contemporary politics. The first socialist opera movie, *Liang Shanbo and Zhu Yingtai* (dir. Sang Hu, Huang Sha, 1954), was screened at several European film festivals in 1954 and 1955 to the delight of audiences and critics. The sight of a long line outside a Paris theater moved Georges Sadoul, and Chaplin reportedly praised this 'extraordinary' film as the 'Chinese *Romeo and Juliet*' (H. Chen 1989: 1: 148). Opening at the end of 1954, the film ran for an entire year in Hong Kong, and was shown in more

Figure 6.5 Five Golden Flowers (1959): romance and exoticism exhibited as national solidarity

than thirty local theaters, sold over one million tickets, grossed HK$1 million and broke all Hong Kong records (M. Yu 2001: 43). Another influential opera movie, *The Heavenly Match* (Tianxian pei, dir. Shi Hui, 1955; b/w), was based on Huangmeidiao opera (yellow plum tune) from Anhui province. The success of these two films was credited for the immense popularity of similar opera movies – many of them 'yellow plum tunes' – that swept Hong Kong, Taiwan and Southeast Asia in the 1960s (see Chapters 4 and 5).

Animation, the third spectacular and entertaining genre in socialist cinema, also achieved a high level of international success. The traditional Chinese arts were squarely behind stylistic experimentation in animation. The ink-and-wash short films, *Where Is Mama?* (Xiao kedou zhao mama, dir. Collective, 1960) and *Cowherd's Flute* (Mudi, dir. Te Wei, 1963) delight the viewer and pay appropriate tribute to two modern Chinese master painters, Qi Baishi and Li Keran. Using paper cuts and puppets, *Gingsen Baby* (Renshen wawa, dir. Wan Guchan, 1961) and *The Cock Crows at Midnight* (Banye jijiao, dir. You Lei, 1964), again both shorts, respectively utilize folk art traditions while structuring their narratives around the class struggle.[5] In the general category of cartoons, the two-part *Uproar in Heaven* (Danao tiangong, dir. Wan Laiming, 1961, 1964) is the first feature-length animation (two hours) in Chinese film history and has remained a favorite. In June 1983 twelve Paris theaters showed *Uproar in Heaven* for a month, and a total number of 100,000 viewers went to see the film (ZDX 1985: 353).

War or military films, a different kind of spectacular genre, dominated the socialist screen (Y. Zhang 2002: 182–5). Among others, *Dong Cunrui* (Dong Cunrui, dir. Guo Wei, 1955; b/w) paid more attention to the human aspect of the war, and was added to the growing list of Communist hagiographies. Major battles continued to be re-staged in films like *The Shanghai Battle* (Zhan Shanghai, dir. Wang Bing, 1959). Small-scale military operations with an emphasis on stratagem formed a sub-category of war film, as in *Guerrillas on the Plain* (Pingyuan youji dui, dir. Su Li, Wu Zhaodi, 1955; b/w). In terms of the historical genre, *Naval Battle of 1894* (Jiawu fengyun, dir. Lin Nong, 1962) offers a lesson of nationalism by foregrounding the humiliating defeat of the entire Manchu naval fleet in the first Sino-Japanese war. Another noticeable development is that of children's war films such as *Zhang Ga, a Boy Soldier* (Xiaobing Zhang Ga, dir. Cui Wei, Ouyang Hongying, 1963; b/w).

There were, of course, excellent children's films as well, such as *The Secret of a Precious Gourd* (Baohulu de mimi, dir. Yang Xiaozhong, 1963; b/w), which teaches a lesson of hard work and self-reliance. Several children's films of the time concentrated on sports, especially soccer, and promoted the collective spirit and discouraged competitiveness solely for championship's sake. In general, sports subjects were more entertaining than other dramas. Unlike satires, urban comedies, for example *It's My Day Off* (Jintian wo xiuxi, dir. Lu Ren, 1959; b/w), stayed away from sensitive political subjects and eulogized altruism as a socialist virtue. Dwelling sympathetically on the realm of everyday life, comedies like *A Woman Barber* (Nü lifa shi, dir. Ding Ran, 1962; b/w) in a sense harked back to the postwar Wenhua tradition of humanism, as exemplified by *Phony Phoenixes.*

In a different way, the postwar Kunlun epic tradition found echoes in *Lin Zexu* (Lin Zexu, dir. Zheng Junli, Cen Fan, 1959), a biography picture dramatizing the rise of patriotism on the eve of the Opium War. Zhao Dan's roles as Lin Zexu and Nie Er (in *Nie Er*) reconfirmed the cinematic bond between the postwar and socialist eras, something the CCP had suppressed as a prohibited subject. Nonetheless, references to the pre-socialist era were inevitable in literary adaptations such as *The Lin Family Shop* (Linjia puzi, dir. Shui Hua, 1959), which can perhaps be seen as screenwriter Xia Yan's effort to reclaim a forbidden territory by reconnecting with May Fourth literature.

Thus, socialist cinema can claim to have broadened an existing genre line-up, and its achievements in animation and opera movies were particularly impressive. However, as hinted by Luo Yijun in 1961, stylistic innovations were often secondary. It is also worth mentioning here that martial arts films disappeared from the socialist screen and genre films in the commercial sense did not mature until the late 1980s.

Figure 6.6 Guerrillas on the Plain (1955): war film as propaganda and entertainment

Figure 6.7 It's My Day Off (1959): altruism as a rewarding socialist virtue

Socialist cinema in perspective: *Stage Sisters* and complexity

With historical hindsight, Shu Xiaoming points out four things that held back film in the first seventeen years of socialist cinema: a direct service to politics, a lack of psychological depth, a distance from the artistic achievements of foreign films, and undeveloped research on the ontology of film (1996: 138–9). Except for the last point, the rest were entirely beyond the control of artists and scholars. Arguably, the supremacy of political correctness was responsible for the tendency to disregard film ontology, or any theoretical considerations outside Marxism and Maoism for that matter.

If framed in Marxism and Maoism, theoretical discussions were allowed and indeed encouraged. An influential artist and leader, Xia Yan published his lectures at the Beijing Film Academy in 1958 as *Problems of Screenwriting* (1985: 93–181), and his emphasis on dramatic structure at the expense of cinematic techniques (except montage) set the agenda of film theory of the time. Leading scholars repeatedly stressed film's literary values. As Yu Min contended in 1962, 'in creating film literature, the general laws of literature are of primary importance, and the special laws of film only secondary' (Luo *et al.* 1992: 1: 541). Decades later, Dai Jinhua evaluates Xia Yan's screenplay theory as an interpretation and perfection of the Chinese *shadowplay theory* (see Chapter 2, pp. 55–6) and argues that his book determined the narrative pattern,

Figure 6.8 Lin Zexu (1959): a historical lesson of the Opium War, featuring Zhao
    Dan

plot construction and technique of films in the 1960s and much of the 1970s
(1993: 157–68).

As in the golden age, Chinese cinema continued to rely on literary and
dramatic concepts in the socialist era. The professionalization of screenwriters
gave them more time to devote to the printed text rather than the moving image,

213

and the publication of 'excellent' screenplays of previous and contemporary films (ZDC 1959–61, 1959–63) helped secure 'film literature' as a legitimate art form (to be studied as words more than images). Not surprisingly, in spite of fundamental changes in the political climate, 'films by literature people' (see Chapter 3, p. 104) continued to dominate the socialist screen, while techniques from popular opera movies started to influence a new generation of film-makers. Apart from dramatic conflicts involving face-to-face confrontation, it is common to see theatrical elements such as exaggerated facial expressions (e.g., the hero's glaring look in a close-up), ritualized gestures (e.g., the clenched fist, the raised arm) and mannered postures (in a low-angle, frontal shot), all supposedly strengthening the revolutionary spirit. Dressed in neat clothes even in implausible situations, characters are all too self-conscious of the camera position and tend to 'freeze' their body in a fashion similar to that of *liangxiang* (fixed on stage) in a traditional opera, as frequently captured in film stills (ZDYYZ 1995: 209, 230, 236, 267). Formulaic as they were, these theatrical elements would be stretched to an extreme in the model play films in the 1970s.

Conformity and *uniformity* thus characterize socialist cinema. Unlike postwar cinema, the socialist system of centralized control and quota production resulted in a conspicuous lack of distinct studio styles. All feature studios – even the military-controlled August First – made similar kinds of films, and leading directors were given a chance to work on various genres. However, the rigidity of the system did not prevent some directors from developing individual styles (D. Ma and Dai 1994). In Xie Jin's case, after experimenting with the opera movie (1954), drama (1955), sports (1957), documentary (1958), war (1960) and comedy (1962), the director turned to *Stage Sisters* (Wutai jiemei, 1965), a project he had planned for years.

The film opens with a series of shots of empty, ancient theater stages of different designs, followed by another series of shots displaying typical rural scenes in southern China, punctuated by the sound of an off-screen female chorus deploring the traveling artists' miserable life. A dramatic chase scene brings the viewer to 1935, as a girl bride named Chunhua (Xie Fang) runs away from an abusive family and hides in a trunk just off-stage from where an itinerant Shaoxing opera troupe is performing. The troupe's head master yields to his daughter Yuehong's pleas to keep Chunhua, and the two girls become sworn sisters. Chunhua learns to specialize in the *wudan* (martial female warriors) and Yuehong the *sheng* (romantic male scholars), and soon the two become popular in the region. Yuehong rejects the sexual advances of a landlord, so he orders the local police to arrest her. Chunhua rescues Yuehong but is caught and humili-atingly tied to a pole in a public square as punishment. The master is wounded in the scuffle and dies soon after. In exchange for the expense of burying their father-master, the two girls sign a contract that forces them to travel with the owner of the troupe to Shanghai and perform without pay for three years.

Their fame grows quickly in Shanghai, and the theater manager, Tang, makes a fortune and lures Yuehong to be his new mistress, replacing an older 'opera

Figure 6.9 Stage Sisters (1965): Xie Jin's humanism and political melodrama

queen' (Shangguan Yunzhu) who subsequently commits suicide. As Yuehong indulges in her new-found wealth, Chunhua turns politically progressive and, with the help of a woman reporter, organizes her own troupe to stage an adaptation of Lu Xun's 'New Year's Sacrifice'. Instructed by a KMT official, Tang has a hooligan throw lime powder in Chunhua's eyes in an aborted attempt to blind her. To cover his role in the attack, Tang forces Yuehong to take the blame, but Chunhua later exposes Tang's scheme in court, where Yuehong (in a fur coat) collapses in fear and shame. After 1949 Chunhua (donning an army cap) joins the touring land reform propaganda team and performs in the play *The White-Haired Girl* in her hometown. She finds Yuehong (now in plain clothes) and convinces her to return to the stage.

Made on the eve of the Cultural Revolution with Xia Yan's support, *Stage Sisters* encountered severe criticism from ultra-leftists during production. The original plan was to conclude the film with the following dialogue:

Yuehong: 'From now on, I'll be a clean person and perform seriously.'
Chunhua (pauses for a moment): 'But to be what kind of person? And to perform what kind of play?'

215

Under political pressure, the completed film ends with Yuehong's promise to restart her life and Chunhua's advice that they reform themselves and perform only revolutionary plays. As if the slogan-like message is not clear enough, the final sequence features the sisters sitting shoulder to shoulder in a motorboat that charges forward, symbolically powered by the socialist engine. Xie Jin's change notwithstanding, the film was killed off right away, damned as a 'poisonous weed' that spread ideas of class compromise and bourgeois humanism (H. Chen 1989: 1: 299). Screened to selected audiences in order to generate criticism, the film was mentioned in national newspapers but did not reach the general public until 1979.

By all standards, *Stage Sisters* is a representative work of socialist realism. On the one hand, the film draws on national traditions and develops an episodic narrative structure of union, separation and reunion that dramatizes the tribulations of the sisters and details their emotional fluctuations (X. Shu 1996: 125–8). The stage as metaphor, the musical score and opera lyrics at times interrupt and comment on the narrative flow, thereby intensifying the film's poetic ambience and providing an effective means to delve into the characters' interior worlds. The inclusion of 'New Year's Sacrifice' and *The White-Haired Girl* ingeniously pays double homage to May Fourth and Communist culture, giving the film an extra historical dimension.

On the other hand, *Stage Sisters* resembles a Hollywood melodrama in terms of its representation of female sexuality, and it is aligned with Soviet socialist realism in its portrayals of those character 'types' that best illustrate the unfolding of history as a grand narrative. Due to its structural parallel to a traditional opera, the film even exhibits certain traits of epic theater as advocated by Bertolt Brecht, such as distanciation and figurative composition that force the audience away from its artistic illusions and contemplate critically the issues presented in front of them. In brief, as Gina Marchetti asserts, 'Xie's style matured in an aesthetic crucible that ground together Hollywood classicism, Soviet socialist realism, Shanghai dramatic traditions, and indigenous Chinese folk opera forms', and *Stage Sisters* therefore contains an already 'very sophisticated' articulation of a 'revolutionary aesthetic' (1997: 60, 75).

This lengthy discussion of *Stage Sisters* is intended to draw attention to the complexity of socialist cinema as embodied in its best examples. In Xie Jin's case, it demonstrates that, as an exception to Shu Xiaoming's generalization, filmmakers had found subtle ways to negotiate with politics and developed artistic means in relation to both domestic and foreign cinematic and theoretical formulations.

THE CULTURAL REVOLUTION AND BEYOND, 1966–78

The Cultural Revolution (1966–76) has often been described as a decade of turbulence and catastrophe. In the early years of the movement, the Red Guards took over much of the nation, cadres and intellectuals were persecuted, schools and government offices shut down, and violence of all kinds permeated everyday life. Insomuch as cinema is concerned, feature production was suspended from 1967 to 1969. A total of 589 features and over 1,000 documentary, animation and educational titles that had been produced in the preceding seventeen years, as well as 883 foreign features, were sealed and stored. Production, distribution and exhibition personnel were dismissed and dispatched elsewhere. During the decade, only seventy-nine features were distributed, including six remakes and thirty-six foreign titles. Under the deranged circumstances, nationwide exhibition incurred a deficit of over RMB20 million between 1974 and 1976, and this period was the time when the new features were released (H. Chen 1989: 2: 274). But for millions of victims and survivors, the financial disaster was nothing compared with the colossal loss of lives and the traumas that the Cultural Revolution created.

The years of devastation

The Cultural Revolution was officially launched in 1966. In May, the CCP central committee called for a fierce attack on bourgeois representatives at all levels in the government. From mid-August to late November 1966 Mao appeared at the Gate of Heavenly Peace (Tiananmen) and greeted tens of thousands of ecstatic – indeed frenetic – Red Guards who had traveled to Beijing from all over the country, and seven lengthy documentaries were made of these events. But in film circles, the Cultural Revolution had arrived two years earlier. In June 1964 Mao had criticized all forms of socialist cultural products as fraught with serious problems and all official organizations as being on the edge of falling into revisionism, feudalism and capitalism. Another nationwide rectification campaign in 1964 produced a large number of casualties. *The Lin Family Shop* was labeled, along with many others, an 'evil film'. Xia Yan's film essays and Cheng Jihua's film history book were selected as targets in the arena of film theory and criticism. In February 1965 Mao commented on Jiang Qing's speech at a military conference on art and literature, describing the seventeen years as 'under the dictatorship of a counter-revolutionary, anti-socialist black line' and called for a socialist revolution in the cultural realm. A 'witch-hunt' even larger than that of 1964 ensued, and the films which were targeted ranged from those depicting artists and intellectuals to revolutionary war films. Even *The Life of Wu Xun* was once again dug out for criticism in 1966. To set an example, Jiang Qing offered her dogmatic, far-fetched comments – the kind of criticism that became the norm in the decade – on sixty-one 'poisonous weed' films at another military conference in May 1966. To warn the audience of what was now deemed 'counter-revolutionary' or at least 'inappropriate' by Jiang Qing's standards, twenty of these films were released nationwide as targets of a massive campaign of film criticism (Zhai 1995: 181–3).

In early 1967 leading newspapers chastised *Sorrows of the Forbidden City*, a

1948 Hong Kong court drama exhibited in the PRC in 1950, as 'a reactionary film'. This old film was singled out partly because Mao had expressed his displeasure as early as 1954 and partly because its depiction of the reformists and the conservatives at the turn of the century served as a rally point for cracking down on those whose loyalty to Mao was in question. Sadly, far away from the political center, Zhu Shilin was rushed to hospital in Hong Kong and died on the same day as he heard about Mao's criticism (Y. Sun 1990: 269). Other casualties in the film world soon followed: Ying Yunwei in January 1967 (at age 63), Cai Chusheng in July 1967 (at age 62), Shangguan Yunzhu in November 1968 (at age 46), Tian Han in December 1968 (at age 70), Zheng Junli in April 1969 (at age 58).[6] Many more connected to or knowledgeable about pre-socialist cinema in Shanghai were incarcerated, some in solitary confinement, for years without appeal or visitation rights. The majority of film workers in the major studios were persecuted or expelled. In Changchun Studio alone, two-thirds of the production staff (521 people) were forced to live in rural areas and their urban registries were taken away (H. Chen 1989: 1: 324-5).

Jiang Qing: from Shanghai through Yan'an to Beijing

The official historiography blames Jiang Qing, the head of the 'Gang of Four' (*siren bang*), as ultimately responsible for the atrocities committed during the Cultural Revolution, thus exonerating Mao and other leaders of their involvement.[7] The 'demonizing' of Jiang was made more acceptable by the revelation of her hidden past in Shanghai during the mid-1930s. An actress starring in *City Scenes*, *Lianhua Symphony* and two other films, Jiang was known as Lan Ping and was the focus of several sensational headlines.[8] She joined a leftist drama troupe and became famous for her role in Ibsen's *Nora*, a stage performance that also cast other rising stars such as Zhao Dan and Jin Shan. Unexpectedly, the troupe soon disbanded because Jiang and Wang Ying both competed for the lead role in Xia Yan's new play, *Courtesan Sai Jinhua* (Sai Jinhua), and no one could settle the dispute. Jiang's marriage with Tang Na (a talented leftist film critic) in a group wedding in Hangzhou and their subsequent separation generated even more publicity in 1936-7. Two months after their honeymoon, Jiang left Tang, first for Yu Qiwei, her second husband/partner and then for Zhang Min (a married playwright with children). Tang subsequently attempted suicide twice within a ten-month period. Amid public condemnation of her 'immoral' behavior, Jiang declared that she was not Ruan Lingyu, who committed suicide in 1935, and would fight back (Y. Luo 1995: 152-3).

Jiang's way of fighting back was neither a direct nor an immediate confrontation with the media. In 1937 she left Shanghai and attended the Yan'an College of Marxism and Leninism. Within a year, at age 24 and after three marriages, she was miraculously wedded to Mao as his third wife. Given her Shanghai record, the CCP approved the marriage on the condition that Jiang would stay out of policy-making decisions for twenty years. Jiang thus kept a low profile until

1950, when she served as director of a film office under the CCP central committee's propaganda department and was appointed as an executive member to the national film advisory committee. She was 'credited' for diagnosing ideological problems in *Sorrows of the Forbidden City* and *The Life of Wu Xun* and influencing Mao's opinions, as well as for vetoing dozens of screenplays in the early 1950s. Prolonged illness forced Jiang out of politics for a decade. Upon her return to the political arena in 1963, she embarked on what she envisioned as a 'revolution in Peking opera' and quickly assumed a leadership position in the Cultural Revolution (Y. Luo 1995: 156–63).

Model play films and a new aesthetic

In 1964 Jiang captured national attention with her comments on 'modern Peking operas' such as *Legend of the Red Lantern* (Hongdeng ji) and *Taking the Tiger Mountain by Stratagem* (Zhiqu Weihushan), as well as the modern ballet *Red Detachment of Women*. In May 1967 all eight model plays were ready and Jiang had them performed in Beijing, an event hailed by the chief CCP organs as a milestone in the development of new proletarian art and literature. In May 1968, sponsored by Jiang Qing, the principle of 'three prominences' was issued as a directive to all artists: 'give prominence to positive characters among all the characters, to heroes among the positive characters, to the principal hero among the heroes'. This principle was duly translated into a set of formulae in film production. In frame composition, the hero must be located at the centre and the villain at the fringes. In camera positioning, the hero must be shot from a low angle and the villain from a high angle. In proportions, the hero must appear large and the villain small. In color scheme, the hero must be bathed in warm colors and the villain in cold tones. In lighting, the hero must be bright and the villain dark. Although formulaic, the principle of three prominences governed film production for almost a decade and left indelible marks on a wide range of artistic works.

Given that feature production had ceased at the time, filming the model plays became an urgent task of implementing and propagating the new aesthetic principle. In 1968 Jiang Qing called on Li Wenhua of Beijing Studio, who recommended that Xie Tieli and a few veteran blacklisted artists be given a chance to redeem themselves by shooting revolutionary films. Soon two film groups were established in Beijing. It was extremely difficult, however, for the group working on *Taking the Tiger Mountain by Stratagem* to meet Jiang Qing's requirements of both 'restoring' and 'exceeding' the stage. First, in their efforts to 'exceed' the stage, Xie Tieli and his group experimented with location shooting in the northeastern forests and with a new spatial-temporal structure of the story, but the result was faulted as resembling neither a film nor an opera. Second, in order to 'restore' the stage, they fixed the camera in front of the stage and basically photographed the entire performance, but again the result failed due to its reliance on mechanical reproduction. After submitting self-criticisms,

219

in the third round the group designed sets in the studio to achieve a three-dimensional 'filmic' perspective but employed long takes to capture the theatrical ambience. They also coordinated camera movements and editing to heighten the operatic tempos and came up with some of the film techniques that exemplified the three prominences mentioned above (Zhai 1995: 188–9).

Taking the Tiger Mountain by Stratagem (Zhiqu Weihushan, dir. Xie Tieli; opera) was finally accepted by the authorities and was released nationwide in October 1970, the first of its kind. Other key model plays followed in succession. It is evident that in the model play films *revolutionary romanticism* overrode any concern of realism, and the artists were routinely blamed if they tried to use realistic makeup, costumes and props. However, more than theatrical rituals, these films intended to erect the artistic models of ultra-leftist ideology for the entire nation. Class struggle was given central spotlight, and Mao's theory of 'continuing revolution under the proletarian dictatorship' was concretized in the staged confrontations against class enemies and revisionists.

The worship of Mao on screen and on the stage paralleled a frenetic personality cult ritualized in everyday life, boosted by the ubiquity of the model plays during the Cultural Revolution. Except for some war films screened for educational purposes, the model plays and their film versions became the only available cinematic entertainment. As the audience was galvanized to emulate the heroes, the model play films gradually acquired the characteristics of 'religious art': 'cinemas took on the functions of the church, the films worked as the bible, the heroes performed like the priests, and the audience acted like the worshipers' (Zhai 1995: 199).

From class struggle to internal struggles in the Party

After scoring a victory with the model play films, the ultra-leftists turned to feature productions in 1973 to further their political agendas. Three types of films are noteworthy in the mid-1970s. First, films of new model plays and other recommended regional operas continued to appear. For example, a film version of the *Legend of the Red Lantern* (dir. Cheng Yin) in the Uygur language was released in 1975. Second, a few color remakes were released in 1974, such as *From Victory to Victory* (Nanzheng beizhan, dir. Cheng Yin, Wang Yan). These remakes preserved the original stories but were shot using the new techniques of the model play films. Third, films dealing with the socialist period became the arenas of intense political confrontation. After January 1974, when three new features opened in theaters, the first such event since the beginning of the Cultural Revolution, class struggles quickly evolved into internal struggles within the Party, masterminded by the ultra-leftists to target their political opponents.

The making of *Breaking with Old Ideas* (Juelie, dir. Li Wenhua, 1975) is representative of the level of political intrigue at the time. In early 1975 Li Wenhua read a screenplay about a Communist labor college and volunteered to direct it.

220

Under political pressure, the original conflict between two schools of educational thought was elevated to that of two opposing Party lines, thus replacing 'contradictions among the people' with confrontations with the enemies. Not surprisingly by then, the enemy figures were defined as two Party leaders who defended the urban-centered, theory-oriented but 'bourgeois' values of education and wanted to shut down the rural-based, practice-oriented but 'proletarian' labor college. Brainwashed by years of ultra-leftist ideology, the crew and the cast enthusiastically embarked on the project in June 1975, experiencing the real life by living on location for a month and collecting details of the Party wrangles.

The film opens with Long Guozheng (Guo Zhenqing), a Yan'an era cadre, riding a raft down the river accompanied by a spirited off-screen song. He reports to his former army superior and assumes the new position as principal of a Communist labor college, which he decides to establish in the mountains against the objection of his deputy Cao Zhonghe and Professor Sun Ziqing. Instead of written examinations, work experience in the field is used as an admission criterion, and barely literate people are accepted as students. The film makes fun of Sun's pedantic way of teaching the functions of the horsetail in the classroom and contrasts it with students' cheerful participation in the field. Principal Long tours an urban university and finds its educational philosophy alienating. Meanwhile, Deputy Cao decides to expel several students who ignored the examinations and helped with the harvest in the village – a decision overturned by Long upon his return. A public meeting to criticize a stubborn student is turned into a denunciation of bourgeois education values. The college is ordered to be shut down, but Long encourages students to post big-character posters in protest, and his political future is secured when the news of Mao's endorsement of their college reaches the campus. Amidst the cheering crowd of students and villagers, Long raises his arm and calls for a resolute breaking with old ideas. A low angle shot of his silhouette against the sky thus projects Long as a larger-than-life hero, a saintly surrogate delegate of the supreme leader Chairman Mao.

Breaking with Old Ideas was completed in October 1975 and was approved without any revision – a sign of its 'perfect' political correctness – because high-ranking ultra-leftists like Zhang Chunqiao had inspected earlier versions of the script (Cleverley 2000: 173–7). When it opened in January 1976, the film received a great deal of attention and was used as an example to counter the so-called 'right-wing restoration' engineered by Deng Xiaoping. In essence, *Breaking with Old Ideas* exemplifies the stereotyping and oversimplification of the ultra-leftist films.

However, ambiguities exist even in stereotypes. As Chris Berry observes, whether the principal hero should be from the Party or the masses remained an unanswered question and meant there was inconsistency in the stereotyping, which the films tried to hide by making him a man of the masses and having him always in agreement with the Party (1982: 57). Yet, being able to gloss over inconsistencies did not solve a more fundamental problem, which was the unpredictability of the outcome of the internal struggles within the Party vis-à-vis filmmakers. After the downfall of the Gang of Four in 1976, *Breaking with Old Ideas* was criticized as a 'reactionary film' and Li Wenhua was investigated for two years (Di 1993: 79).

The unpredictability of political struggles was also evident in the case of *The Pioneers* (Chuangye, dir. Yu Yanfu, 1974), which glorifies workers in the petroleum industry. Stylistically close to ultra-leftist films, the film somehow provoked Jiang Qing, who immediately planned a campaign against it. It was only after Mao commented on a letter of complaint that the film cleared Jiang's obstruction. Evidently, by 1975 Mao was aware of Jiang Qing's political ambition but was too senile to pull her back or bring her down. Only after his death did the CCP moderates, with military support, oust Jiang and her faction in October 1976.

The recovery years, 1977–8

Annual feature production gradually increased from four in 1973 to seventeen in 1974, twenty-four in 1975 and thirty-nine in 1976, with the figure for 1976 approximating that of any given year in the early 1960s (see Table 6.2, pp. 196–7). The output of twenty and forty-four features in 1977 and 1978, respectively, stabilized the situation and prepared for a quantum leap in the new era. But in general, the brief recovery years did not depart from the rigid environment of ideological and artistic confinement. A few films ventured to expose the Gang of Four and vented pent-up frustrations, but they did so in ways similar to the dictates of the three prominences, except that the ultra-leftists were now the villains. A notable development was the return of the spy film, seven in two years, which helped to relax the restrictions on film genres. Ideologically, nonetheless, class struggle was kept as a guiding principle, and film was still required to serve workers, peasants and soldiers. The long-awaited breakthrough in filmmaking occurred only after the third plenary meeting of the CCP eleventh congress in December 1978, which established a new 'open-door' policy of economic reform, modernization and liberalization.

A few positive developments in the recovery years are worth mentioning here. In the exhibition sector, a large number of pre-Cultural Revolution films were released to the public, thus reconnecting the tradition of socialist realism and raising higher expectations for film production in the new era. Movie tickets were sold openly at the box office, ending the units-distribution system implemented since the early 1970s. Hunan (later renamed Xiaoxiang) and Guangxi studios were founded in 1976 and 1978 respectively. The Beijing Film Academy reopened and students were enrolled in directing, photography, design, recording and acting – the same students who would form the fifth generation that would emerge in the mid-1980s (Ni 2003).

CONCLUSION: IDEOLOGY AND SUBJECTIVITY

As Dai Jinhua observes, heroism, collectivism and optimism characterize socialist cinema, which functions primarily as a historical *discourse* designed to legitimatize the CCP regime and its political hegemony in the PRC. As discourse, socialist cinema re-presents the history of modern China as a history of revolutions that, under the CCP leadership, have liberated China from the yoke of imperialism, feudalism and capitalism and will deliver the nation to a bright Communist future. Just as heroism recognizes the sacrifices of the Communist heroes and martyrs, so does collectivism reconstruct a utopian revolutionary or socialist family in which individuals are given critical moments to discard their own private fantasies, discipline and reform themselves by voluntary participation in collective work. The acceptance of individuals into the grand family, most often symbolized by their hard-earned CCP membership (treasured as their second life), is often projected as a group ceremony. Narrative structures of 'obstacle-fighting-victory' and 'ordinary folk-revolutionary-hero' are simultaneously filmic ingredients and key components of socialist revolution, interlocking fiction and reality in the socialist period. Thus, socialist cinema is more than a discourse on Communist revolutions and the maturation of heroes, for it attracted and influenced a whole generation of audiences and turned itself into a meaningful part of modern Chinese history (Dai 1993: 168–79).

Dai's reading of socialist cinema demonstrates the usefulness of Louis Althusser's theory of ideology and subjectivity (1971: 127–86). Indeed, for Dai, *Song of Youth* nicely illustrates the ideal ways that the state ideological apparatuses interpellated the audience into subjection to the dominant ideology. The film chronicles the transformation of Lin Daojing (Xie Fang), a May Fourth woman who divorces her petit-bourgeois husband (a 'reactionary' scholar), identifies with revolution through her unrequited love for a Communist martyr Lu Jiachuan, and finally joins the masses with her new proletarian partner-comrade Jiang Hua. In this film the intellectual is gendered as female (thus demanding paternal guidance from the proletariat), figured as *object* of discursive contestation (between the CCP and the KMT), and interpellated as a potential subject in revolution by the Communist ideology (Dai 1993: 200–17). Certainly, the intertextual link between *Song of Youth* and pre-socialist novels reminds us of the traceable *leftist influence* on such an allegorical representation of the intellectual. But the box-office success of the film points to the audience's enthusiasm in embracing their new subject position in the socialist revolution.

I would argue that not only the general audience but also the third generation of filmmakers were interpellated into the same subject position as the *feminized intellectual* in the socialist period. They were 'feminized' because they were perceived as subordinate to the masses of workers, peasants and soldiers; they were 'subjected' because their political loyalty appears always in doubt and their memberships in revolution had to be earned and periodically renewed. Caught in the powerful state ideological apparatuses, the third generation earnestly sought to live up to the nation-state's expectations and to contribute to the reproduction of new subjects in socialist China by means of cinema. Unlike the second generation, the third generation had a relatively clean start (many from the CCP-controlled areas in the 1940s) and comfortably identified with the new socialist nation-state. Repeated political setbacks only made them more resilient and their characters more elastic, as in the cases of Cheng Yin, Shui Hua, Xie Tieli and Xie Jin, all recruited to film model plays in spite of their earlier films which were critically attacked during the Cultural Revolution. Overdetermination may account for the kind of subjectivity they could obtain, but under the rigid socialist system they never functioned as *agents* acting on their free will. Socialist cinema was, after all, developed as a political weapon, and the filmmakers' status as state employees fixed them squarely in the propaganda machinery (metaphorically as 'bolts and nuts') and made their dream of artistic freedom ultimately nothing but a dream.

Admittedly, the Althusserian model of ideology and subjectivity remains a *theoretical* hypothesis regarding the audience and the artists of socialist cinema. For one thing, it does not explain at what juncture the subject can ignore or reject the interpellation by the dominant ideology, as did political dissidents in different times of the socialist period. For another, it does not recognize the possibility that the subject-in-subjection can and actually does negotiate and maneuver through the cracks and fissures in the ideological system and manage to 'smuggle' alternative or even subversive subtexts in socialist cinema. We must not take the viewer's or the artist's words for granted, for while paying lip service to the CCP policy they might feel and think differently and might react to ideological interpellation in ways other than they openly acknowledged.

In this light, we may reinterpret the questions Chunhua intended to pose in the original script of *Stage Sisters* – 'But to be what kind of person? And to perform what kind of play?' – to be apprehensive, portentous and sarcastic all at the same time. Apprehensive because Chunhua, speaking for artists and intellectuals (e.g., Sun Yu), was truly worried about what would become of them upon entering socialist China. Portentous because Xie Jin and his colleagues, speaking on the eve of the Cultural Revolution, were fully aware of the kind of person they were forced to become and the kind of play they had to perform (hence, Xie Jin's involvement in making the model play film). Sarcastic because, in historical hindsight, we may take Chunhua's questions as rhetorical questions that reveal the fundamental lack of artistic freedom for Chinese filmmakers in the socialist period. As we shall see in Chapter 7, only in the post-Mao era, with ideological controls relaxed and self-conscious cultural reflection, could filmmakers break away from old ideological confinement, reconstruct their personal and artistic identity, and cultivate new subjectivity along with new aesthetics, film language and directorial styles.

7

CINEMA AND NATIONAL/REGIONAL CULTURES, 1979–89

INTRODUCTION: NEW WAVES IN THREE CHINAS

This chapter brings the PRC, Taiwan and Hong Kong together so as to fore-ground the parallel development of the new wave in filmmaking in all three Chinas during the 1980s. Chronologically, the new wave started first in Hong Kong in 1979. It dramatically changed the look of Hong Kong cinema and the way in which filmmakers there negotiated with their colonial history and postcolonial prospects. As in Hong Kong, New Taiwan Cinema developed an increasing awareness of identity issues in Taiwan's own culture and history. Indeed, culture and history were of crucial importance to New Chinese Cinema in the post-Mao period, as cinema became one of the most popular means of rethinking what had gone wrong in the socialist revolution and what people could do to improve their lives. Emerging from the new waves in all three Chinas were new cinematic reflections on national and regional cultures and the common concerns with humanism in the face of the dominant political and economic regimes. Such concerns were put to the test in the 1989 pro-democratic demonstration in Beijing's Tiananmen square, televised live by the Western media and followed by the PLA's brutal crackdown that shocked the entire world. Although the momentum of the new waves had been exhausted by that time, a decade of cinematic innovations, increased interactions among filmmakers from the three Chinas and a number of top international film festival awards had placed Chinese film in a prominent position in world cinema.

In terms of film history, mainland China witnessed the rise of a blooming film industry and film market in the early 1980s. Relieved from decades of political repression, filmmakers of three different generations seized the rare opportunity of relative freedom to launch New Chinese Cinema. Thanks to the low per-centage of household ownership of television sets and the nature of available television programs,[1] film was the preferred form of mass entertainment in the early 1980s, especially in China's vast rural areas, which pushed annual attendance to an all-time high by the mid-1980s. A cultural fever swept over China and engaged intellectuals and professionals in critical reflection on modern

Chinese history and culture. Following the cultural turn engineered by their predecessors, a group of young filmmakers known as the fifth generation revolutionized film language and film styles in Chinese cinema and successfully broke into the circuit of international film festivals.

In Taiwan, young directors like Hou Hsiao-hsien and Edward Yang launched the movement of New Taiwan Cinema in the early 1980s. They re-examined their generation's experience of growing up in Taiwan's environment of fast industrialization and modernization. Furthermore, they integrated Taiwanese dialect into their films in order to capture the indigenous force of Taiwan culture. On the other hand, mainland China received renewed attention in Taiwan cinema, first as the embodiment of a repressive political system and later as the long lost homeland reopened for visits by Taiwan residents. The lifting of the martial law in July 1987 ushered in a new era of democratization in Taiwan, and Hou Hsiao-hsien was quick to confront the taboo topic of the 28 February Incident in *City of Sadness*.

In Hong Kong, new wave filmmakers brought new attitudes toward socio-political issues and new techniques and styles to Hong Kong genre films in the early 1980s. Although many critics believe the new wave was abruptly absorbed by commercial filmmaking, in the late 1980s another group of directors emerged and continued the experimental spirit of their predecessors and launched a second wave that further consolidated Hong Kong's status in international art cinema. As in Taiwan, China loomed large in Hong Kong's cinematic imagination during the 1980s. What critics term 'the China factor' (HKIFF 1990) revealed the anxiety felt about the imminent return of Hong Kong to China's sovereignty (1997) on the one hand, and provided an incentive for filmmakers to explore issues of identity in Hong Kong on the other.

THE PRC: HUMANISM, THE AVANT-GARDE AND COMMERCIALISM

As mentioned in Chapter 6, the third plenary meeting of the CCP eleventh congress in December 1978 ushered in a 'new era' under the leadership of Deng Xiaoping characterized by economic reform, modernization and liberalization. Filmmakers were able to denounce the brutality of the Gang of Four during the Cultural Revolution and tested their new found freedom by exploring previously taboo or sensitive subjects and genres such as political persecution, female sexuality and martial arts. While humanism characterized the entire decade of New Chinese Cinema, from the mid-1980s onward the fifth generation succeeded in introducing the avant-garde as a distinctive feature of Chinese cinema, but the industry as a whole faced a severe challenge from a ferocious tide of commercialism in the late 1980s.

Production and exhibition, 1979–84

Chinese cinema developed rapidly in the new era, and a number of new institutions were established to meet the increased market demand at home and abroad. Inner Mongolia Studio was established in 1979, China Children's Studio in 1980, and Shenzhen and Fujian Studios in 1984. In 1979 China Imports and Exports Company and China Film Coproduction Corporation were founded, the former in charge of purchasing foreign films and distributing Chinese films overseas, while the latter handled Chinese co-productions with other countries and regions. The majority of co-productions were done with Hong Kong, such as Li Hanxiang's *Reign Behind a Curtain* (Chuilian tingzheng) and *The Burning of the Imperial Palace* (Huoshao Yuanmingyuan), two 1983 imperial court dramas endorsing patriotism, which were popular in both China and Hong Kong.

Meanwhile, film education and research charged ahead. In 1982 the Beijing Film Academy graduated its first class admitted after the Cultural Revolution, among them key members of the fifth generation like Chen Kaige and Zhang Yimou.[2] The China Film Art Research Center (Zhongguo dianying yishu yanjiu zhongxin, ZDYYZ) was instituted in Beijing in 1983, which has since overseen the China Film Archive and a new film studies journal, *Contemporary Cinema* (Dangdai dianying) inaugurated in 1984. In May 1980 the Hundred Flowers Awards resumed its annual operations after a lengthy suspension since 1963. In 1981 the Golden Rooster Awards sponsored by the official China Filmmakers Association was set up, and its combined ceremony with the Hundred Flowers Awards became a much publicized, celebrity-filled annual event for film fans. From 1979 to 1985 the Ministry of Culture also issued annual awards for films deemed 'excellent', an event carried over by the Ministry of Radio, Television and Film when the film administration was transferred there from the Ministry of Culture in January 1986.

Annual feature productions grew steadily, from 67 in 1979 to 144 in 1984. Then, after dipping to 126 in 1985, they reached 151 in 1986 (see Table 6.2, pp. 196–7). While each of the three largest studios – Beijing, Changchun and Shanghai – consistently produced between ten and twenty-one features per year, the combined output from other studios such as August First, Emei, Pearl River and Xi'an made up between about 40 and 65 per cent of the annual total. The immense popularity of film as entertainment is evident in the case of *The In-Laws* (Xi yingmen, dir. Zhao Huanzhang, 1981), a rural family melodrama about generational conflict set in the new era. In the first fifteen days of its first run in Beijing, the film had sold 2.75 million tickets. Within a year, the film had sold over 4,000 prints (compared to the average of 100 prints per film); and in a period of two years, it had reached 600 million people – more than one half of the nation's population (H. Chen 1989: 1: 395, 2: 278–9).

At the end of 1984, national exhibition outlets had reached 180,000 and employed 500,000 people, compared with approximately 20,000 employees in

227

the production sector. Annual movie attendance was 25 billion, an all-time high, which means on average 70 million people watched films each day during the mid-1980s (see Table 6.1, p. 192). The nationwide exhibition revenues stood at RMB1.3 billion. A new development was the expansion of exhibition in the rural areas. From March to December 1981 nationwide township theaters increased from 2,000 to 4,000. With further government loans, the figure reached 10,000 by the end of 1984. Geographically, the projection networks covered 97.5 per cent of the nation. Among the rural population an average person watched twenty-four films in 1984, and rural exhibition revenues rose 55.2 per cent from RMB290 million in 1979 to RMB450 million in 1984 (H. Chen 1989: 2: 263–4, 277–8).

Thematic and genre explorations

Against the background of decades of political repression, Chinese filmmakers enjoyed a high degree of creative freedom in the new era and moved quickly to expand their thematic and genre explorations far beyond a mere denunciation of the ultra-leftist Gang of Four. A distinctive feature of New Chinese Cinema was the genuine pursuit of *humanism* – not as an abstract concept but as a *material* force affecting people's daily life with all its emotional and political impact. Filmmakers enhanced film's impact by exploring its audio-visual dimensions. Human emotions, hitherto a sensitive subject in socialist cinema, were explored to the full, sometimes melodramatically, but often they were enacted in a range of quotidian nuances, subtle gestures and facial expressions. By juxtaposing absurd political situations and family dilemmas, several films present intellectuals as the central protagonists, another significant improvement on the post-Mao screen.

The return of intellectuals as legitimate characters does not mean a lack of attention to workers, peasants and soldiers, who had long 'heroically' dominated the socialist screen. The difference was, however, that these characters now appeared not as 'saintly' revolutionaries exemplifying abstract Communist ideas but as *ordinary individuals* struggling with common problems in human relationships such as love, marriage and sexuality, once sensitive subjects which Chinese filmmakers had learned to avoid in the socialist era. *Under the Bridge* (Daqiao xiamian, dir. Bai Chen, 1983), which traces the growing love between a self-employed bicycle repairman and a single mother against social prejudice in Shanghai, in a sense is a return to the social realism tradition of the 1930s. Similarly endorsing the sanctity of love, *Anxious to Return* (Guixin sijian, dir. Li Jun, 1979) depicts an injured soldier who falls in love with a widow while under her care, but who leaves her to rejoin the anti-Japanese troops.

The pursuit of humanism was evident in most genres of the decade. In historical films that feature top CCP leaders, emotions are delicately crafted as an integral part of the narrative. Hence, in *Xi'an Incident* (Xi'an shibian, dir. Cheng Yin, 1981), even the KMT leader Chiang Kai-shek appears as a human being rather than symbolic of the 'evils' of the time. In literary adaptations, rich pictures of local or *regional cultures* often emerge from the humanist treatment. A veteran director, Ling Zifeng offers indigenous Beijing cultural flavors in his adaptation of Lao She's novel, *Camel Xiangzi*, aka *Rickshaw Boy* (Luotuo Xiangzi, 1982). In *Border Town* (Biancheng, 1984), an adaptation of a Shen Congwen novella, Ling captures the distinctive landscape and folk custom of West Hunan.

Admittedly, with all their humanist concerns, filmmakers rarely challenged the CCP legitimacy. On the contrary, in the early 1980s they incorporated officially endorsed reform subjects in their exploration of themes and genres. *In the Wild Mountain* (Yeshan, dir. Yan Xueshu, 1985) recounts the changes in the midst of economic reform through the depiction of two very different rural men – one committed to the age-old agrarian life and the other to modern science – who get divorced and marry each other's former wives. The message of the film – that both the conservative and the reformist will get what he wants – pleased audiences and authorities alike. Likewise, comedies sang the praises of the government, and the new Party policy – 'it's glorious to get rich first' – justifies a comedy series featuring the father–son team of Chen Qiang and Chen Peisi. Nevertheless, the craze for money surfaced as an ironic response to the government's periodic campaigns against 'bourgeois liberalization' in the new era and mocked the persistent anti-capitalist movements of the socialist era. Not surprisingly, even martial arts pictures of the 1980s tended to construct a politically correct narrative. In *A Mysterious Giant Buddha* (Shenmi de dafo, dir. Zhang Huaxun, 1980), which announced the genre's premiere to the PRC screen, KMT agents are featured among the bad guys. But most often in this genre the challenge comes from Japan or Europe, which the Chinese heroes manage to defeat with honor and integrity.

Political melodrama and the Xie Jin model

Xie Jin's films of the 1980s reflect the changing cinematic landscape in the post-Mao years. Contrary to the majority of his contemporaries, who vented anger at the Gang of Four, Xie was courageous enough to push the censorship limits by skillfully integrating a political message into a melodramatic representation. With *The Legend of Tianyun Mountain* (Tianyunshan chuanqi, 1980), he exposed the inhuman treatment the Rightists had suffered after the late 1950s. With *Garlands at the Foot of the Mountain* (Gaoshan xiade huahuan, 1984), he emerged as an exception again because the film has remained the only officially released title on the otherwise forbidden subject of the Sino-Vietnamese border war.[3] In *Hibiscus Town* (Furong zhen, 1986), he told the tale of the political persecution of innocent country folk in the 1960s. Ideologically sensitive and emotionally charged, Xie's films were immensely popular with both audiences and critics alike.

One crucial reason why Xie passed the strict censorship rules in spite of his handling of sensitive subjects is that his films unequivocally acknowledge the ultimate rectitude of the CCP, which heeds the call of history and corrects its errors by rehabilitating the wrongly accused. Another reason is that Xie always introduces an acceptable *presentday* point of view, from which past suffering is turned into a valuable historical lesson and the victims are compensated by a sense of justice projected by filmic representation. Yet another reason is the form of *political melodrama* that Xie helped to craft, which harks back to the early years of socialist realism and extols the virtues of ideological conviction and moral perseverance. Xie's melodramas thus furnish a compelling example of the changing political economy of Chinese filmmaking and of the emergent subjectivity of Chinese filmmakers in the new era (Browne 1994).

Nevertheless, it is precisely Xie's achievement in melodrama that provoked trenchant criticism from the younger generation in a 1986 debate hosted by a Shanghai newspaper. Zhu Dake thus described the problems of the Xie Jin model. First, Xie's augmentation of emotionalism, which solicits tears and manipulates the viewer into a trance in which he or she blindly embraces the artist's traditional ethical views, functions exactly like medieval religious art and runs counter to the modern character of scientism and rationalism. Second, Xie's melodrama follows the procedures of thematic coding, such as 'the suffering of good people', 'the discovery of values', 'moral persuasion' and 'good defeating evil', and creates a myth of compromised solutions to social conflicts. Upon closer scrutiny, the Xie Jin model closely resembles Hollywood's Cinderella narrative, and his trademark melodrama guarantees his box-office appeal. Third, Xie repeatedly portrays his female characters as gentle, kind-hearted, hardworking and self-sacrificing – virtues of traditional womanhood and all 'deformed products of patriarchal culture', in which women discover and endorse male values and offer men their happiness. In short, Zhu believes that the Xie Jin model represents 'retrogress' from the May Fourth spirit and is not representative of the cultural transformation in post-Mao China (Luo *et al.* 1992: 2: 493–5).

The fourth generation: from film theory to cultural reflection

In retrospect, the young critics' prediction that 'Xie Jin's era was over' and his model was 'out of date' proved premature (Semsel *et al.* 1990: 144–6). Melodrama – albeit less didactic and more entertaining – continued to be the favored form of cinematic representation in the 1990s. In theoretical terms, Zhu Dake's criticism of the Xie Jin model would not have come without years of debates on film theory and criticism. As early as 1979, the call for 'throwing away the drama crutch' was heard in film circles, and Zhang Junxiang's 1980 reiteration of the thesis that 'film is literature' was met with counter-arguments that challenge the supremacy of film's 'literary quality' and emphasize film's own aesthetic principles. 'On the Modernization of Film Language', an article written by Zhang Nuanxin and Li Tuo in 1979, exemplifies the turn from literature and drama to the ontology of film in Chinese film theory. The writers argue that, in world cinema, film narrative has moved away from dramatic structuring, and in terms of film language camera movements are privileged over montage editing. The article draws its inspiration from the French new wave, Italian neo-realism and André Bazin's theory of the long take and illustrates aspects of film as a synthetic, expressive art – aspects such as sculptural lighting, shades of color, split screens, variant tempos, natural acting, as well as the relationships between image and sound. Published at the onset of an enthusiastic pursuit of film theory in post-Mao China, Zhang and Li's article was regarded as 'the outlines of experimental film' and as 'the artistic manifesto of the fourth generation' (Luo *et al.* 1992: 2: 3–88).

Zheng Dongtian distinguishes two salient features of the middle-aged directors in the 1980s: simultaneous pursuits of theory and practice and a combination of imitation and creation (Luo *et al.* 1992: 2: 463). Several fourth generation directors, including Xie Fei, Zhang Nuanxin and Zheng Dongtian, were teaching at the Beijing Film Academy when the fifth generation artists were learning their trade. Parallel to their theoretical pursuit, the fourth generation self-consciously imitated foreign accomplishments in an effort to modernize Chinese film language. A documentary aesthetic characterized their early films, such as *Drive to Win* (Sha Ou, dir. Zhang Nuanxin, 1981), which favored long takes, natural lighting and location shooting. The non-dramatic structure emerged as another distinctive mark in such films as *My Memory of Old Beijing* (Chengnan jiushi, dir. Wu Yigong, 1982), which experiments with narrative points of view and creates a poetic ambience comparable to traditional Chinese aesthetics. The exploration of the new film language also enriched the psychological depths of Chinese cinema. The open-ended narrative in *Narrow Street* (Xiaojie, dir. Yang Yanjin, 1981), which stages a film within the film where a director helps the protagonist construct several probable endings, compels viewers to rethink both the tragedy of the Cultural Revolution and their own subjectivity in historical representation.

By the mid-1980s the fourth generation had become increasingly involved in the movement of cultural reflection, and their exploration of cultural traditions took them to uncharted territory. Both *Good Woman* (Liangjia funü, dir. Huang Jianzhong, 1985) and *A Girl from Hunan* (Xiangnü Xiaoxiao, dir. Xie Fei, 1986) examine a peculiar rural practice whereby an adolescent girl is married to a young widow's toddler son, which often results in sexual tension when the girl comes of age. Although both directors endorse the sanctity of female sexuality, their sympathy for victims of patriarchy and their delineation of folk culture can be seen as ideologically ambivalent. On the one hand, they conscientiously set out to expose the inhumanity of the patriarchal repression of female sexuality; on the other, they are fascinated – even mesmerized – by the magic of indigenous culture and inadvertently reproduce the resilience of the patriarchal tradition through filmic representation. Although the young girl in *Good Woman* divorces her toddler husband and marries the man of her choice, her mother-in-law remains a paragon of female virtue, as represented in patriarchal terms by her chastity and diligence. In *A Girl from Hunan*, the household accepts the 'adulterous' young woman thanks to her giving birth to a boy, but the film ends years later with the beginning of another cycle – the wedding of the boy and another adolescent girl.

The fourth generation's ambivalent attitude toward patriarchy is evident in two other films set in contemporary China. In *A Country Wife* (Xiangyin, dir. Hu Bingliu, 1983), a virtuous wife suffers from severe stomach pain but continues all household chores and takes care of her husband and children. Portrayed as being completely submissive, she says nothing but 'I follow you' to her husband, who is later shocked to learn of her cancer and regrets his treatment of her pain with cheap indigestion pills. The film ends with the husband in tears pushing his wife on a one-wheel cart along the mountain path on a trip to see a train for the first – and most likely the last – time in her life. As the absent symbol of modernity, the train remains largely irrelevant to the traditional way of life in a remote village.

More dramatically, *Old Well* (Laojing, dir. Wu Tianming, 1987) champions scientific knowledge that helps Sun Wangquan (Zhang Yimou) locate the first well with water in a mountain village, but the price he pays is his submission to an arranged marriage with a widow for financial benefits to his family. Sun's

Figure 7.1 A Girl from Hunan (1986): a fascination with female sexuality and regional culture

marriage confirms the power of tradition, and his betrayal of his former lover, an educated young woman who, disillusioned, leaves the village, demonstrates the entrenched conservatism of rural China. The television set Sun's lover donates to the village's fundraising event serves as an ironic reminder: a symbol of modernity, the television is a useless device because the signal of modernization cannot penetrate the vast mountains.

Women directors: female consciousness, identity and sexuality

It is worth contemplating the difference between male and female directors when it comes to representing female experience on screen. In general, women directors of the fourth generation differ from their male counterparts in their insistence on *female subjectivity* and gendered experience.[4] They were no longer content with mere gender equality in the workplace, which might have made their admirable predecessor Wang Ping proud as the principal director of *Song of Chinese Revolution* (Zhongguo geming zhi ge, 1985), an officially sanctioned ensemble musical in celebration of Communist achievements. Nor were the middle-aged women directors content with having female characters as protagonists commanding prominent screen time and space. Rather, they wanted to highlight female experience from a *gendered* perspective. Therefore, when women directors chose to confront issues of love, marriage and career, they tended to focus on the psychological processes of their female characters more than the social significance of the issues examined. By concentrating on the texture of 'femininity' (*nüxing*, literally 'female gender') rather than the concept of 'feminism' (*nüquan*, literally 'female power' – a sensitive topic most directors avoid), women directors of the 1980s explored female consciousness and female sexuality in search of female identity (J. Dai 1995).

Sacrificed Youth (Qingchun ji, dir. Zhang Nuanxin, 1985) is an outstanding example by a female director. During the Cultural Revolution a young Han urban woman is dispatched to work in a Dai minority region, where she acquires a sense of feminine beauty and discovers her new identity with the help of her Dai friends. What is remarkable in this film is that, unlike in films by male directors, the female protagonist relies on her own subjectivity rather than her male suitors in the process of redefining her identity. The use of her voice-over throughout the film adds a new psychological dimension to the film, which contributes both to the film's search for female identity and to the trend of cultural reflection.

In comparison, *Woman Demon Human* (Ren gui qing, dir. Huang Shuqin, 1987) is more dramatic and radical in its rendition of female consciousness, identity and sexuality. Rather than acquiring a new identity, the protagonist Qiu Yun is confronted with several identities imposed on her by social discourses. First, her mother's abandonment of her for a man later revealed to be her biological father (who nonetheless refuses to show his face on screen) makes young Qiu Yun a daughter of a 'shameless' mother, who seems to care about sexuality

Figure 7.2 Sacrificed Youth (1985): exploring feminine beauty and female consciousness

more than anything else. As a result of this childhood trauma, Qiu Yun revolts against her mother and her mother's stage role as a charming woman. Second, under her legal father's training, Qiu Yun develops her specialty in masculine martial roles, but her transvestitism (short haircut and boyish manners) engenders an identity crisis when she joins a provincial troupe. She falls in love with her teacher and in one scene makes herself beautiful with make-up. However, as the gossip spreads, her teacher, who is married with several children, is transferred to another unit, and Qiu Yun is seen in a hysterical fit in which she smears make-up on her face so that her stage identity is beyond recognition. Third, Qiu Yun's roles as a wife and mother do not bring her any happiness. Whereas her husband remains an off-screen reference, her admirable screen presence as the male demon Zhong Kui wins her international recognition. In the climatic scene when she revisits her hometown, Qiu Yun seems to embrace her multiple identities by declaring to her alter ego Zhong Kui that she is happily married to the stage (Cui 2003: 219–38).

For critic Dai Jinhua, what makes *Woman Demon Human* a unique 'feminist' film in China is that the ideal man who could save Qiu Yun from trouble exists only in her transgendered performance (J. Wang and Barlow 2002: 151–71).

This idea of *identity as performance* thus represents a breakthrough in Chinese cinema because it distinguishes the 'women's film' as more fluid in gender construction than films by male directors, the latter confined by the age-old construct of identity as rigid and static. Indeed, in a few early films by the female members of the fifth generation, female identity exists more in the processes of female consciousness and female journeys than in the traditional ways of life defined by Party regulations and village rules. For example, *Army Nurse* (Nüer lou, dir. Hu Mei, 1985) ends with the nurse rejecting a Party-arranged marriage, and *Women's Story* (Nüren de gushi, dir. Peng Xiaolian, 1987) concludes with a scene of sisterhood when three women return from their urban journey to confront their patriarchal hometown.

The fifth generation: of avant-gardism and cultural critique

As suggested in the case of women directors above, the fourth and fifth generations shared much in common in the new era. According to Dai Jinhua, in the early 1980s the fourth generation intentionally 'misinterpreted' Bazin's documentary aesthetics so as to indulge themselves in new film techniques and to justify their cultivation of individual styles. The technical and stylistic innovations, which perfectly matched their pursuit of humanism (the priority of humans over politics as well as individuality over collectivity), enabled the fourth generation to 'escape' the previous roles of artists as mere political instrument and moral didacticism. Yet, what they pursued was not an aesthetic of documentary realism *à la* Bazin but rather a *depoliticized* narrative of retrieved memories and rediscovered spiritual realms. A fundamental dilemma arose from their desires simultaneously to indict (past) historical tragedies and to retreat from their (present) historical responsibility.

At the time of the mid-1980s, the fourth generation had outgrown their preference for individual narratives and began to confront larger issues of civilization (industrial modernity) versus ignorance (agrarian values). However, as before, signs of their dilemma were present in their wavering between their declared intention and their ambivalent message, between their rational advocacy for enlightenment and progress and their emotional attachment to cultural China, between their revulsion for repressive patriarchy and their apprehension about industrialization and commercialization. For Dai Jinhua, the fourth generation might have escaped 'history' as they wished, but they frequently fell into the nets of traditional culture which they had reconstructed in the midst of cultural reflection (1999: 15–34).

To a certain extent, the fifth generation took a similar spiritual journey fraught with fundamental dilemmas. They caught the world's attention with such radically iconoclastic avant-garde films as *One and Eight* (Yige he bage, dir. Zhang Junzhao, 1984) and *Yellow Earth*, both featuring Zhang Yimou's eye-catching cinematography characterized by disproportionate framing, natural lighting and barren landscapes (Silbergeld 1999: 15–52). Like their predecessors, the fifth generation favored a non-dramatic structure and depoliticized narration, but they went farther with scant dialogue and music as well as abundant ambiguities in characterization and narration. They insisted on 'showing' their films rather than 'telling' what had happened, which challenged viewers to take up a subject position based in a cultural critique but increased the level of difficulty in film appreciation. Consequently, their films did not appeal to the majority of audiences. In fact, Tian Zhuangzhuang's *On the Hunting Ground* (Liechang zhasa, 1985) sold only two prints for archival collection rather than distribution and his *Horse Thief* (Daoma zei, 1986) fared only slightly better with seven prints nationwide (Berry 1991: 118). Given such an obvious absence of box office, the social impact of the fifth generation's cultural critique was dubious.

Nevertheless, the *discursive* impact of the fifth generation's strategy of historical representation is unmistakable. In their efforts to rewrite revolutionary history, they effectively demythified what had been central to socialist representation. In *Yellow Earth*, the Communist cadre is no longer competent in his ideological indoctrination in a village plagued by drought, and peasants are no longer spontaneous in their response to a call for revolution but instead deeply entrenched in their superstitious belief in the forever-powerful dragon king.

Figure 7.3 One and Eight (1984): realism and symbolism in Zhang Yimou's cinematography

In *One and Eight*, even bandits are courageous in fighting the Japanese, although some of them in the end refuse to submit to the Communist authority. Unlike their predecessors, the fifth generation discursively situated themselves *outside* of official representation and thus felt free to construct their own myths – to remythify Chinese culture and history.

As Dai Jinhua speculates, in order to secure their legitimacy in historical representation, the fifth generation had to accomplish the dual acts of *rebellion* from and *resubmission* to power, as illustrated by the Tibetan outcast in *Horse Thief* (J. Wang and Barlow 2002: 13–48). From the beginning, their rebellion was enacted predominantly in an avant-garde language. This avant-gardism empowered them to question the worshipping of Mao and the dragon king in *Yellow Earth*, to ridicule political absurdity in *Black Cannon Incident* (Heipao shijian, dir. Huang Jianxin, 1985) and to foreground the cruelty of war in *Evening Bell* (Wanzhong, dir. Wu Ziniu, 1988).

Ostensibly, with the fifth generation's unprecedented achievements in the visual realms, Chinese cinema finally broke away from the fifty-year dominance of 'films by literature people' and entered an age contested – albeit not exactly overwhelmed – by 'films by film people'. The following list of contrasts between these two types of films helps to contextualize the young directors' rebellion in question.

Films by literature people	*Films by film people*
literary quality (screenplay)	visual quality (mise-en-scene, camerawork, etc.)
dramatic structure (story)	non-dramatic structure (images)
coherent plot (narrative)	minimal plot (narration)
abundant dialogue (telling)	ambiguous imagery (showing)
fully developed characters (types)	enigmatic characters (icons)
defined message (indoctrination)	ambivalent or contingent meaning (subversion)
diegetic, symphonic music	silence, off-screen sound and space
linear editing (continuity)	jump-cuts (disruption)
theatrical effects (emotion)	documentary effects (cognition)
passive spectator (spoon-feeding)	active spectator (viewer participation)

Whereas literary people – modernist in numerous cases – uphold the supremacy of a film's literary quality, which consists of a coherent plot in a finished narrative product, a dramatic structure of linear development of tension, climax and resolution, film people prefer cinema's visual qualities, which derive from the experimental or modernist use of mise-en-scene, camerawork, lighting, color contrasts and other cinematic devices. The latter's preference for highlighting film's visual aspects also results in the double pursuit of a non-dramatic structure, whereby images take on more significance, and of minimal plot, whereby narration (the way the story is unraveled) may be more important than the narrative itself. Whereas literary people invest in abundant dialogue and fully developed characters in order to convey a definite message, film people delight in ambiguous imagery and enigmatic characters so as to subvert conventional wisdom with ambivalent or contingent meaning. Whereas literary people deploy diegetic, symphonic music and continuity to intensify theatrical effects and to move the spectator emotionally, film people opt for silence, off-screen sound and space, and jump-cuts to approximate a sense of disruption and to achieve documentary effects that challenge the spectator's cognitive ability. In brief, film people no longer treat film as a dramatic rendition of literature that spoon-feeds a preconceived message to the viewer, rather they see it as a process of signification by audio-visual means in which the viewer participates perceptually and conceptually in generating multiple meanings and narratives.

It must be remembered that those features listed under films by film people do not belong exclusively to the fifth generation. As mentioned earlier, the fourth generation aspired to many of these same features in the early 1980s, and certain criteria would be put to more effective use in the 1990s by an even younger generation. As for the fifth generation, after an initial posture of rebellion by way of avant-gardism, most directors turned around in the late 1980s, reclaimed several features typical of literary people and readjusted their ideological positions. It is in this context that Dai Jinhua speaks of the fifth generation's 'resubmission' to power, although power now refers to that of both political and economic regimes.

Commercialization and politicization, 1985–9

Many critics regard *Red Sorghum* (Hong gaoliang, dir. Zhang Yimou, 1987) as a milestone of Chinese cinema that marks an end to avant-gardism and a beginning of commercialism. A surprise winner of the Golden Bear at the 1988 Berlin Film Festival, the first such honor for China, *Red Sorghum* unabashedly fabricated history as myth and pleased a wide spectrum of audiences with its sophisticated cinematic techniques and lavish ethnographic elements (Y. Zhang 2002: 208–20). Unlike previous fifth generation films, which gathered praise abroad but failed in the domestic market, *Red Sorghum* proved a box-office success in China, and tickets for its Beijing showings were sold at RMB0.6–0.7 when the average urban prices stood at RMB0.2–0.3 (Berry 1991: 123). A new possibility was thus confirmed: an art film could be successful in the reform era.

For critics, *King of the Children* (Haizi wang, dir. Chen Kaige, 1987) – a failure both at film festivals and at the box office – and *Red Sorghum* announced the end of the fifth generation as an avant-garde movement (J. Dai 1993: 16). Behind this was the drastically changed economic situation in the mid-1980s. Given the increasing availability of other popular entertainment forms, such as television, concerts and karaoke bars, the urban population was deserting movies at an alarming rate. The 1983 attendance figure was 650 million lower than that of 1982, which translated into a loss of RMB37 million in revenue (H. Chen

1989: 2: 279). Rural audiences also began to shrink, and by 1986 over 40,000 mobile projection teams had folded. Meanwhile, production costs had climbed by as much as 36 per cent since 1980 and studios started to lose money. In 1986 only 20 per cent of feature films (30 out of 151 titles) recouped their investment (Berry 1991: 115).

The economic reform of the film industry further disadvantaged the state studios. Previously, in the centralized planned economy, studios produced features according to the quotas approved by the Film Bureau and received a flat fee of RMB700,000 per title from China Film Corporation regardless of box-office takings. During the late 1980s, however, new reform measures changed this system of guaranteed purchases, and the distributors now either paid RMB9,000 per print or split the revenue by the pre-agreed percentage points (Luo *et al.* 1992: 2: 333). Either way, the emergent market economy pressured studios to consider film's box-office success before it went into production – a situation which studio heads and filmmakers reluctantly learned to confront.

Wu Tianming became the head of Xi'an Studio in 1983 and allocated its limited resources in support of avant-garde filmmaking. His strategy aimed to put Xi'an on the map by producing experimental films by such directors as Chen Kaige, Huang Jianxin, Tian Zhuangzhuang and Zhang Yimou. On this front he succeeded admirably, although he provoked criticism from within and outside his studio. To subsidize art films, Wu foresaw the necessity of the entertainment film (Chen and Rayns 1989: 19–26), which he produced in large numbers, such as *Legend of the Dowager Empress's Tomb, I–V* (Dongling dadao, dir. Li Yundong, 1986–8), an unprecedented long series in the history of PRC cinema. But the entertainment film could also achieve a fairly high artistic standard. A late-comer in the fifth generation, Zhou Xiaowen thus initiated the urban thriller with *Desperation* (Zuihou de fengguang, 1987) from Xi'an.

In 1987, the year when he was appointed head of Shanghai Film Bureau and Shanghai Film Studio, Wu Yigong published a lengthy article, 'We Must Become Film Artists Who Deeply Love the People', in a national newspaper. In it he defends Xie Jin's brand of popular 'realism' and attacks new film theory that champions the experimental film. Wu Yigong's position is clear: 'what's important is what you narrate, not how you narrate'. From the standpoint of 'social responsibility' he faults the avant-garde for indulging in 'salon art, which only a few people appreciate'. Wu had just directed, with Zhang Jianya's assistance, *The Tribulations of a Young Master* (Shaoye de monan, 1987), an adventure comedy adapted from a story by Jules Verne. In response to the accusation of his 'degeneration' into the popular, Wu insisted that his comedy sought to prove that 'box-office value and the pursuit of the entertaining does not have to be seen as "vulgar" and "low" '(Berry 1991: 133–9).

Indeed, the pressure of economic reform compelled critics and filmmakers alike to reconsider the 'entertainment film', a topic addressed by the journal *Contemporary Cinema*, which hosted several round-table discussions and critical forums from 1986 to 1989. Critics began to recognize the importance of the entertainment film in cultural criticism, and filmmakers acknowledged the difficulty of making entertaining features (Semsel *et al.* 1993: 83–139). While critical debates raged on, entertainment films rose to account for 60 per cent of the annual productions in 1988 and 75 per cent in 1989 (ZDYYZ 1995: 428). One type of entertainment film that proved immensely popular was the adaptations of Wang Shuo's tongue-in-cheek satirical fiction, such as *The Trouble Shooters* (Wanzhu, dir. Mi Jiashan, 1988). But behind the comic acts, verbal gags and absurd situations of Wang's 'hooligan' narratives lies a serious undertone of cynicism, which ridicules respectable social values and subverts moral orders, be they Communist, Confucian or commercial (Pickowicz 1995).

For a time, art films continued to appear, albeit in smaller numbers. From the fourth generation came *Film Artist* (Dianying ren, dir. Ding Yinnan, 1988), a surrealist picture, and from the fifth generation came *Evening Bell*, a film shot in 1987 and revised four times before clearing censorship. The censors were troubled by director Wu Ziniu's transcendental concept of humanity, his condemnation of all wars and his hard-to-decipher images (Y. Zhang 2003).

The subversive nature of certain entertainment and experimental films did not go undetected by the government, which had been promoting *propaganda films* dealing with economic reforms but had failed to generate a sustained interest among audiences. In 1987 the CCP central committee approved the establishment of a special committee supervising the production of films and television dramas based on major revolutionary historical events. The upcoming fortieth anniversaries of the PRC provided a timely incentive for the state to reallocate its film resources and heavily subsidize the so-called 'leitmotif films' (*zhuxuanlü dianying*) – productions intent on reinstalling a correct political ideology and nationalistic pride in the population. *The Birth of the Nation* (Kaiguo dadian, dir. Li Qiankuan, Xiao Guiyun, 1989), which features the founding leaders of the PRC, represents this new line of state productions.

By the end of the 1980s, the critical thrust of New Chinese Cinema had largely been spent, and Chinese cinema fell into three large categories: leitmotif films (an increasing presence, state-subsidized, propagandist in nature), art films (a shrinking minority, not necessarily avant-garde) and entertainment or commercial films (a dominant majority, of varied production values). This tripartite categorization would further evolve in the 1990s when Chinese cinema won more international recognition while suffering a series of fundamental financial crises.

NEW TAIWAN CINEMA: RE-IMAGING THE NATIONAL

In the 1980s Taiwan cinema took a historical turn, producing films that explored the cultural roots of Taiwan and re-examined the experiences of growing up in a rapidly modernizing society. The rise of New Taiwan Cinema fundamentally changed the image of Taiwan cinema, but its critics were eager to blame its inherent experimental quality for the decline of Taiwan filmmaking and the dominance of Hong Kong cinema in the Taiwan market.

Market fluctuations and political changes

Amidst the restructuring of the theaters, mentioned in Chapter 4, Taiwan's annual movie attendance peaked in 1981, reaching 250 million viewers or 13.9 cinema visits per capita, up respectively 52.4 per cent from 164 million viewers and 47.9 per cent from 9.4 per capita visits in 1978. Correspondingly, Taiwan feature production grew steadily, from 95 in 1978 to 144 in 1982. However, during the subsequent years of New Taiwan Cinema, the overall production dropped to as low as 58 films in 1984 (see Table 4.4, pp. 129–30). To say the least, such market fluctuations indicate the instability of the industry, which was sustained financially by a quick succession of commercial pictures, from crime thrillers to student films. Crime thrillers rose from eleven in 1979 to forty-two in 1981, and a total of 117 thrillers were produced between 1978 and 1983 (roughly twenty per year). These crime thrillers covered a range of subjects including triad warfare, gambling and female revenge. Another new popular genre was the student film, which addressed adolescent psychology and sexuality and promoted new youth idols. Under pressure from the Hong Kong market, Taiwan also produced slapstick comedies, largely derivative in nature, sometimes mixing sex and violence and resulting in what Lu Feiyi sees as 'across-the-board degradation' (1998: 259–63).

The KMT regime continued to assert its authority in the early 1980s by banning – for bureaucratic rather than ideological reasons – a few Taiwan adaptations of the mainland's post-Cultural Revolution 'scar literature' that exposed CCP corruption and political persecution. In 1980 HKIFF refused to accept certain politically sensitive Taiwan entries, and the Hong Kong censors banned Taiwan's anti-Communist features. Nevertheless, the political tension with Hong Kong did not prevent Taiwan from becoming the largest export market for Hong Kong productions, starting in 1984. Distributors dealing in Hong Kong films thus gained the upper hand in the market competition, and rising companies like Scholar (Xuezhe) and Long Shong (Longxiang) quickly moved to production.

Diversification continued to characterize the early 1980s, which saw the creation of around sixty-nine production companies (compared with eighty-seven in 1979, then a record high) and sixty-nine distribution companies (F. Lu 1998: 248, 292–3). While these figures underscore the speculative mindset in the film market, they further highlight the disintegration of the studio system. As the decade progressed, CMPC no longer dominated the production sector, but instead strengthened its distribution and exhibition lines and started its television and home video business under new branch companies.

On 15 July 1987 the notorious martial law, in effect since May 1949, was officially lifted, and the KMT regime permitted Taiwan residents to visit their relatives on the mainland in November 1987. Such tear-jerking melodramas as *Across the Taiwan Strait* (Haixia liang an, dir. Yu Kanping, 1988), a Long Shong release, quickly captured the outpouring of emotions repressed by the forty-year separation of family members between Taiwan and the mainland. But Taiwan producers were allowed only to shoot documentaries of mainland scenery so long as no actors were involved, and even Hong Kong–PRC co-productions were still banned in Taiwan. Unlike in the cold war era, however, *The Last Emperor* (dir. Bernardo Bertolucci, 1987), an Oscar-winning British–Italian–PRC co-production, was approved for commercial release in Taiwan.

In 1986, two years after placing restrictions on Hollywood imports, the GIO abolished the quota limits for all foreign countries except for Japan (as a special case) and the East European bloc. But the latter was added to the permissible import list in 1988, the year that the GIO implemented a three-tiered film ratings system: G (general audience), PG (parental guidance) and R (restricted).[5] Consequently, imports of all kinds, especially pornography, packed the GIO film office, and the total number of annual films approved for release by the censors increased from 464 in 1986 to 791 in 1989.

In spite of the increase in films approved for release, movie theaters in Taiwan disappeared at an alarming rate: from 736 in 1983 to 456 in 1989 (see Table 4.3, pp. 120–1). The disproportion between the increasing numbers of released films and decreasing numbers of theaters meant that the majority of films had a much shorter run in the late 1980s than before. This was exactly the case with most Taiwan productions, which surged to 158 titles in 1988 – a new height since the decline of Taiwanese-dialect films in 1970. Lu Feiyi offers two reasons for this sudden surge in production. First, the home video business wanted to attract its audience with the assurance of a 'higher' quality by having its films symbolically premiere first in the theater, thereby driving the prices of the video rights from about NT$300,000 to over NT$3 million. Low-budget films thus produced were hastily shown in small theaters for two or three days and then went straight to video sales and rentals.[6] Second, pornographic titles now accounted for over half of Taiwan's annual production, and the much-publicized exhibition of the sexy 'Taiwan sisters' to Hong Kong audiences placed the GIO officials in a moral dilemma. Nonetheless, the GIO could do nothing but issue warnings and attempt to stabilize the market by suspending more than 700 non-existing film companies in 1986–7 and offering film subsidies to the troubled industry (F. Lu 1998: 322–8). By the end of the 1980s all signs pointed to an inevitable decline in Taiwan cinema, this time a steep decline that promised no obvious recovery.

The historical turn and the impasse of nationalism

The rise of New Taiwan Cinema followed a change in filmmaking that started in the late 1970s. A number of veteran directors embarked on a project of 'roots-searching' that traced the cultural origins of Taiwan to an early stage of Chinese settlements in Taiwan and its intimate relations with the mainland, thereby emphasizing a 'shared' sense of Chinese nationalism. A CMPC production that cost over NT$60 million, *The Pioneers* (Yuan, dir. Chen Yaoxin, 1979) focuses on the exploration of petroleum in late Qing Taiwan and dramatizes the Chinese entrepreneurship in competition with foreign explorers. A release from Independence Film, *China, My Native Land* (Yuanxiang ren, Li Xing, 1980) is a biographical film about Zhong Lihe, a founding member of Taiwan's 'nativist literature' movement, producing the kind of literature that focuses on the native soil of Taiwan and its people's experience. Zhong was born in Japanese-occupied Taiwan and was at the time the only Taiwan writer to refuse to write in Japanese (R. Huang 1994b: 229–32). Although no longer as popular as the films of healthy realism two decades before, the roots-searching trend continued with *The Heroic Pioneers* (Tangshan guo Taiwan, dir. Li Xing, 1985), which tells of the immigration experience of early Taiwan settlers and their coexistence with the Taiwan aboriginal tribes. Nonetheless, for an epic film that cost Taiwan Studio NT$50 million to make (Guojia dianying 1996: 112), *The Heroic Pioneers* did miserably at the box office and Li Xing's conventional filmmaking style was blamed for failing to reach younger audiences (see Table 4.2, p. 118).

Another type of historical film was the state-sponsored policy film, which continued to glorify the KMT tradition and promote Chinese nationalism. However, except for *Battle for the Republic of China* (Xinhai shuangshi, dir. Ding Shanxi, 1981), a CMPC–Shaw Brothers co-production, policy films were no longer successful, either in terms of winning awards or at the box office. In commemoration of Chiang Kai-shek's 100th birthday, CMPC co-produced with Hong Kong *The Battle of 23 August 1958* (Ba ersan paozhan, dir. Ding Shanxi, 1986), a large-scale war film set in Jinmen Islands that cost nearly NT$200 million to make (R. Huang 1994b: 141). Its anti-Communist stance meant that it had no overseas market and could never expect to recuperate its investment. After enormous financial losses, the KMT regime restructured Taiwan Studio and renamed it a 'cultural enterprise' company in 1988. Similarly, it restructured China Motion Pictures in 1989, terminating its feature production forever (Guojia dianying 1996).

It is against this background of the declining interest in propaganda and commercial films that a group of young directors found the opportunity to test their professional skills in the early 1980s. Both Chen Kunhou and Hou Hsiao-hsien started directing low-budget films for small companies between 1980 and 1982. In fact, Hou contributed the screenplay to *Good Morning, Taipei*. Although Taiwan did not see as many new talents returning from overseas as did Hong Kong, it had already trained a group of young artists in the island who were eager to project their new cinematic visions. In the early 1980s, the time was ripe for the emergence of New Taiwan Cinema.

The emergence of New Taiwan Cinema

The 1983 release of two films illustrated the simultaneous emergence of new directors and the fading of the older generation. *The Wheel of Life* (Da lunhui, 1983), an omnibus production from Taiwan Studio consisting of three episodes directed by three master filmmakers, King Hu, Li Xing and Bai Jingrui, generated merely a lukewarm reception. By contrast, *Sandwich Man* (Erzi de da wan'ou, 1983), a CMPC omnibus film consisting of three episodes adapted by Wu Nien-chen from Huang Chunming's nativist stories and respectively directed by Hou Hsiao-hsien, Wan Ren and Zeng Zhuangxiang, was greeted with enthusiasm. For critics, the markedly different responses to these two films symbolize the appearance of 'auteur film' and the decline of conventional narrative and 'shadowplay tradition' (see Chapter 2) in Taiwan cinema. A new era dedicated to the cinematic rewriting of Taiwan history thus came into being (F. Lu 1998: 266).

To be exact, New Taiwan Cinema was inaugurated in 1982 when CMPC produced *In Our Time* (Guangyin de gushi, 1982), another omnibus film consisting of four episodes directed by Tao Dechen, Edward Yang and Zhang Yi. CMPC's decision to produce omnibus films reflected its willingness to promote new directors and new cinematic aesthetics on the one hand, and its strategy to reduce risks on the other. Both *In Our Time* and *Sandwich Man* depart from the heroic and melodramatic narratives characteristic of their predecessors and represent two focal areas of New Taiwan Cinema. First, the village is presented as an untainted locale where indigenous cultural practices are increasingly threatened by modernization and urbanization. Second, the city is depicted as an alienating place where individuals have gradually drifted away from their childhood dreams and are now desperately searching for their lost identity and a meaning to their life.

By following schoolchildren through to their teenage then college years and subsequently onto the life of a young couple, *In Our Time*, in its four episodes, details the experiences of *growing up* in Taiwan, which proved to be a favorite theme in New Taiwan Cinema. Admittedly, 'growing up' is only a trope whereby new directors explored the changing Taiwan society, and this exploration was executed in several ways. It could be a dramatic contrast between innocent childhood and confused adulthood, as in *Growing Up* (Xiao Bi de gushi, dir. Chen Kunhou, 1983). The exploration could be to do with female experience, as in *That Day on the Beach* (Haitan de yitian, dir. Edward Yang, 1984), which highlights female subjectivity through the female protagonist's efforts to make sense of her fragmented memories of her childhood and her marriage. The exploration could also take the form of an autobiographic reconstruction of migration and settlement, as in *A Time to Live, a Time to Die* (Tongnian wangshi, dir. Hou Hsiao-hsien, 1985), in which the director presents his Hakka family in Taiwan.

Frustrating urban experiences are captured in a striking manner in Edward Yang's films. His *Taipei Story* (Qingmei zhuma, 1985), which features Hou

Hsiao-hsien as the male lead, contrasts deteriorating tradition with alienating modernity through the altered relationships between two friends growing up together in Taipei. Yang's *Terrorizer* (Kongbu fenzi, 1986) weaves three over-lapping narrative strands into an urban mystery that challenges the 'detective' work perused by an amateur photographer who takes random pictures and stumbles upon a crime scene. True to its modernist intent, the film ends with multiple possibilities of homicide, none of which can save the ruined marriage of a bourgeois couple (Y. Zhang 1994). Yang's configuration of Taipei as dystopia is corroborated in Hou Hsiao-hsien's *Daughter of the Nile* (Niluohe de nüer, 1987). More than Yang, Hou is fascinated with the crime world seen through the eye of a comic book fan who works in a Kentucky Fried Chicken outlet and who, after the death of her mother, finds herself unable to keep the family members together (T. Lu 2002: 95–154).

A unique feature of New Taiwan Cinema is its realistic use of Taiwanese dialect as spoken by ordinary people in the city and countryside alike. Hou Hsiao-hsien's casting of Li Tianlu, a master of Taiwanese puppet theater, in *Dust in the Wind* (Lianlian fengchen, 1986) was so successful that he later devoted an entire film to Li's life, *The Puppet Master* (Ximeng rensheng, 1993). But the KMT position on dialect use in films remained intractable as late as 1988, when Chen Kunhou's request to cut a dialect version of *Osmanthus Alley* (Guihua xiang, 1987) for the best foreign film category at the Oscars was rejected by the GIO on the grounds that the dialect used was not a 'national' language. Luckily for Hou Hsiao-hsien,

Figure 7.4 Taipei Story (1985): urban alienation and the rise of New Taiwan Cinema

a year later the GIO allowed him to send a print of *City of Sadness* directly from a Tokyo processing facility to the Venice Film Festival at the same time as a print was shipped to the Taipei censors. The outcome was the Golden Lion award, the first such honor for any Chinese-language film. Although some conservative critics objected to its inclusion, *City of Sadness*, which is predominantly in Taiwanese dialect and thus violated the rules, won Hou the best director prize in 1989 at the Golden Horse Awards (R. Huang 1994a: 13–14).

With the success of *City of Sadness*, Taiwan cinema reclaimed the legitimacy of using Taiwanese dialect, which had empowered a new generation of directors to set their films on native soil and include indigenous folk custom and local Taiwan history. Typically of Chinese cinema, women's lives received central attention, and New Taiwan Cinema preferred to feature a central female character, showing her long life span in order to capture the changing sociopolitical situations, as in *Kuei-mei, a Woman* (Wo zheyang guole yisheng, dir. Chang Yi, 1985).

A distinguishing mark of New Taiwan Cinema is that ordinary folk are always portrayed as detached from political events of the time. They do not resist Japanese rule, as in *Strawman* (Daocao ren, dir. Wang Tong, 1987), nor do they believe the KMT's rhetoric of reclaiming the mainland, as in *Banana Paradise* (Xiangjiao tiantang, dir. Wang Tong, 1989), a dramatization of a mainlander's lost identity in Taiwan. The plight of the displaced mainlanders, especially those

Figure 7.5 City of Sadness (1989): rewriting history in post-martial law Taiwan

demobilized soldiers, is likewise dramatized in *Lao Mo's Second Spring* (Lao Mo de di erge chuntian, dir. Li Youning, 1984).

'City of sadness': critical responses to New Taiwan Cinema

As discussed in Chapter 4, dispersion, ambivalence and hybridity have been identified as three special characteristics of Taiwan's historical and cultural experiences, which are powerfully demonstrated in *City of Sadness*, the first film to confront the 28 February Incident after the lifting of martial law, and which took second place in the 1989 Taipei Chinese films box-office listings. The film focuses on the Lin brothers. The eldest, Wenxiong, is in charge of the household, since the second brother was drafted by the Japanese as an army physician to Southeast Asia and has never returned after the war. The third brother, who was dispatched to Shanghai as a Japanese interpreter during the war, after the war is persecuted as a 'traitor' and becomes insane. The youngest brother, Wenqing (Tony Leung Chiu-wai [Liang Chaowei]), who is deaf and mute following a childhood accident, relies on written notes to communicate and is a studio photographer. As this epic film progresses, Wenxiong is killed in a feud over a business deal, and Wenqing is arrested because his close friends – a group of Taiwanese intellectuals – have criticized the KMT regime. The film ends with Wenqing's wife listening to her babbling son, looking at their family portrait and writing a new entry in her diary, a seemingly insignificant document that bears her silent testimony to a repressed chapter in Taiwan history.

Geographic dispersion is embodied in a host of characters who arrive from the mainland in postcolonial Taiwan, and ambivalence is heightened by Hou's emphasis on the Lin brothers' utter incomprehension of the rapidly changing sociopolitical situation. The acute sense of hybridity is fully captured in Hou's use of various languages and dialects in the film, including Japanese, Mandarin, Shanghainese and Taiwanese, and the hybrid identity of the Taiwanese is subtly suggested in their Japanese names and their close relationship with the departing Japanese personnel. Above all, Wenqing's muteness best symbolizes the repression that the Taiwanese endured under the Japanese and KMT rule, and his inability to speak metaphorically translates into Taiwan's inability to control and write its own history. Just as Wenqing resorts to photography, Hou uses his film to recover the lost memories, images and voices in Taiwan history (Yip 1997).

Critics were divided in their appraisal of *City of Sadness*. While most applauded Hou's courage in addressing the taboo subject, some were not pleased with his insistence on detached personal observation as opposed to direct political confrontation (P. Liao 1993). Historically, the public attention to New Taiwan Cinema owes much to a group of new film critics, such as Peggy Chiao (Jiao Xiongping) and Huang Jianye, who endorsed new film aesthetics and introduced new film concepts and new ways of watching films in major newspaper columns. Their criticism of conventional film practices angered old-style film critics, and debates between the two groups – simply put, between art film and commercial film – were frequently staged in the media (Chiao 1988: 81–100). By the mid-1980s, however, the troubled film industry convinced the media to reconsider its support of New Taiwan Cinema, and conservatives were quick to reclaim their public forum.

Lu Feiyi comments on two critical positions on New Taiwan Cinema. First, conservatives like Du Yunzhi accuse New Taiwan Cinema of undermining the film industry and precipitating its downfall. But since New Taiwan Cinema made up less than 14 per cent of the total productions between 1982 and 1986, it could not have altered the fate of the entire industry. Second, thanks to its large number of literary adaptations (Hoare 1993), New Taiwan Cinema is believed to have promoted a new type of cinematic realism and a new 'native soil consciousness'. But the fact remains that more titles of New Taiwan Cinema are based on 'modernist literature' in Taiwan, such as *Jade Love* (Yuqin sao, dir. Chang Yi, 1984) adapted from Bai Xianyong, than nativist literature, such as *A Flower in the Rainy Night* (Kanhai de rizi, Wang Tong, 1983) scripted by Huang Chunming. Although not all directors favor the same kind of realism, a fact contrary to neo-realism in Italy, New Taiwan Cinema did start a practice of combining directing and scriptwriting in one role, thereby facilitating the cultivation of individual narrative styles (F. Lu 1998: 277–81).

In terms of its aesthetic pursuit, New Taiwan Cinema resembles the experimental films from the fifth generation in that it strategically positions itself against both commercial and propaganda filmmaking. It avoids didacticism and melodrama and instead prefers ambivalent meanings and subtle emotions. It avoids glamorous stars and plot-driven action scenes and instead favors a slower pace and natural acting. It avoids spoon-feeding messages and instead resorts to film's inherent audio-visual means to create a condition in which the viewer is forced to participate actively in generating meanings. As Douglas Kellner summarizes, 'New Taiwan Cinema favors outdoor locations over studio ones. It utilizes natural rather than artificial lighting as it explores ordinary people's real living and working spaces. Long takes and deep focus shots allow viewers to explore the details in unfamiliar social environments, ones cinema rarely depicted before. Often the directors cast non-professional actors and script dialogue in a way in which the characters' dialects point to their specific region and class' (1998: 105).

Needless to say, because it aimed at a higher level of intellectualism, New Taiwan Cinema alienated a majority of Taiwan audiences accustomed to formulaic comedies, romances and thrillers. Except in a few cases, new directors' films did not fare well at the box office, and from 1986 onwards distributors were reluctant to accept them.[7] For this reason, some critics suggest that New Taiwan Cinema practically ended in 1987 (S. Shen 1995: 6) – the year in which fifty-three film artists published the '1987 Taiwan Cinema Manifesto', in which they vented their frustration about the industry and the government and expressed a hope for 'alternative cinema' (Chiao 1988: 111–18). Incidentally, 1987 is also the year when the fifth generation avant-garde movement allegedly ended. By 1988, disillusioned by the lack of response to their manifesto, many new artists had changed careers; some went to work in the television industry while others made commercials. Indeed, in 1988 Hou teamed up with Wu Nien-chen and others and shot a propaganda television commercial for the ROC Ministry of Defense. This act provoked immediate criticism, accusing the new artists of manufacturing a 'fake public memory' for the authorities and retreating from their previously 'revolutionary' aesthetics.

By the late 1980s, another change had obviously taken place in the field of film criticism. Contrary to the early 1980s when young critics were content with new film aesthetics and textual analysis, the late 1980s saw the emergence of a new critical voice dedicated to exposing ideological subtexts of cultural production informed by critical theory from the West. The antagonistic positioning of the new critique is apparent in the name 'War Machine' (Zhanzheng jiqi), a group that moved film criticism beyond the media and helped professionalize film studies as an ideological intervention from academia (F. Lu 1998: 309–20). A new phenomenon thus emerged to underscore a fundamental irony in Taiwan: as the film industry was going into decline, film studies experienced a boom in the 1990s.

For many, nowhere is the sign of irreversible deterioration clearer than the 1988 Golden Horse Awards, which for the first time since 1964 handed the best picture prize, among others, to *Painted Faces* (Qi xiaofu, dir. Alex Law [Luo Qirui], 1988), a Shaw Brothers–Golden Harvest co-production in Hong Kong. Given the deteriorating condition of filmmaking in Taiwan, film stars like Sylvia Chang (Zhang Aijia) and Brigitte Lin migrated to Hong Kong, where their careers soared to a new height.

THE HONG KONG NEW WAVES: GENRE, HISTORY, IDENTITY

The Hong Kong new waves arrived with much anticipation, but the resilient force of commercial filmmaking quickly assimilated new talents during the 1980s. With the fate of Hong Kong and its return to China sealed in 1984, filmmakers started to rethink issues of history and identity in Hong Kong. At the same time, they proceeded to restructure the industry and rework film genres to produce ever-renewed visual treats to the delight of their loyal audiences.

The 'moment' of the Hong Kong new wave

The harvest moment came for the Hong Kong new wave in 1979. *The Butterfly Murders* (Diebian, dir. Tsui Hark, 1979), a Seasonal Film release mixing a martial arts narrative with Japanese *manga* and new Hollywood science-fiction ingredients, and *The Secret* (Fengjie, dir. Ann Hui, 1979), a murder mystery steeped in a ghost story ambience, are both considered representative of the new wave. But although critically successful, these two films, along with a few other early new wave titles, proved to be box-office failures (Law 2001: 46). Nonetheless, Tsui continued with such remarkable films as *Zu: Warriors of the Magic Mountain* (Xin Shushan jianxia, 1982), a visually striking martial arts-cum-fantasy feature, and *Peking Opera Blues* (Daoma dan, 1986), an action-comedy set in the warlord era (Bordwell 2000: 135–48; S. Ho and Ho 2002). Likewise, Ann Hui showed a social responsibility typical of her television programs and directed *Boat People* (Touben nuhai, 1982), a drama of Vietnamese refugees that won the best picture and best director prizes at the 1983 Hong Kong Film Awards (Jinxiang jiang). Meanwhile, Allen Fong followed the tradition of Cantonese family drama and turned his camera on ordinary people in *Father and Son* (Fuzi qing, 1981) and *Ah Ying* (Banbian ren, 1983) in a realist docu-drama fashion closer to New Taiwan Cinema than to his fellow Hong Kong artists (HKIFF 1999a).

As Law Kar argues, for the new wave directors, 'innovations did not come from a complete rupture with the past or from self-reflexivity. Instead, old genres were freshened up with new approaches' (2001: 47). The pressure to produce within the general parameter of genre filmmaking in Hong Kong thus explains the new wave directors' experiments with popular genres during the decade, and none – except for Allen Fong (who did not make 'genre films') – was committed to one single genre. Ann Hui, for instance, directed an epic martial arts saga, *The Romance of Book and Sword* (Shujian enchou lu, 1987), a two-part co-production with the mainland's Tianjin Studio. The forays into commercial filmmaking like Hui's and Tsui's convinced Paul Fonoroff, a Hong Kong-based critic, that '[t]he "wave" turned out to be a mere ripple, with many of the young filmmakers absorbed by the commercial establishments they had ostensibly sought to transform' (Y. Zhang and Xiao 1998: 42). But, for the new wave promoters, the legitimacy of the name itself remains essential. 'Even if there was no "new aesthetic landscape", the term "Hong Kong New Wave" was still appropriate for the new techniques, daring sensibility, and new genres (and generic mixes) that young television directors and filmmakers brought to Hong Kong cinema' (Law 2001: 50).

As in the case of New Taiwan Cinema, critical endorsement was indispensable for directing public attention to the new wave in Hong Kong. As one scholar notes, the criteria for defining the new wave include: an ethical concept of authorship, the ambivalent image of the commercial film industry as 'other', new filmmakers' unprecedented cosmopolitan orientation, normative realism and a commitment to the specificity of a local identity. Since Hong Kong promoters were anxious to locate in the new wave 'a sense of urgency regarding the recovery of the territory's forgotten history and promotion among the public of the capacity for . . . reflection on their own present situation', the result could not but be disappointing. The new wave did not develop in the direction anticipated by its promoters, who by the end of the 1980s reluctantly admitted that 'the moment of the New Wave, if it ever existed, had in any case come to an end' (Rodriguez 2001: 61–7).

Nevertheless, the contribution of the Hong Kong new wave is undeniable. First, it transformed mainstream filmmaking by reinventing methods of small-scale, high-quality production and packaging. Second, it loosened the rigid genres of martial arts and comedy and helped make *mixed genre films* both aesthetically appealing and commercially viable. Third, contrary to the avant-garde in the mainland, Taiwan and many other countries, the Hong Kong new wave never became narcissistic in its auteur style; instead it cultivated its own audience following not only in Hong Kong but in art-house and cult markets around the world (ZDZ 1998: 237).

Industry and genre restructuring

The power and energy of the commercial industry in Hong Kong are exemplified by Cinema City (Xin yicheng), a film company founded by Carl Mak (Mai Jia), Dean Shek (Shi Tian) and Raymond Wong (Huang Baiming) in August 1980, and initially bankrolled by the Golden Princess (Jin gongzhu) theater chain. To compete with the established Shaw Brothers and Golden Harvest, Cinema City recruited rising stars like Tsui Hark and John Woo (Wu Yusen) and pursued high-budget action comedies. With an astonishing investment of HK$8 million, Cinema City hired an American cinematographer and several stunt experts from Hollywood and Australia for its production of *Aces Go Places* (Zuijia paidang, dir. Eric Tsang [Zeng Zhiwei], 1982). Released in the golden slot of the Chinese New Year, this film and its two immediate sequels satisfied the audience's appetite for chases, stunts and special effects along with paired comic acting. The trio of films topped the box office between 1982 and 1984. Two additional sequels also performed well, ranking third in 1985 and sixth in 1989. For Bordwell, the *Aces Go Places* series demonstrates that, with sufficient investment in Hong Kong, 'a B-plus cinema could become an A-minus one' (2000: 70).

Since Taiwan quickly became Hong Kong's biggest export market, Cinema City set up a Taiwan branch in 1982. Managed by Sylvia Chang in 1983–4, the Taiwan branch produced a few films targeted at the local audience, such as *Papa, Can You Hear Me Sing?* (Dacuo che, dir. Yu Kanping, 1983). Chang had been active in Taiwan and Hong Kong since the mid-1970s in both the film and television industries and won the best actress prizes at the Golden Horse Awards in 1981 and 1986. As the Taiwan market deteriorated, however, Cinema City quickly folded its operations there in 1986.

In a fashion similar to Golden Harvest's efficient 'satellite model of production' (Fore 1994: 45), Cinema City also allowed its key members to set up their own branch companies, such as the famous Film Workshop established by Tsui Hark and John Woo in 1984. Cinema City and Film Workshop teamed up to produce *A Better Tomorrow* (Yingxiong bense, dir. John Woo, 1986), which appealed to the audience with its combination of beautifully choreographed gunfights and sentimental relief and which led to two sequels (1987, 1989) and *The Killer* (Diexue shuangxiong, 1989). Unlike the emotionless knight-errants who represent traditional virtues in other Chinese films, Woo's gangster films depict a 'romantic hero' who doesn't fit the conventional definition of good or evil. Masterfully played by Chow Yun-Fat (Zhou Runfa), Woo's hero, be he a professional killer, an undercover agent, or an overzealous detective, is always tough yet vulnerable, killing in cold blood at one moment and shedding tears in another.

It is obvious that Hong Kong – and by this time Taiwan – audiences displayed a seemingly insatiable appetite for serial productions of hit movies and mixed genres. This is not just true for Cinema City's other releases, such as *A Chinese Ghost Story* (Qiannü youhun, dir. Ching Siu Tung [Cheng Xiaodong], 1987), a ghost story spiced up with martial arts and romance that spawned a sequel in 1990 and an animated feature in 1998. Golden Harvest, along with its satellite companies, especially Jackie Chan's Golden Way Films (Weihe) founded in 1985, was also successful in serial productions. *Project A* (A jihua, dir. Jackie Chan, 1983), an adventure-gongfu picture set in earlier Hong Kong, became the number two hit in 1983, grossing HK$19.3 million (C. Li 1990: 215).

Golden Harvest had tried to duplicate its global success with Bruce Lee in the early 1970s by signing Jackie Chan to Hollywood co-productions such as *The Cannonball Run* (Paodan feiche, dir. Hal Needham, 1981). Chan had delivered super stunt work (refusing to use a double), but his North American ventures in the 1980s were largely unsuccessful, even though *The Cannonball Run* grossed US$160 million worldwide (Fore 1994: 42). Confronted with Cinema City as a formidable new challenger, Golden Harvest, which by now had grown into a large conglomerate managed by Golden Communications, teamed up with its former arch-enemy Shaw Brothers and they began in 1982 to premiere each other's films simultaneously in their theaters. Meanwhile, Shaw Brothers gradually reduced its theater ownership and by November 1985 had given up all its Hong Kong cinemas. After releasing its last six features in 1986, Shaw Brothers suspended feature production for two years, mainly because, at age 80, Run Run Shaw wanted to concentrate on running the highly profitable TVB, of which he commanded the largest percentage of single stock ownership. From 1988 to 1997 Shaw Brothers productions went from no films to five each year, still a far cry from its peak of forty-nine films in 1975 alone (Chan 2000: 676–7).

A new company, D & B Films (Debao), acquired several of Shaw Brothers' most treasured theaters. Founded in 1984 by Dickson Poon (Pan Disheng), D & B productions included *Yes, Madam!* (Huangjia shijie, dir. Correy Yuen [Yuan Kui], 1985), an action comedy that featured the screen debut of Michelle Yeoh (Yang Ziqiong), a rising international star. Unabashedly romantic, *An Autumn's Tale* (Qiutian de tonghua, dir. Mabel Cheung [Zhang Wanting], 1987), is set in New York City and contributed to a trend of filming the Hong Kong diaspora overseas. Another D & B release, *Hong Kong 1941* (Dengdai liming, dir. Leong Po-chih, 1984) is a rare look at the Japanese occupation of Hong Kong, which reminded audiences of a forgotten chapter of Hong Kong's history.

The 1997 anxiety and the complicated 'China factor'

Hong Kong 1941 can be seen to contain an allegorical reference to the impending fate of Hong Kong. This is because the Sino-British Joint Declaration, signed in Beijing in April 1984, had sealed the fate of Hong Kong's return to China's sovereignty in July 1997, albeit with a unique status: 'one country, two systems'. Many Hong Kong residents felt betrayed and abandoned by Margaret Thatcher's British government, which negotiated with China without consulting them, and they started to leave the territory. Since 1984, the emigration rate has stood at around 60,000 people a year, and as Hong Kong's most talented (doctors, bankers and the like) departed in large numbers – even Raymond Chow reportedly obtained a Canadian passport – the potential brain-drain became a serious issue (Fore 1994: 53). However, the Joint Declaration provided an unexpected incentive to an intense, even if belated, exploration of Hong Kong's history and identity. Awareness of Hong Kong's own identity spread quickly. 'By 1988, 80 per cent of respondents to a poll claimed their identity as neither British nor Chinese but Hong Kongers' (Bordwell 2000: 32).

In reality, Hong Kong's relationship with China is much more complicated than a simple declaration of identity or loyalty. Critics have located in two 1984 films opposite modes of response. *Long Arm of the Law* (Shenggang qibing, dir. Johnny Mak [Mai Dangxiong]), a Bo Ho Films (Baohe) release, articulates the suspicion of what is to come, whereas *Homecoming* (Sishui liunian, dir. Yim Ho), a Blue Bird (Qingniao) production, represents an effort to seek mutual understanding. In a *defensive* mode, *Long Arm of the Law* started a trend of portraying violent – and often mainland-related – gangsters in a grimly realistic crime thriller, which may or may not be intended as a political allegory but is often read as such in film criticism (C. Li 1994; Yau 1994). To be sure, the suspicion of the PRC's 'violent' takeover would escalate into paranoia in the wake of the 1989 Tiananmen crackdown. In this context, gangster movies, a staple of the Hong Kong film industry, are seen as cinematic rehearsals of a doomsday scenario, thereby giving these thrillers' graphic emphasis on survival skills a positive twist.

On the other hand, *Homecoming* exemplifies a *proactive* mode of engagement, not at the official level but between ordinary folks separated by drastically different experiences in the capitalist and the socialist systems. Through a Hong Kong resident's return trip to her hometown in Guangdong province and her changed relations with her childhood friends, Yim Ho subtly suggests both the impossibility of reliving one's childhood dreams and the necessity of recognizing each other's historical experience and current situation.

Given that both Johnny Mak and Yim Ho belong to the Hong Kong new wave, it is obvious that the group was not a singular entity and its members were not bound by a unitary artistic or ideological aspiration. Nonetheless, the trope of *border crossing* is central to both Mak's and Yim's works, which illustrate the increasing significance of the 'China factor' in Hong Kong cinema in the 1980s and beyond (HKIFF 1990). Indeed, border crossing could be set in an earlier period, as in *Love in a Fallen City* (Qingcheng zhilian, dir. Ann Hui, 1984). Adapted from Eileen Chang's famous novella, the film symbolically reconnects the largely forgotten link between Hong Kong and Shanghai. Although this 'transregional romance' reveals the anxiety around 1997 in its graphic images of Japan's 1941 attack on Hong Kong, absent in Chang's original, Hui's reconstruction of colonial Hong Kong and Shanghai is said to have initiated a 'nostalgia' cinema trend that peaked in the early 1990s (Y. Zhang 2002: 276–81).

The inventive Hong Kong filmmaker Li Hanxiang conducted another type of border crossing, a series of large-scale co-productions with the mainland that proved popular in both Hong Kong and mainland China. With their patriotic theme, Li's imperial court dramas even won a special prize for excellent films from the PRC Ministry of Culture in 1983. As with Li's New Kunlun, it was mostly small Hong Kong companies which entered into co-productions with mainland studios, and their products concentrated on time-honored genres such as costume dramas, opera movies and martial arts pictures. *Shaolin Temple* (Shaolin si, dir. Zhang Xinyan, 1982), for example, triggered another wave of Shaolin fever and discovered a new gongfu star, Jet Li (Li Lianjie).[8]

The wide spectrum of cinematic responses to the anxiety surrounding 1997 demonstrates that the oversimplified method of reading allegory is itself not sufficient to capture the rich imagination of Hong Kong cinema. In this connection, Bordwell's argument is illuminating: 'Instead of reflecting the mood of the moment, popular cinema is better considered as part of an open-ended dialogue with its culture', because popular cinema is never a crystallization of 'a zeitgeist of a national character' as one wishes (2000: 37). In the second half of the 1980s, such an open-ended dialogue with Hong Kong culture became much more prominent in the early films from Hong Kong's 'second wave' directors.

The second wave: identity, locality and historicity

In terms of numbers, the second wave may not be as impressive as the first wave, but its directors appeared to be more consistent in their aesthetic pursuits and more dedicated to the art film as their preferred option. A key figure of this new group, Stanley Kwan had served as an assistant to Ann Hui and Yim Ho and now attempted to retrieve the repressed memory of 1930s Hong Kong by following a ghost's visit to contemporary Hong Kong in his award-winning *Rouge* (Yanzhi kou, 1987). The ghost used to be a courtesan named Fleur who believes she committed a double suicide with her lover from a rich household (Leslie Cheung [Zhang Guorong]). With the help of a modern-day couple, Fleur realizes that her lover survived and has become a useless film extra. The contrast cannot be more pronounced as Fleur, still as beautiful and young as fifty years ago, resolutely walks into a bright scene of mountain landscape to start her life anew, leaving the burden of history and memory to the old man and, by extension, to the viewer. This ambivalent ending invites an allegorical reading, as 'fifty years' is exactly the length of time the PRC has promised that Hong Kong's current system will remain unchanged. Whereas one may interpret Fleur's departure from her earlier obsession with history and memory as an optimistic outlook on Hong Kong's 'independent' future, Kwan's sheer glamorization of high-class courtesan life – in stark contrast to the dull, mechanical life of the 1980s – inevitably conveys a lingering sense of nostalgia.

Like *An Autumn's Tale*, Kwan's *Full Moon in New York* (Ren zai Niuyue, 1989) is set in New York City. But unlike Mabel Cheung, Kwan extends his exploration of the Chinese diaspora to include a woman each from Hong Kong, Taiwan and the mainland, thereby concentrating on their shared experience of displacement while sorting out their differences in character, education and sexual orientations. Displacement is also central to *The Reincarnation of Golden Lotus* (Pan Jinlian zhi qianshi jinsheng, 1989), in which Clara Law (Luo Zhuoyao) works out a fatalistic parallel between the seductress Pan Jinlian in a traditional Chinese narrative and her modern-day incarnate Lotus. The film starts with political oppression during the Cultural Revolution when Lotus rehearses a revolutionary ballet but is raped by her boss and condemned to work in a factory, where she falls in love with Wu Long. Lotus is then married to a 'dwarf' Hong Kong baker, Wu Dai, whose sexual impotence drives Lotus to have an illicit relationship with Simon after Wu Long, now the family's chauffeur, refuses her advances. As expected, Wu Long kills Simon, but in a break from the classic narrative, the injured Wu confesses his repressed love for Lotus, who drives him over a cliff as the car bursts into flames, leaving behind Wu Dai surviving an overdose of aphrodisiac pills.

Typical of many 1980s Hong Kong features, *The Reincarnation of Golden Lotus* is ambivalent in its ideological stance. Apart from a powerful feminist thrust in its rare endorsement of female sexuality and subjectivity, the film ends on an unsettling note: the heroic, the passionate and the villainous characters all die, whereas the weak 'dwarf' survives but he seems unable to comprehend the historical-fictional drama unfolding in front of him. The multiplicity of identity, locality and historicity Clara Law constructs in this film, therefore, points to a new way of responding to the 1997 anxiety that transcends the bipolar structure as embodied in *Long Arm of the Law* and *Homecoming*. This newly perceived *multiplicity* characterizes the second wave directors more than their pre-decessors, although both groups have ostensibly drawn on personal experience of migration and displacement. Separated by only a few years, the second wave directors appeared more cosmopolitan in their outlook, more global in their subject matter, while at the same time more local or 'translocal' in self-positioning. As they explored the layered historicities and the multiple localities of Hong Kong culture, hybrid identities became something to accept – if not yet to celebrate, as in the 1990s – rather than to evade.

A booming market

Compared with their mainland and Taiwan counterparts, the Hong Kong new wave directors were fortunate to have a supportive market base. During the 1980s Hong Kong audiences continued to prefer homegrown products, as evidenced in the soaring box-office records. *The Young Master* (Shidi chuma, dir. Jackie Chan, 1980) exceeded HK$10.3 million at the box office, a record broken by *Aces Go Places* in 1982 with over HK$26 million. Three years later, *My Lucky Stars* (Fuxing gaozhao, dir. Sammo Hung, 1985) grossed HK$30 million, and by the end of the decade *God of Gamblers* (Dushen, dir. Wong Jing [Wang Jing], 1989) earned HK$37 million at the box office (ZDZ 1998: 232). These figures continued to soar in the early 1990s. As a result, Hong Kong productions regularly accounted for 75 per cent of Hong Kong box-office revenue, relegating Hollywood and other imports to compete for the remaining market share. In 1988, for instance, Hong Kong movie attendance averaged about twelve visits per capita, which was the third highest rate internationally (Fore 1994: 41). Although these figures are high, the peak time was back in 1967, when attendance stood at twenty-seven annual visits per capita (Bordwell 2000: 34), compared with 10.1 in Taiwan in the same year (see Tables 5.1 and 4.3, pp. 154, 120–1).

CONCLUSION: HISTORY, CULTURE AND NATIONHOOD

During the 1980s history became an overriding issue in filmmaking in all three Chinas. In the PRC cinematic interrogation of history began as an emotional response to the Cultural Revolution catastrophes, which then extended back to the Anti-Rightist Campaign and gradually to other significant political and military events. Initially, filmmakers depended on the concept of humanism in their reconstruction of history and were able to confront the CCP 'policy errors' and to render a more balanced view of history, in particular where images of the KMT are concerned. But gradually, culture emerged as an overarching background and films from different generations gained in the richness of cultural representation while losing in the sharpness of ideological critique.

Similar to the mainland, Taiwan cinema first took a historical turn to re-establish its claim to the Chinese heritage by way of 'roots-searching' and policy films that celebrated the KMT tradition. But this brand of state-endorsed Chinese nationalism did not appeal to audiences and was quickly displaced –

if not altogether replaced – by another historical turn: the re-examination of Taiwan experience at the grassroots level by New Taiwan Cinema. As in the mainland, the pursuit of indigenous culture led young artists to challenge official historiography and to reclaim the values of individuals' repressed memories and experiences during the KMT rule. Taiwanese dialect finally gained legitimacy and resurfaced as an effective tool in undermining political repression, but ironically Japan re-emerged from New Taiwan Cinema not so much as a brutal colonizer (as in policy films) but as a culture intimately bound to Taiwan. The significance of *City of Sadness* in this double reconfiguration of the KMT and Japan in cultural terms is both immediate and far-reaching, although the fact remains that New Taiwan Cinema rarely ventured into the culture of Taiwan's aboriginal tribes.

In contrast to the mainland and Taiwan, Hong Kong cinema did not witness a major turn to history, for Hong Kong filmmakers were preoccupied with a more urgent issue: the territory's impending return to China. The immediacy and intensity of the anxiety surrounding 1997 quickly translated into a flourish of gangster films that emphasized their protagonists' survival skills and comedies that exaggerated ordinary folks' – or anti-heroes' – mundane transactions. For critics, the comedian best represents the dilemma facing these forces pulling in opposite directions, as in the case of a 'schizophrenic' text like *Teppanyaki* (Tieban shao, dir. Michael Hui, 1984). 'Michael Hui projects three layers of his personality: ego (the henpecked husband), id (the red-hot lover), superego (the tyrannical father-in-law). Trapped in a love-less marriage to an over-weight aggressive woman, he suffers much humiliation working as a cook for his father-in-law, who runs a Japanese restaurant . . . Is his dilemma a metaphor for Hong Kong?' (HKIFF 1984: 67). If, as *Teppanyaki* might imply, Hong Kong was too preoccupied with its existential urgency to reflect on its history, in the second half of the 1980s more Hong Kong films addressed the question of history as it influenced the unfolding present. Although romance and gangster genres had furnished New York City and Shanghai as two counterpoints of local culture, the historicity and identity of Hong Kong culture did not constitute a prevalent concern until the 1990s.

Nonetheless, the Sino-British Joint Declaration suddenly forced Hong Kong people to realize their fundamental deprivation of nationhood, a realization that would engender the conceptualization of 'culture as disappearance' in Hong Kong cinema in the 1990s (Abbas 1997). On the other hand, both the mainland and Taiwan witnessed a drastic change in the cinematic reconceptualization of nationhood during the 1980s. Filmmakers there insisted on re-imagining the nation from the perspective of the nation-people (characterized by indigenous or local cultures) rather than that of the nation-state or the party-state (charac-terized by ideological indoctrination by and political subjugation to a single party). The politics of nationalism did not disappear overnight but were instead strategically resituated: rather than mere subjects to political nationalism that emphasized institutionalization, instrumentality and unity, filmmakers now emerged as agents of cultural nationalism, reconstructing signs of the nation in its multiple ethnic, cultural and geographic denominations. Ironically, it is precisely these signs of cultural 'authenticity' – together with political repression – that caught the attention of international film circles, exactly at the time when Chinese cinema was developing in the direction of a truly transnational cinema (Y. Zhang 2002: 201–5).

8

CINEMA AND THE TRANSNATIONAL IMAGINARY, 1990–2002

INTRODUCTION: TRANSNATIONAL CHINESE CINEMAS

This chapter brings us up to date with the development of Chinese cinema from 1990, when the PRC attempted to get over a political crisis by speeding up economic reforms nationwide, to 2002, when this narrative film history comes to a closure. At first sight, the military crackdown in Tiananmen of 1989 did not leave any direct impact on mainland filmmaking, but the subsequent CCP investment in leitmotif films has constituted an intensified, prolonged ideological drive to instill patriotism and nationalism in the population, especially the younger generation. The return of Hong Kong to China's sovereignty on 1 July 1997, covered live by the Western media with as much enthusiasm as Tiananmen, proved largely uneventful. This is mainly because Hong Kong cinema had pre-pared for the worst after 1989 and the Asian financial crisis of 1997–8, together with Hollywood's imperial advance in the region, threatened the very foundation of the territory's film industry. At the turn of the millennium, Chinese cinema accelerated its reinvention as *transnational cinemas* (S. Lu 1997: 3). Now that China and Taiwan have both joined the World Trade Organization (WTO), the era of globalization has dawned on all three Chinas, and Chinese filmmakers cannot but confront all its positive, negative and as-yet-uncertain consequences. As the current discussions on the WTO indicate, no one seems able to predict exactly what will happen to Chinese cinema in the near future.

By the century's end, the goal of the 1980s of 'marching to the world' had surely been accomplished, as innumerable awards at international film festivals have brought prestige and popularity to Chinese cinema, albeit ironically at a time when all three industries have experienced an unprecedented decline. In the early 1990s transnational and transregional operations had promised a bright future, when Taiwan and overseas investments were regularly channeled to the mainland and co-productions in commercial genres were all the rage. But since the mid-1990s, when the PRC tightened restrictions on co-productions, Hong Kong's annual production output has plummeted and Taiwan's feature production has come to depend almost entirely on state subsidies. The pro-independence DPP's presidential election victory over the KMT in March 2000 means little to Taiwan cinema, which has now completely lost its exhibition market to Hollywood.

Contrary to the gloomy local prospect, the phenomenal global success of *Crouching Tiger, Hidden Dragon* (Wohu canglong, dir. Ang Lee [Li An], 1999), a multinational co-production featuring a multinational cast and crew, reminds us that a new age of transnational Chinese cinema has arrived.[1] In terms of financing, overseas investments have become customary in all three Chinas, which initially supported art films but now have ventured into commercial films as well. In terms of casting, it has become fashionable to mix stars from all three Chinas as well as from foreign countries, in part to generate audience interest but also to facilitate transnational packaging. In terms of distribution, an increasing number of Chinese films have entered the Western art-house circuits since the early 1990s, and some have successfully made it to the home video market. In terms of exhibition, the PRC is about to open its market to Hong Kong, as it did to Hollywood, and its 'underground films' – those produced without acquiring official permits – are frequently screened at international film festivals and are often better known abroad than at home. In terms of thematic orientation, the transnational imagery has been fundamental to a majority of films in all three Chinas, evidenced not just in urban images but also in plot, characterization, dialogue, music and songs (Y. Zhang 2002: 253–312). In brief, at the beginning of the new millennium, Chinese cinema is transnational in all aspects.

HONG KONG: OF THE GLOBAL AND THE LOCAL

A regional cinema for decades, Hong Kong cinema has become simultaneously more global, as in the cases of Jackie Chan and John Woo, and more local, as in the case of the post-1997 new localism. The years leading to Hong Kong's July 1997 change of status from a crown colony of Great Britain to a special administrative region of the PRC witnessed, on the one hand, a surge of creative energy and, on the other, a steep decline in the local market. The post-1997 adjustment to the fundamentally changed political and economic situation has been agonizing to filmmakers, who nonetheless have managed to beat the odds and have sustained a high level of artistic achievement.

An industry in decline: from the peak to the bottom

The development of Hong Kong cinema peaked in the early 1990s. *All For the Winner* (Dusheng, dir. Jeff Lau [Liu Zhenwei], 1990), a Seasonal Film release featuring the *mo lei-tau* (*wu litou* or 'nonsense') performance by Stephen Chiau (Zhou Xingchi), set a box-office record of HK$41.3 million. The next record of HK$43.8 million came with Chiau's *Fight Back to School* (Taoxue weilong, dir. Gordon Chan [Chen Jiashang], 1991), which was followed by *Justice, My Foot!* (Shensi guan, dir. Johnnie To [Du Qifeng], 1992), another Chiau vehicle, which grossed HK$49.9 million. The new record was exceeded in two years by the film that signifies Jackie Chan's successful break into North America (Fore 1997), *Rumble in the Bronx* (Hongfan qu, dir. Stanley Tong, 1995), which raked in HK$56.9 million in Hong Kong alone.[2]

Nevertheless, signs of an impending crisis surfaced in 1993 when *Jurassic Park* (dir. Steven Spielberg, 1993) grossed HK$50 million in Hong Kong, although Hong Kong products still represented 73 per cent of the total box-office revenue that year. In 1994, between sixty and seventy Hong Kong films (roughly one-third of the year's total) grossed less than HK$4 million, far below the break-even bottom line.[3] Compared with 66 million in 1988, ticket sales dropped to 44 million in 1993, 28 million in 1995, and 22 million in 1996 (see Table 5.1, p. 154).[4] The Eastern (Dongfang) theater chain, which Raymond Wong founded in 1993, closed in 1996, and is survived by three other chains – Golden Harvest, Jinsheng (golden sound) and Xinbao (new treasure), each with approximately twenty-five theaters. In 1992 no single Western film ranked among the top ten, whereas in 1996 five of the top ten films were Hollywood blockbusters (Bordwell 2000: 75–80). Also in 1996, Hong Kong production dropped to 116 titles, less than half of the 1993 total, and for the first time foreign imports earned more in ticket sales (53 per cent) than Hong Kong products. Worse still, as annual production nose-dived to 84 titles in 1997 and 89 films in 1998, the total receipts from Hong Kong features posted a 72.7 per cent loss, from HK$1.24 billion in 1992 to HK$339 million in 1999 (Z. Qi 2002: 84) (see Table 8.1).

Table 8.1 Comparison of box-office revenues in Hong Kong, 1991–2002

Year	Total films	Total b/o (HK$)	% of 1992	HK films	HK film b/o (HK$)	% of total b/o
1991	473	1,370,548,782	—	125	1,034,771,165	75
1992	503	1,551,635,638	—	215	1,239,581,506	78
1993	502	1,538,496,069	down 0.8	242	1,143,984,569	73
1994	474	1,384,072,992	down 10	181	960,278,990	69
1995	461	1,339,029,587	down 13	150	841,560,145	62
1996	430	1,222,300,348	down 21	116	656,574,397	47
1997	410	1,155,842,640	down 25	84	545,875,933	45
1998	453	1,071,720,257	down 30	89	423,907,097	39
1999	423	857,322,610	down 44	100	339,065,080	39
2000	568	952,940,585	down 38	133	346,107,474	36
2001	—	1,040,000,000	down 33	133	—	—
2002	331	862,600,000	down 44	92	347,500,000	40

Sources: Shackleton 2003; Z. Qi 2002: 84.

When Cinema City ceased operation in 1991, Golden Harvest consolidated its market domination, although Win's (Yongsheng) challenged that domination with several hits featuring Stephen Chiau. Golden Harvest consistently maintained its share of total Hong Kong revenues between 20.82 per cent in 1993 and 36.37 per cent in 1998, except in 1994 when its share dropped to 12.27 per cent. But figures like these are misleading. In fact, Golden Harvest's annual production shrank five-fold from twenty in the early 1990s to four in 1999, and its 1998 box-office revenues of HK$154.16 million represented a decrease of 52.3 per cent from its 1992 income of HK$323.09 million (Z. Qi 2002: 85). Golden Harvest Entertainment (GHE), Raymond Chow's distribution–exhibition company, posted a US$6 million loss in the first half of 1998 alone.

Golden Harvest suffered further blows in 1998: the death of its cofounder Leonard Ho, the resignation of Jackie Chan from GHE's board of directors and the forced relocation of its production facilities from Hammer Hill Road. Many observers regard the relocation as the symbolic end of the Hong Kong film industry 'as we know it'. In order to restructure its enterprises, Raymond Chow entered GHE in partnership with Village Roadshow, a powerful Australian exhibition chain. But Golden Harvest's Hong Kong box office continued its slide to HK$73.66 million in 1999, only to rise slightly to HK$86.92 million in 2000 (Z. Qi 2002: 85).

The Asian financial crisis, which had devalued most Southeast Asian currencies by as much as 70 per cent, was a deciding factor in the decline of Hong Kong cinema. So too was the market loss in Taiwan, where exhibition rights per Hong Kong title plunged from HK$5 million (for a blockbuster) or HK$1 million (for an average film) in previous years to HK$70,000 (or NT$0.3 million) in the late 1990s (F. Lie 2002: 60). Many critics also blamed rampant video piracy, expensive ticket prices and skyrocketing production costs. Pirated copies of VCDs (video compact disk, a less advanced form of DVD) could be purchased for US$4 (roughly 43 per cent of a ticket price) shortly after or even at the same time as a film's premiere in the theater. In the late 1990s, theater chains cut ticket prices to US$5 for Hong Kong films and raised the admission for Hollywood blockbusters to US$7.50. But this desperate move could ultimately backfire, as audiences may think that Hong Kong products are not worthy of the big-screen experience and thus further encourage the trend of watching Hong Kong movies at home on VCD (Curtin 1999: 39). Tuesday discounts started in February 1997, then in June 1997 all three theater chains offered discounts for all days, but by the end of 1997 they reverted back to Tuesday discounts only (Chan 2000: 55) (see Table 5.3, p. 170).

As for production costs, a Jet Li film could cost up to HK$35 million in the early 1990s, with one-third of the cost going to the star's salary. A single Jackie Chan production cost US$12 million in 1995, a year when the total investment for all Hong Kong films was US$150 million and the combined Hong Kong exports earned US$130 million.[5] Under heavy financial pressure, producers were forced to slash budgets in the late 1990s. From the earlier break-even bottom line at HK$9 to 10 million, the average production costs per film now stand at HK$4 million, with some features made for as little as HK$1.5 million (Bordwell 2000: 74–83, 119). All these changes have had a dramatic impact on the development of Hong Kong cinema since the early 1990s (see Tables 3.1 and 3.2, pp. 64–5, 90).

'Postmodern, Hong Kong style': of sensations and the sensationalistic

'Hong Kong film celebrates voluptuousness and grotesquerie; it savors cleavages and penises, comic warts and farts, mold-blotched vampires, greedy eaters smeared with sauce and fat, and creatures with gigantic tongues. Nothing gorgeous or hideous is alien to this cinema' (Bordwell 2000: 7). Most of these sensational features mentioned here by Bordwell are captured in the new sub-genre of *mo lei-tau* comedy perfected by Stephen Chiau, whose extravagant acts of nonsense (including his customary toilet jokes) parody 'the rags-to-riches story of Hong Kong's economic development' and who, in his 'witty self-criticism' through farce, humor and pastiche, has emerged as 'the archetypal postmodern (con)man' (Teo 1997: 246). The fact that eight of Chiau's films at the Hong Kong box office exceeded HK$40 million each and a further ten over HK$30 million between 1990 and 1996 proves that his 'postmodern' self-parodies were extremely *meaningful* to contemporary Hong Kong audiences (Chan 2000: 145–6). In postmodern terms, the meaning of Chiau's nonsense or irrationality derives from its outrageous deconstruction of reason and nonsense and its staging of a carnival subversion of normality and decency. Seen in this way, Chiau's *mo lei-tau* may be more than just crudely commercial in nature. Indeed, Chiau has moved on to become a director, and his *Shaolin Soccer* (Shaolin zuqiu, 2001) set a record of HK$60.7 million and was distributed by Miramax in North America (F. Lie 2002: 63–4).

For Stephen Teo, another instance of postmodernism can be located in Tsui Hark's innovative films, which display a mix of diverse features: new wave aesthetics, slapstick comedy, the China syndrome, Hong Kong identity and gender politics (1997: 246). Like Chiau's comedies, Tsui's films abound in self-reflexive moments and references that invite critical examination, but Tsui has been more successful than Chiau in working *allegory* into his parody and pastiche (Lee 1994), and his pictures have more to offer in terms of visual pleasures. In the years leading to the 1997 transition, Tsui conscientiously explored the China–Hong Kong relationship in his large-scale martial arts productions. His spectacular Huang Feihong series and also his swordsman series once again confirm Bordwell's observation: 'In its search for powerful sensations, [Hong Kong] cinema becomes sensationalistic' and serves up 'rapid-fire gratification' (2000: 12).

But the films that best exemplify the sensationalistic nature of Hong Kong cinema are those falling in the newly created *Category 3*, a genre in its own right, albeit deliberately mixing thriller, horror and soft porn. The 1988 film censorship ordinance endorses a ratings system whereby Category 1 denotes films suitable for all, Category 2 unsuitable for children and Category 3 forbidden to viewers under age 18 years.[6] By 1992, about half of the annual Hong Kong releases were Category 3 films, which, even more so than the low-budget eroticism of the 1970s, relished in sexploitation and sadomasochistic porn and gore. One example is *The Untold Story* (Baxian fandian zhi renrou chashao bao, dir. Herman Yau [Qiu Litao], 1993), which 'sensationalizes an incident of rape, murder, and cannibalism in Macao' (Bordwell 2000: 77, 128).

A subgenre of female revenge fantasy quickly surfaced in Category 3 films, most famously represented by *Naked Killer* (Chiruo gaoyang, dir. Clarence Fok [Huo Yaoliang], 1992), a stylistic depiction of lesbian killers, scripted and produced by Wong Jing. Since its theatrical release in New York, this thriller has become a cult classic in the West. A soft-porn office romance, *Pretty Woman* (Qingben jiaren, dir. Yeung Chi Gin [Yang Zhijian], 1991) grossed HK$30 million in two years, and its female lead Veronica Yip (Ye Yuqing), a former Miss Asia, was reportedly paid HK$1 million per title (Davis and Yeh 2001: 14–18). The public's enthusiastic response to Category 3 films meant that mainstream companies were lured into action. Golden Harvest produced *Sex and Zen* (Yuputuan, dir. Michael Mak [Mai Dangjie], 1991), a quality Category 3 film featuring Amy Yip (Ye Zimei), earning HK$20 million and spawning sequels and imitations (W. Wang 1995: 224–5).

As with John Woo's gangster films, Category 3 films have been subjected to allegorical readings in relation to the 1997 anxiety. Julian Stringer argues that the genre 'testified to a severe loss of confidence in the city's political stability' and that the graphic rendition of 'eroticism and cruelty can be read as the death dance of a wicked, economically decadent city'. While acknowledging 'a dystopian postmodern aesthetic' in Category 3 films, Stringer perceptively exposes the genre's 'reactionary' elements, such as 'misogyny, homophobia, repulsed fascination with the naked and open body, and the equation of crime with the working classes' (1999: 362–4). Nonetheless, postmodern or not, the genre is an entertainment vehicle first and foremost, and its reputed 'political function' – testing taboo subjects and exploring the repressed psyche – comes at best as secondary in consideration.

A discussion of postmodernism in Hong Kong cinema would not be complete without reference to Wong Jing, a master of sensations and the sensationalistic whose box-office record has surpassed all directors in Hong Kong history. With incredible ingenuity and at a dizzying speed, Wong launched the gambling cycle, the *mo lai-tau* cycle, the Category 3 sexploitation cycle and the *guhuo zai* (young and dangerous) cycle. He directed five films each in 1991 and 1992, nine in 1993 and seven in 1994, out of which seven exceeded the HK$30 million mark (Chan 2000: 350–1). In addition, Wong was a prolific producer and screenwriter, and the fifteen films he worked on in 1996 accounted for 30 per cent of the territory's theatrical receipts of that year. Wong's products consistently made it to the lists of the annual top ten Hong Kong hits and the combined grosses of his forty-four titles in the 1990s total HK$769.25 million (Z. Qi 2002: 85).[7]

Unlike his father Wang Tianlin, a famous director of Mandarin melodramas of the 1950s and 1960s, Wong is best known for presenting Hong Kong's 'vulgar cinema at its most gleefully appalling', shedding 'plausibility, character consistency, and good taste' and disregarding almost everything except 'the idea of trickery'. With such 'postmodern' tricks as freewheeling intertextuality, cross-referencing and self-referentiality, Wong is unabashed and unapologetic in his parody and pastiche of characters, scenes and music from films East and West, old and new, including his own. In *Whatever You Want* (Zhuguang baoqi, 1994), he depicts a film director named Wong Jing-wai (mocking Wong Kar-Wai), who thus responds to angry viewers of his film *Chungking Expect*: 'You know nothing about postmodernism!' As Bordwell states, Wong Jing represents a kind of 'pop postmodernism', and a line from *Whatever You Want* – 'I change vulgarity into art so as to let you enjoy it' – may well be 'the Wong Jing credo' (2000: 171–7), or, by extension, the credo for commercial filmmaking in Hong Kong.

In the psychosocial realm: nostalgia cinema and melodrama

A different manifestation of postmodernism in Hong Kong cinema is detected in *nostalgia cinema*, a trend that often tapped into the territory's celluloid memory by paying tribute to the Cantonese cinema of the 1960s. Two notable examples are *92 Legendary La Rose Noire* (92 hei meigui dui hei meigui, dir. Chen Shanzhi, 1992) and *He Ain't Heavy, He's My Father* (Xin nanxiong nandi, dir. Peter Chan [Chen Kexin], 1993). By way of humor, farce, satire, parody and pastiche, nostalgia films name their characters after bygone movie stars and mimic their styles, manners, gestures, voices, songs and music scores. Contrary to Wong Jing's films of trickery, however, nostalgia cinema typically builds an ambience of sentimentality in spite of its comic appearance. The past is evoked with fond memory, albeit marked by a melancholy realization that the past is irreversibly lost. In this sense, nostalgia cinema represents a psychosocial response to the 1997 anxiety and a conscientious exploration of Hong Kong identity (Y. Zhang 2002: 280–6). In Teo's judgment, 'there is a genuine attempt to explore history and to acknowledge, even if only grudgingly, Hong Kong's kinship with China's history'. Consequently, 'Hong Kong's type of post-modernism' reveals 'a culture caught in the tension between a desire to construct a non-colonial identity by mobilising a sense of the past, and a profound anxiety about the possibility of that very identity being imposed rather than being constructed autonomously' (1997: 250).

Teo's observation applies to Stanley Kwan's two nostalgic projects. *Centre Stage* (1992) extends nostalgia for old Hong Kong, already palpable in Kwan's

Rouge, to equally strong nostalgia for old Shanghai. In her role as Ruan Lingyu, a tragic star of the 1930s, Maggie Cheung embodies multiple identities criss-crossed by registers of class, language, place, space and time, all of which is heightened by Kwan's self-reflexive structure of multiple narratives. Kwan's *Red Rose, White Rose* (Hong meigui, bai meigui, 1994) doubles the effect of nostalgia for old Shanghai by casting Joan Chen (Chen Chong), formerly a Shanghai award-winning actress, in an adaptation of Eileen Chang's famous Shanghai novel. Another notable adaptation of Chang's Shanghai tale is *Eighteen Springs* (Bansheng yuan, dir. Ann Hui, 1997), but this otherwise nostalgic reconstruction of lost youth and unrequited love ends with a subtle endorsement of the protagonist's courage to face history. Ann Hui's largely *positive* attitude toward the China–Hong Kong relationship is also apparent in her *Song of the Exile* (Ketu qiuhen, 1990), an acclaimed examination of Hong Kong identity that takes its London-educated protagonist to her grandparents' house in Guangdong and her mother's birthplace in Japan.

In the 1990s, nostalgia was often articulated in *melodrama*, which employed the tropes of contrastive temporality, spatiality and referentiality in its exploration of identity, history and locality in Hong Kong. *C'est la Vie, Mon Cheri* (Xin buliao qing, dir. Derek Yee [Er Dongsheng], 1993), for instance, not only refers to *Love Without End* starring Lin Dai but reinforces the cinematic connection by casting Fung Bobo (Feng Baobao), a child star of the 1960s hailed as the 'Hong Kong Shirley Temple'. Fung's melancholy performance of Cantonese opera – now almost a forgotten form of popular culture – provides the melodrama with a structure of feeling, and the premature death of the high-spirited female protagonist drives home a profound sense of fatality and vulnerability. The fact that the film grossed HK$30.6 million at the box office clearly indicates the pervasiveness of nostalgic sentiments prior to 1997.

Needless to say, not all melodramas were nostalgic in the early and mid-1990s. A critically acclaimed production from Sil-Metropole, *Cageman* (Longmin, dir. Jacob Cheung [Zhang Zhiliang], 1992) is a realistic investigation of the crowded living space and inhumane treatment of poverty-stricken seniors in Hong Kong. In the same humanist manner, *Summer Snow* (Nüren sishi, dir. Ann Hui, 1994) dramatizes the everyday struggle of a middle-aged woman who balances her career and her responsibility for taking care of her father-in-law, an Alzheimer patient.

United Filmmaker Organization (UFO, Dianyingren), founded by Eric Tsang in 1990, specialized in socially conscious melodramas during the 1990s. Like D & B, which ceased production in 1992, UFO distinguished itself with medium-budget but artistically sophisticated 'relationship films' targeting local 'chuppies' (Hong Kong yuppies) (Bordwell 2000: 154–5). Two popular UFO films are *He's a Woman, She's a Man* (Jinzhi yuye, 1994) and its equally gender-bending sequel, *Who's the Woman, Who's the Man* (Jinzhi yuye 2, 1996), both directed by Peter Chan. The kind of sentimentality integral to these two 'feel-good' films is intensified in Chan's *Comrades: Almost a Love Story*

(Tian mimi, 1996), a tale of two mainland immigrants who struggle to make a living first in Hong Kong and then in New York City.

Transnational imaginary, transregional imagination

As evident in *Comrades*, the transnational imaginary was essential to the majority of Hong Kong films in the 1990s, and the films of Wong Kar-Wai are the best example of this new, distinctively *cosmopolitan* breed of transregional imagination. Similar to UFO's emphasis on troubled relationships, Wong's *Days of Being Wild* (Afei zhengzhuan, 1990), an In-Gear Film (Ying zhi jie) production, presents through fragmented narratives and kaleidoscopic imagery a rootless man whose desperate search for his birth mother leads him to the Philippines. Simultaneously acclaimed as a postmodern auteur and criticized as a pretentious artist, Wong's triple honors as the best director at the Asia-Pacific Film Festival, Golden Horse Awards and Hong Kong Film Awards marked the beginning of his international career. *Chungking Express* (Chongqing senlin, 1994) is Wong's more balanced look into issues of home, travel, memory and identity, which was shot by Christopher Doyle (Du Kefeng), a cinematographer who also worked on Wong's *Ashes of Time* (Dongxie xidu, 1994) and Edward Yang's film *That Day on the Beach*. Wong's transregional imagination is further exemplified in his casting of Takeshi Kaneshiro (Jin Chengwu), a Japanese-Taiwanese actor, in films like *Fallen Angels* (Duoluo tianshi, 1995). But Wong's transnational imagery is most pronounced in *Happy Together* (Chunguang zhaxie, 1997), a melancholy tale of two self-exiled Chinese gay men in Argentina, which won the best director prize at the 1996 Cannes Film Festival.

Similarly brimming with transnational imaginaries, Clara Law's migration tales, however, are more socially engaged than Wong's philosophical discourses which border on soliloquy. Her *Farewell, China* (Aizai biexiang de jijie, 1990) details the traumas endured by Chinese immigrants in New York City, with a tragic ending where post-Tiananmen pessimism is fully articulated. In comparison, Law's *Autumn Moon* (Qiuyue, 1993) is definitely more optimistic. By tracing the unusual friendship between a young Japanese tourist looking for his lost self and a Hong Kong teenage girl ready to migrate to Canada, Law's affirmation of identity formation in the era of globalization won the Golden Leopard at the Locarno Film Festival. After emigrating to Australia, Law directed *Floating Life* (Fusheng, 1996), a comedy of cultural and generational conflicts set in Australia.

A different kind of transregional imagination is illustrated in Yim Ho's award-winning works. *Red Dust* (Gungun hongchen, 1990) is a story based on Eileen Chang's legendary life during the war and co-produced by Tomson (Tangcheng), which Hsu Feng founded in 1985, and Changchun Studio. *The Day the Sun Turned Cold* (Tianguo nizi, 1994) is an emotionally disturbing psychological drama in which a son turns against his mother, who earlier conspired with her lover to poison her husband (Silbergeld 2004). Collaborating with Zhang Yu, a mainland actress who later studied in California, Yim directed *The Sun Has Ears* (Taiyang you er, 1995), which won him the best director prize at the 1996 Berlin Film Festival.

The foregoing discussion on the new wave directors demonstrates that Hong Kong art cinema has increasingly taken on a new look of cosmopolitanism un-fettered by a narrow focus of geopolitical identity and that the 'reel traffic' among the three Chinas occurred frequently in the 1990s. Apart from regular cultural exchanges between film artists and critics (ZDZ 1998: 232–5), Hong Kong continued its mainland investment, most often through co-productions, but sometimes in studio facilities as well, as when Win's set up a production center in Shenzhen, a growing city adjacent to Hong Kong, in 1993. In particu-lar, Hong Kong producers tapped into cheap mainland manpower and otherwise inaccessible locations like Forbidden City in Beijing. Beijing Studio thus became an ideal partner in co-productions such as *Fong Sai Yuk, I–II* (Fang Shiyu, dir. Corey Yuen, 1993).

However, the kind of transregional imagination that became headline news was the trans-Pacific movement that a number of high-profile Hong Kong film artists made around the mid-1990s. After his last Hong Kong film, *Hard Boiled* (Qiangshen, 1992), John Woo moved to Los Angeles and successfully launched a Hollywood career. He directed big-budget action thrillers like *Broken Arrow* (1996) and *Face/Off* (1997). Woo's Hollywood agent is Terence Chang (Zhang Jiacun), who also manages Chow Yun-Fat's and Michelle Yeoh's Hollywood careers. Yeoh was a valiant Bond girl in *Tomorrow Never Dies* (dir. Roger Spottiswoode, 1997), and Chow delivers great performances in *The Replacement Killers* (dir. Antoine Fuqua, 1998) and other Hollywood films. Like Jackie Chan, Jet Li also entered Hollywood with action flicks like *Romeo Must Die* (dir. Andrzeij Bartkowiak, 2000). In addition, Hong Kong artists who made the trans-Pacific movement in the mid-1990s included Peter Chan, Sammo Hung, Ringo Lam (Lin Lingdong), Stanley Tong, Tsui Hark and Yuen Wo-ping.

Post-1997 film culture: amnesia, new localism and creativity

It must be remembered that since 1997 many Hong Kong directors have also made the trans-Pacific movement the other way around. Tsui Hark, for instance, still manages his Film Workshop in Hong Kong, which produced *Black Mask 2: City of Masks* (Heixia, dir. Tsui Hark, 2001), with dialogue in English. Similarly, Michelle Yeoh starred in *The Touch* (Tianwai chuanqi, dir. Peter Pau, 2002), an English-dialogue adventure film co-produced by Hong Kong – Media Asia (Huanya) and Yeoh's own Mythical Films – and China (Tianjin Studio). Originally scripted in English, these films have added to the *global* image of Hong Kong cinema, which seems characterized by multiple linguistic registers (Cantonese, Mandarin, Taiwanese, English, Japanese and so on) more than ever before.

268

In the immediate post-1997 years, Hong Kong films were classified into schools of 'forgetting' versus 'not forgetting' (W. Huang 1999: 99). For those in favor of 'forgetting', the preferred motif is *amnesia*, which overcomes the identity predicament by relegating personal history and memory to oblivion. *Who Am I?* (Wo shi shui, dir. Jackie Chan, Benny Chan [Chen Musheng], 1998) thus takes Chan's transnational action from Africa to Australia to the Netherlands but specifically bypasses locations in Hong Kong. Similarly, amnesia surfaces in *Purple Storm* (Ziyu fengbao, dir. Teddy Chen [Chen Desen], 1999), which depicts a former Khmer Rouge terrorist working for the Hong Kong police. Crucial to these post-1997 films is the figure of the lone wanderer or drifter, who has 'no identity, no country, no family', no friends and no clear vision of future. The question the audience faces is therefore not so much 'Who am I?' as 'Who do you want to be?' (HKIFF 2000b: 58–62). In this sense, amnesia functions not as a device of forgetting but as a reminder of the unresolved question of identity and the future of Hong Kong. In Tsui Hark's opinion, the future is by any measure more important than the obsessive 1997 allegory: 'at this point in time, it's no longer a question of 1997 but more a question of our future' (HKIFF 1998a: 47).

For those in favor of not forgetting, the best way to prepare for the uncertain future is to confront the reality that is Hong Kong. In this respect, two new developments are particularly noteworthy in post-1997 Hong Kong. First, the low-production model exemplified by Fruit Chan (Chen Guo) challenges the established Hong Kong system of superstars and blockbusters. *Made in Hong Kong* (Xianggang zhizao, 1997) was shot with a budget of HK$500,000 but grossed HK$1.9 million in Hong Kong (Z. Qi 2002: 85), and became an overnight sensation. What is remarkable about *Made in Hong Kong* is not merely its instant critical reputation, its incredible commercial success, its conscientious reference to the rebel youth tradition in Cantonese cinema, or its skillful use of a non-professional cast. More, *Made in Hong Kong* redirects cinematic attention to the underprivileged in a kind of deliberately rugged but effective realism.

To continue his new model, Fruit Chan directed *The Longest Summer* (Qunian yanhua tebie duo, 1998), a docu-drama about a group of unemployed Chinese soldiers dismissed from the British colonial army, which ends with an ironic use of the amnesia motif. *Little Cheung* (Xilu Xiang, 1999) and *Durian, Durian* (Liulian piaopiao, 2000) are two subsequent films linked by Ah Fan, a girl born to an illegal immigrant, who lives under constant threat of deportation to China. Produced for less than HK$1 million each, both films are centered around Portland Street, a Kowloon district notorious for prostitution, which provides an ideal setting for Chan to explore social problems such as child labor, illegal immigration, domestic violence and prostitution, in part from the innocent children's perspective. In addition, Chan's portrayal of Filipino maids and their weekend activities in public places is both refreshing and touching (HKIFF 2000b: 20–5). At times exaggerated but always critical, Chan's films articulate a feeling of community grounded in Hong Kong's lower social strata, and as such they constitute an intentionally unpolished kind of *new localism* in contrast to Wong Kar-Wai's glamorous cosmopolitanism and postmodern aestheticism (F. Lie 2002: 61–2).

The second remarkable post-1997 phenomenon is the consistent output of quality pictures from Milky Way Image (Yinghe yingxiang), established in 1996 by Johnnie To and Wai Ka-fai (Wei Jiahui). Johnnie To had directed box-office hits like *The Heroic Trio* (Dongfang sanxia, 1993), a thriller featuring Maggie Cheung, Anita Mui (Mei Yanfang) and Michelle Yeoh (S. Lu 2001: 122–38), but he did not make a name for himself until after 1997. Wai had worked as a scriptwriter at TVB and as a producer at ATV, and his film about the triads, *Too Many Ways to Be No. 1* (Yige zhitou de dansheng, 1997), subverted the trendy *Young and Dangerous* series. Unlike mainstream Hong Kong cinema, Milky Way productions create a *film noir* version of Hong Kong and capture a profound sense of fatality and pervasive *fin-de-siècle* mentality in the immediate post-1997 years (HKIFF 1999b: 56–88).

One of the most stylistic of Milky Way thrillers is *The Mission* (Qianghuo, dir. Johnnie To, 1999). Critics have noticed that the unexpected ending of *The Mission*, where his colleagues without their boss's knowledge spare a security guard his life, hints at a new type of survival strategy that emphasizes Hong Kong's ability to negotiate its fate. This renewed self-confidence is also apparent in the ways triad gunfights are staged in *The Mission*: not as a pure spectacle of bloody violence but as a game of intellect played with ultimate professional adeptness and dedication. An aesthetic of intrepidity and serenity has thus resulted from To's meticulous attention to frame composition, mise-en-scene, and action choreography (HKIFF 2000b: 41–52).

In connection with the demarcation between forgetting and not forgetting, two other films are worth mentioning. *The City of Glass* (Boli zhi cheng, dir. Mabel Cheung, 1998) unravels a forbidden romance between a married man and a married woman overflowing with sentimental memories and nostalgia for Hong Kong of the 1970s. Significantly, the film pieces together personal histories by making the younger generation responsible for understanding their parents through photos, letters, songs and other unofficial documents. Sentimental in its reconstruction of the 1970s, the film endorses a forward-looking attitude, and its final scene of the fireworks celebrating the return of Hong Kong to China signifies the closing of a chapter in history: the 'city of glass' is shattered, but the new generation must move on. Likewise reminiscent of an earlier Hong Kong, *Ordinary People* (Qianyan wanyu, dir. Ann Hui, 1999) nonetheless activates the trope of amnesia right away and foregrounds the danger of forgetting. Through parallel narratives (street theater performance) and tripartite episodes ('Forgetting', 'Ten Years of Revolution' and 'Never Forget'), the film traces local history from the 1960s Maoists through the 1970s grassroots activism to the 1989 demonstration in support of Tiananmen. In a manner closer to Fruit Chan, Hui's political drama portrays people without adequate shelter and decent jobs and tackles sensitive issues of abortion, date rape and the deportation of illegal immigrant mothers. Her effort to preserve social conscience and memory has earned her critical recognition (HKIFF 1999b: 16–20).

As time passed, however, Hong Kong filmmakers have learned to leave 1997 behind, as suggested by Tsui Hark's comment quoted above. From fatalistic thrillers, Milky Way has therefore proceeded to lighter genres in the new millennium, as exemplified by two titles Johnnie To and Wai Ka-fai co-directed. *Needing You* (Gunan guanü, 2000), an office romance featuring the superstar Andy Lau (Liu Dehua), grossed HK$35.2 million, and the weight-loss comedy *Love on a Diet* (Shoushen nannü, 2001) earned HK$40.4 million. These films demonstrate the potential of the Hong Kong market and indicate Milky Way's awareness of Hong Kong's middle classes, an audience sector D & B and UFO had targeted earlier. Similarly, Media Asia produced *Tempting Heart* (Xindong, dir. Sylvia Chang, 1999), a relationship film that moves its star-crossed lovers between Hong Kong and Japan. Significantly, *Tempting Heart* is neither nostalgic like *The City of Glass* nor political like *Ordinary People*, although all three are sentimental to varying degrees.

In Teo's judgment, 'the level of creativity in Hong Kong cinema has actually increased in spite of the economic downturn' after 1997 (HKIFF 1998a: 13). Like Milky Way, Media Asia, which rose to prominence in the mid-1990s with support from Jackie Chan, has played an important role in the transition. After the failure of its investments in a few mainland projects, such as *A Mongolian Tale* (Hei junma, dir. Xie Fei, 1995), Media Asia has suspended its art film production and instead concentrated on what it sees as quality genre films. *Gen-X Cops* (Tejing xin renlei, dir. Benny Chan, 1999) invested heavily in special effects, such as the spectacular explosion of the Hong Kong Convention Center. The film did well at the box office with HK$15.6 million and was picked up by Columbia TriStar for US distribution, reportedly for US$10 million (F. Lie 2002: 68). Creativity is also evident in a release from Wong Jing's BoB and Partners (Best of the Best, Zuijia paidang), *The Storm Riders* (Fengyun xiongba tianxia, dir. Andrew Lau [Liu Weiqiang], 1998), which beat all Hollywood imports in Hong Kong and ranked first at the 1998 box office.[8] Adapted from a popular *manga*, *The Storm Riders* was a rare blockbuster in post-1997 Hong Kong, produced on a budget of US$10 million and incorporating cutting-edge digital special effects. Even though the pirated VCDs were being sold on the opening day, the film still grossed HK$41.5 million. With successful merchandizing and cross-media promotion, the film was touted as 'the beginning of a new era' for Hong Kong cinema (HKIFF 1999b: 41–5).

TAIWAN: ART CINEMA BEYOND BORDERS

Ironies have beset Taiwan cinema since the early 1990s. On the one hand, Taiwan auteurs and art films have won multiple prestigious international awards (Chiao 2002: 290–315); on the other hand, domestic feature production has been reduced to an inconsequential market factor. Whereas local audiences have practically abandoned Taiwan productions, academics have launched film studies courses and film books have appeared in large numbers.[9] While Hollywood has consolidated its dominance by showcasing blockbusters in Taiwan, Taiwan art cinema has chosen to travel abroad and has targeted audiences beyond its borders.

Changing dynamics of distribution and exhibition

From 1968 to 1992, in spite of the state import quota restrictions, foreign films consistently secured about 50 per cent of Taiwan's exhibition market, whereas Hong Kong films (dubbed in Mandarin and counted as 'domestic') secured around 35 per cent and Taiwan films around 15 per cent. According to Lu Feiyi, the market demand for all three categories had dropped significantly below the annual projected mean of 500 films in 1994, when the combined total of 386 films was the lowest since 1974. Lu attributed the decline in exhibition to the spread of cable and satellite television as well as illegal and unregulated industry practices. Lu thus tracks the changing dynamics based on the 1994 statistics. In terms of films in exhibition, Hong Kong kept its share of 35 per cent, but at 57 per cent foreign films had eroded about half of Taiwan's share, reducing it to merely 8 per cent or twenty-four titles. In terms of film attendance, foreign films represented 87.07 per cent, compared with 10.64 per cent for Hong Kong and 2.29 per cent for Taiwan. In terms of box-office revenue, foreign titles grossed 88.33 per cent because their ticket prices were higher than those for Hong Kong and Taiwan films. Commanding 85.25 per cent of the annual revenue, American films overwhelmed the market, and Hollywood's eight majors raked in 65.9 per cent of the box office with only 22 per cent (eighty-two films) in exhibition (F. Lu 1998: 352–79).

The profitability of foreign, especially Hollywood, films in Taiwan compelled Taiwan companies to compete for foreign distribution rights and to expand theaters specializing in foreign films or both foreign and domestic films. In October 1994 the industry lobby convinced the government to exempt Japanese films from import quotas, to increase prints per foreign film from sixteen to twenty-four, and to expand exhibition venues per foreign film from six to nine each in Taipei and Kaohsiung and four to six each in other cities and counties. In 1996 the state finally abolished all foreign import quotas (F. Lu 1998: 355–70). As a result, the total receipts for foreign exhibition grew steadily in Taipei, from NT$1.499 billion in 1994 to NT$2.617 billion in 1996 and NT$3.146 billion in 1997, an increase of over 100 per cent in three years. *Titanic* (dir. James Cameron, 1997), which ranked first in the top twenty films for 1997, with NT$387,787,110 in Taipei and 1,683,382 tickets sold in Taiwan (both figures 20 June 1998), contributed directly to this unprecedented boom. Significantly, in spite of the dominance of such distribution heavyweights as Buena Vista, Fox and Warner Brothers, Taiwan companies distributed five of the top twenty films (all of which were foreign) in 1997: Spring Cinema (Chunhui) with three, Era (Niandai) and Scholar with one each (Guojia dianying 1998: 84–6). Similarly, in 1998 Era distributed one and Scholar three of the top twenty foreign films (Guojia dianying 1999: 59).

Nevertheless, Taiwan exhibitors to date have not succeeded in negotiating a better deal with Hollywood distributors. The box-office split remains 70 per cent for distributors and 30 per cent for exhibitors in the first week, with a 5 per cent decrease for distributors in each following week until the percentage reaches 50–50. Compared with 60–40 in Japan and 65–35 in Hong Kong, Taiwan exhibitors feel they have been short-changed by Hollywood agencies, even though they are already organized into theater chains like Guobin, Rixin and Lesheng. In general, Taiwan exhibitors followed the trend of building multi-plexes so as to show more films and thus reduce risks. Whereas the total numbers of Taiwan theaters declined from 343 in 1991 to 282 in 1992, the total number of films in exhibition actually rose from 500 in 1991 to 534 in 1992. However, with 255 theaters and 386 total films exhibited in 1994 (F. Lu 1998: Tables 3a, 20e), the declining rates of theaters and films exhibited in Taiwan from 1991 to 1994 are quite similar, respectively 25.7 per cent and 22.8 per cent.

Not surprisingly, the exhibition of Chinese films is far less profitable than foreign films. In 1997 only three Hong Kong star vehicles exceeded NT$10 million, and a mere three out of seventeen Taiwan titles grossed over NT$1 million (Guojia dianying 1998: 89–100). The situation turned worse in 1998, when one-third of Chinese films (twenty-six titles) fell below NT$100,000 and seven titles below NT$10,000, far from sufficient to recoup the minimum promotion costs of NT$500,000. Compared with 1995, when none of the Taiwan titles fell below NT$10,000 and only one below NT$100,000 (Yeh *et al.* 1999: 48–9), the 1998 statistics confirm the disappearance of the market demand for Taiwan productions. No longer competitive with Hollywood since the mid-1990s, Hong Kong cinema also has lost its commanding presence in Taiwan, and the newly approved exhibition of selected mainland titles lends no help in restoring Taiwan audiences' interest in Chinese films.

In short, the decline of Chinese cinema in Taiwan was simply irreversible. In 1992 the Taipei box-office performance of Hong Kong and Taiwan films (7,864,255 tickets and NT$1,063,114,484) was fairly similar to that of foreign films (8,091,082 tickets and NT$1,130,253,176). But by 1998 the gap between the former (NT$158,243,266, down 85.1 per cent) and the latter (NT$2,987,472,720, up 164.3 per cent) had grown so wide (a ratio of 1:18.88) that Hollywood dominance in Taiwan was safely beyond challenge (Liang 2001: 106). Indeed, whereas Chinese and Hollywood films shared the Taipei market equally in 1992, by 2000 Hollywood commanded 93 per cent of the market while Chinese films had a tiny 2.5 per cent, with 4.5 per cent shared by others (Curtin 2003: 245).

Two new phenomena in the Taiwan market are noteworthy. First, to explore viable alternatives, special film exhibitions have been organized to attract special audiences. The practice began with the 'Golden Harvest Shows' in 1995, and since then Era, Spring Cinema and other companies have provided alternative venues for people interested in art cinema from around the world, albeit mostly from France. In 1998 four such exhibitions were devoted to foreign films, two to Chinese (mostly Hong Kong) and one which screened both. With a single print (priced at NT$45,000 each) in circulation and minimal promotion costs, special film exhibitions have carved out a space for art cinema in Taiwan (Guojia dianying 1998: 87).

Second, the seventeen-screen Warner Village Cinemas, a US$50 million investment by Village Roadshow, Warner Brothers and Golden Harvest located in Taipei's commercial East district, opened in January 1998 and has attracted audiences with its fashionable architecture, hip atmosphere and modern management. It predominantly caters to Hollywood fare, but occasionally it also has exhibited Taiwan films such as *Flowers of Shanghai* (Haishang hua, dir. Hou Hsiao-hsien, 1998) and *The Hole* (Dong, dir. Tsai Ming-liang [Cai Mingliang], 1998) for a week or two.[10] At NT$280–300 a piece, its tickets were NT$20 above the average in Taipei, but this did not prevent the Warner Village from selling nearly three million tickets and grabbing between one-quarter to one-third of Taipei's exhibition business in 1998, a spectacular achievement in its first year of operation (Curtin 2003: 243; Guojia dianying 1999: 63–4).

The 'barren soil' of production

As in the case of the Warner Village, Taiwan films have become at best a commercially irrelevant but culturally exotic treat amongst the Hollywood offering of blockbusters in Taiwan. As early as 1995 Hou described Taiwan art films as 'flowers blooming from barren soil' (F. Wang 1995: 17). This sarcastic comment was meant to send out a warning signal because from seventy-six in 1990, Taiwan feature productions nose-dived to forty-three in 1992 (down 43.4 per cent), twenty-four in 1994 and twelve in 1998. Increasingly, and by now almost exclusively, the industry – or what is left of it – has depended for survival on the government's annual 'national film guidance funds' (*guopian fudao jin*).

The guidance funds started in 1989–90 when the GIO decided to allocate NT$30 million to assist production of up to ten features each year, and the amount increased to NT$10 million for some films in 1992. From 1996 to 1999 the annual grants totaled around NT$120 million (or US$3.7 million) for feature production and were allocated to between ten and seventeen winning projects. The guidance funds were also awarded to outstanding screenplays (including those submitted by 'overseas Chinese' like Ang Lee), distribution and exhibition (GIO 1997: 287; GIO 2001: 285). Unfortunately, state subsidies and monetary prizes to award-winning directors did not change the fundamentals of the Taiwan market.[11] In 1997 none of the films produced with state subsidies grossed over NT$1 million in Taipei (Guojia dianying 1998: 91). Worse still, several other productions of the year did not even receive theatrical releases, and the situation remained the same in 1998 when low-budget action films from private companies went directly to video or cable television (GIO 2003).

The government's other attempts to boost Taiwan cinema during the 1990s produced limited positive effects. Launched in 1990, the annual Golden Horse Awards was handled by various non-government organizations, with Li Xing chairing its steering committee for four years, but with the state footing the bill. Controversy often erupted over the Golden Horse Awards operations and the annual allocation of guidance funds, so much so that Edward Yang and Tsai Ming-liang withdrew from Golden Horse competitions in the late 1990s. The government's designation of 1993 as 'national film year', with a budget of US$6 million for various activities masterminded by Peggy Chiao, again failed to arrest the steep decline in domestic production, although it did usher in a period of flourishing film studies and publications (F. Wang 1995: 14). In the late 1990s the government allocated even more money to launch two new film festivals open to international competition, the first a biannual event devoted to documentary films and the second an annual Taipei Film Festival sponsored by the Taipei municipality. Like the Golden Horse Awards, the operating budgets of these new festivals each exceeded NT$20 million (W. Huang 1998: 210–31).

Restricted by the GIO rules for guidance funds competition, whereby a company can apply for only one grant each in the categories of NT$10 million and NT$4 million, but two grants each if the projects are co-produced, CMPC developed its strategy of co-productions in the 1990s. On the one hand, CMPC had no reason to turn away its private Taiwan partners who were willing to cooperate on the basis of its studio facilities; on the other hand, CMPC actively sought co-productions with Hong Kong in order to minimize market risks. From 1990 to 1994 twelve of fifteen CMPC releases were co-productions, including seven with Hong Kong. Many private companies adopted the same strategy in order to survive in the dismal Taiwan market. Long Shong, for instance, benefited tremendously from its investments in Hong Kong productions such as *Swordsman, II–III*.

A new phenomenon in Taiwan production during the 1990s was the high-profile investment in mainland art cinema directors. As will be clearer in the section on cross-strait cooperation below (p. 280), Taiwan money was regularly channeled through Hong Kong to the mainland. To varying degrees Era and Tomson contributed to the global success of Chinese cinema at major international film festivals. As more and more Taiwanese money flowed overseas, Taiwan feature production could only suffer, and by 1994 only twenty-one production companies were in business, down 56.3 per cent from forty-eight in 1990. Annual production is now steady at around fifteen titles, and Taiwan cinema seems to have returned to its starting point in the 1950s, when the industry struggled to invent itself as a viable force in cultural production (F. Lu 1998: 386).

One exception to the 'barren soil' condition for Taiwan production in the 1990s was Chu Yen-ping (Zhu Yanping), labeled 'king of the pop flick' and comparable to Wong Jing in Hong Kong and Feng Xiaogang (see p. 292) in the mainland. In 1994 Chu's *Super Mischievous* (Xin Wulongyuan, 1994), a hilarious comedy featuring two mischievous monks, ranked second among Chinese films in Taipei, beating all but one of the Hong Kong blockbusters and grossing NT$98 million, with island-wide revenues estimated at NT$200 million. A consistently high box-office performer, Chu began directing in 1981 when he teamed up with Hsu Pu-liao (Xu Buliao), a Chaplinesque comedian, and the two cooperated on about forty films in a five-year period. Both started with a salary of NT$60,000 per film, but when Hsu's rose to NT$2.6 million per title, Chu's was NT$0.3 million. After Hsu's death at age 34 in 1985, Chu had his share of ups and downs with genres such as military education, youth idol romance and martial arts (Teng 1996: 102–9). In 1995, Chu's *Super Mischievous, II* (Xin Wulongyuan 2, 1995) had a 33-day run in a Taipei theater, grossed NT$8.8 million in Taipei and sold sixty prints island-wide (Yeh *et al.* 1999: 49, 54–6). But compared with the original, the sequel's reduced drawing power underscores the rapid decline of the Taiwan audience's interest in domestic productions, commercial or otherwise.

Auteurs of New Taiwan Cinema: history and memory

It must be remembered that lower annual productions do not mean lower artistic quality in Taiwan cinema. On the contrary, the 1990s saw the maturation of the auteurs of New Taiwan Cinema and the emergence of a second wave or 'new new wave' (Chiao 2002). Following the success of *City of Sadness*, Hou Hsiao-hsien directed *The Puppet Master*, a documentary-like re-enactment of puppet artist Li Tianlu's life during the Japanese occupation, and *Good Men, Good Women* (Haonan haonü, 1995), a tragic story of political persecution in the KMT era. Together, these three films complete Hou's trilogy interrogating injustices suffered by ordinary Taiwanese, who have no control of their fate in history (Silbergeld 2004). But Hou's films tend to generate more critical enthusiasm than popular response. Era had won prestige with *City of Sadness* but abandoned Hou after financing *The Puppet Master*. Co-produced by Japan and Taiwan, *Good Men, Good Women* grossed only NT$1.77 million in Taipei, but world rights were reportedly sold to a Japanese distributor for US$1 million (Yeh *et al.* 1999: 45). Indeed, Taiwan art film directors like Hou have learned to give up the Taiwan market and count on overseas sales and award monies to recoup part of their production costs.

Hou's fascination with Taiwan's underworld can be traced back to *Daughter of the Nile* and *City of Sadness*, but it receives a more romantic treatment in *Good Men, Good Women*, where an actress reminisces about her dead gangster boyfriend. *Goodbye South, Goodbye* (Nanguo zaijian, nanguo, 1996) continues Hou's fascination and displays the charming southern Taiwan landscape. Set in contemporary Taiwan, the film lacks Hou's earlier obsession with history and memory but expresses his view of post-martial law Taiwan as a society plagued by corruption and crime. *Flowers of Shanghai*, an adaptation of a famous late Qing Wu-dialect novel set in Shanghai, represents yet another attempt at a new style. Without any outdoor location scenes, the film builds a claustrophobic environment where courtesans and their lovers fight over trivial matters and engage in a convoluted game of emotions. With *Millennium Mambo* (Qianxi manbo, 2001), Hou seems eager to embrace MTV-style visuals and to reach out to the 'Gen-X' audiences. The film stars Shu Qi (Shu Kei) as a voluptuous young rebel caught up in restless, sadomasochistic romances with young and middle-aged men. Her character thrives on drugs, cigarettes, wine, sex and pop music.

Compared with Hou's apparent indulgence in decadence in *Millennium Mambo*, Edward Yang has maintained a relentlessly critical view of contemporary Taiwan as an affluent but spiritually impoverished society. While *Mahjiong* (Majiang, 1996) also exposes the gangster world, Yang's position is never that of romantic infatuation but rather a sober investigation that reveals the bankruptcy of moral principles in the entire Taiwan population. Similarly attacking the frenzied capitalist drive, *A Confucius Confusion* (Duli shidai, 1995) ridicules the otherwise decent middle classes and their hypocritical moral appearances (Y. Zhang 2002: 299–305). Arguably Yang's most brilliant picture, *A One and a Two* (Yiyi, 2000) documents two generations' largely failed endeavors to register the meaning of love and life in contemporary Taipei. Not surprisingly, the film won the best director award at the 2000 Cannes Film Festival, once again confirming Yang's status as an international auteur.

Yang's critique of transnational capitalism and his philosophical meditation on the human condition in the era of globalization make him almost unique among his Taiwan peers. It is true that his earlier investigation of history and memory in *A Brighter Summer Day* (Gulingjie shaonian sharen shijian, 1991) succeeds in depicting Taiwan culture as heterogeneous and Taiwan identity as hybrid. But compared with his contemporaries, Yang is more critical of the status quo and less susceptible to nostalgia, narcissism or obsession that characterize the works of other New Taiwan Cinema directors in the 1990s.

For instance, an obsession with mine workers is elaborated in two epic accounts: *The Hills of No Return* (Wuyan de shanqiu, dir. Wang Tong, 1992) and *A Borrowed Life* (Duosan, dir. Wu Nien-chen, 1993). Whereas Wang's dramatization of poverty and exploitation is set against a history of mainland migration to Taiwan, Wu chooses to identify with the Japanese era (*duosan* is the Japanese term for 'father'), making it both an object of nostalgia and a site of resistance to mainland culture. Wu's strategy of native resistance is more pronounced in *Buddha Bless America*, which pits innocent Taiwan villagers against various 'colonizing' powers – the KMT regime, the US army (which uses the village land for military exercises during the Vietnam War) and American culture. Like Hou's Taiwan trilogy, Wang and Wu seem obsessed with Taiwan native soil and tend to situate Taiwan more within a postcolonial than a transnational context, as further exemplified in *Red Persimmons* (Hong shizi, dir. Wang Tong, 1996), yet another rural Taiwan saga.

The second wave: fluid identities and urban sensibilities

The 1990s saw the emergence of a second wave in Taiwan. Most notable among new talents is Ang Lee, who completed his training in the US and secured CMPC support for his inaugural family drama trilogy, sometimes called 'father knows best' (Dariotis and Fung 1997). Lee's transregional, diasporic imagination is evident in *Pushing Hands* (Tuishou, 1991), a story set in the US about interracial marriage and cultural difference that introduces his trademark humanistic position on cross-cultural, intergenerational conflicts. These themes are further elaborated in *The Wedding Banquet* (Xiyan, 1993), a comic but positive portrayal of homosexuality in New York, and *Eat Drink Man Woman* (Yinshi nannü, 1994), on a Taipei widowed father's bewilderment with his three daughters' sexual life and their eventual surprise by his marital decision. At a time when Taiwan cinema suffered tremendous financial losses, Lee proved to his peers and CMPC that well-crafted art films could succeed in both winning awards and generating profits.

There are two other prominent second wave members who are commercially less successful but artistically more adventurous than Lee. Stan Lai (Lai Shengchuan), a famous theater artist in Taiwan, crossed over to feature production with *Peach Blossom Land* (Anliang taohua yuan, 1993), an experimentalist juxtaposition of two stage dramas, and *The Red Lotus Society* (Feixia A Da, 1994), a sarcastic probe into the myth of flying and magical powers. Like Stan Lai and Ang Lee, Tsai Ming-liang worked closely with CMPC and relied heavily on film guidance funds, although his 'overseas Chinese' status caused him some problems.[12] After announcing his iconoclastic intent in *Rebels of the Neon God* (Qingshaonian nezha, 1992), which began his illustrious career, Tsai delivered *Vive l'amour* (Aiqing wansui, 1994), an existential investigation of the absurdity of life distinguished by little dialogue and no music score. Although its Taiwan revenues of NT$11 million broke even with its production costs, *Vive l'amour* won the Golden Lion at the 1994 Venice Film Festival and the exhibition rights were sold to Italy for US$150,000 (Yeh *et al.* 1999: 46).

Backed by more substantial guidance funds than his first two features, Tsai continued to tackle the themes of alienation, depression, desperation and solitude in his next two films. *The River* (Heliui, 1997) is a sober look at a dysfunctional family of a gay father and son, and *The Hole* is a dramatization of existential crisis enhanced by Ge Lan's melodious songs. Co-produced by Peggy Chiao's Arch Light (Jiguang) and a French company, *What Time Is It There?* (Ni na er jidian le, 2001) furthers Tsai's exploration of psychological traumas and the collapsed family in a transnational context, linking Taipei and Paris via the fluidity of space and time and the incomprehensible cycle of life and death.

Fluid identities and urban sensibilities characterize Ang Lee, Stan Lai and Tsai Ming-liang more than their predecessors from New Taiwan Cinema, with the exception of Edward Yang. Cosmopolitan in their outlook, these three talented directors perceive new Taiwanese identities as conditioned less by an idealized projection of Taiwan native soil than by the incessant *flow* of capital, commodity, desire and traffic, which constantly transgress boundaries of all kinds – spatial, temporal, cultural, ethnic, moral and sexual. No longer obsessed with retrieving memory and reconstructing history, they choose to confront existential crises and private emotions of ordinary urbanites caught in a disintegrating post-modern world.

Lee, Lai and especially Tsai, who is said to have invented a new cinematic style distinct from that of New Taiwan Cinema (T. Wen 2002: 92, 120), are closer to an even younger group of second wave directors. Just as *Eat Drink Man Woman* opens with rushing traffic in Taipei, *Treasure Island* (Zhiyao weini huo yitian, dir. Chen Kuo-Fu [Chen Guofu], 1993) follows the trafficking of illegal money through an urban labyrinth to a literal dead end in Taipei (a portion of the highway under construction). Likewise, in an allegorical but comic manner, *Tropical Fish* (Redai yu, dir. Chen Yu-hsun [Chen Yuxun], 1995) demonstrates through kidnapped children that the otherwise 'fixed' identities of perpetrators and victims are shown in an extremely fluid form. Fluid identities come under more critical scrutiny in *The Personals* (Zhenghun qishi, dir. Chen Kuo-Fu, 1997), in which a young woman interviews a host of potential suitors after she posts a newspaper ad seeking dates. Emotionally engaged, *The Personals* resembles *Mahjiong* but tackles hypocrisy and moral corruption in a more personal way.

Like the previous generation, the second wave directors won critical acclaim but their films often failed miserably at the box office. Except for *Tropical Fish*, which grossed NT$4.62 million in a 35-day run at two Taipei theaters, all other films from the second wave approved for release in 1995 did poorly. In Taipei *The Peony Pavilion* (Wode meili yu aichou, dir. Chen Kuo-Fu, 1995) took NT$678,210 and *Heartbreak Island* (Qunian dongtian, dir. Hsu Hsiao-ming [Xu Xiaoming], 1995) a mere NT$193,980. Worse still, *Lonely Hearts Club* (Jimo fangxin jule bu, dir. Yee Chih-yen [Yi Zhiyan], 1995) was not released until 1997, and as late as 1998 *Ah Chung* (Zhongzai, dir. Chang Tso-chi [Zhang Zuoji], 1995) and *A Drifting Life* (Chunhua menglu, dir. Lin Cheng-sheng [Lin Zhengsheng], 1995) had not been exhibited at all (Yeh *et al.* 1999: 42–9).

Critical opinions differ sharply with regard to the second wave. Whereas Peggy Chiao argues that the younger generation had come to maturity by the mid-1990s (Chiao 2002), Liang Liang blames them for neglecting local audiences and catering to international jurors by showcasing taboo subjects such as incest and homosexuality as proof of their artistic courage. In their efforts to become the second Hou Hsiao-hsien, many of these directors have ignored the limits of rural subject matter and the long-take aesthetic typical of New Taiwan Cinema. In short, Liang is worried about the apparent stagnation not only in Taiwan's film market but also in Taiwan directors' artistic imagination in the late 1990s (2001: 106).

Reel contacts across and beyond the Taiwan strait

In the 1990s, co-productions with mainland China became particularly attractive for Taiwan producers because of its natural resources, acting talents and inexpensive manpower. Since Taiwan's relaxation of the restriction on cross-strait travels in 1989, around 140 Taiwan-funded films had been shot in the mainland by the mid-1990s, which was more than the total shot in the island during the same period (F. Wang 1995: 11). However, many of these co-productions initially did not get released in Taiwan due to a government imposed '50 per cent rule', stipulating that a film would be banned in Taiwan if the mainland cast and crew numbered more than half. *Five Girls and a Rope* (Wuge nüzi yu yigen shengzi, dir. Ye Hongwei, 1991) thus became an early victim of such arbitrary censorship rules. By the mid-1990s, the 50 per cent rule was revoked. *Accidental Legend* (Feitian, dir. Wang Shau-di, 1995) was the first Taiwan feature to be shot entirely on the mainland, and its budget was NT$40 million. Unfortunately, the film was not released commercially in Taiwan due to a perceived lack of box-office potential (Yeh *et al*. 1999: 38–42).

In October 1994, Taiwan officially lifted its ban on the import of mainland films, but the annual quota was limited to ten titles, each with up to thirty-six prints. A maximum of thirteen theaters each in Taipei and Kaohsiung can screen a single mainland film simultaneously, in addition to eight other theaters in the rest of the island. Clearly, mainland imports are regulated more strictly than those from other countries, which after 1996 have no quota restrictions and can have up to fifty-eight prints in circulation throughout the island, simultaneously signing up to eighteen screens each in Taipei and Kaohsiung and ten additional screens in other cities and counties. However, not many mainland films have been commercially released in Taiwan, and those which are released are often partially funded by Taiwan companies (GIO 2001: 286).

As stated earlier, in the early 1990s Taiwan producers set up shop in Hong Kong to bypass Taiwan regulations and co-produced films with noted mainland directors. Among the first major international hits was *Raise the Red Lantern* (Dahong denglong gaogao gua, dir. Zhang Yimou, 1991), which Qiu Fusheng produced for Era and which won the Silver Lion at the 1991 Berlin Film Festival. Era also co-produced *To Live* (Huozhe, dir. Zhang Yimou, 1994) with Shanghai Studio, a dramatization of the absurd socialist revolution that landed the best actor award for Ge You at the Cannes Film Festival. In a more glamorous way, Hsu Feng brought Tomson to the international spotlight when *Farewell My Concubine* (Bawang bieji, dir. Chen Kaige, 1993) won the Golden Palm at the Cannes Film Festival. As if to speed up competition with his Taiwan peers, Wang Yingxiang also signed up fifth generation directors for his Long Shong productions, such as *Nanjing 1937* (Nanjing da tusha, dir. Wu Ziniu, 1994).

The most successful co-production to date is *Crouching Tiger, Hidden Dragon*, which assembled a multinational production line-up from the US, Hong Kong, Taiwan and China. Location shooting was done, among other picturesque places, in the Gobi Desert and the Taklamakan Plateau in western China. Studio work was done in Beijing, music recording in Shanghai, vocals added in Los Angeles and post-production completed in Hong Kong. For James Schamus, the film's executive producer and screenwriter, the film 'is really bringing together almost every conceivable idea you could have of China' (Sunshine 2000: 46, 140–2). Perhaps more than anticipated, this co-produced imaging of China swept through the global market and garnered four awards at the 2000 Oscars, including best foreign language film.

Ang Lee's case highlights on the one hand the immense attraction mainland China has for filmmakers and audiences alike and, on the other, the inevitable slippery nature of geopolitical boundaries in the era of globalization. The case further demonstrates the prevalence of a cosmopolitan outlook in Taiwan or Taiwan-co-produced films. Indeed, at the start of the new millennium, Taiwan cinema has relied on transnational, transregional operations and its appeal has reached far beyond the island's geographic borders.

THE PRC: POST-SOCIALIST CINEMA

Post-socialist cinema in the PRC has traveled down an uneven path since the early 1990s. The state has invested heavily in propaganda films while encouraging private companies to produce ideologically acceptable art and commercial films. Whereas the fifth generation moved from ethnographic to historical and contemporary subjects, the sixth generation filmmakers emerged from the margins of the studio system and earned their reputation through underground or semi-official modes of production and distribution. Meanwhile, genre films, especially comedies, have climbed to the top of the box office, attracting transnational capital along the way. In brief, art, capital and the state have formed an uneasy partnership and all involved proceed cautiously toward an uncertain future.

The political economy of post-socialist cinema

Like its Hong Kong counterpart, mainland Chinese feature production started strongly in the early 1990s and reached an all-time high with 166 films in 1992, although many of these were co-productions with Hong Kong and Taiwan. For instance, of 146 features released in 1995, co-productions accounted for thirty-five (or 24 per cent). Due to the new state policy requiring that most post-production work be done in the mainland, the number of co-productions dropped to around ten (or 9.1 per cent) out of a total of 110 in 1996. Similar to what happened in Hong Kong, in 1997 annual feature production declined to eighty-five (down 22.7 per cent). Although official figures indicate eighty-two features produced in 1998 and ninety-nine in 1999, some scholars estimate the actual number of films exhibited to be thirty-seven in 1998 and around forty in 1999 (W. Huang 1999: 133–4; Yin 1999: 23). The official figures for the new millennium stayed in the same neighborhood: ninety-one in 2000, around eighty in 2001, and 100 in 2002, the latter including thirteen titles shot for exclusive rural screening, fifteen co-productions, seven in 16mm and two in digital format (S. Huang 2003; J. Liu 2003: 1) (see Table 6.2, pp. 196–7).

Similar declines also occurred in movie attendance and exhibition revenues. In 1991 annual attendance stood at 14.4 billion, down 42.4 per cent from 25 billion in 1984, but in 1994 the number fell to 3 billion, down another 79.2 per cent from 1991 (Yeh *et al.* 1999: 180). The annual exhibition revenues likewise declined from RMB2.36 billion in 1991 to RMB1.44 billion in 1998, RMB0.85 billion in 1999 and rebounded only slightly to RMB0.96 billion in 2000, but the 2002 figure of RMB 0.9 billion still fell below the estimated break-even level of RMB1.05 billion (S. Huang 2003) (see Table 6.1, p. 192). Poor as these figures are, the actual percentage of revenue raked in by domestic films is even more depressing.[13] Cheap pirated VCDs, rundown exhibition venues, relatively expensive ticket prices (RMB40), and low production values are frequently blamed for the declining numbers in movie attendance and box-office revenues for domestic films.[14]

Two new developments changed the balance of the political economy in post-socialist cinema in the mid-1990s. First, the CCP augmented ideological pressure and sponsored productions of leitmotif films that endorse state policy and support Party propaganda. The implementation of the '9550 project' in 1996 set an annual quota of ten 'excellent' leitmotif films in the ninth five-year plan and encouraged state studios to compete for government subsidies (Yin 1998: 6–7). Second, to attract audiences back to cinema, the state allowed China Film Corporation to enter partnership with transnational capitalism and distribute 'mega imports' (*dapian*) from Hollywood (and occasionally Hong Kong) on a split box-office arrangement. Starting in October 1994 and limited to ten each year up to 2002, these blockbusters attracted viewers immediately.[15] For example, in 1995 movie attendance was up as much as 40 per cent from the previous year in Shanghai's Yongle theater chain.

The import of blockbusters also boosted high-budget private investments such as *Red Cherry* (Hong yingtao, dir. Ye Daying, 1995), a co-production with Moscow's Gorky Studio and Youth Studio in Beijing that cost Hong Kong-based Ocean Films (Dayang) RMB27 million and four years to make. This film about two Chinese orphans' sufferings in the Soviet Union during the Second World War broke records in many Chinese cities, pushing it to the top of the 1995 domestic box office and beating most Hollywood imports of that year (Pan 1996: 6). Ocean Films also co-produced with Beijing Studio *Blush* (Hongfen, dir. Li Shaohong, 1994), which won the Silver Lion at the Berlin Film Festival, and with Xi'an Studio *The Emperor's Shadow* (Qinsong, dir. Zhou Xiaowen, 1996), which cost RMB40 million but ranked second in the 1996 domestic chart (see Table 8.2).

The high-profile successes of commercially oriented art cinema soon brought official partners into new 'private' (*minying*) companies. Forbidden City

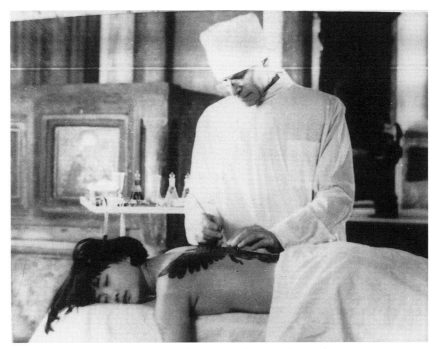

Figure 8.1 Red Cherry (1995): commercial packaging of art and memory

Table 8.2 Selected production costs in the PRC, 1959–2002

Year	Film	Cost (RMB)	Profit (RMB)
1959	*Song of Youth*	310,000	360,000
mid-1980s	average	600,000	—
late 1990s	average	3,000,000	—
1993	*The Days* (black and white)	100,000	—
1995	*Red Cherry*	27,000,000	—
1996	*Warrior Lanling*	20,000,000	—
1996	*The Emperor's Shadow*	40,000,000	—
1996	*The Decisive Turning Point, I-II*	100,000,000	—
1997	*The Opium War*	100,000,000	—
1998	*Dreams Come True*	4,000,000	—
2000	*Sorry, Baby*	10,000,000	—
2001	*Big Shot's Funeral*	29,000,000	—
2002	*Hero*	250,000,000	—

Sources: Dai 1993: 201; Dai 1999: 369; Deng 2002: 17; Pan 1996: 6; Semsel *et al.* 1993: 87; Shackleton 2003; Zhongguo yishu 2002: 58.

(Zijincheng), for example, was set up in 1996 with state money totaling RMB5.18 million from these government units: Beijing Television Station (25.5 per cent), the Beijing Television Art Center (25.5 per cent), Beijing Film Company (24.5 per cent), and the Beijing Culture and Arts Audio-Visual Press (24.5 per cent) (ZDX 1997: 342). Two of Forbidden City's 1998 releases topped the domestic feature rankings. *A Time to Remember* (Hongse lianren, dir. Ye Daying, 1998) continued the commercial packaging of revolutionary subjects by casting Leslie Cheung as an underground communist, while *Dreams Come True* (Jiafang yifang, dir. Feng Xiaogang, 1998), a hilarious comedy, inaugurated 'new year's pictures' (*hesui pian*) as a competitive new genre.[16]

Nevertheless, it must be remembered that a majority of state studios tended to lose money in the 1990s. An official report lists August First, Changchun and Pearl River studios as three of the biggest loss-makers, RMB1.3–1.9 million each in their 1995 distribution year, while Beijing and Shanghai Studios squeezed a meager profit of RMB4.2 million each. The latter amount is roughly equivalent to the profit generated by *Shanghai Triad* (Yao a yao, yao dao waipo qiao, 1995), Zhang Yimou's stylish foray into the gangster genre produced by Shanghai Studio (ZDX 1996: 206–7). From 1997 to 1999, more than 70 per cent of features failed to recover their production costs, which averaged around RMB3 million per title (Rosen 2002b). In 1998 only the top ten films grossed over RMB3 million. A government regulation that requires that each year two-thirds of a theater's screening time must be reserved for domestic films obviously has failed to save the 'sinking ship' of the mainland film industry (W. Huang 1999: 134).

Whereas the state seems to have loosened its policy on profit-sharing distribution with Hollywood, it has never relaxed its ideological control, and film censorship actually became more stringent in the aftermath of Tiananmen in 1989. *The Blue Kite* (Lan fengzheng, dir. Tian Zhuangzhuang 1993), a critique of socialist revolution co-produced by Hong Kong's Longwick Film and Beijing Studio, was entered at the 1993 Tokyo Film Festival without prior official approval. Even though the film won the Tokyo grand prize and was widely distributed and acclaimed abroad, it was banned in China and Tian was immediately prohibited from filmmaking along with a number of 'underground' filmmakers. When Tian returned to directing, he chose *Springtime in a Small Town* (Xiaocheng zhichun, 2002), a remake of Fei Mu's 1948 masterpiece, which shows little if any subversive intent. Jiang Wen, a famous actor-turned-director, met a similar fate. His *In the Heat of the Sun* (Yangguang canlan de rizi, 1995), a revisionist but nostalgic picture of army kids' adolescent life during the Cultural Revolution, was given the green light by the censors. But the government banned Jiang's next feature, *Devils on the Doorstep* (Guizi laile, 2000), a black-and-white dramatization of the absurdity of war. Yet, at the turn of the new millennium, CCP censorship was such that Jiang Wen himself was not politically sanctioned and has continued his spectacular acting career.

Figure 8.2 In the Heat of the Sun (1995): nostalgia for the Cultural Revolution

Leitmotif films: politics, ideology and art

From 1991 to 2000 a total of thirty-five titles and forty-eight parts of the CCP-designated 'major revolutionary historical films' were produced, four times as many as those of the 1980s (Zhongguo yishu 2002: 54). Several factors contributed to the heavy investment in these leitmotif films in the 1990s. First, the 1989 Tiananmen event prompted the CCP to launch new initiatives to re-educate the population and instill the spirit of nationalism (Berry 1994). Second, a number of celebrations, such as the seventieth anniversary of the CCP in 1991 and the fiftieth anniversary of the PRC in 1999, necessitated the production of leitmotif films as tributes to the party-state. Third, both state studios and individual directors realized that, due to substantial subsidies, shooting leitmotif films actually helped them accumulate political capital without incurring any financial burden.

In terms of genre, many leitmotif films are large-scale war films recounting the CCP victory over the KMT. Seen together, *The Decisive Engagements, I–III* (Da juezhan, dir. Li Jun *et al.*, 1991–2), *The Decisive Turning Point, I–II* (Da zhuanzhe, dir. Wei Lian, 1996) and *The Decisive Further Advances, I–IV* (Da jinjun, dir. Yang Guangyuan *et al.*, 1996–9) restage all major battles during the civil war of 1946 to 1949. Historical and biographic genres also account for a large number of leitmotif films. They either depict key historical events or portray the CCP and PLA founding fathers such as Mao Zedong, Zhou Enlai,

Liu Shaoqi and Deng Xiaoping, and together with war films they are classified as major revolutionary historical films.

Significantly, in spite of mandatory viewing from schools and free tickets from work units, only five major revolutionary historical films made it to the annual top ten list and the remainder failed miserably at the box office. Indeed, for war epics like *The Decisive Engagements, I–III*, a series budgeted at RMB100 million, there is no way one could ever estimate the exact costs of military involvements (Zhongguo yishu 2002: 58). Take Xiaoxiang Studio as a more manageable example: only one out of five revolutionary films generated some profit (RMB1 million). Nonetheless, even the worst performer, *Autumn in Hometown* (Guyuan qiuse, dir. Zheng Dongtian, 1999), which drew only fifty-eight viewers in Zhejiang province and the Chongqing municipality combined and grossed RMB500,000 nationwide, might still be profitable once one factors in state subsidies and government award monies. In the case of *The National Anthem* (Guoge, dir. Wu Ziniu, 1999), the RMB9.6 million in subsidies nearly canceled out the RMB9.93 million it made in losses. But because the film won an excellent film prize at the Huabiao Awards (worth RMB1 million), a special prize from the Golden Rooster Awards and the best picture at the Hundred Flowers Awards, it actually gained financially as well as politically for the studio (Zhongguo yishu 2002: 55–7).[17] This explains why a studio like Xiaoxiang would continue producing leitmotif films.

It is worth observing that directors otherwise known for art films have been recruited for leitmotif productions. From the fourth generation came Zheng Dongtian and Huang Jianzhong, the latter directing *My 1919* (Wode 1919, 1999), a patriotic film set in Paris. Earlier, Xie Jin directed *The Opium War* (Yapian zhanzheng, 1997), a RMB100 million production that grossed RMB72 million in China and NT$3 million in Taipei (Deng 2002: 17; Guojia dianying 1998: 99). Released in Hong Kong in July 1997 to mark the return of the territory, the film was the first PRC feature to premiere there on a split-revenue basis. Representing the fifth generation in leitmotif films is Feng Xiaoning, whose *Red River Valley* (Honghe gu, dir. Feng Xiaoning, 1997) stages the solidarity of Tibetan and Han Chinese in defense against British invaders. Like Wu Ziniu and Ye Daying, Feng repackages nationalism, revolution and romance in the age of post-socialist commercialization.

'Ethnographic cinema': spectacles of ethnicity, sexuality and history

In terms of international reputation, the type of Chinese film making headlines in the early 1990s is 'ethnographic cinema' – films that showcase exotic landscape and architecture and exhibit female sexuality and gender oppression (Y. Zhang 2002: 220–39). Zhang Yimou's *Ju Dou* (Ju Dou, 1989) set the pattern for ethnic, erotic exhibitionism (Cui 2003: 127–49), and further refined the style in his *Raise the Red Lantern*, a theatrical rendition of the tension between a master and his four wives (T. Lu 2002: 157–72). *The Story of Qiuju* (Qiuju da guansi, 1992) brought Zhang from a mythical, 'timeless' China to a contemporary rural setting, and this co-production with Hong Kong's Sil-Metropole won the Golden Lion and the award for best actress (Gong Li) at the 1992 Venice Film Festival.

International reputation, foreign festival demand and transnational investment soon lured more Chinese directors of different generations into ethnographic filmmaking. Ling Zifeng directed *Ripples Across Stagnant Water* (Kuang, 1991), a tale of a woman with three men. *Red Firecracker, Green Firecracker* (Paoda shuangdeng, dir. He Ping, 1994), which won a grand jury prize at the Hawaii Film Festival, metaphorically releases repressed sexuality as a spectacular firecracker show by the Yellow River.

In the beginning, the CCP censors were not pleased with the increasing focus on sexuality as a potent symbol of patriarchal oppression. Hence, *The Black Mountain Road* (Heishan lu, dir. Zhou Xiaowen, 1990) and *Bloody Morning* (Xuese qingchen, dir. Li Shaohong, 1990) were shelved for a few years before receiving limited releases, the latter probably due more to its graphic depiction of violence in contemporary rural China. But after *The Woman from the Lake of Scented Souls* (Xianghun nü, dir. Xie Fei, 1992) was co-winner of the Golden Bear with *The Wedding Banquet* at the 1993 Berlin Film Festival, the subject of sexuality seemed no longer a taboo. Set in the age of globalization where economic reform has brought fundamental changes to a remote mountain village, *Ermo* (Ermo, dir. Zhou Xiaowen, 1994) won several jury's awards at the Locarno Film Festival and might have convinced the censors to release Zhou's earlier film, *The Black Mountain Road*.

Even if sexuality is not a principal concern, ethnic Chinese culture remains foregrounded in art films such as *Life on a String* (Bianzou bianchang, dir. Chen Kaige, 1991) and *The King of Masks* (Bianlian, dir. Wu Tianming, 1995). Both films depict traditional folk artists and both exemplify 'diasporic' filmmaking from the two eminent directors who took up residence in the US in the wake of Tiananmen and who depended on overseas investment. Nonetheless, the 'ethnographic turn' in the first half of the 1990s appeared to be taken over by a 'historical return' by the mid-1990s. More than *The Blue Kite*, Chen Kaige's *Farewell My Concubine* dramatizes the political violation of Peking opera art through a turbulent century. By the time Chen completed *The Emperor and the Assassin* (Jingke ci Qinwang, 1998), a glamorized epic about the murderous First Emperor Qin, it is clear that his return to history reveals the ambivalence of his ideological positioning.

In the case of Zhang Yimou, the return to history – or re-imagined history – is equally problematic. Spanning a shorter period than that of *Farewell My Concubine*, *To Live* highlights the absolute necessity of tolerance as a time-honored survival skill for ordinary people in socialist China (Chow 1998: 113–52). What distinguishes Zhang from Chen is the former's willingness to experiment with new styles in urban settings, as in *Keep Cool* (Youhua haohao shuo, 1997), which is distinguished by its use of improvised acting. Primarily known for his rural films, Zhang did not re-emerge in the international spotlight until *Not One Less* (Yige dou buneng shao, 1999), a docu-drama about a poverty-stricken rural school and featuring a non-professional cast. Winner of the Golden Lion at the 1999 Venice Film Festival, *Not One Less* received funding from Columbia Asia, which also invested in *The Road Home* (Wode fuqin muqin, 1999), Zhang's nostalgic, romanticized recollection of the Anti-Rightist years, again set in a rural village. As if to confirm Zhang's inexhaustible talent and Columbia Asia's vision, *The Road Home* won the Golden Bear at the 2000 Berlin Film Festival (Sunshine 2000: 142).

Urban cinema: between post-socialist nostalgia and postmodern farce

Zhang Yimou's forays into urban subjects reflect the increasing importance of the city in cinematic landscapes of post-socialist China. Two women directors are noteworthy in this new development. With compassion and restraint, Li Shaohong probes the psychological crisis of a middle-aged man in *Family Portrait* (Sishi buhuo, 1992), and addresses the dilemma of some newly unemployed workers in *Red Western Suit* (Xinfu dajie, 1998). Using the distinctive style of documentary realism, which thrives on a non-professional cast and long takes, Ning Ying unravels sympathetic pictures of retirement life in *For Fun* (Zhaole, 1992) and of routine operations in a police branch in *On the Beat* (Minjing gushi, 1995), both set in present-day Beijing.

In a manner different from these two late female bloomers of the fifth generation, Huang Jianxin continued his political satire in films like *Back to Back, Face to Face* (Beikaobei, lianduilian, 1994), which dramatize the absurdity of political life and the remnants of socialist ideology in contemporary China. In the new millennium, however, Huang has re-emerged with new-style urban pictures centered on emergent middle-class values. More than his female colleagues, Huang appeals to widespread *post-socialist nostalgia* for the lost simplicity and naiveté of the earlier decades in *Tell Me Your Secret* (Shuochu nide mimi, 2000) and *Marriage Certificate* (Shuishuo wo bu zaihu, aka Jiehun zheng, 2001). The fact that these two films made it to the domestic top ten list in 2000–1 indicates the convergence of critical art and popular entertainment in post-socialist China. Indeed, ranked second in the 2002 box office is *Together with You* (He ni zai yiqi, 2002), a sentimental drama about a father and son relationship set in contemporary Beijing, which represents Chen Kaige's turn to local, everyday concerns.

A large number of urban films are comedies of various stripes. Some critics consider *Mr Wang: Flames of Desire* (Wang xiansheng zhi yuhuo fenshen, dir. Zhang Jianya, 1993) to be a 'postmodern' pastiche whereby an old Shanghai cartoon character is revived to mock, in a tongue-in-cheek manner, contemporary moral decadence. Like Zhang Jianya, Xia Gang is a latecomer of the fifth generation, but his light urban comedies such as *After Separation* (Da saba, 1992) drew him closer to the more cynical comedy style perfected by Wang Shuo in the late 1980s. By the late 1990s, Ge You and Xu Fan, two leads in *After Separation*, had become a regular pair in a milder sort of comedy, Feng Xiaogang's feel-good new year's pictures.

Feng Xiaogang, who co-wrote *After Separation*, became well known after cooperating with Wang Shuo on television dramas. In the mid-1990s, Wang and Feng's satire and humor ran into censorship problems. Two of their works were banned in mid-production: *Papa* (Wo shi ni baba, dir. Wang Shuo, 1996) and *An Awkward Life* (Guozhe langbei bukan de shenghuo, dir. Feng Xiaogang, 1997). Miraculously, Feng reinvented himself as the number-one commercial film director in China. After *Dreams Come True* completed its domestic dream making, Feng flew to Los Angeles and delivered a bitter-sweet immigration tale in *Be There or Be Square* (Bujian busan, 1999), the biggest hit in China at the time, and second only to *Titanic*. Feng's two 2000 features, *Sorry, Baby* (Meiwan meiliao) and *A Sigh* (Yisheng tanxi), topped the domestic box office again. In spite of criticism of his tendency to cater to the audience's 'lowly tastes', Feng's commercial fare hypes a postmodern farce on screen. As will be discussed below, his consistent box-office record soon brought him transnational investment.

The sixth generation and beyond: underground and peripheral

An urban focus is similarly typical of the sixth generation directors who started their career in the 1990s when economic reform took away the kind of state sponsorship of art cinema the previous generation had enjoyed. Instead of waiting patiently in the state system, several young directors decided to work 'underground', shooting films without acquiring official permits and shipping them overseas for exhibition. Three noted members of the sixth generation made their debuts this way. Mixing rock music with documentary footage of rebel singer Cui Jian, Zhang Yuan's *Beijing Bastards* (Beijing zazhong, 1993) represents 'outlawed' filmmaking against the repressive regime. More constrained and artistic in nature, Wang Xiaoshuai's black-and-white debut, *The Days* (Dong Chun de rizi, 1993), exposes feelings of despair, desperation and derangement in post-socialist China, feelings captured in a similar manner by He Yi (He Jianjun) in *Red Beads* (Xuanlian, 1993) and *Postman* (Youchai, 1995). These films foreground a deep-seated crisis of male subjectivity in a changing sociopolitical environment, in which the male artist is alienated from and outraged by both the political and commercial mainstreams (Donald 2000: 105–12).

In these films, urban landscapes thus take on a predominantly gloomy appearance. By way of investigating marginal and repressed lifestyles, such as alcoholics in *Sons* (Erzi, 1996) and gays in *East Palace, West Palace* (Donggong xigong, 1997), Zhang Yuan has maintained his trademark defiance. Even in *Seventeen Years* (Guonian huijia, 1999), his first domestically released feature shot in a state prison with official approval, Zhang builds up a sinister ambience in which any hope of compromise between the grieving parents and the reformed daughter seems suspect. A similar trajectory of moving from the underground to the peripheral is visible in Wang Xiaoshuai's career. Before directing a performance artist's protest in *Frozen* (Jidu hanleng, 1996) under the pseudonym Wu Ming (literally 'no name'), Wang had completed *So Close to Paradise* (Biandan, guniang, 1998), which had to wait three years before its limited release in China. A sober investigation of urban problems like prostitution, *So Close to Paradise* is still critical of the status quo, but Wang's *Beijing Bicycle* (Shiqi sui de danche, 2001) is more lyrical and more nostalgic in its rendition of the fast disappearing Beijing cityscape.

By the mid-1990s a different group in the sixth generation emerged from the peripheries of the studio system. They raised funds from private sources, purchased studio labels and embarked on low-budget filmmaking. Like their underground colleagues, these new directors resorted to rock music, alternative lifestyles and sadomasochistic acts to express their anger at and estrangement from society. Their anger erupts like a volcano in such rock music movies as *Dirt* (Toufa luanle, dir. Guan Hu, 1994) and *Weekend Lovers* (Zhoumo qingren, dir. Lou Ye, 1995), and their estrangement finds articulation in *Rainclouds Over Wushan* (Wushan yunyu, dir. Zhang Ming, 1995) and *The Making of Steel* (Gangtie shi zheyang liancheng de, dir. Lu Xuechang, 1997, completed in 1995). By the late 1990s, however, their restless 'adolescent' phase seemed to be over and the establishment gradually accepted or supported their subsequent films. *No Visit After Divorce* (Lihun le, jiu bie zailai zhaowo, dir. Wang Rui, 1997) was among the first from this group to make it to the domestic top ten (Cui 2001; Han 1995 and 1999).

Regardless of their underground or peripheral modes of production, insistence on personal perspective and commitment to a new vision of 'truth' or 'objectivity' characterize the sixth generation directors (Dai 1999: 382). To a great extent, they conscientiously distinguish themselves from their fifth generation predecessors. Whereas the latter are associated with rural landscape, traditional culture, ethnic spectacle, grand epic, historical reflection, allegorical framework, communal focus, and depths of emotion, the former are sided with an urban milieu, modern sensitivity, a narcissistic tendency, initiation tales, documentary effects, uncertain situation, individualistic perception, and precarious moods. For the new generation, their films are definitely more 'truthful' to reality than the fifth generation's glamorization of ethnicity, sexuality and history (Y. Zhang 2004).

The sixth generation's professed adherence to truth has not prevented them from engaging in formal experiments. Indeed, a new visual sensibility is evident in MTV-style rapid cross-cuts of images, and episodic narration is integrated in *Call Me* (Huwo, dir. Ah Nian [Xu Hongyu], 1999) and *Dazzling* (Huayan, dir. Li Xin, 2001). Cinematic doubling is built into both the narrative structure and characterization in *Lunar Eclipse* (Yueshi, dir. Wang Quan'an, 1999) and

Suzhou River (Suzhou he, dir. Lou Ye, 2000), two fantastic tales each featuring an enigmatic woman who lures the male protagonist into an urban labyrinth of desires and disappointments (Silbergeld 2004). Seeking a documentary aesthetic grounded in real characters in real settings, Jia Zhangke has earned an international reputation with his trilogy set in a poverty-stricken district in Shanxi province – *Pickpocket* (Xiao Wu, 1998), *Platform* (Zhantai, 2000) and *Unknown Pleasures* (Ren xiaoyao, 2002) – a trilogy that exposes the underside of the glorious façade of economic reform buttressed by official rhetoric and commercial filmmaking.

Diaspora filmmaking and transnational investment

The 1990s was a time when Chinese diasporic filmmaking congealed into a critical mass. High-profile directors like Chen Kaige aside, Hu Xuehua returned from the US and directed *Warrior Lanling* (Lanling wang, 1996), a RMB20-million fantastic myth film with dialogue in an imaginary 'ethnic minority' language (S. Huang 2000: 43). Joan Chen, best known for her lead role in *The Last Emperor*, also returned to direct *Xiu Xiu: The Sent Down Girl* (Tianyu, 1998), a tale of political and sexual oppression set in the Cultural Revolution. Indeed, Dai Sijie, a Chinese-French director, also approached the Cultural Revolution in *China, My Sorrow* (Niupeng, 1989) and again in *Little Chinese Seamstress* (Xiao caifeng, 2002).

Most diasporic filmmakers have preferred cultural rather than political subjects and have sought legitimacy by means of co-production, as exemplified by two Chinese-American women producers. Ann Hu (Hu An) directed *Shadow Magic* (Xiyang jing, 2000), a co-production of China, Taiwan, Germany and the US that traces the making of the first Chinese opera movie short *Conquering the Jun Mountain*. Similarly, Luo Yan invested in *The Pavilion of Women* (Tingyuan lide nüren, dir. Yim Ho, 2000), a Beijing Studio–Universal co-production that sees her play the lead in an orientalist tale of forbidden love between a Chinese housewife and an American missionary. Albeit released commercially in China, both films are rooted in a Euro-American perspective and both return to the Hollywood tradition of representing China as an exotic land.

A more stable mode of co-production is found in Imar (Yima), a Beijing-based company founded by American Peter Loehr (Luo Yi), with financial support from Taiwan's Rock Records and with production assistance from Xi'an Studio. Loehr concentrates on low-budget (RMB3 million), upbeat urban projects. By negotiating the best possible exhibition deals in major Chinese cities, he was able to successfully launch *Spicy Love Soup* (Aiqing malatang, 1998) and *Shower* (Xizao, 1999), both directed by Zhang Yang, and which respectively ranked fifth in 1998 and fourth in 2000. Obviously, Loehr shares the same emphasis on urban cinema as do the sixth generation, but his preference for bright, optimistic pictures, colorful images and lucid narratives distinguishes his mode of producer-centred commercial operations from that of underground or peripheral art cinema pursued by the auteur-minded sixth generation. In short, Zhang Yang's two films point to a new aesthetic from a younger group willing to assert its presence in mainstream culture.

If Loehr represents the small-scale transnational investment, then *Big Shot's Funeral* (Dawan, dir. Feng Xiaogang, 2001) can be seen as an attempt by Hollywood to explore the best way to profit from the enormous market in China at the time of its official entry into the WTO in December 2001. A US$3.5 million production partially funded by Columbia Asia, the film is a postmodern urban farce staged in Forbidden City and featuring stars from mainland China, Hong Kong and North America. The Chinese co-producers (China Film Group and Huayi Brothers Taihe) were responsible for the target box office of RMB26 million in China, but frenetic promotion and a combination of bids for exhibition rights and split box office produced a better than expected result. From its premiere on 21 December 2001 to 31 January 2002, nationwide revenue totaled RMB38 million, with RMB11 million from Beijing, RMB5.2 million from Shanghai and RMB2 million each from Shenzhen and Sichuan province (Deng 2002). In the WTO age of transnational capitalism, post-socialist China has proved its worth in generating record box-office revenues.

CONCLUSION: ART, CAPITAL AND POLITICS IN THE AGE OF THE WTO

As illustrated by *Big Shot's Funeral*, commercial operations have dominated the mainland market in recent years. The intensity of business competition is such that *Hero* (Yingxiong, dir. Zhang Yimou, 2002) soon broke the record set by *Big Shot's Funeral*. With an astonishing production cost of RMB250 million (US$31 million) and a promotion cost of RMB15 million (see Table 8.2, p. 283), Zhang's martial arts epic features leading Hong Kong and mainland stars. Backed by Miramax, this China–Hong Kong co-production aimed to compete with *Big Shot's Funeral* and *Crouching Tiger, Hidden Dragon*, two money-makers distributed overseas by Sony Pictures. After a long period of intense media hype, *Hero* premiered on 20 December 2002 on the mainland. It grossed RMB98 million in one week and more than doubled the four-week domestic receipts of Feng's comedy a year before, moving eventually to claim a record RMB241.68 million in the domestic market and an equally extraordinary record in East and Southeast Asia by February 2003 (S. Huang 2003; Y. Yu 2003).[18]

If the production and promotion of *Big Shot's Funeral* was predominantly commercial in nature, as evidenced by a long list of sponsoring Chinese companies whose names and products are on display in the film, the promotion for *Hero* was as much political as – if not more than – commercial. As Chen Kaige did with *The Emperor and the Assassin*, Zhang Yimou held a much-publicized premiere of *Hero* inside the Great Hall of People on Tiananmen Square, thereby reinforcing the impression of state sponsorship of his 'entertainment' project. But Zhang's complicity with the state did not escape public scrutiny. Arguably, the government's diligent crackdown on video piracy of *Hero* constituted the favor the state returned for Zhang's outstanding service to mainstream ideology since the late 1990s. Indeed, Zhang was commissioned to shoot the promotional video for China's bid for the 2008 Olympics in Beijing, and the surge of nationalist pride in the wake of China's success situates Zhang in a new alliance of art, capital and politics. Just as capital is complicit with politics in Feng Xiaogang's postmodern farce about post-socialist China, in the eyes of many Chinese critics, art is complicit with politics in Zhang's symbolic submission to tyrannical power in a new allegory of the unified China as *tianxia* (literally, 'under the heaven').

Nonetheless, the politics of commodification of art aside, blockbusters from Feng and Zhang are merely part of the flourishing scene in mainland feature production. What deserves our attention equally is the emergence of a newer group of talents in the new millennium. In 2002 alone eleven young directors made their debuts, in part because the Film Bureau now permits private companies to enter production without using studio labels. Contrary to early sixth generation films, which dwell on personal frustration and symbolic rebellion, new directors address social issues without always compromising their artistic visions and, in some cases, demonstrate a high level of sophistication in making genre films. At the 2002 Beijing College Film Festival, *The Missing Gun* (Xunqiang, dir. Lu Chuan, 2002), a detective film mixing humor and suspense with Sichuan dialect, won the best first film prize, and *Spring Subway* (Kaiwang chuntian de ditie, dir. Zhang Yibai, 2002), a study of triangular love relationships, was voted as the audience's favorite. From the perspective of the industry, the recent flourish of new private productions simultaneously announces the disintegration of the state studios' monopoly on film production and the advent of a new *horizontal* mode of risk-sharing co-productions open to media and cultural enterprises.

While small-budget productions provide a venue for aspiring new directors, the WTO pressure has compelled the state industry to proceed with large-scale *vertical* integration of production, distribution and exhibition. In 2001 the Film Bureau approved the establishment of three more film groups (*jituan*) in China. In addition to Beijing-based China Film Group, Shanghai Film Group, Shanghai Yongle Film Group and Changchun-based North China Film Group, three more cross-regional corporations came into being: South China Film Group centered on Guangzhou-based Pearl River Studio, Northwest Film Group centered on Xi'an Studio and Southwest Film Group centered on Chengdu-based Emei Studio. Ostensibly, the PRC leadership believes that *size* matters in competition with Hollywood, especially when the latter will soon triple its annual import of blockbusters and is allowed to own up to a 49 per cent stake in a Chinese exhibition venue or in an audio-visual product company.

In general, the opposite line of thinking has prevailed in Taiwan, where the leadership has long abandoned state-run film production and has been content with giving out annual guidance funds as token support for island-made award-winning features. After the success of *Double Vision* (Shuangtong, dir. Chen Kuo-Fu, 2002), a Nan Fang Film and Columbia Asia co-production, the GIO has expressed interest in promoting Taiwan cinema and has proposed to require theaters to reserve 20 per cent of their screen time for Taiwan-produced films and to subsidize those theaters that comply with the proposed requirements (Rosen 2002a). How it will actually proceed remains to be seen.

The earlier success of *Crouching Tiger, Hidden Dragon* has certainly boosted the confidence of some private companies. For example, Peggy Chiao's Arc Light teamed up with Pyramide Production in France and launched a transregional project of six city films, ambitiously titled 'Tales of Three Cities' (Taipei, Hong Kong and Beijing). At the 2001 Berlin Film Festival, their first films generated critical acclaim. *Betelnut Beauty* (Ai ni ai wo, dir. Lin Cheng-sheng, 2001), set in Taipei, won the Silver Bear for best director and *Beijing Bicycle* won another Silver Bear as well as a grand jury prize. The third film, *Blue Gate Crossing* (Lanse damen, dir. Yee Chih-yen, 2002), a sweet Taipei tale of adolescent romance, also met with a warm reception in Europe. As planned, Chiao's subsequent films will similarly feature young directors and address Hong Kong, Beijing and then Taipei again.

Chiao's geocultural mapping of changing Chinese cities represents an alliance of art and capital drastically different from that of Zhang Yimou. First, Chiao does not seek high-profile political support either in mainland China or in Taiwan; rather, she prefers to fashion an identity for her projects as artistic or even auteur-based. Second, Chiao's projects cultivate emerging talents and emphasize both the multiplicities that constitute China and the similarities beyond geopolitical boundaries – similarities discerned in the visions and styles of young filmmakers from different Chinese cities. Third, as products of transnational investment, Chiao's projects are *export oriented* and therefore no longer tied to one market in particular. Like her Taiwan colleagues such as Edward Yang and Tsai Ming-liang, Chiao has become a globetrotting cosmo-politan who targets overseas sales more than the local market in Taiwan, where foreign films accounted for 96 per cent of exhibition revenues in 2001 (GIO 2001: 280).

Compared with Hollywood's absolute domination in Taiwan, the 60 per cent of foreign representation of Hong Kong's 2002 box-office may look pretty good to outsiders, but the Hong Kong film industry has suffered great losses in the new millennium. After a steady increase in overall box-office receipts of 11 per cent in 2000 and 9 per cent in 2001, total receipts declined 17 per cent to HK$862.6 million and the box office for Hong Kong features dropped 24 per cent to HK$347.5 million in 2002. Whereas 239 foreign films were exhibited in 2002, only ninety-two Hong Kong features were released in the same year; sixty-seven of these were film releases and twenty-five were released on digital video (see Tables 5.2 and 8.1, pp. 155–6, 261).

One encouraging sign was that *Infernal Affairs* (Wujian dao, dir. Andrew Lau, Alan Mak, 2002), a Media Asia production, grossed HK$43.7 million in late December 2002, beating *Harry Potter and the Chamber of Secrets* (dir. Chris Columbus, 2002), which ranked second with HK$29.2 million. Yet, besides *Infernal Affairs*, only three other Hong Kong productions made it to the bottom of the 2002 top ten (Shackleton 2003). Moreover, the miserable 4 per cent Taiwan box-office receipts shared by Hong Kong and Taiwan features in 2001 indicates the extent to which Hong Kong cinema has lost this crucial offshore market to Hollywood. Nonetheless, another positive development in 2002 was the promise from the PRC authorities that, in the age of the WTO, Hong Kong films will be excluded from the annual import quotas of blockbusters and instead will be given access to the mainland market once certain provisions are met. Again, exactly how this new 'domestic' treatment of Hong Kong films will translate into practice remains to be seen.

At this point it is appropriate to contemplate Bordwell's assessment of Hong Kong cinema: 'A local cinema definitely, but with fast-diminishing resources. A regional cinema for decades, but retreating before Hollywood's imperial advance. A diasporan cinema, chiefly on video' (2000: 82). Admittedly, after decades of successful regional expansion and global marketing, Hong Kong cinema has repositioned itself locally in economic and cultural realms since the late 1990s, and Fruit Chan's and Ann Hui's recent features represent such a new localism at work. Evidence for this 'local turn' is also found in the acquisition of Shaw Brothers film collections by Hong Kong-based Celestial Pictures (Tianying), which selects classic Hong Kong titles and releases them in digitally restored DVD and VCD formats to the delight of film fans, not necessarily 'diasporan', around the world. However, the fact that the CEO of Celestial Pictures, William Pfeiffer, used to work for Disney in Tokyo and Sony Pictures in Hong Kong and India only reveals the surface of a complicated network of multinational operations (including Malaysia and Singapore) behind a fierce competition over 'regional' dominance in entertainment and media industries (Curtin 1999). Indeed, to position Celestial Pictures further in line with transnational capitalism, Miramax has bought the North American rights to its Shaw Brothers package.

In comparison, Taiwan cinema has never successfully sustained itself as a regional cinema for long and has now almost lost its identity as a local cinema insomuch as its local audience is concerned. Not without irony, the 'local' or the 'national' in Taiwan cinema has received increasing attention in academic studies as well as international film festivals, when all the while Taiwan filmmakers have pushed Taiwan cinema far beyond the island's borders and made it an appreciable presence in international art cinema. Among all three Chinas, the mainland is the only place where the pride of 'national cinema' is still accentuated in media coverage, but official nationalism propagated by leitmotif films pales in comparison with new directors' conscientious local concerns and the transnational packaging of big-budget commercial productions.[19]

In conclusion, Chinese cinema – as exemplified by film production, distribution and exhibition in the mainland, Hong Kong, Taiwan and overseas – has definitely exceeded the model of a national cinema. Locally situated, regionally connected, transnationally imagined and globally circulated, Chinese cinema has entered the new millennium with a cosmopolitan outlook, a flourish of transnational imaginaries, an urgent sense of crisis and an eagerness to compete in the era of globalization.

NOTES

1 INTRODUCTION: NATIONAL CINEMA AND CHINA

1 The Taiwan government has revised its policy and now classifies films in three categories: 'domestic' (exclusively Taiwan productions), 'Hong Kong' (which ironically includes mainland productions) and 'foreign' (GIO 2003).

2 CINEMA AND NATIONAL TRADITIONS, 1896–1929

1 Throughout the book, all currencies are Chinese unless otherwise noted. Yuan is the Chinese dollar used in China up to 1949; NT$ (new Taiwan dollar) used in Taiwan since June 1949; HK$ (Hong Kong dollar) used in Hong Kong throughout; RMB (Renminbi or mainland dollar) in the PRC since October 1949. For approximate exchange rates, see Table 2.1.

2 The first Chinese theater devoted entirely to film screening is believed to be the Quanxian Garden in Tianjin, which featured American titles as early as 1906 (Min 1998).

3 Many individuals shared the kind of high rhetoric issued by Commercial Press. In the early 1920s Gu Kenfu, Zhou Jianyun and Wang Xuchang called on Chinese filmmakers to resist the offensive portrayals of the Chinese in foreign films (Luo *et al.* 1992: 1: 9, 21). Li Minwei advocated 'national salvation through film' (*dianying jiuguo*) with the conviction that 'only through education can we strengthen China, and developing the film industry is an important aid to spread education' (M. Li 1993: 86).

4 For example, a ticket for Mei Lanfang's performance in Shanghai cost 3 yuan in the early 1920s, whereas with 0.2 yuan or so one could watch a Hollywood film that had cost 1 million dollars to produce (Luo *et al.* 1992: 1: 25).

5 In addition to the superimposition of images of a giant 'golden-eyed eagle' and human characters, *Swordswoman of Huangjiang, VI* presents a high-angle point-of-view shot from the bird chasing terrorized villagers.

6 A 1960 China Film Archive catalog lists 227 films of martial arts/immortals and demons produced between 1928 and 1931: thirty in 1928, eighty-five in 1929, sixty-nine in 1930 and forty-three in 1931. Another fourteen came in 1932, thus making a total of 241 in five years (S. Li and Hu 1996: 239).

7 According to a Mingxing report, the studio made a profit of 57,394.99 yuan in 1926, lost 19,028.42 yuan in 1927, made 47,363.59 yuan profit in 1928, 25,595.79 yuan in 1929 and 25,505.94 yuan in 1930 (ZDZ 1996a: 43, 1418). The surge in 1928 owed a great deal to *The Burning of Red Lotus Temple*.

8 Apart from Shanghai, the rest of China was divided into six regions, each allocated one print in circulation: central China (Hunan, Hubei, Jiangxi and Anhui provinces), north China (Hebei, Henan, Shandong and Shanxi provinces), west China (Sichuan, Yunnan and Guizhou provinces), northeast China (Jilin, Liaoning and Helongjiang provinces), east China (Jiangsu, Zhejiang and Fujian provinces), south China (Guangdong and Guangxi provinces as well as Hong Kong and Macao). The box office in all these regions was not as predictable as that in Shanghai (Du 1988: 129).

9 Hou's 'appropriate' subjects include equality, humanism, elevation of laborers' and women's status, honesty, forgiveness, altruism, martyrdom, optimism, filiality, lofty heterosexual love and creativity (Luo *et al.* 1992: 1: 56–7). Interestingly, Hou's list of 'inappropriate' subjects resembles a great many items from the censorship laws issued by the State of Pennsylvania in 1918 and by the British government in 1922, both translated and published in *Eastern Miscellanies* (ZDZ 1996a: 144–7).

10 After the reel of 200 feet came the reel of 400 feet, and by 1926 Hou Yao noted the reel of 1,000 feet as standard (Luo *et al.* 1992: 1: 51).

3 CINEMA AND THE NATION-PEOPLE, 1930–49

1 I leave the 'golden age' in quotation marks because more research is needed to determine whether there are two distinct golden ages and, if so, what exactly distinguishes them. An alternative is to consider the 1930s and 1940s together as a 'golden age' period in which creativity was interrupted by the war.

2 In this chapter, unless otherwise specified, all titles up to and including 1936 are silent pictures; all unspecified titles following this time are sound.

3 Lianhua's fixed assets, estimated at 105,000 yuan, consisted of the studio facilities of Great China-Lily (45,000 yuan), Shanghai Minxin (40,000 yuan) and Hong Kong Minxin (20,000 yuan). In addition to Wu Xingzai's pledge of 55,000 yuan in cash, Lianhua raised over 250,000 yuan from its other cofounders, most of them in Hong Kong. The Lianhua stocks were offered at 10 yuan a share, and 150,000 yuan was thus raised from Hong Kong and Macao (M. Yu 1997: 14–15).

4 Laikwan Pang lists seventy-two such 'leftist films' (2002: 241–4) included in an official Chinese publication (ZDYYZ 1993), but I contend that listing films like *Twin Sisters* and directors like Fei Mu as 'leftist' is problematic and symptomatic of the revisionist Communist historiography of the 1980s.

5 *Chenbao* was under the control of Pan Gongzhan and *Minbao* (formerly *Minguo ribao*, Republican news) under Ye Chucang, then secretary of the KMT central committee.

6 Besides Xia Yan, the group consisted of Ah Ying, Chen Wu, Ling He and Situ Huimin.

7 For instance, the nightclub scenes, where Hu Rongrong – labeled the 'Chinese Shirley Temple' – tap dances to a cheering crowd, greatly reduce the ideological message hidden behind a series of contrasts between the rich and the poor in *A New Year's Coin* (Yasui qian, dir. Zhang Shichuan, 1937), a film based on a script by Xia Yan.

8 The numbers of Hollywood films Lu Xun watched are as follows: nine in 1928 (plus one German film), seven in 1929, one in 1930, twenty in 1931, two in 1932, five in 1933 (plus two Soviet), thirty in 1934 (plus one German and two Soviet), thirty in 1935 (plus one Soviet) and fourteen in 1936 (plus four Soviet). In terms of genre, Lu Xun preferred historical and religious subjects, but interestingly

he watched at least three Charlie Chan detective films (S. Liu and Xing 1981: 222–31).

9 Another source lists 421 imported features, 309 or 73.4 per cent of them Hollywood, in 1933 (J. Cheng *et al.* 1981: 2: 161).

10 In 1932–3, a film magazine organized China's first public election of a movie queen or king, which resulted in the crowning of Hu Die (13,582 votes), with Ruan Lingyu as close second (13,490 votes) and the actor Jin Yan in third place (13,157 votes) (ZDZ 1996a: 1338).

11 Cai Chusheng briefly served as Zheng Zhengqiu's assistant director and had worked with Sun Yu in Lianhua since 1931 (ZDZ 1996a: 1276).

12 After the release of *New Woman* in 1935, Ruan Lingyu could no longer tolerate the media coverage of her triangular love affairs and committed suicide; her funeral was a public event unprecedented in scale by any other star in Chinese film history (M. Chang 1999).

13 Some surmise that Liu Na'ou's assassination was a mistake on the KMT's part because Liu had worked for the regime before he assumed a pro-Japanese position. He co-directed a 20,000-yuan Central Film production, *Secret Codes* (Mi dianma, 1937), with Zhang Daofan, a noted KMT cultural leader who wrote the screenplay (Gongsun 1977: 2: 206–9). Liu also contributed the screenplay to *Smile Forever* (Yongyuan de weixiao, dir. Wu Cun, 1937), a Mingxing release. Earlier, Liu had worked for Yihua and contributed his first screenplay, *Romance in Tribal Mountains* (Yaoshan yanshi, dir. Yang Xiaozhong, 1933), shot on location in Guangxi province by Huang Yicuo's Yilian (Du 1988: 251). Before his assassination, Mu Shiying had stayed in Hong Kong and had directed *Night Pearl* (Ye mingzhu, 1937), a tragic story about a dance hostess (M. Yu 1997: 156).

14 However, both *Mulan Joins the Army* and *Princess Iron Fan* had been shown in Japan (G. Zuo and Yao 2001: 63).

15 The KMT regime never relaxed its censorship during the war. From 1939 to 1941, for instance, the censors in the hinterland banned 961 books and magazines and frequently harassed artists and intellectuals (D. Li 2000: 61).

16 Note these exponential rates of postwar inflation: in terms of Shanghai's wholesale price index, December 1945 was 885 times that of the early half of 1937, December 1946 was 6,816 times, December 1947 was 100,000 times, and August 1948 was 5.64 million times (Z. Wang 2000: 26). If the same index was set at 100 in September 1945, then it rose to 1,475 in September 1946, 12,534 in September 1947 and 1,368,049 in August 1948 (Eastman 1984: 174). To control the situation in 1947, Hollywood demanded that ticket prices be set in US dollars and even suspended its film releases when Chinese exhibitors refused to cooperate for fear of losing attendance. After two months, Hollywood gave in to the exhibitors because audiences were drawn to theaters showing Chinese films (Z. Wang 1998: 61).

17 There were approximately fifty theaters, with a total of 50,000 seats, in postwar Shanghai (Cambon 1995: 42; Z. Wang 2000: 30).

18 In prewar Shanghai, a movie ticket could cost up to 2 yuan, as much as that for Peking opera and double that for a dance hall. In 1947, however, an average movie ticket cost only 15.6 per cent of the price for Peking opera and 42 per cent for the dance hall. In August 1948, movie ticket prices soared to 200,000 yuan at the lowest and 1.2 million at the highest (see Table 2.2). But surprisingly, in terms of purchasing power, the cheapest movie ticket in 1948 equaled 0.313 kilogram of rice, whereas the cheapest ticket in 1936 (0.2 yuan) was equivalent to 1.875 kilogram, enough for a person's daily allowance (Z. Wang 2000: 27). A Chinese silver dollar (*yinyuan*) could exchange for US$0.218–0.363 prior to the monetary reform in November 1935. After that, China switched to *fabi* (legal tender), and

the rate was set at 1 yuan versus US$0.295 (Z. Wang 1998: 64) (see Table 2.1). For an overview of the complicated monetary situation in Republican China, see Z. Zhang 1990: 297–305.

19 These ratios were inflation-adjusted. Otherwise, at a minimum 30 billion yuan per film (in the US numerical system, as throughout this book), the postwar production cost stood at 3 million times that of the prewar one, and in Nanjing the postwar ticket soared to 1.2 million times that of the prewar price (Y. Ding 1998: 45).

20 Ironically, Zhang Daofan's edits – 'no darkness but brightness, no satire but eulogy' (Y. Ding 1998: 94) – sounded exactly like what Mao Zedong imposed on Yan'an artists in 1942, which would remain guiding CCP policy for decades.

21 In a recent selection of 200 Chinese film classics in a Hong Kong Film Critics Society poll, *Spring in a Small Town* tops the list of all-time ten best Chinese-language films (Zhao 2002: 403).

22 Sun Yu acknowledged his influence by a newspaper article on Gorky's revolutionary romanticism back in 1932 (C. Li 1991: 54).

23 For instance, Cheng Bugao recalled that, inspired by *Sunrise*, he and his cinematographer had installed the camera on a tripod and succeeded in their experiment with tracking shots without actually using tracks in the production of *Spring Silkworms* (S. Li and Hu 1996: 315). Cheng also expressed his admiration for the editing techniques that made the ending of *Way Down East* (dir. D.W. Griffith, 1920) so impressive, and one scholar suggests that Griffith's influence is visible in Cheng's rendition of the flood sequence at the end of *Wild Torrents* (Pang 2002: 148).

24 For example, one critic sees in Yuan Muzhi's *Street Angel* a successful integration of the bitter-sweet Chaplin comedy, the heavy ambience of German expressionism and the smooth flow of Jean Renoir's camera movements and images (Hong Kong Art Center 1984). Yet, Ma Ning argues that *Street Angel* goes beyond foreign influences such as the point-of-view shot and montage because it has incorporated two distinctively Chinese types of discourse: 'journalistic' (insertion of newspaper clippings) and 'popular' (folk songs and magic shows) (1989: 26).

25 Zheng Zhengqiu's rhetoric sounded nearly identical to that of Chen Wu, who also charted out the anti-imperialism, anti-feudalism direction for Chinese cinema (ZDYYZ 1993: 66–74). Both Wang's and Zheng's articles were published in the inaugural issue of *Mingxing Monthly* (May 1933), edited by Ke Ling, a leftist affiliate not as radical as many of his colleagues.

4 CINEMATIC REINVENTION OF THE NATIONAL IN TAIWAN, 1896–1978

1 After its relocation to Taiwan in 1949, China Motion Pictures reduced its personnel from 200 plus to 106 (L. Ye 1995: 44). As late as 1963, including twenty-four new posts, Taiwan Studio had merely seventy-eight employees (Guojia dianying 1996: 110). In comparison with the PRC, there were about 1,700 employees in Shanghai Studio alone in 1953.

2 Ye Longyan lists seven titles, one as 'reportedly' (1998: 233–43), but Chen Feibao mentions only five (1988: 15). In this chapter, unless otherwise indicated and excluding titles mentioned in the previous chapters, all titles before 1960 are sound films in black and white (b/w) and all titles since 1960 are color sound films.

3 During her first visit to Taiwan in January 1941, Li Xianglan gave three concerts a day for three days at Taipei's 1,500-seat Great World Theater to full-house audiences, who paid 0.7–1.3 yen per ticket. In 1943 Li came to Taiwan to star in a

film co-produced by the Taiwan governor's office and managed to visit Liu Na'ou's tomb (L. Ye 1998: 300–9).

4 Robert Chen uses the word 'destruction' to describe this postwar phase (Y. Zhang and Xiao 1998: 50), while Ye Longyan sees it as 'the darkest period' in Taiwan film history (1995: 23).

5 More specifically, a theater owner might get just NT$1.57 out of the NT$10 ticket price after paying the producer and the government. The latter typically charged NT$2 for the nation-building fund, NT$1.25 for defense, NT$1 for assistance for military families, NT$0.4 for the relief fund for suffering mainland compatriots, entertainment taxes and other contemporary taxes for flood relief, education and so on (R. Chen 1993: 32). However, the exact percentage of taxes varied from year to year. A 1971 government report indicates that three kinds of taxes accounted for 32.138 per cent of a ticket's price. At NT$19 per ticket, the theater received NT$6.1 after splitting the revenue with the distributor, but the report also mentions the education tax soon to be added to theater tickets (Z. Wei 1993: 98).

6 Lu Feiyi questioned the legitimacy of KMT's ownership of CMPC because the company was in part based on twenty or so Japanese-owned theaters and should therefore belong to the state rather than the Party. In addition, Agricultural Education Studio itself was a state enterprise and its structures built on loans provided by the state-owned Agricultural Bank (F. Lu 1998: 47).

7 For Japan, the 1956 quota was eight films, but the 1957 quota rose to twenty-four. Because Chiang Kai-shek was reportedly upset by the front-page newspaper ads for Japanese films, the government ruled that Japanese films could open only at two theater chains and could not run beyond fifteen days (R. Huang 2001: 64).

8 The state subsidies to overseas Chinese producers could be as high as HK$300,000 in 1956. The export ratio to Japan at the time was worth NT$200,000–300,000 a piece, which was approximate to the production cost of a Taiwanese-dialect picture (F. Lu 1998: 74–8).

9 There were two ways to gain tax advantages. First, one could import more negatives than needed and sell the remainder for profits since negatives were in high demand. Second, one could conspire with an overseas company and report more negatives than were actually imported, thus applying for more US dollars and selling the difference on the black market. From 1951 to 1958, for private companies, exchange rates for imports (NT$32.28 = US$1) were considerably higher than those for exports (NT$26.35 = US$1). These tax advantages provided extra incentives to Taiwan film production during the 1950 and 1960s, until the margins of exchange rates for imports and exports became insignificant (F. Lu 1998: 57, 80).

10 The KMT censors shut down ten periodicals in the mid-1950s, among them *Film and Theater Magazine*. A large number of martial arts novels were also banned. Although no confrontation with the regime occurred in film circles, several people were investigated for various reasons (F. Lu 1998: 69, 97–8). Bai Ke, the first head of Taiwan Studio, was executed after his wife was identified as an underground Communist. Another account has it that Bai committed suicide in prison (L. Ye 1995: 48).

11 The Amoy-dialect film arrived in Taiwan in 1949, but this subgenre did not become popular until 1954 (L. Ye 1999: 60–1). For sample titles as well as their production companies in Hong Kong, see F. Chen 1988: 95.

12 Twenty-three Amoy-dialect films were exhibited in Taiwan in 1955, thirty-seven in 1956, twenty-six in 1957, thirteen in 1958, twenty-four in 1959, only one in 1960 (L. Ye 1999: 81–3).

13 One source indicates a temporary halt of Japanese imports in 1962 (Z. Wei 1993: 89).

14 Li Quanxi, a dialect director elected by newspaper readers in 1965 as one of the ten best directors in Taiwan, confirms that he used to shoot three films per month for three years even during the low season between the two waves. Including work on postproduction, he could still turn out two films per month. Not surprisingly, he was credited with twenty-one titles in 1962 (Guojia dianying 1994: 67–76).

15 As Lu Feiyi observes, while Italian neo-realism exposes social evils without prescribing easy solutions, healthy realism entrusts solutions to traditional ethics and humanism and thus distinguishes itself from socialist realism, which entrusts the future to Communist practice in the era of socialism (1998: 104).

16 Based on this information, the average ticket price was NT$11.64 in 1963, compared with NT$2.3 in 1949 (up 406.1 per cent).

17 *Dragon Gate Inn* had a 41-day run in Seoul and grossed HK$2.25 million, setting a record in Hong Kong in 1968.

18 NT$5,518,642 from *Storms Over the Yangtze River* in 1969 was comparable to NT$5,606,174 from *Hsi Shih* in 1965 and was not surpassed until 1972, when the craze for Bruce Lee films hit Taiwan (R. Huang 2001: 53–5).

19 In 1975 CMPC invested NT$10 million and built a culture city on its Taipei premises, which was opened to the public interested in the history of costumes, architecture, film technology and underwater photography (F. Chen 1988: 187).

20 The numbers of Qiong Yao's romances among the annual top ten Chinese films in Taipei and their respective rankings are as follows: two in 1966 (placed second and seventh), two in 1968 (fourth and ninth), one in 1969 (fourth), one in 1971 (second), two in 1973 (second and fourth), two in 1974 (second and seventh), two in 1975 (first and second) and one in 1976 (place unknown) (R. Huang 2001: 27).

21 Ranked first and second in 1975, Bai Jingrui's two films grossed NT$12.6 and 11.5 million respectively, then the record highs.

22 Liao Jinfeng admits that he was not aware of Taiwanese-dialect films before 1989. The official documentation of the time was such that only five dialect titles were recorded for 1963 when eighty-nine were actually produced (2001: 11–13).

5 CINEMATIC REVIVAL OF THE REGIONAL IN HONG KONG, 1945–78

1 From 1960 to 1965 Hong Kong's production output exceeded that of Hollywood but trailed behind Japan and India (Jarvie 1977: 75). From 1960 to 1965 Hong Kong's economy sustained an average growth of 13.6 per cent a year (HKIFF 1996: 66). From 1969 to 1978, the average growth rate was 9.3 per cent, in spite of the 1974 oil crisis (with 2.1 per cent growth) and the 1975 recession (0.4 per cent) (Cheuk 1999: 19).

2 During the strike, over 200,000 Hong Kong workers crossed the border to Guangzhou, where local agencies provided them with food and shelter. The strike ended after the appointment of a new Hong Kong governor, who offered HK$20 million to the workers in compensation and approved Chinese representation in the legislative council (M. Yu 1996: 159–61).

3 According to Yu Muyun, *Two Orphan Girls on the Battlefield*, a film Tianyi shot for a Guangzhou company in 1932, was the first Cantonese talkie and the first partial color picture in China (1997: 31–2). Yu's view is corroborated by a 1934 Tianyi document, which lists the film as sound (ZDZ 1996a: 59). In this chapter,

unless otherwise indicated and except for those already mentioned in the previous chapters, all films produced after 1932 are Cantonese talkies and all films after 1960 are in color.

4 As early as May 1919 a Hong Kong newspaper reported activities of three film censors, who ordered cuts to those parts of films that had already passed the American or the British censorship but were deemed inappropriate for Hong Kong audiences (M. Yu 1996: 92).

5 One exception was Zi Luolian who, at age 17, was misled by a false advertisement and served as a supporting actress in the sole Japanese-produced occupation-era feature, *The Attack on Hong Kong* (Xianggang gonglüe zhan, 1942).

6 Out of all the films produced before 1942 merely four titles survived in extant prints, most of them collected by the China Film Archive in Beijing.

7 The fact Zhang Shankun was in debt is further corroborated by the KMT regime's decision to lift its sanctions on those titles Zhang had produced before Great Wall pledged its allegiance to the PRC. Zhang was able to profit from the Taiwan market to help settle his debt (R. Huang 2001: 28).

8 The Hong Kong Overseas Chinese Education Association launched the first purification campaign in 1935 in imitation of a similar effort in Australia that attempted to resist Hollywood sex and violence (Du 1988: 79). Luo Mingyou and Li Minwei, with support from Hong Kong Christian groups, initiated the second purification campaign in Hong Kong in 1938 (M. Yu 1997: 115–16, 188–9).

9 Union Film Enterprises' *Spring* and *Autumn* were shown in mainland cities (most likely with Mandarin soundtracks). In 1957 the readers of *Beijing Daily* cast 6,853 votes to elect these two titles as among their five most favorite films and cast 4,424 votes to elect Ng Cho-fan as among their five most favorite stars (ZDZ 1998: 75).

10 The most famous postwar radio storyteller was Li Wo, who improvised tear-jerking tales for Radio Fengxing in Guangzhou (1945), Radio Rediffusion in Hong Kong (Lidi husheng, 1949), Radio Villa Verde in Macao (Lücun, 1951) and Commercial Radio in Hong Kong (Shangye, 1957). He later printed his tales in newspaper installments, which were then collected and published in book form. From 1949 to 1964, over forty of Li Wo's airwave novels were adapted into Cantonese films (HKIFF 1986: 57–66).

11 Eileen Chang's other contributions include *Tale of Two Wives* (Rencai liangde, dir. Yue Feng, 1957), *June Bride* (Liuyue xinniang, dir. Tang Huang, 1960; b/w), *Father Takes a Bride* (Xiao ernü, dir. Wang Tianlin, 1963; b/w) and *Please Remember Me* (Yiqu nanwang, dir. Zhong Qiwen, 1964) (HKIFF 1998b: 126–76).

12 The slight decrease of those below age 15 was matched by a gradual increase in the percentage of those between the age of 15 and 34 in the population: from 29.7 per cent in 1971 to 35.1 per cent in 1976 and 40.7 per cent in 1981 (HKIFF 1988: 76). The population was estimated at four million in 1970 and would grow to five million in the 1980s. Given the stronger purchasing power of Hong Kong residents in the 1970s, the number of potential movie viewers was tremendous. A 1971 report indicates that on average Hong Kong residents watched twenty-one movies per year (Cheuk 1999: 11–20). Although this was down from the peak of 100 million attendances in 1967 (or twenty-seven times per capita), it remained comparable to 1959 (twenty-two times) when the city had a population of close to 3 million (Bordwell 2000: 34, 66) (see Table 5.1).

13 Sil-Metropole's releases are counted as 'domestic' productions in PRC film publications, thus revealing its source of funding.

14 Before Tang Shuxuan's case, *Yesterday, Today and Tomorrow* (Zuotian, jintian, mingtian, dir. Lung Kong, 1970) fell victim to 'probably the first instance of

303

political censorship in the Hong Kong cinema' when an order came to cut and re-shoot the film. The pre-release censorship order came as a result of a protest by the New China News Agency, the official Beijing representative in Hong Kong before the 1997 handover (Teo 2000: 103–4)

15 RTV would become ATV (Asian Television, Yazhou dianshi) in 1982 and waged an all-out war against TVB, then controlled by Run Run Shaw.

16 Teo uses the term 'cultural nationalism' to refer to the tendency of Chinese directors in Hong Kong and Taiwan to instill morale and pride in the audience (1997: 23).

6 CINEMA AND THE NATION-STATE IN THE PRC, 1949–78

1 A report from July 1949 indicates that 130 American and British features were shown in Shanghai (roughly 63.7 per cent of the total exhibited) and their viewers were around 932,000 or 51.2 per cent of total attendance. By June 1950 audiences for Hollywood movies had dwindled to 270,000 or 14 per cent of total attendance (Du 1988: 395–6).

2 In this chapter, all films are color unless otherwise indicated.

3 Among these film casualties of the Anti-Rightist Campaign, three did not survive to see themselves officially rehabilitated in 1979. Shi Hui apparently committed suicide in 1957 at age 42, Sha Meng died in 1964 at age 57, and Lü Ban in 1976 at age 63.

4 In terms of shot composition, *Third Sister Liu* represents an attempt to approximate the viewing experience afforded by the traditional hand-scroll painting, something Zheng Junli also sought in his *Spring Comes to the Withered Tree* (Kumu fengchun, 1961). In addition to drawing inspiration from traditional theater and folk songs, Zheng intentionally used the horizontal panning and tracking shots of interrelated images to capture the changing perspectives of scroll painting (N. Lin 1985; Luo *et al.* 1992: 1: 638–49).

5 Another new sub-category of animation is folded-paper figures, which is not as popular as other animation styles.

6 According to an official estimate, sixteen film industry people were persecuted to death in Shanghai, seven in Beijing, and an unspecified number in Changchun (H. Chen 1989: 1: 324). Another source indicates that 126 film artists died during the Cultural Revolution (Du 1988: 398).

7 In 1981 China's Supreme Court sentenced Jiang Qing to death, a verdict reduced to life imprisonment in 1983. In 1991 Jiang committed suicide in prison.

8 Jiang Qing was born to a shop-owner and his concubine. Unable to tolerate the abuse from Jiang's father, her mother left the family, taking Jiang with her. Jiang's mother took a job as a maid in a household whose second son, Kang Sheng, would decades later become Jiang's political sponsor and collaborator. Jiang studied drama in 1929, got married and divorced in 1930 at age 16, and in 1931 became the partner of Yu Qiwei, upon whose recommendation she joined the CCP in 1933.

7 CINEMA AND NATIONAL/REGIONAL CULTURES, 1979–89

1 In around 1980 very few households had television sets in mainland China, and the programs were predominantly propagandist, educational and informational

(e.g., news, weather forecast and adult learning classes). As late as 1988, household television ownership was only 48 per cent nationwide (Berry 1991: 115).

2 The 'fifth generation' was so named because many members came from the fifth directing class (of 1982) in the Beijing Film Academy's history. Their education included staging spoken dramas and watching Chinese and foreign film classics (Ni 2003).

3 Two subsequent films on the subject were banned: *The Dove Tree* (Gezi shu, dir. Wu Ziniu, 1985) and *In Their Prime* (Tamen zheng nianqing, dir. Zhou Xiaowen, 1986), both fifth generation works.

4 In addition to those mentioned in this chapter, women directors active in the 1980s include Dong Kena, Shi Shujun, Shi Xiaohua, Wang Haowei and Wang Junzheng (J. Dai 1995).

5 In 1994 the GIO added a fourth category, 'protection advised', which requires that children between 6 and 12 years of age be accompanied by parents, relatives, friends or teachers.

6 The impact of videotapes is noticeable in Taiwan. Annual movie attendance stood at 250 million in 1981 when the ownership of VCRs was 3.75 per cent. In 1982 VCR ownership increased to 5.83 per cent whereas movie attendance dropped to 192 million (down 23.2 per cent). In 1983 VCR ownership surged to 9.09 per cent, and movie attendance fell to 135 million (down another 29.7 per cent) (F. Lu 1998: 245). Of course, other factors contributed to the decline in attendance.

7 Only five titles (about 10 per cent) of New Taiwan Cinema were box-office hits: *Papa, Can You Hear Me Sing?*, *A Flower in the Rainy Night*, *Growing Up*, *Lao Mo's Second Spring* and *Kuei-mei, a Woman*, all produced between 1983 and 1985.

8 Two former left-wing studios, Great Wall and Sun Luen, produced *Shaolin Temple* under a temporary name, 'Zhongyuan' (central plain), in 1982. Later that year, the two studios and Phoenix merged to form Sil-Metropole.

8 CINEMA AND THE TRANSNATIONAL IMAGINARY

1 In Hong Kong the film ranked fifteenth at the box office in 2000 with HK$14,764,598 (from 6 July to 20 September) but it also grossed HK$2,309,145 in a second run from 4 January to 9 May 2001. The combined revenues should make it eleventh in the 2000 chart. The film's global exhibition revenues are estimated at US$205 million (S. Huang 2003).

2 These statistics are taken from S. Chang 2002: 88; F. Lie 2002: 63–4; ZDZ 1998: 233–4. In addition, *Royal Tramp, I–II* (Luding ji, dir. Wong Jing, 1992) features Stephen Chiau and took HK$77 million, the combined gross takings of the film's two parts shown separately (Teo 1997: 248).

3 In the mid-1990s the typical bottom line was between HK$9 and 10 million, of which one-third went to the cast (normally including at least one big star), one-quarter to other personnel, and one-quarter to production and post-production. Exhibition required twenty-five to thirty prints at HK$10,000 each, and advertising consumed a maximum HK$1 million (Bordwell 2000: 119). As indicated by the box-office figures, even top-grossing features with Jackie Chan and Stephen Chiau could only rake in between HK$40 and 50 million, which means that Hong Kong cinema depended entirely on overseas sales to generate profits. This was also the case in the early 1980s, when the average production costs per title were between HK$0.7 and 0.8 million and a box-office gross of

HK$1 million was considered a hit. Typically, after splitting 60 per cent of the revenue with the exhibitor, the producer could expect only HK$0.2 million in income once all other expenses were subtracted, such as 17.5 per cent for entertainment taxes, 15 per cent for distribution and 12 per cent for promotion. The resulting HK$0.6 million deficit could be reversed by overseas sales, which normally generated a total of between HK$0.75 million and 0.3 million in Singapore and Malaysia, HK$0.2 million in Taiwan, HK$0.15 million in Europe and North America, and HK$0.1 million from the rest of the world. But if a film failed to generate HK$0.8 million at the Hong Kong box office, the producer would most likely lose money (HKFA 1997a: 15–18).

4 Compared with HK$1.24 billion grossed by Hong Kong releases in 1992, the 1996 figure of HK$656.57 million represents a decrease of 47 per cent in four years (see Table 8.1). The increased ticket prices partially made up for the 100 per cent decline in the number of ticket sales. Indeed, since the early 1990s ticket prices had almost doubled to US$7 (or HK$55) in the late 1990s (Curtin 1999: 39). For instance, in 1991 ticket prices were raised from HK$26–30 to $30–36, an increase of 15 to 20 per cent (S. Chang 2002: 87) (see Table 5.3).

5 Nonetheless, Jackie Chan's star power was unmistakable overseas. From 1982 and 1994, films directed by or starring Chan topped the Taipei Chinese box office ten times (T. Li 1997: 264–9). Also in Taipei, Chan's *Mr Nice Guy* (Yige haoren, dir. Sammo Hung, 1997) alone grossed NT$43.1 million, compared with NT$11.36 million for *Once Upon a Time in China and America* featuring Jet Li in the same year. Even so, *Mr Nice Guy* failed to rank among the top twenty of the 1997 Taipei box-office hits, which were all Hollywood blockbusters with revenues ranging from NT$43.4 to 387.8 million, the latter an all-time record set by *Titanic* (Guojia dianying 1998: 85–90). In comparison, while *Titanic* ranked first at the 1997 Hong Kong box office, *Mr Nice Guy* ranked third and *Once Upon a Time in China and America* fifth. Once a dominant force, by 1998 Hong Kong films had but a meager market share of less than 2.4 per cent in Taiwan, where a Hong Kong title earned a pitiable amount of NT$3,210 (or US$100) in the golden slot of the January holidays (Guojia dianying 1999: 65; Rosen 2002a).

6 The new ratings were first imposed administratively in 1987 when the news broke that film censorship, in place since 1953, was illegal and that the colonial government knew about the situation as early as 1972. In 1994 an amendment to the 1988 ordinance was approved, which differentiates between children and young persons by dividing Category 2 to 2A (unsuitable for those under 12) and 2B (unsuitable for all under 18) (Davis and Yeh 2001: 20).

7 Wong Jing's record is second only to Stephen Chiau, whose forty-four films in the 1990s grossed a total of HK$1.124 billion (F. Lie 2002: 64). Not surprisingly, Wong directed several Chiau films early in the decade.

8 The story was very different in Taipei, where *The Storm Riders* grossed NT$20.3 million but did not make it to the top thirty in 1998 (Guojia dianying 1999: 59–67).

9 Inaugurated in 1995, the film book series from Yuanliu, one of Taiwan's leading publishers, stood at ninety-eight titles in June 2001.

10 In Taipei, *Flowers of Shanghai* grossed NT$2,690,990 and *The Hole* NT$321,960, both insignificant amounts compared with the NT$33,794,700 made by *Scream, II* (dir. Wes Craven, 1997), which ranked a mere thirtieth in the 1998 Taipei box office (Guojia dianying 1999: 68). *Flowers of Shanghai* and *The Hole* each received a GIO guidance fund of NT$10 million.

11 In 1990 the GIO announced the increased monetary prizes to winners at major international film festivals: NT$30 million for the best picture award and

NT\$3 million for an individual's award. Earlier in 1983, as the GIO director, James Soong (Song Chuyu) set the prize at NT\$10 million for the winner of the best picture award at the Asia-Pacific Film Festival.

12 Originally from Malaysia, Tsai stayed in Taipei after his college education and received a total of NT\$28 million for his first four projects. After he withdrew from the 1998 Golden Horse Awards in protest against some 'incompetent' jurors, his detractors called for the government to demand repayment of his guidance funds because legally Tsai was not a Taiwan citizen. After consulting with the Overseas Chinese Commission, the GIO confirmed Tsai's resident status was equivalent to that of a Taiwan citizen (W. Huang 1999: 240–2).

13 In 2001, for instance, domestic films accounted only for RMB280 million or one-third of the total annual revenue. In 2002, domestic films accounted for RMB500 million or 55.6 per cent of the total – a dramatic increase thanks largely to Zhang Yimou's co-production *Hero*.

14 In early 2000, fifteen Chengdu theaters in Sichuan province reduced ticket prices from RMB40 to RMB5 for both domestic and foreign films and movie attendance surged six times accordingly, setting a box-office record of RMB70,000 per day.

15 For various reasons, blockbuster imports did not reach the limit of ten titles in most years (Rosen 2002b). Now that China has officially joined the WTO, Hollywood imports will gradually increase to fifty; twenty of them will be split and the rest for flat fees.

16 A RMB30 million production, *A Time to Remember* managed to gross RMB6 million in Beijing and RMB25 million nationwide but still incurred a loss of RMB10 million after splitting revenues with exhibitors. On the other hand, *Dreams Come True* cost less than RMB4 million to produce but raked in RMB11.5 million in Beijing and over RMB30 million nationwide. In comparison, *Titanic* earned a record of RMB320 million or 22.2 per cent of the 1998 box office in China (Deng 2002: 16; S. Huang 2003; W. Huang 1999: 150–9; Yin 1999: 24).

17 The State Administration of Radio, Television and Film (Guangdian zongju), formerly the Ministry of Radio, Television and Film, supervises the 'Huabiao Awards', which is the new name for the excellent film awards administered by the same ministry and, before it, the Ministry of Culture.

18 Although *Hero*'s performance in Hong Kong was not as impressive as in mainland China, with HK\$19.8 million in ten days the epic ranked fourth in the top ten Hong Kong features and tenth in the overall top ten in 2002 (Shackleton 2003). By mid-February 2003, the film had grossed HK\$26.7 million in Hong Kong, US\$10 million in South Korea, US\$7 million in Taiwan and Southeast Asia. The film's exhibition rights were sold at US\$20 million to North America and US\$8 million to Japan. Additionally, while the film's overseas audio-video rights reached US\$10 million, its domestic audio-video rights were auctioned for RMB17.8 million and its tie-in domestic theater advertising took in RMB20 million (Dangdai dianying 2003: 5; Y. Yu 2003: 30).

19 One example of such recent local concerns is *Cala, My Dog* (Kala shi tiao gou, dir. Lu Xuechang, 2002), a Beijing tale featuring Ge You as an ordinary worker who desperately tries to save his unregistered pet dog confiscated by the police.

BIBLIOGRAPHY

Abbas, Ackbar (1997) *Hong Kong: Culture and the Politics of Disappearance*, Minneapolis: University of Minnesota Press.

Althusser, Louis (1971) *Lenin and Philosophy and Other Essays*, translated by Ben Brewster, New York: Monthly Review Press.

Berry, Chris (1982) 'Stereotypes and Ambiguities: An Examination of the Feature Films of the Chinese Cultural Revolution', *Journal of Asian Culture* 6: 37–72.

—— (ed.) (1991) *Perspectives on Chinese Cinema*, London: BFI Publishing.

—— (1994) 'A Nation T(w/o)o: Chinese Cinema(s) and Nationhood(s)', in W. Dissanayake (ed.) *Colonialism*, 42–64.

—— (1998) 'If China Can Say No, Can China Make Movies? Or, Do Movies Make China? Rethinking National Cinema and National Agency', *Boundary 2* 25,3: 129–50.

Bordwell, David (2000) *The Planet Hong Kong: Popular Cinema and the Art of Entertainment*, Cambridge, Mass.: Harvard University Press.

Browne, Nick (1994) 'Society and Subjectivity: On the Political Economy of Chinese Melodrama', in N. Browne *et al.* (eds), *New Chinese Cinemas*, 40–56.

Browne, Nick, Paul G. Pickowicz, Vivian Sobchack and Esther Yau (eds) (1994) *New Chinese Cinemas: Forms, Identities, Politics*, London: Cambridge University Press.

Cambon, Marie (1995) 'The Dream Palaces of Shanghai: American Films in China's Largest Metropolis Prior to 1949', *Asian Cinema* 7,2: 34–45.

Chan, Ching Wai (Chen Qingwei) (2000) *Xianggang dianying gongye jiegou ji shichang fenxi* (The structure and marketing analysis of Hong Kong film industry), Hong Kong: Dianying shuangzhoukan.

Chang, Michael G. (1999) 'The Good, the Bad, and the Beautiful: Movie Actresses and Public Discourse in Shanghai, 1920s–1930s', in Y. Zhang (ed.) *Cinema and Urban Culture in Shanghai*, 128–59.

Chang, Shi (2002) '90 niandai Xianggang dianying dashi ji' (Chronicle of major events in Hong Kong cinema of the 1990s), *Dangdai dianying* 2: 87–90.

Chen, Feibao (1988) *Taiwan dianying shihua* (A history of Taiwan cinema), Beijing: ZDC.

—— (1994) 'Chutan Taiwan dianying daoyan jiegou jiqi dianying meixue tezheng' (Generations of Taiwan directors and their aesthetic features), *Dianying yishu* 1: 36–9, 2: 24–30.

Chen, Huangmei (ed.) (1989) *Dangdai Zhongguo dianying* (Contemporary Chinese cinema), 2 vols, Beijing: Zhongguo shehui kexue chubanshe.

Chen, Kaige and Tony Rayns (1989) *King of the Children and the New Chinese Cinema*, London: Faber and Faber.

Chen, Mo (1996) *Daoguang xiaying mengtaiqi: Zhongguo wuxia dianying lun* (Montages of swords and knights: Chinese martial arts films), Beijing: ZDC.

Chen, Ru-shou Robert (1993) *Taiwan xindianying de lishi wenhua jingyan* (Historical and cultural experiences in New Taiwan Cinema), Taipei: Wanxiang.

Chen, Wei (ed.) (1992) *Ke Ling dianying wencun* (Ke Ling's film essays), Beijing: ZDC.

Cheng, Jihua, Li Shaobai and Xing Zuwen (eds) (1981) *Zhongguo dianying fazhan shi* (History of the development of Chinese cinema), 2 vols, Beijing: ZDC; first published in 1963.

Cheng, Shuren (S.J. Benjamin Cheng), Gan Yazi (Atsun Kann) and Chen Dingxiu (D.S. Chen) (eds) (1927) *Minguo shiliunian Zhonghua yingye nianjian* (China cinema year book 1927), Shanghai: Zhonghua yingye nianjian she.

Cheuk, Pak-Tong (1999) 'The Beginning of the Hong Kong New Wave: The Interactive Relationship Between Television and the Film Industry', *Post Script* 19,1: 10–27.

Chiao, (Peggy) Hsiung-Ping (ed.) (1988) *Taiwan xindianying* (New Taiwan Cinema), Taipei: Shibao chuban gongsi.

—— (1993) *Gaibian lishi de wunian: Guolian dianying yanjiu* (Five years that changed history: studies of Guolian studio), Taipei: Wanxiang.

—— (ed.) (2002) *Taiwan dianying xin xin langchao* (New new wave of Taiwan cinema 90's), Taipei: Maitian.

Chongqing shi wenhua ju dianying chu (ed.) (1991) *Kangri zhanzheng shiqi de Chongqing dianying* (Chongqing films during the resistance war against Japan), Chongqing: Chongqing chubanshe.

Chow, Rey (1995) *Primitive Passions: Visuality, Sexuality, Ethnography, and Contemporary Chinese Cinema*, New York: Columbia University Press.

—— (1998) 'Introduction: On Chineseness as a Theoretical Problem', *Boundary 2* 25,3: 1–24.

Clark, Paul (1987a) *Chinese Cinema: Culture and Politics Since 1949*, London: Cambridge University Press.

—— (1987b) 'Ethnic Minorities in Chinese Films: Cinema and the Exotic', *East–West Film Journal* 1,2: 15–31.

Cleverley, John (2000) *In the Lap of Tigers: The Communist Labor University of Jiangxi Province*, Lanham: Rowman and Littlefield.

Crofts, Stephen (1993) 'Reconceptualizing National Cinema/s', *Quarterly Review of Film and Video* 14,3: 49–67.

—— (1998) 'Concepts of National Cinema', in Hill and Gibson (eds), *The Oxford Guide to Film Studies*, 385–94.

Cui, Shuqin (2001) 'Working from the Margins: Urban Cinema and Independent Directors in Contemporary China', *Post Script* 20,2–3: 77–93.

—— (2003) *Women Through the Lens: Gender and Nation in a Century of Chinese Cinema*, Honolulu: University of Hawaii Press.

Curtin, Michael (1999) 'Industry on Fire: The Cultural Economy of Hong Kong Media', *Post Script* 19,1: 28–51.

—— (2003) 'The Future of Chinese Cinema: Some Lessons from Hong Kong and

Taiwan', in Chin-Chuan Lee (ed.) *Chinese Media, Global Contexts*, London: RoutledgeCurzon, 237–56.

Da Zhonghua Baihe (ed.) (1926) *Zhibian waishi tekan* (Special magazine on *The Migration Act*), Shanghai: Da Zhonghua Baihe gongsi.

Dai, Jinhua (1993) *Dianying lilun yu piping shouce* (Handbook of film theory and criticism), Beijing: Kexue jishu wenxian chubanshe.

—— (1995) 'Invisible Women: Contemporary Chinese Cinema and Women's Film', *Positions* 3,1: 255–80.

—— (1999) *Xieta liaowang: Zhongguo dianying wenhua, 1978–1998* (Looking from a slanted tower: Chinese film culture, 1978–1998), Taipei: Yuanliu.

Dangdai dianying (ed.) (2003) 'Dianying *Yingxiong* xianxiang fenxi' (Decoding the *Hero* phenomenon), *Dangdai dianying* 2: 5–27.

Dariotis, Wei Ming and Eileen Fung (1997) 'Breaking the Soy Sauce Jar: Diasporas and Displacement in the Films of Ang Lee', in S. Lu (ed.) *Transnational Chinese Cinemas*, 187–20.

Davis, Darrell W. and Yeh Yueh-yu (2001) 'Warning! Category III: The Other Hong Kong Cinema', *Film Quarterly* 54,4: 12–26.

Deng, Guanghui (2000) 'Piaofang gushi: guochan dianying 1995–1999' (Box-office stories: domestic productions, 1995–1999), *Dianying yishu* 5: 15–9.

—— (2002) 'Shichang faxing lunli ji qita' (Distribution ethics and other observations), *Dangdai dianying* 2: 24–6.

Desser, David (2000) 'The Kung Fu Craze: Hong Kong Cinema's First American Reception', in Fu and Desser (eds) *The Cinema of Hong Kong*, 19–43.

Di, Di (1993) '*Juelie* jishi yu fenxi' (*Breaking with Old Ideas*: chronicle and analysis), *Dianying yishu* 2: 76–84.

Dianying yishu (ed.) (1996) '1995 nian guochan maizuo yingpian paihang bang qian shiming' (1995 top ten domestic films), *Dianying yishu* 3: 4–5.

—— (ed.) (1997) '1996 nian guochan yingpian piaofang shouru paihang bang qian shiming' (1996 top ten domestic films), *Dianying yishu* 3: 4–5.

—— (ed.) (1998), '1997 nian guochan yingpian piaofang shouru paihang bang' (1997 top grossing domestic films), *Dianying yishu* 3: 4–5.

—— (ed.) (1999) '1998 nian guochan yingpian piaofang shouru paihang bang' (1998 top grossing domestic films), *Dianying yishu* 3: 4–5.

—— (ed.) (2000) '1999 nian guochan yingpian piaofang shouru paihang bang' (1999 top grossing domestic films), *Dianying yishu* 3: 4–5.

—— (ed.) (2001) '2000 nian guochan yingpian piaofang shouru paihang bang' (2000 top grossing domestic films), *Dianying yishu* 3: 4–5.

—— (ed.) (2002) '2001 nian guochan yingpian piaofang shouru paihang bang' (2001 top grossing domestic films), *Dianying yishu* 3: 12–13.

Ding, Xiaodi (1984) *Yingshi chunqiu* (Records of film events), Beijing: ZDC.

Ding, Yaping (1998) *Yingxiang Zhongguo: Zhongguo dianying yishu, 1945–1949* (Imaging China: Chinese film art, 1945–1949), Beijing: Wenhua yishu chubanshe.

Dissanayake, Wimal (ed.) (1993) *Melodrama and Asian Cinema*, London: Cambridge University Press.

—— (ed.) (1994) *Colonialism and Nationalism in Asian Cinema*, Bloomington: Indiana University Press.

Donald, Stephanie (2000) *Public Secrets, Public Spaces: Cinema and Civility in China*, Lanham, MD: Rowman and Littlefield.

Du, Yunzhi (1978) *Zhongguo de dianying* (Chinese cinema), Taipei: Huangguan.
—— (1988) *Zhonghua minguo dianying shi* (A history of cinema in the Republic of China), 2 vols, Taipei: Wenjianhui.
During, Simon (1997) 'Popular Culture on a Global Scale: A Challenge for Cultural Studies?' *Critical Inquiry* 23: 808–33.
Eberhard, Wolfram (1972) *The Chinese Silver Screen: Hong Kong and Taiwan Motion Pictures*, Taipei: Orient Cultural Service.
Eastman, Lloyd E. (1984) *Seeds of Destruction: Nationalist China in War and Revolution 1937–1949*, Stanford: Stanford University Press.
Elsaesser, Thomas (1989) *New German Cinema: A History*, New Brunswick, NJ: Rutgers University Press.
Farquhar, Mary Ann and Chris Berry (2001) 'Shadow Opera: Towards a New Archeology of the Chinese Cinema', *Post Script* 20,2–3: 25–42.
Feng Min, Shao Zhou and Jin Fenglan (1992), *Zhongguo dianying yishu shigang* (An outline history of Chinese film art), Tianjin: Nankai daxue chubanshe.
Fonoroff, Paul (1997) *Silver Light: A Pictorial History of Hong Kong Cinema, 1920–1970*, Hong Kong: Joint Publishing.
Fore, Steve (1994) 'Golden Harvest Films and the Hong Kong Movie Industry in the Realm of Globalization', *The Velvet Light Trap* 34: 40–58.
—— (1997) 'Jackie Chan and the Cultural Dynamics of Global Entertainment', in S. Lu (ed.) *Transnational Chinese Cinemas*, 239–62.
Fu, Poshek (1997) 'The Ambiguity of Entertainment: Chinese Cinema in Japanese-occupied Shanghai, 1942 to 1945', *Cinema Journal* 37,1: 66–84.
—— (1998) 'Projecting Ambivalence: Chinese Cinema in Semi-occupied Shanghai, 1937–41', in Wen-hsin Yeh (ed.) *Wartime Shanghai*, London: Routledge, 86–109.
—— (2000a) 'Between Nationalism and Colonialism: Mainland Emigres, Marginal Culture, and Hong Kong Cinema 1937–1941', in Fu and Desser (eds) *The Cinema of Hong Kong*, 199–226.
—— (2000b) 'The 1960s: Modernity, Youth Culture, and Hong Kong Cantonese Cinema', in Fu and Desser (eds) *The Cinema of Hong Kong*, 71–89.
Fu, Poshek and David Desser (eds) (2000) *The Cinema of Hong Kong: History, Arts, Identity*, London: Cambridge University Press.
Gao, Xiaomei (ed.) (1996) *Xiaocheng zhichun* de dianying meixue: xiang Fei Mu zhijing (Aesthetics of *Spring in a Small Town*: a homage to Fei Mu), Taipei: Guojia dianying ziliao guan.
Gong, Jianong (Robert Kung) (1967) *Gong Jianong congying huiyi lu* (Gong Jianong's memoirs of his silver screen life), 3 vols, Taipei: Wenxing shudian.
Gongsun, Lu (1977) *Zhongguo dianying shihua* (A history of Chinese cinema), 2 vols, Hong Kong: Nantian.
GIO (Government Information Office) (ed.) (1997) *Republic of China Yearbook 1997*, Taipei: GIO.
—— (2001) *Republic of China Yearbook 2001*, Taipei: GIO.
—— (2002) *Republic of China Yearbook 2002*, Taipei: GIO.
—— (2003) GIO film-related website: ⟨http://www.gio.gov.tw/taiwan-website/7-av/film_industry/mframes_eg.htm⟩.
Guan, Wenqing (Moon Kwan) (1976) *Zhongguo yintan waishi* (Unofficial history of the Chinese screen), Hong Kong: Guangjiaojing chubanshe.

311

Guojia dianying ziliao guan (National Chinese Taipei film archive) (1994) *Taiyu pian shidai* (The era of Taiwanese-dialect films), Taipei: Guojia dianying ziliao guan.

—— (1996) *Taiying wushi nian: Lishi de jiaozong* (Fifty years of the Taiwan Studio: footprints of history), Taipei: Guojia dianying ziliao guan.

—— (1998) *1998 dianying nianjian* (Cinema in the Republic of China 1998), Taipei: Guojia dianying ziliao guan.

—— (1999) *1999 dianying nianjian* (Cinema in the Republic of China 1999), Taipei: Guojia dianying ziliao guan.

—— (2001) *2000 Taiwan dianying wenhua ditu* (Map of 2000 Taiwan film culture), Taipei: Yuanliu.

Gunning, Tom (1998) 'Early American Film', in Hill and Gibson (eds) *The Oxford Guide to Film Studies*, 255–71.

Han, Xiaolei (1995) 'Dui diwudai de wenhua tuwei: houwudai de geren dianying xianxiang' (A cultural breakaway from the fifth generation: the phenomenon of individualist film in the post-fifth generation), *Dianying yishu* 2: 58–63.

—— (1999) 'Tuwei hou de wenhua piaoyi' (Driftings after the breakaway), *Dianying yishu* 5: 58–65.

Hansen, Miriam Bratu (2000) 'Fallen Women, Rising Stars, New Horizons: Shanghai Silent Film as Vernacular Modernism', *Film Quarterly* 54,1: 10–22.

Harris, Kristine (1997) '*The New Woman* Incident: Cinema, Scandal, and Spectacle in 1935 Shanghai', in S. Lu (ed.) *Transnational Chinese Cinema*, 277–302.

—— (1999) 'Adaptation and Innovation: Costume Drama Spectacle and *Romance of the Western Chamber*', in Y. Zhang (ed.) *Cinema and Urban Culture in Shanghai*, 51–73.

Hayward, Susan (1993) *French National Cinema*, London: Routledge.

He, Ma (1956) *Shanghai jiuhua* (Old stories from Shanghai), Shanghai: Shanghai wenhua chubanshe.

Higson, Andrew (1989) 'The Concept of National Cinema', *Screen* 30,4: 36–46.

—— (1995) *Waving the Flag: Constructing a National Cinema in Britain*, London: Oxford University Press.

Hill, John and Pamela Church Gibson (eds) (1998) *The Oxford Guide to Film Studies*, London: Oxford University Press.

HKFA (1997a) *50 Years of the Hong Kong Film Production and Distribution Industries: An Exhibition*, Hong Kong: Urban Council.

—— (1997b) *Hong Kong Filmography*, vol. 1 (1913–1941), Hong Kong: Urban Council.

—— (1998) *Hong Kong Filmography*, vol. 2 (1942–1949), Hong Kong: Urban Council.

—— (2000) *Hong Kong Filmography*, vol. 3 (1950–1952), Hong Kong: Urban Council.

—— (2002) *The Cathay Story*, Hong Kong: HKFA.

—— (2003) *Hong Kong Filmography*, vol. 4 (1953–9), Hong Kong: HKFA.

HKIFF (1981) *A Study of the Hong Kong Swordplay Film, 1945–1980*, a publication for the 5th HKIFF (rev. edition, 1996), Hong Kong: Urban Council.

—— (1982) *Cantonese Cinema Retrospective, 1960–69*, a publication for the 6th HKIFF (rev. edition, 1996), Hong Kong: Urban Council.

—— (1984) *A Study of Hong Kong Cinema in the Seventies*, a publication for the 8th HKIFF, Hong Kong: Urban Council.

—— (1986) *Cantonese Melodrama, 1950–1969*, a publication for the 10th HKIFF (rev. edition, 1997), Hong Kong: Urban Council.

—— (1987) *Cantonese Opera Film Retrospective*, a publication for the 11th HKIFF (rev. edition, 1996), Hong Kong: Urban Council.

—— (1988) *Changes in Hong Kong Society Through Cinema*, a publication for the 12th HKIFF, Hong Kong: Urban Council.

—— (1990) *The China Factor in Hong Kong Cinema*, a publication for the 14th HKIFF (rev. edition, 1997), Hong Kong: Urban Council.

—— (1991) *Hong Kong Cinema in the Eighties*, a publication for the 15th HKIFF, Hong Kong: Urban Council.

—— (1993) *Mandarin Films and Popular Songs: 40's–60's*, a publication for the 17th HKIFF, Hong Kong: Urban Council.

—— (1995) *Early Images of Hong Kong & China*, a publication for the 19th HKIFF, Hong Kong: Urban Council.

—— (1996) *The Restless Breed: Cantonese Stars of the Sixties*, a publication for the 20th HKIFF, Hong Kong: Urban Council.

—— (1998a) *Hong Kong Panorama, 97–98*, a publication for the 22nd HKIFF, Hong Kong: Provisional Urban Council.

—— (1998b) *Transcending the Times: King Hu & Eileen Chang*, a publication for the 22nd HKIFF, Hong Kong: Provisional Urban Council.

—— (1999a) *Hong Kong New Wave: Twenty Years After*, a publication for the 23rd HKIFF, Hong Kong: Provisional Urban Council.

—— (1999b) *Hong Kong Panorama, 98–99*, a publication for the 23rd HKIFF, Hong Kong: Provisional Urban Council.

—— (2000a) *Border Crossings in Hong Kong Cinema*, a publication for the 24th HKIFF, Hong Kong: Leisure and Cultural Services Department.

—— (2000b) *Hong Kong Panorama, 1999–2000*, a publication for the 24th HKIFF, Hong Kong: Leisure and Cultural Services Department.

Ho, Sam and Wai-leng Ho (eds) (2002) *The Swordsman and His Jianghu: Tsui Hark and Hong Kong Film*, Hong Kong: HKFA.

Hoare, Stephanie (1993) 'Innovation through Adaptation: The Use of Literature in New Taiwan Film and Its Consequences', *Modern Chinese Literature* 7,2: 33–58.

Hong Kong Arts Center & Hong Kong Chinese Film Association (eds) (1984) *Early Chinese Cinema: The Era of Exploration*, a programme for the Hong Kong Arts Festival 1984.

Hong Kong Motion Picture Industry Association (2003) Online box office figures: <http://www.mpia.org.hk/mpia/index.htm>.

Hong, Shi (1995) 'Diyici langchao: mopian qi Zhongguo shangye dianying xianxiang shuping' (The first wave: a discussion of commercial films in the silent era of Chinese cinema), *Dangdai dianying* 2: 5–12.

Hou, Xisan (1996) *Beijing lao xiyuan zi* (Old theaters in Beijing), Beijing: Zhongguo chengshi chubanshe.

Hu, Die (1988) *Hu Die huiyi lu* (Hu Die's memoirs), Beijing: Wenhua yishu chubanshe.

Hu, Ke (1996) 'Cong duo jiaodu lijie Zhongguo wusheng dianying' (Comprehend Chinese silent films through multiple perspectives), *Dangdai dianying* 5: 51–9.

Hu, Xu (1986) *Xin Zhongguo dianying de yaolan* (The cradle of film in new China), Changchun: Jilin wenshi chubanshe.

Hu, Xu and Gu Quan (1990) *Manying – Guoce dianying mianmian guan* (Man'ei: perspectives on national policy films), Shanghai: Zhonghua shuju.

Huang, Ailing (1983) 'Shilun sanshi niandai Zhongguo dianying dan jingtou de xingzhi' (On the nature of single shots in Chinese films of the 1930s), *Zhongguo dianying yanjiu* 1: 31–57.

Huang, Ren (1994a) *Beiqing Taiyu pian* (Sorrowful Taiwanese-dialect films), Taipei: Wanxiang.

—— (1994b) *Dianying yu zhengzhi xuanchuan* (Film and political propaganda), Taipei: Wanxiang.

—— (2001) *Lianbang dianying shidai* (The era of the Union Film), Taipei: Guojia dianying ziliao guan.

Huang, Shixian (2000) 'Hu Xuehua' (Hu Xuehua), *Dazhong dianying* 1: 42–4.

—— (2003) 'Quanqiuhua chaoliu yu Zhongguo bentu dianying de wenhua xuanze – duiyu "hou WTO shiqi" Zhongguo dianying shengcun jingyu jiqi qianjing de jidian sikao' (Cultural options for Chinese domestic film amid the globalization tide: thoughts on the existential context and prospects of Chinese cinema in the WTO era), in Ji'nan Liu (ed.) *Rushi (WTO) yu Zhongguo dianying de da qushi* (The WTO and the trends of Chinese cinema), Beijing: Beijing guangbo xueyuan chubanshe.

Huang, Wulan (ed.) (1998) *Dangdai Zhongguo dianying: 1995–1997* (Contemporary Chinese cinema: 1995–1997), Taipei: Shibao wenhua.

—— (1999) *Dangdai Zhongguo dianying: 1998* (Contemporary Chinese cinema: 1998), Taipei: Shibao wenhua.

Jarvie, Ian C. (1977) *Window on Hong Kong: A Sociological Study of the Hong Kong Film Industry and Its Audience*, Hong Kong: Centre of Asian Studies, University of Hong Kong.

Kam, Tan See (1993) 'The Hongkong Cantonese Vernacular as Cultural Resistance', *Cinemaya* 20: 12–15.

Kellner, Douglas (1998) 'New Taiwan Cinema in the 80s', *Jump Cut* 42: 101–15.

Kubo, Akira (1986) 'Bizhi gaige yihou de Zhongguo jingji' (Chinese economy after the currency reform)', *Zhongguo jindai jingjishi yanjiu ziliao* (Research materials on modern Chinese economy history), 5: 49–86.

Law, Kar (2000) 'The American Connection in Early Hong Kong Cinema', in Fu and Desser (eds) *The Cinema of Hong Kong*, 44–70.

—— (2001) 'An Overview of Hong Kong's New Wave Cinema', in E. Yau (ed.) *At Full Speed*, 31–52.

Lee, Leo Ou-fan (1991) 'The Tradition of Modern Chinese Cinema: Some Preliminary Explorations and Hypotheses', in C. Berry (ed.) *Perspectives*, 6–20.

—— (1994) 'Two Films from Hong Kong: Parody and Allegory', in N. Browne *et al.* (eds) *New Chinese Cinemas*, 202–16.

—— (1999) *Shanghai Modern: The Flowering of a New Urban Culture in China, 1930–1945*, Cambridge, Mass.: Harvard University Press.

Lent, John A. (1990) *The Asian Film Industry*, Austin: University of Texas Press.

Leyda, Jay (1972) *Dianying: An Account of Films and the Film Audience in China*, Cambridge, Mass.: MIT Press.

Li, Cheuk-to (Li Zhuotao) (1990) *Bashi niandai Xianggang dianying biji* (Notes on Hong Kong cinema of the 1980s), vol. 1, Hong Kong: Chuangjian.

—— (1991) 'Eight Films of Sun Yu', *Cinemaya* 11: 54–63.

—— (1994) 'The Return of the Father: Hong Kong New Wave and Its Chinese Context in the 1980s', in N. Browne *et al.* (eds) *New Chinese Cinemas*, 160–79.

Li, Daoxin (2000) *Zhongguo dianying shi, 1937–1945* (Chinese film history, 1937–1945), Beijing: Shoudu shida chubanshe.

Li, Hanxiang (1984) *Sanshinian xishuo congtou* (Detailed accounts of my thirty-year career), 3 vols, Hong Kong: Tiandi tushu.

Li, Jin (1997) 'Xin ganjue pai he ersanshi niandai Haolaiwu dianying' (New perceptionists and Hollywood films of the 1920s–30s), *Zhongguo xiandai wenxue yanjiu congkan* 3: 32–56.

Li, Jinsheng (1995) 'Lun Zhang Shichuan dui Zhongguo zaoqi dianying fazhan de gongxian' (Zhang Shichuan's contribution to early Chinese cinema), *Dianying yishu* 2: 37–42.

Li, Minwei (1993) 'Wo yu Zhongguo dianying', *Dangdai dianying* 6: 83–6.

Li, Shaobai (1991) *Dianying lishi ji lilun* (Film history and film theory), Beijing: Wenhua yishu chubanshe.

Li, Suyuan and Hu Jubin (1996) *Zhongguo wusheng dianying shi* (A history of Chinese silent films), Beijing: ZDC.

Li, Tianduo (1997) *Taiwan dianying, shehui yu lishi* (Taiwan cinema, society and history), Taipei: Yatai.

Li, Yizhuang (1994) 'Xianggang dianying yu Xianggang shehui bianqian' (Hong Kong cinema and Hong Kong social changes), *Dianying yishu* 2: 15–23.

Liang, Liang (2001) 'Jiushi niandai Taiwan dianying de zhengce' (Taiwan film policy in the 1990s), *Dianying yishu* 4: 103–6.

Liao, Jinfeng (2001) *Xiaoshi de yingxiang: Taiyu pian de dianying zaixian yu wenhua rentong* (The disappeared images: representation and cultural identification in Taiwanese-dialect films), Taipei: Yuanliu.

Liao, Ping-hui (1993) 'Rewriting Taiwanese National History: the February 28 Incident as Spectacle', *Public Culture* 5: 281–96.

Lie, Fu (2002) '90 niandai Xianggang dianying gaishu' (An overview of Hong Kong cinema of the 1990s), *Dangdai dianying* 2: 59–68.

Lin, Niantong (1985) 'A Study of the Theories of Chinese Cinema in their Relationship to Classical Aesthetics', *Modern Chinese Literature* 1,2: 185–200.

Liu, Jianzhong (2003) 'Zai fazhan zhong qianjin, zai jianshe zhong wanshan – jianshu 2002 nia Zhongguo dianying ye' (Advance in development, improve in construction: a brief survey of China's film industry in 2002), *Zhongguo dianying bao* 731 (13 Feb.): 1–2.

Liu, Siping and Xing Zuwen (eds) (1981) *Lu Xun yu dianying* (Lu Xun and film), Beijing: ZDC.

Lu, Feiyi (1998) *Taiwan dianying: zhengzhi, jingji, meixue, 1949–1994* (Taiwan cinema: politics, economy, aesthetics, 1949–1994), Taipei: Yuanliu.

Lu, Hongshi and Shu Xiaoming (1998) *Zhongguo dianying shi* (Chinese film history), Beijing: Wenhua yishu chubanshe.

Lu, Sheldon Hsiao-peng (ed.) (1997) *Transnational Chinese Cinemas: Identity, Nationhood, Gender*, Honolulu: University of Hawaii Press.

—— (2001) *China, Transnational Visuality, Global Postmodernity*, Stanford: Stanford University Press.

Lü, Shushang (1961) *Taiwan diangying xiju shi* (History of Taiwan cinema and drama), Taipei: Dongfang chubanshe.

Lu, Si (1962) *Yingping yijiu* (Film criticism in recollection), Beijing: ZDC.

Lu, Tonglin (2002) *Confronting Modernity in the Cinemas of Taiwan and Mainland China*, London: Cambridge University Press.

Luo, Yijun (ed.) (1988) *Zhongguo xinwenyi daxi, 1949–1966* (Anthology of modern Chinese literature and arts), *Film Sections*, 2 vols, Beijing: Zhongguo wenlian chubanshe.

—— (1995) 'Jiang Qing yu dianying' (Jiang Qing and cinema), in ZDX (ed.) *Lishi yu xianzhuang*, 151–78.

Luo, Yijun, Li Jinsheng and Xu Hong (eds) (1992) *Zhongguo dianying lilun wenxuan, 1920–1989* (Chinese film theory: an anthology), 2 vols, Beijing: Wenhua yishu chubanshe.

Ma, Debo (1995) 'Yingyun huanliu: jiushi nianjian "zaidao" yu "yule" zhizheng' (Cycle of fates in Chinese film: ninety years of struggles between 'moral education' and 'entertainment'), in ZDX (ed.) *Lishi yu xianzhuang*, 1–32.

Ma, Debo and Dai Guangxi (1994) *Daoyan chuangzuo lun: lun Beiying wuda daoyan* (On five major directors of Beijing Film Studio), Beijing: ZDC.

Ma, Ning (1989) 'The Textual and Critical Difference of Being Radical: Reconstructing Chinese Leftist Films of the 1930s', *Wide Angle* 11,2: 22–31.

Manzhou zazhi she (ed.) (1935–43) *Dianying huabao* (Screen pictorial), formerly *Manzhou yinhua* (Manchurian screen), monthly, vols 1–8, Xinjing (Changchun).

Marchetti, Gina (1997) 'The Blossoming of a Revolutionary Aesthetic: *Two Stage Sisters*', in S. Lu (ed.) *Transnational Chinese Cinema*, 59–80.

Mast, Gerald (1976) 'Film History and Film Histories', *Quarterly Review of Film Studies* 1,3: 297–314.

Meng, Fanhua (2001) 'Zhongguo dianying wenhua de minzuxing yu zhengzhi xiangxiang: chuqi shehui zhuyi Zhongguo dianying wenhua de zai pingjia' (Nationality and political thinking in Chinese film culture: a reassessment of Chinese film culture of the early socialist period), *Dianying yishu* 4: 70–3.

Meng, Liye (1995) 'Lun wuliushi niandai Zhongguo dianying de shehui wenhua huanjing yu meixue tezheng' (Socio-cultural environments and aesthetic features of Chinese cinema of the 1950s–60s), in ZDX (ed.) *Lishi yu xianzhuang*, 130–50.

Min, Jie (1998) *Jindai Zhongguo shehui wenhua bianqian lu* (Records of social and cultural transformations in early modern China), vol. 2, Hangzhou: Zhejiang renmin chubanshe.

Miyoshi, Masao (1993) 'A Borderless World? From Colonialism to Transnationalism and the Decline of the Nation-State', *Critical Inquiry* 19: 726–51.

NFCC (ed.) (1934) *Dianying jiancha weiyuanhui gongzuo baogao* (The work report of the National Film Censorship Committee), Nanjing: NFCC.

Ni, Zhen (2003) *Memoirs from the Beijing Film Academy: The Genesis of China's Fifth Generation*, trans. Chris Berry, Durham, NC: Duke University Press.

Nowell-Smith, Geoffrey (ed.) (1996) *The Oxford History of World Cinema*, London: Oxford University Press.

O'Regan, Tom (1996) *Australian National Cinema*, London: Routledge.

Ouyang, Yuqian (1984) *Dianying banlu chujia ji* (Entering the film world in my mid-career), Beijing: ZDC.

Pan, Ruojian (1996) '*Hong yingtao* zai shangye yunzuo zhiwai' (*Red Cherry*: beyond commercial operations), *Dianying yishu* 3: 6–8.

Pang, Laikwan (2002) *Building a New China in Cinema: The Chinese Left Wing Cinema Movement, 1932–1937*, Lanham, MD: Rowman & Littlefield.

Pickowicz, Paul (1993) 'Melodramatic Representation and the "May Fourth" Tradition of Chinese Cinema', in E. Widmer and D. Wang (eds) *From May Fourth to June Fourth: Fiction and Film in Twentieth-Century China*, Cambridge, Mass.: Harvard University Press, 295–326.

—— (1995) 'Velvet Prisons and the Political Economy of Chinese Filmmaking', in Deborah Davis, Richard Kraus, Barry Naughton and Elizabeth Perry (eds) *Urban Spaces in Contemporary China: The Potential for Autonomy and Community in Post-Mao China*, London: Cambridge University Press, 193–220.

—— (2000) 'Victory as Defeat: Postwar Visualizations of China's War of Resistance', in Wen-hsin Yeh (ed.) *Becoming Chinese: Passages to Modernity and Beyond*, Berkeley: University of California Press, 365–98.

Qi, Zhiyong (2002) '90 niandai Xianggang dianying gongye zhuangkuang' (The condition of Hong Kong film industry in the 1990s), *Dangdai dianying* 2: 83–7.

Rodriguez, Hector (1997) 'Hong Kong Popular Culture as an Interpretive Arena: The Huang Feihong Film Series', *Screen* 38,1: 1–24.

—— (1998) 'Questions of Chinese Aesthetics: Film Form and Narrative Space in the Cinema of King Hu', *Cinema Journal* 38,1 (Fall): 73–97.

—— (2001) 'The Emergence of the Hong Kong New Wave', in E. Yau (ed.) *At Full Speed*, 54–69.

Rosen, Stanley (2002a) 'Hollywood, Globalization and Film Markets in Asia: Lessons for China?', paper delivered at Fudan University, Shanghai, 23–4 November 2002.

—— (2002b) 'The Wolf at the Door: Hollywood and the Film Market in China, 1994–2000', in Eric J. Heikkila and Rafael Pizarro (eds) *Southern California in the World and the World in Southern California*, Westport, CT: Praeger, 49–77.

Semsel, George S. (ed.) (1987) *Chinese Film: The State of the Art in the People's Republic*, New York: Praeger.

Semsel, G., Chen Xihe and Xia Hong (eds) (1993) *Film in Contemporary China*, New York: Praeger.

Semsel, G., Xia Hong and Hou Jianping (eds) (1990) *Chinese Film Theory: A Guide to the New Era*, New York: Praeger.

Shackleton, Liz (2003) 'Hong Kong Box Office Slumps 17% in 2002', *Screen Daily* 2 Jan. ⟨http://www.screendaily.com⟩.

Shen, Hao and Shen Yanzhe (eds) (1928) *Dianying yuebao* (Film monthly), 7 (10 Oct.), Shanghai: Liuhe gongsi.

Shen, Shiao-ying (1995) 'Where Has All the Capital Gone: The State of Taiwan's Film Investment', *Cinemaya* 30: 4–12.

Shimizu, Akira (1995) *Shanghai soka eiga watakushi-shi* (History of Shanghai *zujie* films), Tokyo: Shinchosha.

Shu, Xiaoming (1996) *Zhongguo dianying yishu shi jiaocheng* (Textbook history of Chinese film art), Beijing: ZDC.

Shu, Yan (1994) 'Dianying de "lunhui" – jinian zuoyi dianying yundong 60 zhounian' (The cycles of film – in commemoration of the sixtieth anniversary of the leftist film movement), *Xin wenxue shiliao* 1: 72–93.

Silbergeld, Jerome (1999) *China Into Film: Frames of Reference in Contemporary Chinese Cinema*, London: Reaktion Books.

—— (2004) *Hitchcock with a Chinese Face: Cinematic Doubles, Oedipal Triangles, and China's Moral Voice*, Seattle: University of Washington Press.

Stephenson, Shelley (1999) ' "Her Traces Are Found Everywhere": Shanghai, Li Xianglan, and the Greater East Asia Film Sphere', in Y. Zhang (ed.) *Cinema and Urban Culture in Shanghai*, 222–45.

Stringer, Julian (1999) 'Category 3: Sex and Violence in Postmodern Hong Kong', in Christopher Sharrett (ed.) *Mythologies of Violence in Postmodern Media*, Detroit: Wayne State University Press, 361–79.

Su, Yun (ed.) (1986) *Yi Dongying* (Northeast studio in recollection), Changchun: Jilin wenshi chubanshe.

Sun, Yu (1990) *Dalu zhige* (Song of the big road), edited and proofread by Shu Qi and Li Cheuk-to, Taipei: Yuanliu.

—— (2000) 'Sun Yu zishu' (Sun Yu in his own account), *Dianying yishu* 6: 56–60.

Sunshine, Linda (ed.) (2000) *Crouching Tiger, Hidden Dragon: A Portrait of the Ang Lee Film*, New York: Newmarket Press.

Talens, Jenaro and Santos Zunzunegui (1997) 'Toward a True History of Cinema: Film History as Narration', *Boundary 2* 24,1 (Spring): 1–34.

Tam, Kwok-kan and Wilmal Dissanayake (1998) *New Chinese Cinema*, Hong Kong: Oxford University Press.

Tan, Chunfa (1992) *Kai yidai xianhe – Zhongguo dianying zhifu Zheng Zhengqiu* (Opening a new road – Zheng Zhengqiu, the father of Chinese cinema), Beijing: Guoji wenhua chuban gongsi.

—— (1995) 'Changqi bei wudu bei lengluo de yiye – zaoqi de Zhongguo dianying' (A period long misunderstood and long neglected – early Chinese cinema), *Dangdai dianying* 2: 13–20.

Tang, Xiaobing (2000) *Chinese Modern: the Heroic and the Quotidian*, Durham, NC: Duke University Press.

Teng, Sue-Feng (1996) 'King of the Pop Flick – Film Director Chu Yen-ping', *Sinorama* (Feb.): 102–9.

Teo, Stephen (1997) *Hong Kong Cinema: The Extra Dimensions*, London: BFI Publishing.

—— (2000) 'The 1970s: Movement and Transition', Fu and Desser (eds) *The Cinema of Hong Kong*, 90–110.

Tian, Benxiang and Jiao Shangzhi (1993) *Zhongguo huaju shi yanjiu gaishu* (An overview of the studies of the history of Chinese spoken drama), Tianjin: Tianjin guji chubanshe.

Wang, Ban (1997) *The Sublime Figure of History: Aesthetics and Politics in Twentieth-Century China*, Stanford: Stanford University Press.

Wang, Fei-yun (1995) 'Flowers Blooming in Barren Soil', *Free China Review* (Feb.): 4–17.

Wang, Jing and Tani E. Barlow (eds) (2002) *Cinema and Desire: Feminist Marxism and Cultural Politics in the Work of Dai Jinhua*, London: Verso.

Wang, Wei (1995) *Yiyi yu kongbai: dangdai Xianggang dianying guancha* (Meaning and blank: an examination of contemporary Hong Kong cinema), Taipei: Wanxiang.

Wang, Zhaoguang (1998) 'Minguo nianjian Meiguo dianying zai Hua shichang yanjiu' (A market analysis of Hollywood films in China during the republican era), *Dianying yishu* 1: 57–65.

—— (2000) 'Zhanhou Shanghai guochan dianyingye de qishi' (Lessons from the postwar Shanghai film market), *Dianying yishu* 5: 26–32.

Wei, Zhuo (1993) 'Niuqu de chengzhang: Taiwan dianying chanye fenxi, 1945–1975' (Twisted development: an analysis of Taiwan film industries, 1945–1975), *Con-Temporary* 81: 74–99.

Wen, Tianxiang (2002) *Guangying dingge: Cai Mingliang de xinling changyu* (Framed by lights and shadows: Tsai Ming-liang's mindscape), Taipei: Hengxing.

Wu, Cheng (ed.) (1979) *Yong yanjing kan de Zhongguo dianying shi* (A history of Chinese cinema seen through the eyes), Taibei: Longjiang.

Xia, Yan (1984) 'Zai "ershi-sishi niandai Zhongguo dianying huigu" kaimu shi shangde jianghua' (Speech at the opening ceremony of 'Retrospective of Chinese cinema of the 1920s–1940s'), *Xin wenxue shiliao* 1: 21–9.

—— (1985) *Dianying lunwen ji* (Collection of film essays), Beijing: ZDC.

Xiao, Zhiwei (1997) 'Anti-Imperialism and Film Censorship During the Nanjing Decade, 1927–1937', in S. Lu (ed.) *Transnational Chinese Cinemas*, 35–57.

—— (1999) 'Constructing a New National Culture: Film Censorship and the Issues of Cantonese Dialect, Superstition and Sex in the Nanjing Decade', in Y. Zhang (ed.) *Cinema and Urban Culture in Shanghai*, 183–99.

Xu, Chihen (1927) *Zhongguo yingxi daguan* (Aspects of Chinese shadowplays), Shanghai: Hezuo chubanshe.

Xu, Zhuodai (1924) *Yingxi xue* (Film studies), Shanghai: Huaguang shangyeshe tushu bu.

Yang, Yan (2001) 'Kangzhan shiqi guomin zhengfu de guanying yingye kaolüe' (A study of the film industry sponsored by the nationalist government during the resistance war), *Dianying yishu* 3: 117–20.

Yau, Esther C.M. (1994) 'Border Crossing: Mainland China's Presence in Hong Kong Cinema', in N. Browne *et al.* (eds) *New Chinese Cinemas*, 180–201.

—— (ed.) (2001) *At Full Speed: Hong Kong Cinema in a Borderless World*, Minneapolis: University of Minnesota Press.

Ye, Longyan (1995) *Guangfu chuqi Taiwan dianying shi* (A history of Taiwan cinema in the early postwar period), Taipei: Guojia dianying ziliao guan.

—— (1997) *Taibei Ximending dianying shi* (History of film activities in Taipei's Ximending), Taipei: Guojia dianying ziliao guan.

—— (1998) *Rizhi shiqi Taiwan dianying shi* (History of Taiwan film during the Japanese colonization), Taipei: Yushan she.

—— (1999) *Chunhua menglu: zhengzong Taiyu dianying xing shuai lu* (Spring flowers, dream dews: the ups and downs of the authentic Taiwanese-dialect films), Taipei: Boyang wenhua.

Yeh, Yueh-yu (1998) 'Defining "Chinese" ', *Jump Cut* 42: 73–6.

—— (2002) 'Historiography and Sinification: Music in Chinese Cinema of the 1930s', *Cinema Journal* 41,3: 78–97.

Yeh, Yueh-yu, Zhuo Botang and Wu Hao (eds) (1999) *Sandi chuanqi: Huayu dianying ershi nian* (Romance between three territories: Chinese-language cinema in the past two decades), Taipei: Guojia dianying ziliao guan.

Yi, Ming (ed.) (1993) *Sanshi niandai Zhongguo dianying pinglun wenxuan* (Selection of film criticism from 1930s China), Beijing: ZDC.

Yin, Hong (1998) *Shiji zhuanzhe shiqi de Zhongguo yingshi wenhua* (Chinese film and television culture in the transition period of the century), Beijing: Beijing chubanshe.

—— (1999) '98 Zhongguo dianying beiwang' (Memorandum on 1998 Chinese films), *Dangdai dianying* 1: 21–30.

Ying, Xiong (1993) '*Xiaocheng zhichun* yu "dongfang dianying" ' (*Spring in a Small Town* and 'eastern cinema'), *Dianying yishu* 1: 11–18, 2: 46–51.

Yip, June (1997) 'Constructing a Nation: Taiwanese History and the Films of Hou Hsiao-hsien', in S. Lu (ed.) *Transnational Chinese Cinemas*, 139–68.

Yu, Muyun (1996) *Xianggang dianying shihua* (A historical account of Hong Kong cinema), vol. 1, Hong Kong: Ci wenhua.

—— (1997) *Xianggang dianying shihua* (A historical account of Hong Kong cinema), vol. 2, Hong Kong: Ci wenhua.

—— (1998) *Xianggang dianying shihua* (A historical account of Hong Kong cinema), vol. 3, Hong Kong: Ci wenhua.

—— (2000) *Xianggang dianying shihua* (A historical account of Hong Kong cinema), vol. 4, Hong Kong: Ci wenhua.

—— (2001) *Xianggang dianying shihua* (A historical account of Hong Kong cinema), vol. 5, Hong Kong: Ci wenhua.

Yu, Yuxi (2003) '*Yingxiong* de shangye chenggong yu youxiao de shichang cehua' (*Hero*'s commercial success and its effective marketing), *Dianying yishu* 2: 27–30.

ZDC (ed.) (1959–61) *Wusi yilai dianying juben xuanji* (Selected screenplays since the May Fourth), 2 vols, Beijing: ZDC.

—— (1959–63) *Zhongguo dianying juben xuanji* (Selected Chinese screenplays), 8 vols, Beijing: ZDC.

ZDX (ed.) (1982–6) *Zhongguo dianyingjia liezhuan* (Biographies of Chinese film people), 7 vols, Beijing: ZDC.

—— (1996) *Zhongguo dianying nianjian 1996* (China film yearbook), Beijing: ZDC.

—— (1997) *Zhongguo dianying nianjian 1997* (China film yearbook), Beijing: ZDC.

—— (1998–9) *Zhongguo dianying nianjian 1998–1999* (China film yearbook), Beijing: ZDC.

—— (2000) *Zhongguo dianying nianjian 2000* (China film yearbook), Beijing: ZDC.

ZDYYZ (ed.) (1993) *Zhongguo zuoyi dianying yundong* (The leftist film movement in China), Beijing: ZDC.

—— (ed.) (1995) *Zhongguo dianying tuzhi* (Illustrated annals of Chinese film), Guangxi: Zhuhai chubanshe.

ZDYYZ and ZDZ (eds) (1995) *Zhongguo yingpian dadian, 1977–1994* (Encyclopedia of Chinese films, 1977–1994), Beijing: ZDC.

ZDYYZ and ZDZ (eds) (1996) *Zhongguo yingpian dadian, 1905–1930* (Encyclopedia of Chinese films, 1905–1930), Beijing: ZDC.

ZDZ (ed.) (1996a) *Zhongguo wusheng dianying* (Chinese silent cinema), Beijing: ZDC.

—— (ed.) (1996b) *Zhongguo wusheng dianying juben* (Scripts of Chinese silent cinema), 3 vols, Beijing: ZDC.

—— (ed.) (1998) *Xianggang dianying tuzhi, 1913–1997* (Records of the Hong Kong cinema, 1913–1997), Hangzhou: Zhejiang sheying chubanshe.

Zhai, Jiannong (1995) 'Wenge dianying: ershi shiji teshu de wenhua xianxiang: 1966–1972 nian Zhongguo dianying shi pingxi' (Cultural Revolution cinema: a special cultural phenomenon in the twentieth century – an analysis of Chinese film history, 1966–1972), in ZDX (ed.) *Lishi yu xianzhuang*, 179–99.

Zhan, Youpeng and Lan Chao (1996) *Shao Yifu zhuan* (Biography of Run Run Shaw), Hong Kong: Mingliu.

Zhang, Che (1989), *Huigu Xianggang dianying sanshinian* (30 years of Hong Kong cinema in recollection), Hong Kong: Sanlian shudian.

Zhang, Junxiang (ed.) (1989) *Zhongguo kangri zhanzheng shiqi dahoufang wenxue shuxi: diba bian, dianying* (Series of Chinese hinterland literature during the resistance war against Japan: vol. 8, films), Chongqing: Chongqing chubanshe.

Zhang, Junxiang and Cheng Jihua (eds) (1995) *Zhongguo dianying da cidian* (China cinema encyclopedia), Shanghai: Shanghai cishu chubanshe.

Zhang, Xudong (1997) *Chinese Modernism in the Era of Reforms: Cultural Fever, Avant-garde Fiction, and the New Chinese Cinema*, Durham, NC: Duke University Press.

Zhang, Yingjin (1994) 'The Idyllic Country and the Modern City: Cinematic Configurations of Family in *Osmanthus Alley* and *The Terrorizer*', *Tamkang Review* 25,1: 81–99.

—— (1996) *The City in Modern Chinese Literature and Film: Configurations of Space, Time, and Gender*, Stanford: Stanford University Press.

—— (1997) 'Building a National Literature in Modern China: Literary Criticism, Gender Ideology, and the Public Sphere', *Journal of Modern Literature in Chinese* 1,1: 47–74.

—— (ed.) (1999a) *Cinema and Urban Culture in Shanghai, 1922–1943*, Stanford: Stanford University Press.

—— (1999b) 'Prostitution and Urban Imagination: An Aspect of Chinese Film in the 1930s', in Y. Zhang (ed.) *Cinema and Urban Culture in Shanghai*, 160–80.

—— (2000) 'A Typography of Chinese Film Historiography', *Asian Cinema* 11,1: 16–32.

—— (2002) *Screening China: Critical Interventions, Cinematic Reconfigurations, and the Transnational Imaginary in Contemporary Chinese Cinema*, Ann Arbor: University of Michigan, Center for Chinese Studies Publications.

—— (2003) '*Evening Bell*: Wu Ziniu's Visions of History, War and Humanity', in Chris Berry (ed.) *Chinese Films in Focus*, London: BFI Publishing.

—— (2004) 'Rebel without a Cause? China's New Urban Generation and Post-socialist Filmmaking since the Early 1990s', in Zhen Zhang (ed.) *The Urban Generation: Chinese Cinema and Society at the Turn of the Twenty-First Century*, Durham, NC: Duke University Press.

Zhang, Yingjin and Zhiwei Xiao (1998) *Encyclopedia of Chinese Film*, London: Routledge.

Zhang, Zhen (1999) 'Teahouse, Shadowplay, *Bricolage*: *Laborer's Love* and the Question of Early Chinese Cinema', in Y. Zhang (ed.) *Cinema and Urban Culture in Shanghai*, 27–50.

—— (2001) 'Bodies in the Air: The Magic of Science and the Fate of the Early "Martial Arts" Film in China', *Post Script* 20,2–3: 43–60.

Zhang, Zhongli (ed.) (1990) *Jindai Shanghai chengshi yanjiu* (Study of modern urban Shanghai), Shanghai: Shanghai renmin chubanshe.

Zhao, Jiawei (ed.) (2002) *Jingdia 200 – Zuijia huayu dianying erbai bu* (200 classics: two hundred best Chinese-language films), Hong Kong: Xianggang dianying pinglun xuehui.

Zheng, Yimei (1982) *Yingtan jiuwen – Dan Duyu he Yin Mingzhu* (Old stories about the film circles – Dan Duyu and Yin Mingzhu), Shanghai: Shanghai wenyi chubanshe.

Zhong, Dafeng, Zhen Zhang and Yingjin Zhang (1997) 'From *Wenmingxi* (Civilized Play) to *Yingxi* (Shadowplay): The Foundation of Shanghai Film Industry in the 1920s', *Asian Cinema* 9,1: 46–64.

Zhong, Dafeng and Shu Xiaoming (1995) *Zhongguo dianying shi* (A history of Chinese cinema), Beijing: Zhongguo guangbo dianshi chubanshe.

Zhongguo yishu yanjiu yuan yingshi yishu yanjiu suo (Film and TV Arts Institute, China Arts Academy) (2002) 'Jiushi niandai zhongde geming lishi ticai yingpian chuangzuo diaocha baogao' (Report on the production of films about major subjects in revolutionary history in the 1990s), *Dianying yishu* 3: 54–9.

Zhou, Xiaoming (1985) *Zhongguo xiandai dianying wenxue shi* (A history of film literature in modern China), 2 vols, Beijing: Gaodeng jiaoyu chubanshe.

Zhu, Ying (1998) 'Commercialism and Nationalism: Chinese Cinema's First Wave of Entertainment Films', *Cineaction* 47: 56–66.

Zuo, Guifang and Yao Liqun (eds) (2001) *Tong Yuejuan* (Actress Tong Yuejuan), Taipei: Wenjianhui.

SUBJECT INDEX

323

NAME INDEX

Cai Chusheng (1906–68) 61, 74, 79–82, 91–2, 96, 110, 157, 191, 218, 299

Chan, Fruit (Chen Guo, b. 1959) 269, 295

Chan, Jackie (Cheng Long, b. 1954) 179, 252, 256, 260–2, 269–71, 305–6

Chang, Eileen (Zhang Ailing 1920–95) 103, 165–6, 187, 254, 266–7, 303

Chen Kaige (b. 1952) 7, 227, 238–9, 280, 287–8, 292

Cheng Bugao (1898–1966) 32, 42, 52, 67–8, 93, 300

Cheng Yin (1917–95) 193, 204–6, 220, 224, 228

Chiau, Stephen (Zhou Xingchi, b. 1962) 260–3, 305–6

Chiu Shu-sun (Zhao Shushen, b. 1904) 62, 89, 152, 157

Chor Yuen (Chu Yuan, b. 1934) 174–6, 180

Dan Duyu (1897–1972) 21–2, 33–5, 42–3, 156

Fei Mu (1906–51) 50, 54, 81, 86, 101–6, 110–11, 157, 284

Feng Xiaogang (b. 1959) 276, 284, 289, 292–3

Hong Shen (1894–1955) 27–9, 35, 53–4, 62, 67–8, 74

Hou Hsiao-hsien (Hou Xiaoxian, b. 1947) 7, 226, 243–9, 274–7

Hou Yao (1903–40) 28–32, 38–42, 50–1, 54–6

Hu Die (aka Buttefly Wu 1907–89) 42, 51, 77–9, 107, 160, 299

Hu, King (Hu Jinquan 1931–97) 114, 141, 145, 148, 178, 187, 244

Huang Jianxin (b. 1954) 237–9, 288

Hui, Ann (Xu Anhua, b. 1947) 183–4, 249–50, 254, 266, 270, 295

Hui, Michale (Xu Guanwen, b. 1942) 180–1, 257

Jiang Qing (aka Lan Ping 1914–91) 218–19, 222, 304–5

Kwan, Stanley (Guan Jinpeng, b. 1957) 7, 254–5, 265–6

Law, Clara (Luo Zhuoyao, b. 1957) 255, 267

Lee, Ang (Li An, b. 1954) 260, 278–9

Lee, Bruce (Li Xiaolong 1940–73) 144, 151, 162, 175, 178–9, 187

Li Hanxiang (1926–96) 168–9, 176–80, 186, 227
in Taiwan 114, 137–9, 141, 143

Li Minwei (Lai Man-wai 1893–1953) 31, 54, 60, 152, 297

Li Xing (b. 1930) 130, 133–5, 140, 144–8, 243–4, 275

Ling Zifeng (1917–99) 193, 229, 287

Liu Na'ou (1900–40) 76, 86–8, 106–9, 119, 299, 301

Lung Kang (Long Gang, b. 1935) 174–6, 303

Luo Mingyou (1900–67) 49–50, 60–2, 81, 111

Mei Lanfang (1894–1961) 31, 34, 60, 101

FILM INDEX

327